INDIAN CITIES

INDIAN
CITIES
Histories of Indigenous Urbanization

Edited by
KENT BLANSETT, CATHLEEN D. CAHILL,
and ANDREW NEEDHAM

UNIVERSITY OF OKLAHOMA PRESS : NORMAN

This book is published in cooperation with the William P. Clements Center for Southwest Studies, Southern Methodist University, and with the generous assistance of The McCasland Foundation, Duncan, Oklahoma.

Library of Congress Cataloging-in-Publication Data

Names: Blansett, Kent, editor. | Cahill, Cathleen D., editor. | Needham, Andrew, 1971– editor.
Title: Indian cities : histories of indigenous urbanization / edited by Kent Blansett, Cathleen D. Cahill, and Andrew Needham.
Description: Norman : University of Oklahoma Press, [2022] | "This book is published in cooperation with the William P. Clements Center for Southwest Studies, Southern Methodist University, and with the generous assistance of The McCasland Foundation, Duncan, Oklahoma." | Includes bibliographical references and index. | Summary: "A collection of essays that explores the history of Indigenous peoples as city makers and city dwellers, showing how, from colonial times to the present day, Indigenous people have shaped and been shaped by urban spaces"—Provided by publisher.
Identifiers: LCCN 2021034639 | ISBN 978-0-8061-7663-5 (paperback)
Subjects: LCSH: Indians of North America—Urban residence. | Indians of North America—Social conditions. | Indians of North America—Ethnic identity. | Urbanization—North America—History. | City and town life—North America— History.
Classification: LCC E98.U72 I53 2022 | DDC 970.004/97—dc23
LC record available at https://lccn.loc.gov/2021034639

The paper in this book meets the guidelines for permanence and durability of the Committee on Production Guidelines for Book Longevity of the Council on Library Resources, Inc. ∞

CONTENTS

ACKNOWLEDGMENTS

This volume began as a series of conversations facilitated by Southern Methodist University's Clements Center for Southwest Studies symposium series. One of the joys of collaborative scholarship lies in the creation of new connections between people in recognition of shared intellectual pursuits. The editors thank all the contributors for their efforts to strengthen each others' essays and the volume as a whole through suggestion and critique. We mark the willingness of all the contributors to offer constructive criticisms, and of the authors to listen and consider those criticisms, as one of the most rewarding intellectual experiences of our careers. We would also like to thank the authors' familial and support networks that allow the time for scholarly work to take shape and the vital assistance while participants were away.

The contributors of this volume met twice, first near Taos, in the lands of the people of Taos and Picuris Pueblo, and second in New York City, in the lands of the Lenape people and the city with the largest urban Native population in the United States. We hope this volume can provide some measure of support to raise historical awareness of Indigenous exclusion and erasure, both in the cities of the Americas and its educational institutions.

Any volume such as this one, which involved collaboration between twelve authors, three editors, two universities, and a university press, rests on the work of innumerable people at those institutions. We would like to thank the Clements Center for Southwest Studies at Southern Methodist University for developing the format of paired symposia that has consistently created edited collections that are more than the sum of their parts. We would like to especially thank

Andy Graybill and Neil Foley for their institutional support, warm hospitality, and thoughtful suggestions about the shape and scope of the symposia and book. Ruth Ann Elmore provided invaluable logistical assistance, event planning, and the kind of enthusiastic, generous welcome that proved crucial in bringing the participants together both physically and intellectually. At SMU-in-Taos, we thank Cyndy Gimble for coordinating the meetings on campus, Mike Adler for arranging a visit to Pot Creek Pueblo, and Mark Henderson for leading our tour. We would also like to thank the people of Taos Pueblo, who welcomed the participants to their community and provided a tour.

At New York University, we would like to thank the Native Studies Forum, the History Department, the Cities Collaborative at NYU, and the Provost's Office for financial support of our NYU meeting. We thank Liz Ellis, Thomas Sugrue, and Dean Itsuji Saranillo for their support, their thoughtful commentary at the public symposium and private suggestions on particular essays. The editors would also like to extend an additional thanks to Liz for her reading of and suggestions on the introduction. For their extensive, behind-the-scenes logistical support, we thank Laura Chen-Shultz and the Asian/Pacific/American Institute, Karen Burrell and Guerline Semexant in the History Department, and Nou Moua in the Department of Social and Cultural Analysis. We also thank the building staff at each location for their work in preparing the spaces where we met and in cleaning them after our meetings. We are also grateful for the support of Pennsylvania State University's History Department and the University of Kansas.

At the University of Oklahoma Press, we thank Adam Kane for his initial support and Alessandra Tamulevich for her enthusiasm for the project, as well as her assistance and patience in seeing this book through the publication process. Our thanks also to Zubin Meer for his careful eye in copyediting, to Stephanie Evans for her help with the production process, and to Kerin Tate for writing the index. Additionally, we would like to thank Cheyenne and Arapaho artist Brent Learned for permission to use his piece "Trouble on the Plains" for the book's cover.

A NOTE ON INDIGENOUS USAGE

As readers will note, many of the essays use names, terms, and place names from a range of Indigenous languages. The volume does not place these words in italics, as they are neither foreign nor exotic to the Indigenous spaces and communities the essays detail and explore.

INTRODUCTION

Indian Cities

Today 70 percent of Indigenous peoples in the United States, a population of more than 3.7 million people, live in cities. In Canada, 867,415 First Nations people, roughly half the nation's Indigenous population, reside in metropolitan areas.[1] City life is not new to Indigenous people. Long before European settler colonists arrived in North America, Native peoples constructed Pueblo Bonito and Casa Rinconada, and Cahokia and Tenochtitlán, calling those cities home for centuries. In the centuries since, cities have become new frontlines in the struggle against colonization, oppression, and exploitation. In the seventeenth and eighteenth centuries, Indigenous people claimed areas of Charleston, Santa Fe, and Detroit as their own. In the nineteenth century, they made spaces for themselves in Washington, D.C., and Ottawa, as well as the smaller capitals of North America's emergent and imperial nation-states. And in the twentieth and twenty-first centuries, even as both popular culture and scholarly discourse positioned "Indian" and "city" as incommensurate abstractions, Indigenous people built the skylines of New York, Toronto, and Los Angeles and made areas of Rapid City, Winnipeg, and Tulsa into centers of Indigenous power. Within the urban landscape of buildings, streets, lights, signs, alleyways, and sidewalks, Native peoples came together in a gathering of nations, creating intertribal arenas and, collectively, building what we term "Indian cities."

Indian Cities offers a methodological intervention in urban and Indigenous histories. By foregrounding Indigenous peoples as city makers and city dwellers, as agents and subjects of urbanization, the essays in this collection simultaneously highlight the work of Indigenous peoples in shaping urban places and the role that urban spaces play in shaping Indigenous communities and politics. The essays provide multiple perspectives on urban Indigeneity and experiences of city life across centuries. Some speak to urban dangers: cities as sites or spaces where the hate that generated the genocidal violence at Mankato and Sand Creek found voice, where property lines excluded people from ancestral burial grounds, and where policing and plunder produced death and dispossession. At other times, the essays reveal landscapes of hope: places, openings, and opportunities where new communities and new politics took shape, where existing cities could be reclaimed or new cities could be made out of collective action, where Indigenous people could offer direct challenges to erasure and colonization, or where Indigenous people literally (re)claimed and (re)made place. Collectively, though, they demonstrate how urban history and Indigenous history are incomplete without each other.

The essays in this collection analyze the particular urban places created and maintained by Indigenous people within larger metropolitan areas. By foregrounding Indigenous peoples as city makers and city dwellers, these chapters highlight Indigenous people's impact on urban structures and urbanity itself, as well as the effects of urbanism on Indigenous people and politics. We use the term "Indian cities" to represent collective urban spaces organized by a range of institutions and organizations, including churches, businesses, activist networks, and public health units. Sometimes these urban institutions strengthened tribal identities, but they have often also been intertribal, creating new forms of shared experience, allegiance, and affectivity and giving rise to new shared practices of Indigeneity. "Indian cities" thus play a critical role in advancing sovereignty and rearticulating identity while also forging common bonds of spatial control and local identity. Living within and amid settler states and empires, however, the residents of "Indian cities" have constantly confronted challenges to their very presence in urban areas. In cities, Native people struggled to both control their own spaces and to challenge dominant ideologies of so-called Native apathy, backwardness, and primitivity that frame "Indian cities" as a contradiction in terms. Nonetheless, as many of the essays in the volume attest, "Indian cities" were and are more than places of oppression or victimization; they speak, also, to the beauty, sophistication, and resilience of Indigenous lives and communities. Indigenous inhabitants of "Indian cities" created spaces that encouraged Indigenous organization, nationalism, and resistance, spaces that existed—and continue to exist—in the face of still-dominant realities of Indian erasure and nonrecognition.

"Indian cities," both as description of historical and contemporary reality and as politically charged scholarly intervention, then, reveal how Indigenous peoples from the eighteenth century to the present have reimagined and "produced" urban spaces to respond to the challenges of settler colonialism.[2] The "Indian cities" explored in this collection range in time from colonial Charlestown to contemporary Winnipeg and, in type, from global metropolises, regional centers, and small towns to the unconventional urban space of the 2016 Oceti Sakowin encampment at the Standing Rock Sioux Reservation in North Dakota. A common thread running throughout this volume is that these places amount to more than mere sites of oppression and victimization. These "Indian cities" also attest to the autonomy and creativity of Indigenous lifeways, personal and collective. Their very existence offers a direct challenge to erasure in the form of vital places of decolonization and Indigenous futures. The study of these "unexpected places"—to adopt Philip Deloria's phrase—has prompted the scholars in this collection to grapple with and debate the historical truths bound up in the Indigenous experiences of the Indian city.[3] Collectively, they demonstrate that the varied histories of Indigenous peoples are inseparable from those of North American urban experience.

Indigenous peoples of the Americas have been building and living in cities since long before the arrival of European colonizers. Hundreds of ancient metropolises were located throughout the hemisphere, from the southernmost reaches of Argentina and Peru to the northern stretches of Canada. These ancient cities included the Maya cities of Caracol, El Pilar, and Tikal, which all held more than 100,000 residents. Those cities formed centers of a largely urban empire populated by at least 2 million people, and as many as 11 million, at its height between the third and tenth centuries B.C.E. Tikal alone had an urban core that sprawled over six square miles, comprising more than 3,000 built structures, rivaling any Roman city in late antiquity.[4] Further south, the Inca Empire contained infrastructural marvels like the 25,000-mile network of paved roads that linked the cities of Jauja and Cuzco, as well as the majestic citadel at Machu Picchu. More than a 150,000 people lived in Cuzco, the largest Incan city, in 1400, equaling the population of Paris at the same time.[5]

Just prior to conquest, the great Aztec island capital of Tenochtitlán supported a population of up to 400,000, rendering it the world's third largest city. It contained enormous trade plazas that served urban consumers who strolled along paved streets and lived in distinct neighborhoods. Tenochtitlán's residents could browse exotic zoos that contained a diversity of wildlife and attended schools and universities where engineering, astronomy, history, medicine, the arts, and military and agricultural science were taught. Massive temples, some larger than European cathedrals, marked the city's skyline. Beyond this urban core was an impressive layout of residential neighborhoods with waste management and a dual-pipe aqueduct that supplied fresh spring water to city residents. Tenochtitlán's engineers linked the metropolis together with networks of paved roads, canals, streets, and bridges as well as advanced agricultural technologies, including floating gardens, that sustained its immense population.[6]

In the American Southwest, from 1020 to 1120 B.C.E., ancient Puebloan structures such as Pueblo Bonito and Casa Rinconada served more than 10,000 people with a complex network of roads that reached into what is now Mexico, California, and the Great Plains.[7] Roads also led west to the extensive settlements of the Akimel and Tohono O'odham peoples, later called "Hohokam," a series of urban nodes occupied by as many as 150,000 people who lived amid 100,000 acres of farmland served by 500 miles of irrigation canals—canals that nineteenth-century settlers would excavate to build the aptly named city of Phoenix, born, as they saw it, from the ashes of a "long-lost civilization."[8] Farther east, at the confluence of the Mississippi and Missouri Rivers, Cahokia in 1100 C.E. supported a population larger than that of London or Jerusalem at the time. Cahokia comprised more than one hundred earthen superstructures or mounds, some larger in circumference than the pyramids of Egypt. Known today as Woodhenge (after England's Stonehenge and Woodhenge), a circular structure of strategically placed wooden poles acted as a solar calendar providing the city with a detailed record of the seasons—critical to managing the crops needed to sustain a vast population.[9] Indigenous residents of these cities occupied cosmopolitan worlds where neighbors spoke multiple languages and visitors exchanged exotic imports that moved through trade networks that connected South, Central, and North America and the Caribbean.

Despite this long history of urban development, colonists and European intellectuals, perhaps unsurprisingly, would actually use the Indigenous urban past to erase the Indigenous urban present and to create an image of Native primitivity irreconcilable with urban modernity. In the hands of these settlers and scholars, ancient archaeological remnants served not to highlight a venerable urban Indigenous heritage but to deny it. Indeed, at the beginning of the twentieth century, popular and academic historians of ancient Indigenous metropolises emphasized the supposedly fleeting nature of these bygone ancient cultures. Links between the inhabitants of those cities and subsequent Indigenous populations were all but erased from most historical narratives. The marvels of colossal mounds or now-ruined cities were falsely attributed to earlier Europeans, or even superhumans, giants, or extraterrestrials—anyone but Indigenous peoples.[10]

A "deurbanization" of Indigenous people has been central to both the discourse and reality of colonization. In other words, settler societies have denied the existence of Indigenous urban pasts—and presents and futures—insisting that urbanity and Indigeneity are antithetical. Even as Indigenous peoples continued to make Indian cities, their complex urban histories have remained largely hidden, and the chapters within this volume explicitly address this erasure. Invariably cast as "communal," "tribal," and "traditional," Native peoples have long been portrayed as having no place in urban society. Indeed, the tropes of deurbanization suggested they were either exiled from or overwhelmed by urban society, leaving them out of place in urban spaces. As historian Jean O'Brien argues, "Historical narration implicitly argued that Indians can never be modern because they cannot be the subjects of change, only its victims." Residents of Indian cities became, as Philip Deloria suggests, not unexpected urbanites that disrupted colonial understandings of Indigeneity but, rather, anomalies that reinforced reigning prejudices.[11]

The two primary means of deurbanization, which we detail here as "dispossession" and "dislocation," exist in treaties, public ceremonies and symbols, and scholarly and professional rhetoric, as well as fictionalized accounts of Indigenous people in urban spaces. Deurbanization wrongly suggests not only that Native presence is a matter solely of the urban past, but also that the presence of Indigenous people in urban space poses a threat to their own social and psychological well-being. It argues that "urban" and "Indigenous" are irrevocably incommensurate terms.

Indigenous dispossession has deeply shaped the development of U.S. and Canadian cities and this process is ongoing. In the North American cities of the past three centuries, the dispossession of Native nations enabled the privatized property and capital accumulation that became key components of modern urban economies. Take Chicago, for example. After its defeat of the Sauk and Meskwaki confederation led by Black Hawk in 1832, the U.S. government moved to legally extinguish all remaining Native claims to territory in Illinois, including lands held by the Neshnabé, or Potawatomi, people along the terminal moraine that separated Lake Michigan from the Illinois River. Despite informing the U.S. representative that someone had "told him a lie" and that "far from wishing to sell their land, they wished to keep it," Neshnabé leaders were coerced into signing two legally dubious treaties, in 1833, that became the legal basis for American possession of much of the land surrounding the booming city of Chicago.[12] While most Neshnabé people were exiled west of the Mississippi (though significant numbers likely returned, at least for a time, to their homes), the land from which they were forcibly dispossessed quickly gained near-astronomical values in the new economy of privatization, with lots priced at $33 in 1833 soon selling for $100,000 only four years later. Over the following decades, the historic Neshnabé homelands became, perhaps, the most important node of nineteenth-century global capitalism. The pattern of physical and legal dispossession repeats in almost every contemporary city in the United States and Canada.

The dispossession of Native peoples from urban spaces was not only a matter of violence and coercion. Rather, Native dispossession emerged as a key element of urban "origin stories," explaining and commemorating how modern cities came to be. For example, in 1928, the city of Chicago erected a series of four sculptures to adorn the DuSable Bridge, which crosses the Chicago River near where the 1833 treaties were signed. These sculptures, material manifestations of those stories, display dispossession as a key step in the city's early history. While the first two sculptures—"The Discoverers" and "The Pioneers"—depict stately scenes of "New World" "contact" and settlement—the third "Defense" displays a soldier with sword drawn (commemorating settler "martyrdom"), protecting frightened women and children from menacing "savage" Indians. "Defense," predictably, leads to "Regeneration," featuring equally heroic laborers building the modern city. In sum, this collection produced and reinforced a public narrative in which the dispossession of dangerous Indians played a vital role in creating Chicago's urban greatness. That this sculpture reversed the actual historical events—in which settler violence threatened Indigenous communities—suggests not only "defensive conquest" as integral to the *idea* of the modern American city but also cities as sites of both actual and symbolic violence.[13]

Master narratives of dispossession proffered other civic lessons. Well into the twentieth century, Indigenous dispossession was "performed"—or staged—by urban elites eager to display the broad societal transformations they sought to create. In Florida, in 1927, a self-appointed Seminole "chief" (actual Seminole political structure involved a council) named Tony Tommie stood on stage beside the president of the Miami Chamber of Commerce and declared, "The white man is the child of Destiny . . . the red man is the child of Nature. . . . The child of Nature must allow the child of Destiny his way." What followed, as historian N. B. D. Connolly recounts, was a bizarre ceremony of dispossession. On the field that lay before the stage, Seminole women planted corn using wooden implements. Then, seven tractors plowed the field before a celebratory parade of young white women (each representing a different state, following Miss Miami) scattered fresh seeds onto the land symbolically cleared of Native possession. This ceremony advanced ideas of historical and technological progression and, in the process, symbolized the replacement of Seminoles with white settlers.[14] Other such civic displays and representations held a similar message: There was no possibility of an Indigenous urban present or future. And whether violently or consensually, Indian people had been erased from the city itself.

This lesson took root not only in public commemorations of the urban past but also in much of the scholarship on urban history. Focused on the explosive growth and expansion of North American cities, urban histories frequently portrayed Indigenous people as present only at the outset of urban development, and then only as subjects that exit the narrative so that the work of urban growth could commence. To choose but one example, Chicago's Potawatomi (Neshnabé) people depart the narrative of William Cronon's magisterial *Nature's Metropolis* following the land cessions of 1833, a moment that supposedly represents the origins of the modern city. As Cronon writes, "The hybrid cultural universe of Indians and Euroamericans that had existed in the Chicago area for decades was finally to be shattered by different conceptions of property and real estate."[15] Dispossession became disappearance within Cronon's narrative of the explosive transformation that those conceptions of property and real estate wrought in Chicago and its hinterlands. However, as Rosalyn LaPier and David Beck have shown, numerous Potawatomi extended families retained their property within Chicago's city limits. Some Indigenous persons, such as To-gah Bertrand, who sued in 1876 "to assert her title to 126 acres of valuable land in South Chicago," attempted to use the treaties to contest both the new regime of property and their own dispossession. While her suit was unsuccessful, Bertrand's actions suggested the ways in which, as LaPier and Beck write, "Chicago remained Indian Country to the Indian people who stayed there, visited, or moved to the city."[16]

In their narratives of expansion, urban histories have often too easily borrowed rhetorical terms and conceptual frameworks from frontier histories, denying, inadvertently perhaps, the role of Indigenous people in city making. Important works of urban history with titles or subtitles such as *Crabgrass Frontier*, *The Metropolitan Frontier*, and *Life on the New Frontier* convey a Turnerian understanding of urban history.[17] In such frameworks, urban expansion serves as a force that completely remakes land and its meaning and, at the same time, severs connection between those spaces existing on either side of the urban frontier. The essays that follow resist these tendencies and illustrate the often-invisible histories of Indigenous endurance and revitalization. They illustrate the persistent power of Native people to carve out spaces in Rapid City, Prescott, Minneapolis, Winnipeg, and other places within which they claimed autonomy and authority. At the same time, these essays demonstrate the connections that Native people built between urban and nonurban Indigenous communities— between Dallas and the many reservations in Oklahoma, between Washington, D.C., and myriad Native nations—and in the process created new Indigenous modernities. In these ways, the creation of Indian cities served to challenge dispossession and the characteristics it ascribed to Native people.

The second way settler society has deurbanized Indigenous people is by perpetrating narratives of dislocation. Such narratives admit the possibility of Indigenous people occupying urban space, yet invariably cast such urban existence as negative. Rather, narratives of dislocation envisioned urban life as creating trauma for Native people, portrayed now as facing psychological disorientation and social isolation. Vital to these narratives is the idea that collective trauma emerged not out of the effects of colonialism and racism but, rather, out of Native people's supposed unpreparedness for urban life. The experience of urban life, with its large crowds, mass culture, and complex economic situations, was thought inimical to Native people, producing only crisis or dysfunction. Dislocation thus drew from the same assumptions that characterized narratives of dispossession: that Indigenous people lacked the capacity to be city makers and that merely living in cities would produce alienation and maladjustment.

The idea that urban experiences produced dislocation increased in potency through the twentieth century. The 1928 study *The Problem of Indian Adminis-tration*, better known as the Meriam Report, represented the first institutional study of the urban Indian experience. It dedicated one chapter on "The Migrated Indian." Produced by the Brookings Institution for the Bureau of Indian Affairs (BIA), and grounded in the methods of the Chicago School of urban sociology, this chapter provided a fine-grained look at a variety of off-reservation Native communities, ranging from informal camps located near border towns to fami-lies living in a variety of major cities in the Midwest and West Coast. While the report painted a dire portrait of the experience of people living in border towns, it portrayed those in cities as well adjusted, "absorbed" into "the several social or economic classes to which the Indians would naturally belong by virtue of the kind of work and earnings his talents and personality have made available to him." The report did reflect the BIA's assimilationist assumptions, praising the supposed tendency of Indians living in cities to abandon "traditional Indian hospitality in its most aggravated form" or "sponging." At the same time, it revealed that the same people had formed their own communities with nearby Native people, particularly "their former classmates in the Indian schools." In contrast, Native people living in border towns faced rampant discrimination, owing to the "probability certain elements in these communities are far more interested in the Indians as a supply of cheap mobile unskilled labor than in the Indians as future productive, skilled workers, capable of maintaining themselves at a reasonable American standard of living."[18] In short, the Meriam Report found exploitation and discrimination the root cause of the social challenges faced by Native people, and that those challenges lessened as Native people migrated to major cities.

By the late 1940s, federal perspectives on urbanization had undergone a significant shift in both the United States and Canada. Reservations and tribal governments themselves were increasingly seen as dead ends, subject to unilat-eral "termination" by federal authorities. From 1953 to 1970, the U.S. Congress pushed through numerous pieces of legislation to strip Native nations of their federal recognition. Known popularly as the Termination Acts, altogether they eradicated the federal recognition and trust responsibilities for more than

109 sovereign Native nations.[19] In Canada, the "White Papers" expanded pro-
termination agendas that increased the powers of the revised provisions of
the 1951 Indian Act to abrogate the sovereign status of Indigenous peoples.[20]
At the same time, the BIA launched the relocation program, actively seeking
to disenfranchise and "detribalize" Native peoples by offering government-
sponsored relocation assistance to Indian families. As a result, one in seven
Native peoples volunteered to relocate to one of the six participating cities. In
contrast to the tenor of the Meriam Report, the BIA viewed these relocatees as
requiring extensive federal supervision to navigate urban life. Relocation was
deeply influenced by, first, modernization theory, which understood Native
people as existing at a "primitive" stage of development. One federal official
testified to Congress that "the Navajos are passing through a stage of development that the rest of American society experienced fifty to one hundred year[s]
ago," suggesting that collectively Navajos would require extensive education
in the ways of urban modernity if they were they to succeed.[21] Relocation was
equally informed by the culture-and-personality school of anthropology, which
emphasized that sudden cultural changes could cause extensive psychological
damage to individuals whose psyches had been shaped by the norms of their
childhoods.[22] Together, culture-and-personality and modernization theory
informed the architects of relocation policy that urban residence, while necessary, would leave Native people psychologically vulnerable and incapable of
managing their own affairs. Those theories also suggested that any challenges
Native people faced in urban America would not be caused by colonial under-
development or racial discrimination but by the temporal and psychological
dislocation created by relocation to cities.

The termination and relocation era witnessed a dramatic rise in urban Native
migration. The 1950 U.S. census reported that 56,000 Native peoples resided in
cities. Ten years later, this number jumped to 146,000, with one in four Native
peoples living in urban zip codes. Thirty thousand Indians moved to Chicago,
Denver, Dallas, Cleveland, San Francisco, and Los Angeles under the auspices
of the BIA's Relocation Authority. Efforts at cost cutting, however, quickly gave
the program a bad reputation among Indians for providing few of the promised
social services, for allocating housing in "skid row sections" and "slum areas,"
and for placing Indians in unskilled jobs. As one relocatee in Denver commented,
"Heck, if I wanted to work in a junkyard, I could've stayed at home."[23]

The failures of relocation spurred some of the first academic work examining
the experiences of urban Indian communities, as the following section details.

It also led to new negative portrayals of urban life by Indigenous writers. Most famously, the Kiowa author N. Scott Momaday's 1968 novel *House Made of Dawn* (the only book by a Native author to win the Pulitzer Prize for fiction) follows an Indigenous veteran's BIA relocation from Jemez Pueblo to Los Angeles. Momaday's main character, Abel, experiences a series of misadventures and finds himself unable to adjust to the labor demands, social structure, and urban culture of Los Angeles. Distraught, Abel retreats from urban modernity to Jemez Pueblo and a life of Native tradition. The book is rightly considered a literary masterpiece, but it nonetheless reinforced some clichés regarding urban dislocation. Actual dichotomies exist between urban and reservation spaces: Abel's connections to his culture and community do not survive in Los Angeles. Abel is shattered by his experience of urban modernity and must retreat to Jemez Pueblo to reclaim his identity. But rather than the BIA's underfunded and poorly managed relocation program, Los Angeles serves as the novel's chief antagonist, a force of unrelenting oppression for Native people.[24] Yet this was not the experience of all Native people in Los Angeles. As Nicholas Rosenthal has shown, despite significant challenges, Indian migrants to Los Angeles formed a dynamic, artistically vibrant Indian city.[25]

To many, the frames, ideas, or structures of dispossessions and dislocation denied and continue to deny the possibility of urban Indigeneity. In suggesting that Indigenous people exist only in the city's past or that urban modernity causes psychological trauma unique to Native people, such ideas serve to obscure the actual causes of Native oppression, both within and outside urban spaces and involving the ongoing legacy of colonialism and inequalities of health, wealth, and power. Traditional notions of dispossession and dislocation also deny the possibility of the urban worlds that Indigenous people have created. They deny the very possibility of Indian cities. But even as they denied that possibility, Indigenous people built those worlds. It is to that history we now turn.

While deurbanization limited governmental and scholarly understanding of urban Indigenous communities, Native people have long created their own spaces within larger metropolitan areas. As the essays in the first half of this collection detail, urban Indigenous communities took shape in cities across North American for centuries prior to the BIA's urban relocation program. While often marginalized, decried, and exploited by urban authorities, those spaces often allowed Native people to garner personal and collective strength.

While relocation policy led Momaday and others to disaggregate urban and Indigenous spaces in fiction and the arts, urban Native communities built and worked to document their Indian cities. In 1955, Reverend Dr. David Cory, a non-Native Presbyterian minister who worked for decades with Brooklyn's Mohawk ironworkers, published *Within Two Worlds*, one of the first books devoted to documenting the urban Indian experience. Based on extensive interactions with Mohawk ironworkers and their families in their own language, Cory's book documented the various challenges urban Indian communities faced as well as their struggles to assert their right to the city.[26]

During the 1960s, increasing opposition to the patently destructive policies of termination and relocation led to new Indigenous urban policies and to novel scholarly attention. Urban Indian communities began to challenge termination legislation by collectively organizing and demonstrating in order to change public opinion and reform government policy. Various national meetings, including the National Congress of American Indians (in 1944), American Indian Chicago Conference (1961), and National Indian Youth Council (1961), brought urban residents together with reservation leaders to discuss and formulate programmatic solutions to shared problems. At the same time, an army of sociologists, ethnographers, and anthropologists hit the streets armed with tape recorders and notepads to conduct field research on the urban Indian experience. These interdisciplinary scholars wrote some of the first studies of Indian cities informed by oral histories and census data pulled from many cities, including Los Angeles, Denver, Albuquerque, Phoenix, San Francisco, and Seattle.[27] As Kent Blansett has shown, this combination of an increasingly politicized Native community building and novel scholarly energy at San Francisco State College provided the impetus and setting for the 1969 occupation of Alcatraz Island. That same year, Vine Deloria Jr. addressed some of these same issues in his 1969 manifesto, *Custer Died for Your Sins*.[28]

Though mainly published in scholarly journals, this early research also appeared in five seminal book-length studies: Jack O. Waddell and O. Michael Watson's *The American Indian in Urban Society* (1971), an interdisciplinary anthology on a range of cities; Elaine M. Neils's *Reservation to City* (1971); sociologist-anthropologist Murray Wax's *Indian Americans Unity and Diversity* (1971); sociologist Jeanne Guillemin's *Urban Renegades* (1975), which explored Mi'kmaq identity in Boston; and economist Alan Sorkin's *The Urban American Indian* (1978), which identified key institutions within Indian cities.[29]

The first scholarly histories examining Native people in cities emerged soon afterward. Drawing on the ethnographic fieldwork of anthropologists and sociologists of the prior decade, historians combed archival records to reveal the anti-Indigenous prejudice of federal policymakers who had developed the dual policies of termination and relocation. In 1986, Donald Fixico published his *Termination and Relocation*, a landmark early work that definitively linked the two policies.[30] Other historians were slow to take up the topic, although anthropologists and sociologists contributed valuable studies, notably Joan A. Weibel-Orlando, on Los Angeles; Susan Lobo, on the Bay Area; Terri Snyder and Grant Ardent, on Chicago; and Frances Sanderson and Heather Howard-Bobiwash, on Toronto.[31]

Scholars also began to address the urban Indian activism of the Red Power era. For example, *Like a Hurricane: The Indian Movement from Alcatraz to Wounded Knee*, appeared in 1996, coauthored by Paul Chaat Smith, associate curator of the Smithsonian's National Museum of the American Indian, and literary scholar Robert Allen Warrior. Susan Applegate Krause and Heather A. Howard (also known as Heather Howard-Bobiwash) called particular attention to women's urban activism in their 2003 special issue of *American Indian Quarterly*, parts of which were later republished as the edited collection *Keeping the Campfires Burning*.[32] Such studies focused on the post–World War II era.

The first decade of the twenty-first century saw an exciting explosion of scholarship addressing the question of Indigenous urbanism. In 2007, Coll Thrush's groundbreaking *Native Seattle* united the fields of urban history and Native history, weaving together the Indigenous places that became the city of Seattle and the Native people who lived and worked there. This book launched a productive conversation that, in turn, led to excellent studies on Los Angeles, Chicago, Albuquerque, and Tucson, including Nicholas Rosenthal's *Reimagining Indian Country*, Rosalyn LaPier and Dave Beck's *City Indian*, Myla Vincenti Carpio's *Indigenous Albuquerque*, and Victoria Haskins's *Maids and Matrons*. These authors all took seriously the idea that Native peoples had history with cities long before the mid-twentieth century. They also examined Indians in unexpected places, including labor unions, railroad switchyards, and movie lots, but also in familiar places—performing at fairs, for example—but with a twist, as economic agents and strategic choice makers.[33]

As Thrush elaborates in his second book, *Indigenous London* (2016), "Identifying Indigenous histories of the spaces of the city challenges the absence that others have assumed . . . and moves not just toward the limning of presence, but . . . to the idea that Indigenous people in London were not just there, but that they mattered to the city's history."[34] Inherent within Thrush's argument, and applicable from ancient times to the present, is that Indigenous peoples possess rich urban histories that continue to shape and influence the development of urban spaces around the world. Specifically, the continuing and contemporary presence of Indians in cities offers a direct challenge to the various myths of colonization that justified dispossession, genocide, discrimination, and anti-Indian legislation. Beyond the mythology of their victimization, Native peoples continue to Indigenize and redefine modern urban development, politics, and landscapes. The essays within this anthology accordingly challenge traditional notions of the urban Indian experience or how scholars have traditionally defined Indian cities.

In 2007, when *Native Seattle* appeared, Ho-Chunk anthropologist Renya K. Ramirez also made important contributions to the field of urban Indigenous studies. Her idea of cities as "Native hubs" conceptualized urban areas as places connected to many different Indigenous spaces by the movement of Native people within cities as well as between cities and reservation communities. Emphasizing similar connections between cities and their hinterlands, Andrew Needham demonstrated that Native reservations' extractive "energy" landscapes are just as much modern creations as urban areas like Phoenix. Kent Blansett, likewise, explored Native community building within cities, but he also traced Native activist networks connecting multiple cities.[35]

In this volume, the authors build on these exciting and important works to further challenge the conceptual separation of urban communities and Indian communities. Moreover, they push us to consider overlooked cities. Rather than focus on cities that have already garnered considerable scholarly attention— Chicago, Los Angeles, San Francisco, and New York—they look to regional centers with large Indigenous populations such as Buffalo, Rapid City, and Winnipeg. The authors also look to reservation border towns as flash points for intense conflicts over Indigenous urban rights. And they look to the ways that Native people made their own spaces within major metropolitan centers and their environs, such as Minneapolis–Saint Paul and Dallas–Fort Worth. Rather than characterizing Indian urbanization as beginning in the mid-twentieth century, this volume reaches back to the eighteenth century to investigate how Native peoples have navigated and remade centers of colonial, imperial, and national power at the early stages of North American settler colonialism. And, finally, they present accounts of Indigenous resilience, of the ability to create community and claim sovereign authority in the face of political forces that presumed to predict Indigenous peoples' demise and pursued their elimination.

The essays in part I demonstrate the continuity of Native urban sensibilities and traditions in the era of early Euro-American colonialism. Focused on the labor grievances of common Cherokee men in early seventeenth-century Charlestown, Nathaniel Holly reveals how Cherokees incorporated early Charlestown into their urban lives, political and economic. Most dynamically, he utilizes Cherokee-language terms and locutions in such a way as to not only center Cherokee perspectives and sensibilities but also defamiliarize complacent readerly expectations.

Similarly, Daniel Usner demonstrates how Indigenous peoples of the lower Mississippi drew colonial New Orleans into their trade and diplomatic networks. In Usner's terms, Natives "beg[a]n creatively establishing their own trade and ceremonial grounds in New Orleans in order to negotiate and even resist colonialism," by transforming colonial towns meant to assert settler dominance into useful spaces. These chapters highlight Native diplomacy and trade between Native and settler societies as vital factors in the formation of these cities.

Part II moves to the middle of the nineteenth century to reveal how all kinds of cities grew in tandem with Indigenous dispossession. We cannot divorce growing urban areas from the Indigenous sites upon which they developed, or their originary violence and their continued resource exploitation. Moreover, many of the urban patterns that continue to shape our world were developed in this period.

Urbanization and imperialism were "inextricably intertwined" by the mid-nineteenth century, Ari Kelman argues. Western cities like Saint Paul and Minneapolis played key roles as hubs of an expanding U.S. empire. They became nodes in networks of trade and information as the United States expanded into Indigenous lands. When Native people resisted these incursions, those cities also became the "stage upon which settlers and public officials could host morality plays . . . [and] perform the sanctity of white civilization and the inviolability of federal authority and the rule of law." This was most clearly displayed in Mankato, Minnesota, with the hanging of the Dakota thirty-eight, the largest mass execution in U.S. history.

Considering Niagara Falls and Buffalo, critical geographer Mishuana Goeman examines how stories about place create affective landscapes that work to erase

Native people and reconfigure Indigenous spaces into settler places. At Niagara Falls, Americans, at once, celebrated sublime nature and the development of hydroelectric power while effacing local Native presence through promotion of the tourist romance on the death of the Maid of the Mist. In truth, the Tuscarora and Seneca peoples were removed to reservations and their reservation lands flooded. In the wake of hydroelectric "development," this pattern was replicated across the continent through the twentieth century.

Maurice Crandall challenges the conventional idea of Indians moving to cities and, instead, shows that cities also came to the Indian. In Arizona and elsewhere, U.S. military violence and forced removals cleared territory for the development of new forms of land use and urbanization by white settlers. Yavapai and Dilzhe'e Apaches were exiled from the Verde Valley to the San Carlos Reservation for twenty-five years. When they returned to their homelands, they found them dramatically changed, overlaid by a landscape of small towns serving the ranching and mining industries. Apache people persisted, maintaining their communities by living in the in-between spaces and engaging in manual labor, insisting on their status as "original inhabitants trying to reclaim at least a small portion of what was already [theirs]."

Though far removed from the colonial outposts, Washington, D.C., as the nation's capital, nonetheless enshrines the symbolism of U.S. conquest. Joe Genetin-Pilawa contrasts notions of conquest, literally inscribed into the art and architecture of the capital, with the lived experiences of Native visitors to, and inhabitants of, the city. In art and architecture, Native men were portrayed as irrationally violent, justifying conquest for the legislators who regularly passed by such images in the halls of the Capitol and elsewhere. Yet in recovering the actual Indigenous histories of Washington, Genetin-Pilawa reminds us that imperial metropoles are also Indian cities.

The twentieth-century stories told in part III may seem the most familiar. But appearances can be deceiving. Some of them reexamine the U.S. relocation policies of the mid-twentieth century that have shaped so many earlier discussions. Although policymakers posited that Native people who moved to cities would be "changed" or made "non-Native" by the experience, setting up a false binary that continues to shape our understanding of the urban Indian experience, these essays explode that binary by revealing the vibrant, creative, and diverse experiences of Native people as they sought to create lives, communities, and institutions in a variety of cities, some nestled in their traditional homelands, others far-flung but nonetheless still imbued with a sense of "home." In all cases, they practiced Indigenous placemaking and shaped the city in essential ways.

The section opens with Elaine Marie Nelson's essay on Rapid City, South Dakota, at the turn of the century. The town of Rapid City was located on unceded Lakota land at the gateway to the sacred Black Hills, long a place of intertribal gatherings. Nelson argues that Native people were good for the local settler economy; for example, the establishment of a federal boarding school for Native children and the tourist draw of "real live Indians" meant town boosters encouraged limited Native presence. For their part, Native people used the opportunities in Rapid City, financial and social, to congregate in larger numbers, forge intertribal political coalitions, and assert claims to their land, especially the Black Hills.

Sasha Suarez reflects on what it means for members of one Indigenous nation to "claim urban space in the homeland of other Indigenous nations"? Acknowledging Minneapolis as Dakota land requires a different lens for analyzing the experiences of non-Dakota Indigenous people in the city. Focusing on Ojibwe women who moved to Minneapolis from the White Earth Reservation, Suarez explores how they created "social groups that acted as adaptive social networks from home" fostering an urban Indigenous community that would facilitate the Indigenous placemaking manifest in today's Minneapolis Indian Center and the American Indian Cultural Corridor.

Drawing on oral histories and other firsthand sources, Douglas K. Miller suggests that too often scholars focus on how cities disconnect people from tribal communities when, in fact, as he explains, "there are no urban Indians, there are only Indians living in urban places." By relating the rich variety of Indigenous life in Dallas, a federal relocation city, Miller reveals how people fostered Native nationalism as well as intertribal community. Drawing on Renya K. Ramirez's notion of cities as Native hubs connected to reservations, he highlights the movements of people and ideas both to and from cities as well as ancestral communities. Such movement nurtured tribal identity while community spaces and Indigenous institutions in the city helped foster intertribal connections.

Whereas the other essays in this volume focus on areas that became part of the United States, David Hugill's essay turns to the Canadian context with a focus on Winnipeg, Manitoba. Hugill refutes the tendency to see urban Indigenous people as victims and, instead, offers up a view of "Indigenous people as active agents of the city's production." In particular, he explores postwar community organizers' efforts to create an Indigenous enclave in Winnipeg, Neeginan or "our place" in Cree. Writing against the often-triumphalist tenor of urban history, he relates Indigenous activists' decades-long attempt to "construct a different kind of urbanity."

The final section pushes our notions of cities and the urban even further, challenging us to consider the temporality of cities as well as the often-unseen connections between urban areas and rural reservations. Anthropologist Dana Powell uses participant observation in the NoDAPL Encampments protesting the Dakota Access Pipeline in 2016–17 to describe an "alterNative" Indigenous configuration of a city: a temporary congregation of people who come together for a common purpose but whose ideas and social relations persist after the Encampment's wood and canvas structures and urban infrastructures disappear. Powell describes the protest camp as a "fluid social field" that at one point, with almost ten thousand people, made up "the tenth largest population hub in South Dakota." She urges us to consider that it was "a mode of social practice anchored in relations, mobility, and infrastructure," that made the encampment "a historically significant, if fleeting, Indigenous *city.*"

Jennifer Denetdale concludes the volume with a poignant personal essay on the impact of the COVID-19 pandemic on the Navajo people. Considering the relationship between the reservation and its border towns, her piece reveals how the structures of colonialism and their attendant social disparities have long been etched into the landscape and continue to wreak havoc in Native communities.

In the interests of robust collaboration, the authors met twice in seemingly very different places. First, we met in Taos, New Mexico, in the fall of 2018. Five months later, we reconvened in New York City. Together, these two places suggest the long history of Indigenous urbanism. First established in the eleventh century, Taos Pueblo is, with Acoma Pueblo and Oraibi, the oldest continually occupied structure in what is today the continental United States. New York City today has a population of 112,000 Native Americans, the largest population of Native people in any place in the United States. For centuries, Native peoples in both places have faced the realities of dispossession and dislocation. They have been portrayed as giving up the most valuable land in the world for mere beads, as being primitive counterpoints to modernity, as disappearing or no longer existing at all. And yet Indigenous peoples in Taos and New York, as in a range of other Indian cities across North America, have consistently claimed their right to make these cities sites of social and cultural renewal, where long-extant communities can be revitalized and new intertribal communities can be made as Indigenous migrants from across the Americas continue to move to urban areas. In this moment, when Indigenous futures are threatened by present-day colonialism—manifest in threatened lands, waters, and human and other than human bodies—we call on scholars in Native American and Indigenous studies and urban studies to continue to recognize, after the essays in this collection, not only the Indigenous pasts in the cities they study but also the ways in which Native peoples have continuously endeavored to make cities into homes.

NOTES

1. Urban Indian Health Commission, "U.S. Census Marks Increase in Urban American Indians and Alaska Natives," Feb. 28, 2013, www.uihi.org/wp-content/uploads/2013 /09/Broadcast_Census-Number_FINAL_v2.pdf; and Statistics Canada, "Aboriginal Peoples in Canada: Key Results from the 2016 Census," *The Daily*, October 25, 2017, www150.statcan.gc.ca/n1/daily-quotidien/171025/dq171025a-eng.htm.

2. We define settler colonialism as the ongoing effort of settler societies to displace Indigenous people and polities and dispossess them of their land and resources. For an introduction to settler colonialism, see Patrick Wolfe, *Settler Colonialism and the Transformation of Anthropology* (London and New York City: Continuum International Publishing Group, 1998), 2. We use "produced" following Henri Lefebvre's understanding of distinct tripartite spatial formations created (a) through vernacular practices of daily life, (b) in attempts by political and economic actors to impose order upon space, and (c) in the representation of spaces as distinct. Henri Lefebvre, *Production of Space*, trans., Donald Nicholson-Smith (Oxford: Blackwell, 1991), 37–40. For an excellent account of how these three levels of spatial production intersect, see Richard White, "What Is Spatial History?" Spatial History Lab, working paper, Feb. 1, 2010, https:// www.stanford.edu/group/spatialhistory/cgi-bin/site/pub.php?id=29.

3. Philip Deloria, *Indians in Unexpected Places* (Lawrence: University Press of Kansas, 2004).

4. Simon Martin and Nikolai Grube, *Chronicle of the Maya Kings and Queens* (New York: Thames & Hudson, 2008), 9. Recent studies using LIDAR technology have suggested previous estimates of 2 million people may have radically underestimated Mayan populations. This recent work suggests an upper bound of 11 million people residing in the area in the late classic period of 650 to 800 B.C.E. Marcelo A. Canuto, et. al., "Ancient Lowland Maya Complexity as Revealed by Airborne Laser Scanning of Northern Guatemala," *Science* 361 (Sept. 28, 2018), a.k.a. issue no. 1355, https://science.sciencemag .org/content/361/6409/eaau0137/tab-pdf. For more information on Mayan city building, see Michael D. Coe, *The Maya*, 4th ed. (New York: Thames and Hudson, 1987), 91.

5. For details on the Incan road network, see Charles Mann, *1491: New Revelations of the Americas before Columbus* (New York: Vintage Books, 2011), 74

6. Matthew Restall, *When Montezuma Met Cortés: The True Story of the Meeting that Changed History* (New York: HarperCollins, 2018), 3–9, 128–29.

7. Alvin M. Josephy Jr., ed., *America in 1492: The World of the Indian Peoples before the Arrival of Columbus* (New York: Vintage Books, 1991), 237, 376–77, 399.

8. James Bayman, "The Hohokam of the American Southwest," *Journal of World Prehistory* 15 (Sept. 2001): 257–311. For an account of Hohokam infrastructure inspiring the naming of Phoenix, see Arthur Horton, *An Economic, Political, and Social Survey of Phoenix and the Valley of the Sun* (Phoenix: Southside Progress, 1941), 15.

9. Timothy R. Pauketat, *Cahokia: Ancient America's Great City on the Mississippi* (New York: Viking, 2009).

10. For fantastical accounts of the building of Cahokia, see Jacob F. Lee, *Masters of the Middle Waters: Indian Nations and Colonial Ambitions along the Mississippi* (Cambridge, Mass.: Harvard University Press, 2019), 1–3, 18–21.

11. Jean M. O'Brien, *Firsting and Lasting: Writing Indians Out of Existence in New England* (Minneapolis: University of Minnesota Press, 2010), 107; and Deloria, *Indians in Unexpected Places*.

12. Quoted in William Cronon, *Nature's Metropolis: Chicago and the Great West* (New York: Norton, 1991), 28. For discussion of the treaties, see Ann Keating, *Rising Up from Indian Country: The Battle of Fort Dearborn and the Birth of Chicago* (Chicago: University of Chicago Press, 2012).

13. For additional details, see Boyd Cothran, *Remembering the Modoc War: Redemptive Violence and the Making of American Innocence* (Chapel Hill: University of North Carolina Press, 2014).

14. N. B. D. Connolly, *A World More Concrete: Real Estate and the Remaking of Jim Crow South Florida* (Chicago: University of Chicago Press, 2014), 65–66.

15. Cronon, *Nature's Metropolis*, 29.

16. Rosalyn LaPier and David Beck, *City Indian: Native American Activism in Chicago, 1893–1934* (Lincoln: University of Nebraska Press, 2015), 6 and 3.

17. For examples of urban histories employing frontier language, see Carl Abbott, *The Metropolitan Frontier: Cities in the Modern American West* (Tucson: University of Arizona Press, 1993); Joel Garreau, *Edge City: Life on the New Frontier* (New York: Anchor Books, 1991); and Kenneth T. Jackson, *Crabgrass Frontier: The Suburbanization of the United States* (New York: Oxford University Press, 1985). Frederick Jackson Turner established the so-called frontier thesis or paradigm with "The Significance of the Frontier in American History," a paper first read at the American Historical Association in Chicago in 1893.

18. Institute for Government Research, *The Problem of Indian Administration* (Baltimore: Johns Hopkins University Press, 1928), 705 and 668.

19. Donald Fixico, *Termination and Relocation;* Kenneth Philp, *Termination Revisited: American Indians on the Trail to Self-Determination* (Lincoln: University of Nebraska Press, 1999); and Douglass K. Miller, *Indians on the Move: Native American Mobility and Urbanization in the Twentieth Century* (Chapel Hill: University of North Carolina Press, 2019).

20. Roger Nichols, *Indians in the United States and Canada: A Comparative History* (Lincoln: University of Nebraska Press, 2018), 344–45.

21. William Warne, testimony before House Committee on Public Lands, Subcommittee on Indian Affairs, *Navajo and Hopi Rehabilitation*, 81st Cong., 1st sess., April 18, 19, 22, May 16–18, 1949, 32.

22. On the culture-and-personality school's influence on midcentury social scientific thought, see Joanne Meyerowitz, "'How Common Culture Shapes the Separate Lives': Sexuality, Race, and Mid-Twentieth-Century Social Constructionist Thought," *Journal of American History* 96 (March 2010): 1057–84. For the application of culture-and-personality thinking to an Indigenous group, see Clyde Kluckhohn and Dorothea Leighton, *The Navajo* (Cambridge, Mass.: Harvard University Press, 1946).

23. Larry Burt, "Roots of the Native American Urban Experience: Relocation Policy in the 1950s," *American Indian Quarterly* 10 (Spring 1986): 90.

24. N. Scott Momaday, *House Made of Dawn* (New York: Harper and Row, 1968). The 1961 film *The Exiles* featuring an all-Native cast, offers a similar portrait of Native Los Angeles. See Liza Black, "*The Exiles:* Native Survivance and Urban Space in Downtown Los Angeles," *American Indian Culture and Research Journal* 42, no.3 (2018), 155–82.

25. Nicholas Rosenthal, *Reimagining Indian Country: Native American Migration and Identity in Twentieth-Century Los Angeles* (Chapel Hill: University of North Carolina Press, 2012).

26. David M. Cory, *Within Two Worlds* (New York: Friendship Press, 1955).

27. On such early studies, see Joan Weibel-Orlando, "Urban Communities," in *Handbook of North American Indians*, vol. 2, *Indians in Contemporary Society*, ed. Garrick A. Bailey (Washington, D.C.: Smithsonian Institution, 2008), 312.

28. Kent Blansett, *Journey to Freedom: Richard Oakes, Alcatraz, and the Red Power Movement* (New Haven, Conn.: Yale University Press: 2018); and Vine Deloria Jr., *Custer Died for Your Sins: An Indian Manifesto* (New York: Macmillan, 1969).

29. Jack O. Waddell and O. Michael Watson, *The American Indian in Urban Society* (Boston: Little, Brown, 1971); Elaine M. Neils, *Reservation to City: Migration and Federal Relocation* (Chicago: University of Chicago Department of Geography, 1971); Murray Wax, *Indian Americans: Unity and Diversity* (Englewood Cliffs, N.J.: Prentice-Hall, 1971); Jeanne Guillemin, *Urban Renegades: The Cultural Strategy of American Indians* (New York: Columbia University Press, 1975); and Alan L. Sorkin, *The Urban American Indian* (Lexington, Mass.: Lexington Books, 1978).

30. Fixico, *Termination and Relocation*. For recent discussions of these policies, see Laurie Arnold, *Bartering with the Bones of Their Dead: The Colville Confederated Tribes and Termination* (Seattle: University of Washington Press, 2012). In *Indians on the Move*, Douglas Miller suggests we need to disentangle our studies of the particularities of termination and relocation policies from Indigenous urban experiences more broadly to reveal a much longer history of movement to cities.

31. Joan A. Weibel-Orlando, *Indian Country, L.A.: Maintaining Ethnic Community in Complex Society* (Urbana: University of Illinois Press, 1991); Susan Lobo, ed., *Urban Voices: The Bay Area American Indian Community* (Tucson: University of Arizona Press,

2002); Terry Straus and Grant P. Arndt, eds., *Native Chicago*, (Chicago: Albatross Press, 2002); and Frances Sanderson and Heather Howard-Bobiwash, eds., *The Meeting Place: Aboriginal Life in Toronto* (Toronto: Native Canadian Center of Toronto, 1997).

32. Paul Chaat Smith and Robert Allen Warrior, *Like a Hurricane: The Indian Movement from Alcatraz to Wounded Knee* (New York: New Press, 1996); Troy R. Johnson, *The Occupation of Alcatraz Island: Indian Self-Determination and the Rise of Native Activism* (Urbana: University of Illinois Press, 1996); and Susan Applegate Krause and Heather A. Howard, eds., *Keeping the Campfires Burning: Native Women's Activism in Urban Communities* (Lincoln: University of Nebraska Press, 2009).

33. Coll Thrush, *Native Seattle: Histories from the Crossing-Over Place* (Seattle: University of Washington Press, 2007); Rosenthal, *Reimagining Indian Country*; LaPier and Beck, *City Indian*; Myla Vincenti Carpio, *Indigenous Albuquerque* (Lubbock: Texas Tech University Press, 2011); and Victoria Haskins, *Maids and Matrons: Regulating Indian Domestic Service in Tucson, 1914–1934* (Tucson: University of Arizona Press, 2017). See also James B. LeGrand, *Indian Metropolis: Native Americans in Chicago, 1945–1975* (Urbana: University of Illinois Press, 2002).

34. Coll Thrush, *Indigenous London: Native Travelers at the Heart of Empire* (New Haven, Conn.: Yale University Press, 2016), 24.

35. Renya K. Ramirez, *Native Hubs: Culture, Community and Belonging in Silicon Valley and Beyond* (Durham, N.C.: Duke University Press, 2007); Andrew Needham, *Power Lines: Phoenix and the Making of the American Southwest* (Princeton, N.J.: Princeton University Press, 2014); Blansett, *Journey to Freedom*. See also Miller, *Indians on the Move*; and Cathleen D. Cahill, "Urban Indians, Native Networks, and the Creation of Modern Regional Identity in the American Southwest," *American Indian Culture and Research Journal* 42, no. 3 (2018): 71–92.

PART I

REMAKING URBAN SPACES
IN EARLY AMERICA

"OTHERS OF A MORE ORDINARY QUALITY"

Cherokee Commoners in Charlestown
during the Winter of 1717

"He intended to deceive [me]," Hootleboyau lamented. And "he cheated [me] likewise," Yorogotogaskee chimed in. As their interpreter relayed their claims to the powerful ugvwiyuhi across the table in the winter of 1717—months after dozens of Cherokee towns came to the aid of the English gaduhv'i in their war with Yamasees and other Muskogee-speakers—these two relatively unremarkable lower towns laborers must have wondered if the beloved man called John Barnwell would take their complaints seriously. On this particular occasion, an Ani-Charlestown warrior had "deluded" them during a routine economic transaction. While John Jones promised to pay them for some skins and a basket during their stay in the English gaduhv'i, the two anisogwili had yet to receive any recompense. For whatever reason, these burdeners decided they could not abide such treatment. But rather than lash out at Jones or quietly accept their economic fate, these Cherokees "of a more ordinary Quality" put their hard-won urban knowledge to use. Like their more prominent headmen, Hootleboyau and

Yorogotogaskee knew their way around Charlestown's paths of power. Indeed, when the aggrieved laborers finally left the English gaduhv'i some weeks later, they had each secured a pair of matchcoats for their trouble.[1]

As this story indicates, the "silent files of Indian burdeners" so often evoked by scholars like Verner Crane were not so quiet.[2] Indeed, their cries of dissatisfaction illuminate an aspect of Cherokee history that has largely gone unnoticed. Yet historians have adopted Crane's poetic phrase as historiographical gospel. Nearly fifty years after Crane quieted ordinary Cherokees, John Phillip Reid mourned their absence from the historical record: "We will never know the Cherokee until we hear from these lesser individuals: the nonheadmen, the warriors, hunters, farmers, and traders who did not negotiate or played secondary roles in negotiations with the Europeans."[3] Aside from some moderately fruitful archaeological work, historians have scoured the same colonial sources in search of "lesser" folk with little success.[4]

And when Cherokees like the frustrated Hootleboyau and Yorogotogaskee do make cameo appearances in studies of the Indigenous Southeast, historians hardly ask any questions of them—especially questions motivated by urban, labor, or personal concerns: Why were Cherokee commoners in Charlestown? Where were they from? What did they do while they resided for weeks in town? How might they have interpreted their urban experiences? And what role did their labors play in those experiences? Answering these sorts of questions does more than help us to "know the Cherokee" better. It also accomplishes something more important than simply pointing out the seemingly anomalous presence of Cherokees in Charlestown or their persistence in the face of intentionally restrictive colonial trade regulations. By paying attention to *these* Cherokees *in* Charlestown, we gain a more complete picture of their particular ways of being in the world and the urban nature of that world.

Though examining seemingly out-of-place Cherokees in a colonial urban center might seem strange to historians of early America who routinely flock to the frontier in search of such interactions, for all of the Cherokee-speaking characters in this essay, Charlestown was just another urban place in a world characterized by urban places. As their very names indicate, the Ani-Dugilu and Ani-Itsa'ti were urban peoples living in an urban world. They organized their lives around their own disgaduhv'i, which operated as political, social, legal, and economic centers. The urban nature of Cherokees was readily apparent to anyone who paid attention. "The *Cherokees*," an Ani-Charlestown observed, "allow no settlements to be called towns, except where they have a house for public consultations."[5] More than just a collection of houses and people at a particular spot, a gaduhv'i was a community of people. A "townhouse"—often large enough to hold an entire gaduhv'i—rendered a simple settlement something more than a group of built structures. "Symbolically," anthropologist Christopher Rodning argues, "townhouses 'housed' towns, anchoring them within the southern Appalachian landscape."[6] Like their own disgaduhv'i, Charlestown also had "a house for public consultations" that visiting Cherokees called a "beloved House." Cherokees treated colonial disgaduhv'i like Charlestown as recognizable variations on a familiar theme. So while Charlestown and its inhabitants were new and different, they were not strange. They were all part of the same urban world.[7]

Examining overlapping visits during the winter of 1717 offers an opportunity to illuminate how Cherokees "of a more ordinary Quality" navigated this urban world.[8] While colonial recordkeepers often made mention of "Cherikee Indians now in town," they rarely elaborated on the experiences of their Indigenous guests.[9] The only Cherokee visitors who usually merited mention were those whom colonial officials deemed important—chiefly headmen. Because the voices of common Cherokees are sparse in the *Journals of the Commissioners of the Indian Trade*, this essay also follows two headmen from Cherokee towns—Caesar from the middle town of Itsa'ti, and Charitey Hagey from the lower town of Dugilu—as they mediated a labor dispute between their anisogwili and Charlestown's unigvwiyuhi. Elite Cherokees had more than just geopolitical concerns on their diplomatic plates, as it turns out. By bringing the stories of Hootleboyau and Yorogotogaskee to the fore, we see the "silent files" of "lesser individuals" emerge as people with an intimate knowledge of how power operated in the English gaduhv'i and, more important, how to put that knowledge to good use. Whether that meant pushing one of their headmen to intervene on their behalf or seeking out powerful Ani-Charlestown on their own, common Cherokees were an urban people central to the story of the early modern Atlantic world.

USING UNIGVWIYUHI

Standing in Robert Daniell's Bay Street house in the winter of 1717, Caesar threatened the Ani-Charlestown ugvwiyuhi. Unless his anisogwili "might be at liberty to trade with whomsoever they thought fit, they would leave the town that night, and go home and sit down."[10] Even when Caesar asked for "three hundred men to head" his warriors against their mutual Ani-Ka'wita enemies during a meeting with the South Carolina Commons House of Assembly a week earlier, he made sure to mention the good that such men would do for the trade between his town and the English gaduhv'i. The Ani-Charlestown warriors would, he assured the beloved men, help the Ani-Itsa'ti anisogwili "bring down their skins securely and not fear the waylaying of the paths." In addition to the geopolitical motivations for his visit to Charlestown, then, Caesar's threat revealed an equally pressing reason for braving the bloody path to Charlestown.[11] Driven at least partially by his men who labored as anisogwili, this visit was something of a labor dispute. The ninety-one lower towns laborers who accompanied Charitey Hagey to Charlestown were motivated by similar concerns. They all wanted a proper place to sell their individual wares. If Charlestown's unigvwiyuhi would not send traders to their urban centers, then traveling to the English gaduhv'i was the next best option. For Cherokee commoners, the ability to freely exchange the fruits of their labor with the Ani-Charlestown—in the English gaduhv'i—was central to their alliance.

By examining the dramatic lengths Caesar and Hagey adopted to secure permission for their anisogwili to trade with "whomsoever they thought fit" while in Charlestown during the winter of 1717, it is clear that these headmen knew how important the labor of more common Cherokees was to their interurban alliances. And, while hierarchy certainly shaped the urban world of the colonial Southeast, the effort that each headman put forward in securing concessions from Charlestown's headmen also reveals the power that common Cherokees had over their headmen. As Daniell, Caesar, and Hagey well knew, Cherokee commoners were central to the smooth operation of their intertwined worlds.[12]

Caesar and Hagey used dramatically different—but equally effective—means to accomplish their diplomatic ends. Caesar started at the top. In a private audience with Governor Daniell, he went to work for his laborers. "They cannot," Caesar told his counterpart, "sell their skins where they please." And if his people could not be supplied with goods in their own urban centers, Caesar continued, the Ani-Itsa'ti would take drastic measures. Either they would trade with individual colonists while in the English gaduhv'i as they had for years, or they would "go to those who will seek their friendship." Clearly shaken by these forceful demands, Daniell assured them that he would do all he could to accommodate their demands. But he would first have to consult his beloved men in the Commons House of Assembly. Caesar must have felt confident that his work was nearly done. And Daniell did his part, telling the Commons House the next morning, "This is a matter of so great importance that I may safely say the welfare of the whole settlement depends upon the same."[13] But Charlestown's beloved men saw the situation differently than their governor.

As Caesar sat in the Indian House near the town gates awaiting word that he could release his people to trade with individual colonists, a trader and translator he called Uweti Tsisdu appeared in the doorway with some news for his friend. The Commissioners of the Indian Trade had asked to see Caesar and Hagey the next morning to discuss the situation. When Caesar asked what the governor's beloved men had said, the translator, Eleazar Wigan, probably hesitated before paraphrasing their decision that "these demands are impossible for us to comply with" because "we think the altering of . . . the present Indian trading law . . . will very much endanger the safety of this Province."[14] Probably equally frustrated by this setback, Caesar and Hagey settled on different plans for getting what they wanted. Caesar would use war to his advantage; Hagey, peace.

Whether it resulted from a willful ignorance of how Cherokee-speakers organized their identities and allegiances around particular urban centers or from a desire to get these foreign people out of town as quickly as possible, the Commissioners agreed only to see these two headmen together. Speaking through Uweti Tsisdu, the Commissioners told the headmen from Itsa'ti and Dugilu what they already knew. That the Commons House had found "the present Establishment to be the most safe and fair for a constant Commerce and Trade with them."[15] The Commissioners then quickly reassured the headmen that they had prepared "a handsom present" for each of them to smooth over any frustrations. Yet this offer betrayed the Commissioners' fundamental misunderstanding of what was at stake here. While Caesar and Hagey would certainly take any gifts they were offered, leaving Charlestown without securing permission for their anisogwili to trade their skins with individual colonists would represent a serious failure. Not only would their personal power likely diminish, but their towns' alliances with Charlestown would be in serious jeopardy.

At this point Caesar put his plan into action. After expressing his frustration with Charlestown's "great Men on this affair," he informed the Commissioners "that their faces were painted . . . their Minds were bent on War (towards St. Augustin [Florida]), and that they could stay no longer at the Board."[16] As Caesar stormed out the door to visit Charlestown's most powerful ugvwiyuhi, he promised the Commissioners they would be back to "deliver their Minds, fully." Hagey, however, sat quietly and waited for Caesar to finish. When the

Commissioners asked him "what was the Cause of their going away so abruptly," Hagey declined to provide an answer. While he did not agree with Caesar's tactics, he had to admit the Itsa'ti headman had a point. And rather than oppose him in public, Hagey decided to wait and see what happened. So, like Caesar, he left the Commissioners to contemplate what they had just witnessed. But on his way out Hagey decided to plant the seed of an idea. After mentioning that he planned to head home shortly, Hagey mentioned that he intended to go "Home by Way of the Catapaws" with his anisogwili.[17] Hoping that he could secure some employment for his anisogwili, Hagey offered the Commissioners a way to save face. In this scenario, his men would leave Charlestown with goods to trade with the Catawbas and the Ani-Charlestown would not have to formally compromise on their aversion to Indigenous trade in their town. And if Caesar wanted to act like a lunatic, all the better. Not only would that make Hagey's demands seem reasonable by comparison, but he might also curry favor with Charlestown's unigvwiyuhi.

As Hagey orchestrated his own brand of diplomacy, the spitting-mad Caesar barreled over to Daniell's private house at the end of Bay Street to begin the next scene in his drama. Whatever Caesar said to Charlestown's ugvwiyuhi after storming through the English headman's doors made quite an impression. As the Commons House discussed the sort of presents they could offer Caesar and Hagey so as to persuade them to drag their people out of town without allowing them to trade, Governor Daniell began beating at the door. Once the House Speaker managed to convince Daniell to sit down, the ugvwiyuhi told the entire house about what had just happened. At a meeting with Caesar "at his house," the headman "told him there, that unless their people might be at liberty to trade with whomsoever they thought fit, they would leave town that night, and go home and sit down."[18] After discussing the matter with his beloved men for a while, Daniell retreated to allow them time to consider their options.

The Commons House, "having spent some time therein," settled on two seemingly contradictory motions. The first addressed the current predicament: "whether the Cherikee Indians now in Town shall have the liberty to sell and dispose of what skins they now have to whom and where they shall think fit?" Yes, the House resolved. The Ani-Itsa'ti and Ani-Dugilu would be able to do what they wanted with their skins. But only the ones who were "now in town." Like the Cherokees they hoped to satisfy, these colonial officials recognized the importance of the Cherokees' presence in Charlestown to the success of their petition. A breath later, however, the Commons House resolved that they would also "stand by the Indian trading law." In their eyes, this was a one-time exception.[19] By beating down the doors of the right people, Caesar had won his people a victory. But he did not know that yet.

While his rival went door to door ruffling the feathers of the most powerful colonists in Charlestown, Hagey returned to visit the Commissioners to see if they would agree to his earlier proposal. As he informed the unigvwiyuhi, he planned to head "Homewards Tomorrow or the next Day at furthest."[20] Finding that the Commissioners had not understood his earlier offer, Hagey tried again—this time more explicitly. Since he and his men planned to visit the Catawbas on their way home, he told the Commissioners, they "will be willing to carry Burdens there for Pay in order to be sold to them Indians."[21] As if thinking out loud, Hagey also mentioned that this effort would "appear as a Token of joynt Friendship to the said Catapaws." The Commissioners finally got the hint. After giving Hagey the presents they promised him some days earlier, the Dugilu ugvwiyuhi left to "view the Goods in Store" so he could personally select what was most in demand in his town, Dugilu, and what he thought the Ani-ta'gwa might most appreciate. About a week later Hagey looked over £1,500's worth of goods laid out for his ninety-one anisogwili. His laborers had received the usual two yards of blue duffel's worth of compensation and were ready to go. As Hagey headed south on the path along the bay and then turned west on the broad path, he must have felt relieved his diplomatic labor was done for now.[22]

In the midst of Hagey's measured labor negotiations, Caesar visited the Commissioners with his third act rehearsed and ready to go. After the usual greetings, the Commissioners presented Hagey with his presents. And with that, the curtain raised. Because he was headed toward St. Augustine bent on war, Caesar requested the Commissioners hold onto his gifts until he returned—"[I]t being their Intention," the Commissioners noted, "to carry the Rum and Sugar to their respective Towns, there to assemble the Warriers, and drink the same in a Bowl of Punch, in Commemoration of the English." Caesar knew the currency of flattery worked particularly well with the Ani-Charlestown. But Caesar was not done. "[I]f he should die," Caesar desired the beloved men to give his brother "his Part of the Rum and the Sugar . . . in order to fulfill his aforesaid Will and Intention." If he was prepared to die in service of their alliance, Caesar must have reasoned, surely the Commissioners would be willing to allow his people to trade in Charlestown. The scene was not quite over, however. It turns out that Caesar had used the previous day or so to examine the contents of the public store. While poring over kettles and knives, earbobs and looking glasses, he spotted a box of guns. How could the Commissioners deny him weapons of war if he was, in fact, headed off to war? So "Cesar moved to have Guns provided for him, insisting that he heard they may be obtained for ready Money." Here the Commissioners hesitated. Caesar must have known he was going just a bit too far, so he quickly assuaged their concerns by saying, "he would speak to the Governour about them."[23]

Although no record of another meeting with Charlestown's ugvwiyuhi survives, Caesar must have had mixed feelings when Daniell informed him that his men would be allowed—this one time only—to dispose of their skins however they thought fit. By now, however, Caesar was committed to his story. They had to at least make it appear that they were serious about going to war. Plus he did not want to lose the guns promised him by the governor. So, on their way out of town Caesar, Partridge (another headman), ten more men, and nine women visited the Commissioners to gather their guns.[24] Where they went after that is a mystery. Presumably they exited Charlestown through the usual gates, caught a ferry over the Ashley River, and headed toward St. Augustine. Yet wherever the war party went, it did not get far. There was no need to risk their lives now. Although the closest Yamasees lived nearly three hundred miles to the south, one short week later Caesar appeared before the Commissioners and informed them that his "Expedition to the Southward, against the Yamasees was frustrated."[25] Because he intended to head home soon, he asked for—and received—the rum and sugar he had left behind. That same day his thirty-seven anisogwili loaded up £915 worth of goods and prepared to head back to Itsa'ti.

While Caesar's diplomatic style differed drastically from his rival's, the Itsa'ti headman also left Charlestown with everything he wanted and his people demanded. For Caesar and Hagey, Charlestown was quickly becoming a familiar place. While they used their growing knowledge of Charlestown differently, they both wielded it for similar ends. In both cases, that meant satisfying the demands of their people. While Caesar seemingly got what he wanted, his theatrics failed to live up to the expectations of more common Cherokees. A few months after these Cherokees returned home, Uweti Tsisdu reported that "Charikee Warriours had beaten Cesar very much, and do threaten to kill him, for his bad Behaviour to the English and some of their own . . . Men, when last in Charles Town."[26] While it is unclear why exactly Caesar was beaten, it is clear that what happened in Charlestown *mattered* to Cherokee commoners.

ANISOGWILI ON THE STREET

While Caesar and Hagey labored to secure official permission for their men to trade in Charlestown, their anisogwili pursued their own interests. Because this was not the first time these laborers had visited Charlestown in search of trade, most of their transactions went smoothly. Or at least well enough to warrant neither comment nor complaint from colonial officials. On this particular trip, however, a few anisogwili were "cheated" by individual Charlestonians. Although this was almost certainly not the first time Cherokee-speaking laborers found themselves shortchanged by their new allies, perhaps they finally felt comfortable enough with Charlestown's power to put up a fight. Goading their headmen into demanding an official allowance to trade from Charlestown's unigvwiyuhi was one thing. Powerful people like Hagey and Caesar had already fostered connections to the leading men in this powerful English gaduhv'i. But commoners like the two aggrieved laborers who open this essay were a different story.

While the voices of common Cherokees were usually stifled by colonial indifference, their periodic visits to Charlestown created situations that forced Ani-Charlestown officials to publicly deal with their complaints. These frustratingly infrequent occasions provide the opportunity to hear common Cherokees and note their use of a seemingly foreign gaduhv'i to their advantage. The urban setting for these encounters, in other words, plays a central role in their social—and historiographical—preservation. By eavesdropping on anisogwili complaints during the winter of 1717, it becomes clear that headmen were not the only Cherokees who knew how to navigate Charlestown's geography of power. These men often carried skins of their own to the colonial capital with hopes of exchanging them for specific goods. And on most occasions, their transactions went smoothly. The misfortune of one anonymous middle towns sogwili, however, provides us with a rare glimpse of the tenor of such transactions and illuminates the urban knowledge that even the least remarkable Cherokee possessed.

With only one skin left to sell before heading out of town, the sogwili from Itsa'ti was willing to deal with just about anyone. Unfortunately for him, his chosen Charlestonian turned out to be after a steal. While the exact setting and circumstances of the exchange remain unclear, the Itsa'ti burdener gave an Ani-Charlestown named Thomas Cutler his last deerskin in exchange for a yard of caddis and a small, otherwise useless inch-wide remnant of silk. It probably made a difference to this burdener that neither caddis nor silk was usually available. Indeed, he must initially have been satisfied by the exotic deal he managed to secure on the eve of his departure.[27]

Something happened, however, to convince the Itsa'ti man than he had been swindled. Perhaps he swaggered into his lodgings to show off his score only to be enlightened by some of his more experienced brethren. Whatever the reason for his dissatisfaction, he immediately complained to Caesar. The headman must have told the sogwili that there was little he could do at this point. Remember Caesar had already begun his drama. So, the simple laborer from Itsa'ti set out on his own in search of satisfaction. He could not just appear before the Commissioners or knock on Daniell's door. He did, however, know of a Charlestonian who could get him an audience with some of Charlestown's beloved men. As the frustrated man from the middle towns left his house in Charlestown, he followed a familiar path to the bay. He had decided to visit the one man whom he knew would recognize him. After all, the Itsa'ti sogwili visited Thomas Barton each time he entered the gaduhv'i and each time he left. Barton was the government-appointed storekeeper responsible for receiving skins and doling out trade goods for return trips and he was the burdener's last best hope.[28]

Upon arriving at the storehouse, the Itsa'ti laborer must have been relieved when Barton recognized him and offered to hear his complaint. Whether they conversed through signs, broken English, or confident Cherokee with the aid of an interpreter, Barton got the picture. As he would later relate to his superiors, "A white Man took a Skin of him, for a Streak of the Fag End of a Piece of Silk, and about a Yard of Cadis." But if the Itsa'ti laborer could only identify his antagonist as a "white Man," he had little chance of success. Yet just as the Itsa'ti man was in the middle of his harangue, he spotted a familiar face "passing by the Shop."[29] Thomas Cutler, it turns out, was in the wrong place at the wrong time. The sogwili simply pointed at Cutler and "affirm[ed] that he was the Man, who had injured him."[30]

Now Barton had little choice but to take the laborer's complaint to the Commissioners. After enlisting Caesar as his interpreter, the Itsa'ti burdener and Barton appeared before the board. Once Barton had introduced the man and provided the Commissioners with an abridged version of his complaint, the Charlestonian unigvwiyuhi posed some questions to the Itsa'ti sogwili. Speaking through Caesar, the Commissioners asked the man what had happened. Grasping the remnant of silk in his hands, the laborer related his tale. And, while they listened to the complaint, the Commissioners took no immediate action on the

Itsa'ti man's behalf—at least according to their clerk. They ordered Barton to give Caesar a knife out of the public store for his interpretive labors and then adjourned. Perhaps they decided that caveat emptor served well enough here. The Itsa'ti man had, after all, received *something* in return for his skin.[31]

The exact contours of the resolution of *Itsa'ti burdener v. Cutler*, however, is relatively unimportant. That a common laborer—who was so unimportant that his name was not recorded—was able to navigate Charlestown's geography of power well enough to have his case heard before some of the most powerful unigvwiyuhi in the English gaduhv'i is remarkable. Sure, luck played a part. But the Itsa'ti man's familiarity with Charlestown contributed to the creation of that luck. If he had barged into the Commissioners' tavern in search of redress or went in search of Cutler to exact his own retribution, he might have never been able to receive the audience he desired. The Itsa'ti sogwili bent the power that dwelled in Charlestown to his own purposes. Like Caesar, he knew how the colonial city's power operated and he used that knowledge to his advantage.

As the Itsa'ti man's tale demonstrates, exchange in Charlestown had become more difficult since Charlestown's unigvwiyuhi had ordered individual colonists not to trade with Indigenous visitors. While Cherokee-speaking commoners usually had little trouble finding a market for their skins and their women's baskets in Charlestown, residents of the colonial capital had begun to either refuse to trade with the anisogwili or offer them less for their wares. As a result, people like Hootleboyau and Yorogotogaskee had to seek out other alternatives. Before arriving in Charlestown to unload the deer skins they carried, a few Ani-Dugilu accompanied Col. Alexander Mackey to the garrison at Edistoe in search of a more welcoming environment of exchange.

Upon arriving at the small outpost, Mackey introduced his lower towns companions to the garrison's commander, John Jones. Because Jones seemed an "honest man," Hootleboyau decided to see what the colonist would offer him for some of his skins.[32] Relatively quickly, the two settled on an agreeable price for eleven of Hootleboyau's deerskins and seven of his beaver.[33] But when Jones asked the Dugilu laborer about some of the "painted Baskets" he also carried, Hootleboyau refused to part with those commodities.[34] While trading them with the seemingly honest Jones would be easy, Hootleboyau knew these baskets would fetch a much higher price in Charlestown. Although he managed to fend off Jones's advances, one of his companions decided to take the Edistoe commander up on his offer. Hailing from one of Dugilu's smaller satellite settlements, Yorogotogaskee of Noyowee agreed to give Jones a single basket

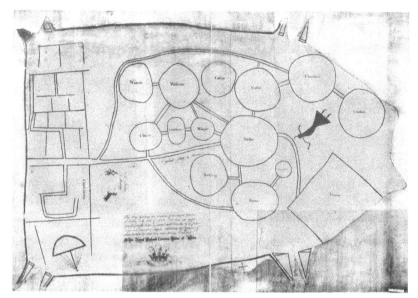

Detail from *Map of the several nations of Indians to the Northwest of South Carolina*, c. 1721. Library of Congress, Geography and Map Division. This map provides a view of Charlestown (*bottom left*) through Indigenous eyes. It is no coincidence that the largest path leads directly to where the "beloved House" sat. Although most historians refer to this map colloquially as the "Catawba Deerskin Map," Cherokees were also asked to "mark the boundaries of the lands between them and the English settlers" in 1721. Even if this is not their map, in other words, it is as close to a visual representation of their Charlestown as we can get. Such a map demonstrates that all sorts of Indigenous people knew Charlestown's paths and paths of power. This version of Charlestown is remarkably similar to one created by an Ani-Charlestown some years earlier.

in exchange for a shirt.[35] Perhaps Yorogotogaskee only had the one basket and he decided not to press his luck in Charlestown. Or maybe he had a clutch of baskets and figured that throwing one to Jones was not the worst idea. Whatever his reasoning, the Noyowee laborer would come to regret his decision.

Rather than press for payment immediately, Hootleboyau and Yorogotogaskee agreed to let Jones "come down along with him to Charles Town, and satisfie him for them" there. While this seems like an easily avoided mistake in hindsight, these two lower towns laborers must have agreed to dozens of similar transactions in the past. These successes, of course, went unrecorded.

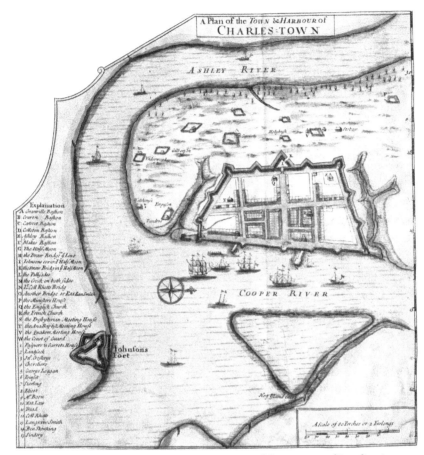

Detail from Edward Crisp, *A Complete Description of the Province of Carolina in 3 Parts*, c. 1711. Library of Congress, Geography and Map Division. This detail of Charlestown from Crisp's map of Carolina provides a view of the English town from the perspective of an Ani-Charlestown. While there seems to be more detail here—buildings labeled, walls drawn, wharves present—the Indigenous view seems to include more footpaths than this one, suggesting their particular way of experiencing the gaduhv'i.

After continuing on to Charlestown, Hootleboyau "importuned" anyone who would listen that he and his mate had been cheated—Jones had not yet paid his debts. He surely asked Mackey to intercede on his behalf, but their traveling companion either could not force the garrison commander to pay or refused to meddle in a clearly illegal transaction.

In desperation, Hootleboyau and Yorogotogaskee used their knowledge of Charlestown and its geography of power to their advantage. While Mackey had failed them, plenty of other powerful people haunted the taverns of the gaduhv'i. Amid the cadre of powerful unigvwiyuhi in Charlestown, of course, was their own headman. Hagey was almost certainly the first person they approached with tales of their plight. Although the Conjuror of Dugilu had larger problems to deal with, he likely reassured his people that he would present their complaint to the Commissioners at the right time. But as days passed without any hint of resolution or restitution, the two lower towns laborers decided that they had to find another way to get their complaint in front of the Commissioners.[36]

Perhaps they knew Colonel Mackey in his capacity as one of the newly appointed Commissioners of the Indian Trade. Whatever their acquaintance with the beloved man called John Barnwell, Hootleboyau and Yorogotogaskee hoped he would listen to their complaint.[37] Because they were not confident in their English-language skills, the two aggrieved laborers secured the services of an "Interpretess" named Elizabeth Bedon.[38] Although Bedon only spoke Yamasee, she was the best they could do on short notice. Whether they found a local enslaved Yamasee who spoke Cherokee or one of them happened to speak Yamasee, Hootleboyau and Yorogotogaskee related their plight to Barnwell through Bedon.

While they admitted they had "heard the Talk the white Men have about [not] buying their Skins," the two anisogwili claimed they had been "deluded by" Jones.[39] For these two lower towns laborers, the questioned legality of their unsuccessful attempt at trade hardly mattered. They had participated in similar sorts of exchange countless times previously and they knew that the Commissioners had no authority to punish them. Indeed, Hootleboyau intended to continue the practice with the baskets he carried to the English gaduhv'i. By bringing their complaint to Barnwell's attention, they probably hoped Jones would, at the very least, be punished for violating the trading act. What these two really wanted, however, was the payment Jones promised them. Now that they had deputized Barnwell, as it were, they would have to wait and see if the Commissioners would act in an official capacity to compensate them for their lost labor.

For his part, Barnwell knew how quickly this small complaint could become fatal to a town still fighting a war. Charlestown could not afford to lose its alliance with Dugilu—both militarily and economically. And because he was a sitting Commissioner, he had already heard the complaints lodged by Hagey about the faltering trade and Caesar's threat to seek friendship elsewhere. So Barnwell did what Hootleboyau and Yorogotogaskee had counted on. Calling a special meeting of the Commissioners, Barnwell laid the laborers complaint before the board. After hearing the complaint from Barnwell's mouth, the Commissioners ordered a copy of it drawn up and delivered to the Commons House immediately. While no record survives detailing their deliberations on the laborers' complaint, their willingness to suspend the trading act and allow Cherokees like Hootleboyau and Yorogotogaskee to trade with individual Charlestonians was almost certainly related to the complaints of these commoners. The knowledge of Charlestown and its inner workings displayed by these virtually anonymous lower towns laborers highlights the connections a wide range of Cherokee-speakers had with the English gaduhv'i. It was not just a place for clever headmen. Not only did they force a special meeting of the Commissioners, but their precisely directed complaints received an audience from an even more powerful body of beloved men. They were not headmen, yet they had a sort of power that Charlestown's unigvwiyuhi could not ignore.[40]

Probably encouraged by the earlier actions of Charlestown's beloved men, the Conjuror decided that this was a perfect time to seek satisfaction for Hootleboyau and Yorogotogaskee. So two days after Barnwell had presented their complaint, Hagey repeated the testimony of Hootleboyau and Yorogotogaskee to the Commissioners. "John Jones," he affirmed, "hath cheated his People."[41] It turns out that Hootleboyau and Yorogotogaskee were not alone in complaining to their headman. Hagey also took this opportunity to lodge the grievances of two more nameless Ani-Dugilu laborers. A Charlestonian "Joyner" had borrowed a horse from one sogwili, promising him "Rum and a Coat" in exchange. The colonist had not only neglected to fulfill his end of the bargain but had still not returned the horse. And finding two stray horses on his way down, another laborer had returned those horses to Alexander Mackey, who "hath given no Reward to the Indian."[42] On this occasion, Hagey received assurances that "due Satisfaction" and "full Amends made him for his People's wrongful usage."[43] The Commissioners also gave him a message to pass along to his mistreated people. "[I]t was their own fault," the Board claimed, "for not hearkening to the Great Men's talk to them, and occasioned by their choosing rather to deal with private Persons."[44] Furthermore, these Charlestonian unigvwiyuhi warned that if this happened in the future, they would be powerless to offer any restitution.

Upon returning to his lodgings near the town gate, Hagey must have given his people the happy news. Satisfaction was on its way in the next day or so. The wheels of justice in Charlestown, however, turned slowly. Rather than take Hootleboyau, Yorogotogaskee, and Hagey at their word, the Commissioners decided to issue a warrant of seizure for John Jones to compel his appearance before the Board. As Charlestown's beloved men well knew, this would take days.[45] Hootleboyau and Yorogotogaskee knew nothing about this change of plans when they walked into the Commissioners' tavern the next day expecting their promised payment.

They waited patiently while Caesar and Partridge performed a scene about their intentions to head off for war. The two laborers must have felt confident in their case as they watched the two middle towns headmen accept elaborate gifts. Buoyed by this display, Hootleboyau and Yorogotogaskee approached the board and "moved for Restitution for the Skins and Baskets John Jones defrauded them of."[46] But the anisogwili could hardly believe what they were hearing from Charlestown's beloved men. Any satisfaction, the Charlestonians said cooly, would be deferred "til Munday."[47] Hootleboyau and Yorogotogaskee were outraged. While their exact protestations went unrecorded, the clerk noted that it was only through "Cesar's Perswasion" that one of them agreed to wait. The other wronged worker "was hardly prevailed with to consent to" the additional delay.[48] Whether Hootleboyau and Yorogotogaskee thought they were in the midst of another Charlestonian scheme to deceive them or were simply sick of waiting for their promised compensation, they had clearly had enough with the way Charlestonians did business. They left the Commissioners' tavern that afternoon resolved—more than ever—to fight for their satisfaction.

While the lower town laborers simmered in their house near the gates, John Jones ambled into town ready to defend himself. But when the two complainants appeared before the board ready to mount their last offensive, they were met with more than the usual suspects. Jones they would have expected. But seeing Daniell awaiting their arrival must have been a bit of a welcome shock to Hootleboyau and Yorogotogaskee. What began as a complaint to their own headman had now become the concern of Charlestown's most powerful ugvwiyuhi. Well informed as to the Indians' side of the story, Daniell asked Jones to share his perspective on the troubling transaction. After swearing an oath, Jones "denied the Fact" of the accusations leveled against him. Whether he denied ever having seen Hootleboyau and Yorogotogaskee or just his alleged deception remains unclear. Whatever the grounds of his defense, however, his lower towns accusers vociferously "affirm[ed] the Truth of their Assertion."[49]

While the Commissioners' clerk dismissively noted that the Indigenous laborers continued to use only "Indian Evidence" to support their accusations, Governor Daniell and his beloved men knew that such a species of evidence was clearly enough in this case. Dripping with contempt, the clerk recorded that "for the pretended Injuries of the said Jones, to them" the two burdeners received "two striped Duffield Matchcoats and two Strouds Matchcoats" as "Compensation."[50] Although the Commissioners' clerk clearly felt that these two common laborers did not deserve any sort of reward for their illegal behavior, more powerful men knew better. While Hootleboyau and Yorogotogaskee were not remarkable in virtually any way, sending these men back to their towns without satisfaction was out of the question. The alliance with their gaduhv'i was far too important. If these two men traveled back to their urban center with tales of poor treatment in Charlestown, the alliance might be dead. Navigating Charlestown's geography of power, then, was not just the bailiwick of the most powerful Cherokees. Otherwise unremarkable commoners were just as creative and just as adept with that skill.

As dozens of Cherokee commoners still strolled the streets of his gaduhv'i during the winter of 1717—some perhaps right outside his Bay Street windows—Robert Daniell penned a letter to his superiors in London. "The Cherikees . . . Kings and head Warriors are now with us," he began. This particular bit of correspondence, however, was not so much about Caesar and Hagey as about what they demanded while in town—and whom they registered those requests on behalf of. "The Charge We are at to maintain them," Daniell continued, "and the Demands they make are so unreasonable that We may properly say We are become their Tributaries." The "them" here clearly references the Cherokee commoners who sauntered along Daniell's sandy streets. While they all required food and lodging for their weeks-long residences, the currency the governor really worried about was power. According to his calculus, the wrong people were "Tributaries." And as he drafted this missive, news of further complaints from common Cherokee laborers like Hootleboyau or Yorogotogaskee crossed his desk. While he had no desire to hear what they had to say, Daniell knew their protests required his attention. Dealing with the demands of Cherokee

"Kings" was one thing. Handling the comparatively petty problems of laborers was quite another story. Cherokees of all persuasions were becoming far too familiar with Charlestown.[51]

NOTES

1. Jan. 23, 1717, *Journals of the Commissioners of the Indian Trade: September 20, 1710–August 29, 1718*, ed. William L. McDowell Jr. (Columbia: South Carolina Archives Department, 1955), 150–51; hereafter cited as JCIT. "Of a more Ordinary quality" quoted from Frank J. Klingberg, *The Carolina Chronicle of Dr. Francis Le Jau* (Berkeley: University of California Press, 1956), 169. As is apparent from the first paragraph, this essay uses Cherokee-language terms to help illuminate Indigenous perceptions and understandings of lived reality, especially as they pertain to the urban world Cherokees moved through in the eighteenth century. In the estimation of Cherokees, places like Charlestown and Itsa'ti, 350 miles distant, were *both* disgaduhv'i. Realizing that fact changes our understanding of Cherokees and their colonial world. In his recent book on Hawaiian "geographies of exploration," David Chang notes that the use of the "Hawaiian-language" is necessary for fully "understanding the Hawaiian past." Without understanding Hawaiian, we cannot understand how Hawaiians experienced or made sense of the past. The same goes for Cherokee. Using the term *gaduhv'i* to describe Cherokee towns and Charlestown demonstrates that Cherokees understood both places as fundamentally similar. By employing Cherokee terms, then, this essay strives to reinterpret English-language sources from a Cherokee perspective and, thereby, defamiliarize and subvert readerly expectations. And rather than offer a glossary, the chapter provides contextual clues so as to help readers infer for themselves, perhaps through rereading, the meanings to Cherokee terms used herein; see David H. Chang, *The World and All the Things upon It: Native Hawaiian Geographies of Exploration* (Minneapolis: University of Minnesota Press, 2016), xi. For another example of Indigenous language as a method of interpretation, see Michael Witgen, *An Infinity of Nations: How the Native New World Shaped Early North America* (Philadelphia: University of Pennsylvania Press, 2012), 25–26. For more on the Yamasee War, see Steven J. Oatis, *A Colonial Complex: South Carolina's Frontiers in the Era of the Yamasee War, 1680–1730* (Lincoln: University of Nebraska Press, 2004); William L. Ramsey, *The Yamasee War: A Study of Culture, Economy, and Conflict in the Colonial South* (Lincoln: University of Nebraska Press, 2008); and Larry E. Ivers, *This Torrent of Indians: War on the Southern Frontier, 1715–1728* (Columbia: University of South Carolina Press, 2016). For the urban dimensions of that conflict, see Nathaniel Holly, "From Itsa'ti to Charlestown: The Urban Lives of Cherokees in Early America" (PhD diss., College of William and Mary, 2019), 95–133.

2. Verner W. Crane, *The Southern Frontier, 1670–1732* (1929; repr., Tuscaloosa: University of Alabama Press, 2004), 108.

3. John Phillip Reid, *A Better Kind of Hatchet: Law, Trade, and Diplomacy in the Cherokee Nation during the Early Years of European Contact* (University Park: Penn State University Press, 1976), 117.

4. For examples of archaeologists' work on Cherokee commoners, see Jon Bernard Marcoux, *Pox, Empire, Shackles, and Hides: The Townsend Site, 1670–1715* (Tuscaloosa: University of Alabama Press, 2010), and Christopher B. Rodning, "The Archaeology of Gender and Women in Traditional Cherokee Society," *Journal of Cherokee Studies* 20 (1999): 3–27. In two of the most recent—and most important—books devoted to Cherokees, neither author mentions the likes of Hootleboyau or Yorogotogaskee by name. Yet while one, Tom Hatley, does devote a few paragraphs to burdeners, the other, Tyler Boulware, only mentions anisogwili on a single page. See, respectively, Tom Hatley, *The Dividing Paths: Cherokees and South Carolinians through the Revolutionary Era* (New York: Oxford University Press, 1995), 37–39; and Tyler Boulware, *Deconstructing the Cherokee Nation: Town, Region, and Nation among Eighteenth-Century Cherokees* (Gainesville: University Press of Florida, 2011), 37.

5. "LIST of all the CHEROKEE TOWNS," *South Carolina Gazette*, July 5, 1760. Another Ani-Charlestown distinguished between towns, small villages, and places with just a few houses; see Christopher French, "Journal of an Expedition to South Carolina," *Journal of Cherokee Studies* 2 (Summer 1977): 275–301, especially 284–88.

6. Christopher Rodning, "Mounds, Myths, and Cherokee Townhouses in Southwestern North Carolina," *American Antiquity* 74, no. 4 (2009): 632.

7. July 3, 1753, "Proceedings of the Council Concerning Indian Affairs," in *Documents Relating to Indian Affairs, May 21, 1750–August 7, 1754*, ed. William L. McDowell Jr. (Columbia: South Carolina Archives Department, 1958), 437. On Indigenous urbanism in colonial North America, see Boulware, *Deconstructing the Cherokee Nation*; Christopher B. Rodning, *Center Places and Cherokee Towns: Archaeological Perspectives on Native American Architecture and Landscape in the Southern Appalachians* (Tuscaloosa: University of Alabama Press, 2015); and Joshua Piker, *Okfuskee: A Creek Indian Town in Colonial America* (Cambridge, Mass.: Harvard University Press, 2004). And for more on Indians in colonial cities, see Daniel Usner, *American Indians in Colonial New Orleans: From Calumet to Raquette* (Baton Rouge: Louisiana State University Press, 2018); Christine DeLucia, *Memory Lands: King Philip's War and the Place of Violence in the Northeast* (New Haven, Conn.: Yale University Press, 2018), 29–120; and Jay Gitlin, Barbara Berglund, and Adam Arenson, eds., *Frontier Cities: Encounters at the Crossroads of Empire* (Philadelphia: University of Pennsylvania Press, 2012).

8. Klingberg, *The Carolina Chronicle*, 169.

9. January 26, 1717, JCIT, 233.

10. January 24, 1717, Journals of the Commons House of Assembly, Green Transcripts, South Carolina Department of Archives and History, Columbia, South Carolina, 5:227; hereafter cited as JCHA (Green). Caesar had learned English while he was enslaved in Charlestown, so impromptu talks like this one would have been possible without an interpreter.

11. January 17, 1717, JCHA (Green), 5:222. While John Phillip Reid devotes a few pages to Caesar's demand, he largely ignores the anisogwili Caesar championed; see Reid, *Better Kind of Hatchet*, 105–9. For his part, Hatley mentions Caesar's demand in the context of his two-page section on burdeners but with little analysis of the threat

or significance of location; see Hatley, *Dividing Paths*, 37. Stern, moreover, neglects to mention the demand entirely; see Jessica Yirush Stern, *Lives in Objects: Native Americans, British Colonists, and Cultures of Labor and Exchange in the Southeast* (Chapel Hill: University of North Carolina Press, 2017).

12. January 24, 1717, JCHA (Green), 5:227.

13. January 17, 1717, JCHA (Green), 5:222.

14. January 18, 1717, JCHA (Green), 5:223–24.

15. January 23, 1717, JCIT, 150.

16. January 23, 1717, JCIT, 150–51.

17. January 23, 1717, JCIT, 151.

18. January 24, 1717, JCHA (Green), 5:227.

19. January 24, 1717, JCHA (Green), 5:227.

20. January 25, 1717, JCIT, 152.

21. January 25, 1717, JCIT, 152

22. January 30, 1717, JCIT, 155, and 1717/1/31, JCIT, 157.

23. January 26, 1717, JCIT, 153.

24. January 29, 1717, JCIT, 154.

25. February 5, 1717, JCIT, 158.

26. May 9, 1717, JCIT, 178

27. January 20, 1717, JCIT, 156.

28. January 20, 1717, JCIT, 155–56.

29. January 20, 1717, JCIT, 156.

30. January 20, 1717, JCIT, 156.

31. January 20, 1717, JCIT, 156.

32. January 23, 1717, JCIT, 150.

33. January 25, 1717, JCIT, 151.

34. January 23, 1717, JCIT, 150.

35. January 23, 1717, JCIT, 150.

36. Jessica Stern calls on the complaints of Hagey, Hootleboyau, and Yorogotogaskee as evidence for the "advocacy" of headmen and the shared concerns of individual Indians. See Stern, *Lives in Objects*, 82, 85. Reading Hootleboyau's complaint through a gendered lens, Michelle LeMaster sees it as evidence of "[l]ong-distance trade" being the "responsibility of men"; see Michelle LeMaster, *Brothers Born of One Mother: British-Native American Relations in the Colonial Southeast* (Charlottesville: University of Virginia Press, 2012), 138.

37. Walter B. Edgar and N. Louise Bailey, eds. *Biographical Directory of the South Carolina House of Representatives: Volume 2, The Commons House of Assembly, 1692–1775* (Columbia: University of South Carolina Press, 1977), 52–54.

38. She was active in the Ashley River Antipedo Baptist Congregation, which almost certainly sought to preach the gospel to Indigenous neighbors. As a result of her participation in that effort, Bedon acquired a fluency in the Yamasee language that proved useful to the two aggrieved laborers; see Edgar, *Biographical Directory*, 66–67.

39. January 23, 1717, JCIT, 150–51.

40. January 23, 1717, JCIT, 149. The Journal notes that on this particular occasion, "their met by special Summons."

41. January 25, 1717, JCIT, 151.

42. January 25, 1717, JCIT, 151.

43. January 25, 1717, JCIT, 151–52.

44. January 25, 1717, JCIT, 152.

45. January 26, 1717, JCIT, 152–53.

46. January 26, 1717, JCIT, 153.

47. January 26, 1717, JCIT, 153.

48. January 26, 1717, JCIT, 153.

49. January 28, 1717, JCIT, 154.

50. January 28, 1717, JCIT, 154.

51. January 26, 1717, Governor and Council to the Lords Proprietors, CO 5/1265 fol. 129, National Archives, Kew, United Kingdom.

DANIEL H. USNER

2

COMMUNICATING SOVEREIGNTY IN *BALBANCHA*

The Performance of Native American Diplomacy
in Early New Orleans

The ceremony began when a delegation of about forty Chitimacha Indians—
including a headman and his wife—landed in several dugout canoes at the Mississippi River's bank fronting New Orleans, a colonial town still being cleared
and surveyed. Singing to the cadence of gourd shakers and waving a calumet
pipe toward the sky, the Chitimachas marched solemnly to the makeshift cabin
of Jean-Baptiste Le Moyne, Sieur de Bienville. Once all of these visitors were
seated on the ground, the pipe was lit and presented to Louisiana's governor.
After war with the French had ravaged his people for more than a decade, the
Chitimachas' "word-bearer" expressed joy over Bienville's willingness to accept
peace. "Our hearts and our ears are filled with it," he declared, "and our descendants will preserve it as long as the ancient word shall endure." After presenting
a gift of deerskins to the governor, this orator further elaborated on the causes
and consequences of the costly war. With a brief speech, Bienville received
this promise of peace, along with the pipe itself as a gift. He commanded the

Chitimachas to return all colonists taken captive during the war but refused to return any Chitimacha people captured and enslaved by the French. Bienville then closed this ceremony by insisting that the chief relocate his village closer to New Orleans, a city that would henceforth take its rituals quite seriously.[1]

As this performance of a calumet ceremony begins to suggest, the birth and early growth of New Orleans depended intricately on French relations with Indigenous people of the Lower Mississippi Valley. Countless Indian delegations frequented colonial towns across the hemisphere to negotiate with imperial officials and conduct diplomatic rituals, communicating their interests and identities in urban spaces that bluntly signified European occupation.[2] Even after American cities stopped being centers of Indian diplomacy, an Indigenous presence persisted in diverse and dynamic ways. And all of this was certainly the case for New Orleans, which would be visited periodically by formal delegations of Indian leaders and regularly by informal groups of Indian traders and workers throughout the nineteenth century. Whether engaging government officials in diplomatic ceremonies, peddling cultural objects in marketplaces, playing traditional stickball matches in and around town, performing songs and dances before city spectators, or becoming residents, American Indians have managed to keep New Orleans as a crucial place in their homeland.[3]

The riverfront site chosen for New Orleans, at the crescent-shaped bend in the Mississippi, had long been used by Indigenous people to transport goods between waterways and to seasonally gather food sources. Natural conditions making this site ideal for portage and fishing, however, also reduced any likelihood of it becoming a place for permanent occupation, an environmental challenge that to this day demands expensive engineering and constant vigilance.[4] In the year 1699, on the Saturday after Mardi Gras, Bienville's older brother, Pierre Le Moyne d'Iberville, was slowly ascending the Mississippi River when he encountered a group of Biloxi Indians just below the future site of New Orleans. On the lush but spongy shoreline of the river, covered with thick canebrakes and shaded by cypress and oak trees, one of these Biloxi travelers treated the French naval officer to a customary show of friendship by first passing both hands over his own face and breast and then passing them over Iberville's face and breast before raising them toward the sky. In return for knives, glass beads, and axes offered by Iberville, the Biloxi gave him some buffalo and bear meat. This was Iberville's first time voyaging on the Mississippi, and its banks surely seemed exotic to someone born and raised in Canada. But for someone who, along with other members of his family, had accumulated plenty of experience in Indian diplomacy, the Biloxi's greeting would not have appeared so strange. Two days following that initial encounter, Iberville's party, including Bienville, reached a point along the river where Indians portaged to and from Lake Pontchartrain. "They drag their canoes over a rather good road," Iberville reported, "at which we found several pieces of baggage owned by men that were going there or were returning." After his guide, another Biloxi man, pointed out that the distance from river to lake was short, "the Indian picked up a bundle from there." Within only a few days, the French Canadian Le Moyne brothers learned from American Indians the importance of both ceremony and commerce right where the Crescent City was born two decades later.[5]

The years that passed between the Le Moynes' initial journey along these banks of the Mississippi and young Bienville's founding of Nouvelle Orleans were violent and deadly for the region's Native inhabitants. Imperial rivalry between France and England—especially slave raiding by Indian allies of South Carolina—wreaked widespread havoc among Lower Mississippi Valley people.[6] In 1715 a Frenchman witnessed English traders upriver at Natchez purchasing Chaouacha captives, whose village below the future site of New Orleans had been attacked by a party of Natchez, Chickasaw, and Yazoo raiders. To avoid slave-raiding attacks on this edge of homelands suddenly shattered by violence and disease, groups of Houma and Natchitoches Indians took temporary refuge along bayous and ridges between the Mississippi River and Lake Pontchartrain. It did not take long for French colonial officials to launch their own raids for Native captives. A twelve-year-long war against the Chitimachas yielded numerous slaves for early Louisiana settlers. Once the Company of the Indies began sending settlers and slaves to develop plantations along the lower Mississippi, however, stable and peaceful relations with American Indians became essential. Within months of New Orleans's founding in 1718, destructive warfare between Chitimachas and Frenchmen finally reached its end with the calumet dance that marked one of the city's earliest public rituals.[7]

Whether relations between Native and colonial groups were violent or peaceful at any given time, representation of American Indian people in words and images printed to promote colonization of Louisiana reveals more about imperial fantasies than about actual interactions. One Paris magazine published a fictionalized letter from an imaginary colonist who expected Louisiana to "one day become France's Peru." Typical of attempts to publicize opportunities for trade and settlement at the new colonial port of New Orleans, an engraving that circulated to promote investment in John Law's Company of the Indies depicted Indians in supplicatory postures—expressing submissive gratitude toward missionaries and merchants.[8]

What was actually happening on the ground, however, did not match promotional imagery. While slaves, convict workers, indentured servants, and soldiers grudgingly cleared flood-prone land for New Orleans, American Indians used their knowledge of river currents, lakes, bayous, and wetlands to draw the new colonial space into their trade and diplomatic sphere. Europeans might worry about its perilous location—fearing floods, insects, hurricanes, and diseases—but Indians were used to blending their harvests, travels, and rituals with the region's natural rhythms. Indians would now begin creatively establishing their own trade and ceremonial grounds in New Orleans in order to negotiate and even resist colonialism. For thousands of years Southeastern Indians had constructed mounds as spaces for ritual performance and aesthetic expression, many of them constituting urban centers. In a project studying many different mound sites, Choctaw writer LeAnne Howe associates ball games, dances, and other ceremonies with the layering of soils. Post-Mississippian societies perpetuated this tradition on village square grounds and eventually on colonial plazas where gift exchanges and calumet dances secured political alliances.[9]

Thanks to an unnamed Chitimacha woman's interpretation of the negotiations ending her people's war against the French, Antoine Simon Le Page du Pratz—the colonist holding her in slavery—was able to record in his *Histoire de la Louisiane* many details about that calumet ceremony performed at the very start of New Orleans. In order to establish any new alliance or restore peace after a war, American Indians throughout the region performed ceremonies centered on the use of a pipe made of river cane or some other reed-like material and attached to a carved bowl made of red or black stone. Along with the pipe decorated with bird feathers and waved during an opening dance and the smoking of tobacco with the opposite party—as depicted in Le Page du Pratz's engraving *Marche du Calumet de Paix*—there were some other sensory features: the sound made by gourd shakers, wooden drums, cane flutes, and human voices, the smell and taste of bountiful meals, and the feeling of bodies being rubbed and seated on mats or skins.[10] A ceremonial system linking different levels of the natural world and forming kinship ties between strangers, this elaborate ritual of diplomacy extended from the northern Great Plains and western Great Lakes across the eastern woodlands. French officials and travelers like Bienville, who received the Chitimachas' gift of a pipe in 1718, were quick to adopt the calumet ritual in order to establish necessary trade alliances with Indigenous nations.[11]

Antoine Le Page du Pratz, *Marche du Calumet de Paix*, engraving in *Histoire de La Louisiane* (1758). The Historic New Orleans Collection, Gift of Mrs. Henry C. Pitot in memory of Henry C. Pitot.

Describing one of many subsequent ceremonies performed in New Orleans by American Indian delegates during those early decades, a clerk working for the Company of the Indies vividly described how they regularly turned the formative colonial town into their own ritual space. He also partly captured the multiple sensory dimensions of those diplomatic performances. Numbering anywhere between one hundred and fifty and five hundred men and women, the Indians sang and danced before lining up outside the governor's house gate. Chiefs and other dignitaries then entered carrying plenty of gifts and placing a calumet in the governor's hands. After everyone present took a puff from the pipe, the delegation spokesmen delivered a series of speeches through a French interpreter familiar with their language, which might last for hours. "Since the great sun of the French sent you here to govern the country, and he has found in you much valor and the necessary qualities to make you obey," as the lead orator would typically open with, "we come here, with my nation, to present to you our fealty and assure you that, when you need our small services, we will always be ready to follow your orders, whether it is to second you in a war you may have against your enemies, as well as for any other thing that regards the usefulness of the French nation, which we have always loved, and which we continue to cherish." Once all speeches ended, "four worthies get up, along with four Indians, and dance the calumet dance, all painted and ornamented with different types of feathers, to the sound of an earthen pot covered with a deerskin, ornamented with many bells and accompanied by their voices." Written about a place fast becoming a creative confluence of diverse rhythms and tones, Marc-Antoine Caillot added, "This makes music as bizarre as their movements and dances. When they have danced for a while, by making extraordinary contortions that make you want to die laughing, they sit down again on their bottoms, whereupon one of them gets up and takes the calumet." After the pipe was passed around for a final round of smoking, deerskins and other gifts were placed at the governor's feet. On the next day the governor spoke to the chief and his closest entourage and then gave them an array of goods that commonly included cloth, combs, mirrors, muskets, and vermillion. "When they return to their village, the chief has it all divided."[12]

In such moments of cross-cultural negotiation, it is impossible to capture adequately what Indian diplomats intended to convey to newly arrived French counterparts, as well as what spiritual power and Indigenous knowledge was being invoked—the "mental space," as Henri Lefebvre would put it. After all, we are at the mercy of colonial texts like that of Caillot's, written for audiences far removed from those engaging the ceremonial action on the ground—Lefebvre's "real space."[13] Nor can we know with confidence what the performances in New Orleans meant for their Indian performers in the moment or when back in their own communities: How were these events narrated? What impact did they have on the status and prestige of participants? How did negotiation with colonial officials enhance the prestige and power of participants, or how did it cause controversy and rivalry among community leaders? It is safe to say that colonial interpreters and recorders missed most of the spiritual and epistemological import of Indian emissaries' words and actions. We should nevertheless make attempts, through advanced Indigenous studies, to recover Native American spaces and networks still unfortunately considered remote and foreign.[14]

What can be gathered, for now, is a rough understanding of the innovation and improvisation that Indians applied to their own diplomatic traditions when visiting New Orleans, thereby contributing to the production of civic culture in a new urban space. Without any doubt, perception and interpretation of Indigenous public performances differed across a transoceanic cultural divide, expressed frequently through Europeans' condescending complaints over cost and time spent. Accommodation to protocol practiced by Native peoples, however, was an economic and political necessity for colonial officials. A mutual desire for things, knowledge, and power from each other required reliable means of communication and even a degree of trust crossing even the widest of cultural divides.[15] A place of performance, as Matt Cohen shows for colonial New England, constitutes "a momentarily stable and readable ground for communication" that we can examine with some confidence by considering "the materiality of oral performance." The spaces in which Indian delegates and colonial officials negotiated their respective interests and reached mutual agreements certainly involved representational contests as important as warfare and commerce. Even when directed mainly at colonial audiences in towns like New Orleans, performance of the calumet ceremony's symbolism, dance, and oratory preserved also a network of Indigenous communication. Explaining construction of an even wider semiotic space elsewhere in North America, Michael Witgen persuasively demonstrates that European imperial interpretations of diplomatic protocol never accurately represented the complex and dynamic webs of kinship actually formed by Native allies.[16]

Although Indian diplomacy instantly became an important feature of public life and civic culture in New Orleans, the city's survival and early growth depended more immediately upon goods and services provided by nearby Indian communities. Ensuring that colonial cityscapes never belonged to any single group, as Christine DeLucia has recently emphasized about early Boston, Native people resourcefully put "urban homelands" to uses that included everything from ritual reclamation to material interaction.[17] From many different communities and nations, American Indians brought to the new port town on the Mississippi River a growing volume of deerskins for exportation and an essential supply of grain and meat for urban consumption. Through a frontier exchange economy already underway in the countryside, they began in quick time to regularly deliver an array of products to New Orleans and occasionally to work as guides for travelers or as fugitive-catchers for slaveowners.[18]

Indian labor as well as Indian trade contributed heavily to the city's formative economy, but most Native people working inside the colonial town were enslaved captives taken during early warfare. Long before New Orleans was founded, tens of thousands of captured Indigenous North Americans had been sold into transatlantic slavery, at first by European explorers and eventually by colonial officials and merchants. Many of these captives, mostly taken during war, were shipped to British or French Caribbean colonies; others worked as plantation slaves or household servants up and down the eastern seaboard. Many enslaved Indians lived in cities like Montreal, Boston, New York, Charleston, and—by the 1720s—New Orleans. From Louisiana's beginnings, Indian people, especially Chitimacha women and children, formed a substantial part of the French colony's slave population. While some entered into legal marriage with their owners, most suffered the psychic and physical violence facing enslaved persons in general. Indian slaves frequently collaborated with African slaves in attempting escape and rebellion, which predictably heightened anxiety among owners and officials. When the Natchez launched upriver their war of resistance against the French, Chaouacha—the Native community nearest New Orleans— was totally destroyed by African slaves armed by the colonial government solely for that purpose. Soon thereafter, hundreds of Natchez men, women, and children were being transported through the city as prisoners and shipped as slaves to France's island colonies. Because tens of thousands of African and African American slaves would be transported there for nearly a century and a half, initially from across the Atlantic world and later from other parts of the United States, New Orleans is rightfully seen as one of North America's most infamous slave markets. But less recognized was its position also as an entrepôt for the exportation of many enslaved American Indians, sharing this role with other colonial port towns. In 1731 two ships embarked from New Orleans to Saint-Domingue with some four hundred Natchez captives on board.[19]

For most of the eighteenth century, however, peaceful exchange between American Indians and town residents remained the norm in and around New Orleans. Providing the colonial town with foodstuffs and services was the mainstay of nearby Indian communities' relationship with the colonial town, contributing significantly to its foodways, material life, and public culture. For larger Indian nations located farther inland, like the Choctaws, commerce in deerskins constituted their most important and longest-lasting connection with New Orleans. The Choctaws started using the name Balbancha for New Orleans, a "place of foreign languages," a name derived from *balbaha*, their word for talking in an unknown language or for prattling like an infant. American Indian people obviously recognized that the French colonial town had become a pivotal place for intercultural communication and exchange.[20]

Indian delegations to New Orleans were essential for securing alliances with Indians across the Mississippi Valley, and whatever promises and presents Native emissaries might bring back home really mattered. With the Natchez War well underway in 1730, an Illinois chief named Chikagou led a diplomatic party to the city, offering military support to the French. One of several Upper Mississippi Valley delegates who had visited Paris several years earlier,[21] Chikagou spread on the ground before Governor Étienne Périer a deerskin bordered with porcupine quills and placed upon it two calumets along with other ceremonial objects. The pipes, he told the governor, represented two messages: his people's religious devotion to Roman Catholicism and their political allegiance to the French Crown. "We have come from a great distance to weep with you for the death of the French, and to offer our Warriors to strike those hostile Nations whom you may wish to designate." Many Illinois families had been converted by Jesuit missionaries, and Chikagou was seeking assurance that Périer would protect the Illinois as well as "our Black Robes." "When I went over to France," he reminded the governor, "the King promised me his protection for the Prayer, and recommended me never to abandon it." The need for protection, of course, was mutual, as the Illinois would become especially important participants in France's ensuing campaigns against the Chickasaws—powerful allies of the British situated in the heart of the Lower Mississippi Valley.[22]

During the three weeks spent in New Orleans, Chikagou and his delegation dramatically demonstrated their Roman Catholic faith to town residents.

Lodging at the Ursuline nuns' residential school, these Illinois Indians impressed Father Mathurin le Petit "by their piety, and by their edifying life." As the Jesuit priest reported, "every evening they recited the rosary in alternate choirs, and every morning they heard me say Mass. . . . In the course of the day, and after supper, they often chant, either alone or together different prayers of the Church. . . . To listen to them, you would easily perceive that they took more delight and pleasure in chanting these holy Canticles, than the generality of the Savages, and even more than the French receive from chanting their frivolous and often dissolute songs."[23] Missionary work never reached many Indigenous people in the Lower Mississippi Valley during the colonial period, in contrast with the heavy Jesuit influence upriver in the Illinois country. Capuchin priests and Ursuline nuns made some effort to teach and convert Native youth inside their New Orleans establishments, but with minimal results.

Admitted into the Ursuline convent in 1749, Marie Turpín—not surprisingly an Illinois woman—experienced the longest religious residency in the city by an Indigenous person. Daughter of a wealthy merchant in the town of Kaskaskia and of an influential and pious Illinois woman, Turpín left for New Orleans shortly after the death of her mother. Not unlike Chikagou's blended expression of Native and Catholic identity in the ritual of diplomacy, Turpín was likely representing the interest of her family while also committing herself to religious faith. But limitations that the Ursuline order imposed upon an Indian woman—even one with measurable prestige and piety by colonial standards— became manifest in the confinement of young Marie to the status of a lay sister. Lay nuns performed mostly domestic labor at the convent, while choir nuns learned to read and write, taught residential and day-school pupils, and carried out the order's administrative work. Marie Turpín took her final vows in 1752 but was never allowed to advance to choir status. With the name of Sister St. Marthe, she died a decade later with tuberculosis at the age of thirty-two.[24]

Only months before Chikagou's diplomatic visit in 1730, New Orleans was the scene of a sharply contrasting public ritual. Tunica allies of France brought five Natchez prisoners to the capital, including the Female Sun of the Flour Village. While a colonist smashed the skulls of the others (a woman and three children) and threw their bodies into the fire, the Female Sun—believed to be an instigator of the Natchez War—was tortured and burned by her Tunica captors. Strategically masking the violence of colonial occupation, repression, and enslavement, officials commonly expected public torture and execution to be carried out by Indigenous allies. As one observer explained in this case, Governor

Périer wanted the Indians instead of the French to commit this gruesome act of retribution. While imperial authority was being publicly enforced, the sight of Native people performing the cruel task would also fuel the colonial audience's fearful disdain toward them. After preparing themselves with dance and song known as "the calumet of death," the Tunicas carried the Natchez woman from the town watchhouse and tied her to a frame made of river-cane poles. The Female Sun "taunted her torturers with threats and insults," directing much of this at a Natchez man who had betrayed his own people and joined the Tunicas. Before this terrible spectacle of slow cutting, piercing, and burning ended, both a French woman who had been earlier captured by the Natchez and an outraged French soldier added their own assaults against her body. For their role as captors and executioners on behalf of the French, the Tunicas would soon suffer a devastating raid by vengeful Natchez warriors that cost the lives of two of their chiefs. Other executions performed in New Orleans during the months of war against Natchez enemies included the burning of three Chickasaw prisoners by France's Choctaw allies.[25]

Shortly into the second half of the eighteenth century, a force beyond the will of colonial and Native peoples in the Lower Mississippi Valley brought political and economic changes on a scale significantly greater than those experienced since the founding of New Orleans. After losing the Seven Years' War, France ceded to Britain all territory that it had claimed east of the Mississippi. Meanwhile, royal cousins Louis XV and Carlos III secretly agreed to transfer from French to Spanish possession what remained of Louisiana west of the river. Although resting sinuously along the east bank of the river, the "Île d'Orléans"—that important slice of Louisiana between Lakes Borgne, Pontchartrain, and Maurepas and the Mississippi—remained part of Louisiana. How American Indians would adapt to this sudden loss of France as their familiar ally and to newly made claims on their allegiance by Spain and Great Britain after 1763 mattered not only inside and between their own nations, but also in their continuing relationship with New Orleans.

Although Indian trade in and around the port town remained important to many of its resident merchants and administrators, sudden growth in the size of the Lower Mississippi Valley's colonial population—slave and free—and rapid development of its urban and plantation economy began testing their diplomatic mettle and cultural resilience like never before. This transformation of the region also provided American Indian nations a short-lived chance to play one empire off against the other, to the chagrin of colonial officials demanding exclusive allegiance from them. As Chief Latanash of the Tunicas told a British official at Manchac, "We are free men. . . . We want to be friends with all the white people near us—as we live among them." "Are we not free," he asked, "to go to which side of the River we please?"[26] Regardless of which European empire was claiming their loyalty, American Indians worked hard to keep New Orleans within their own economic and political network as much as possible. To optimize their own advantages in a newly configured imperial borderland, Indians dodged colonial demands from Spain and Britain for exclusive allegiance. They even managed to avoid implication in a revolt against Spain's first Louisiana governor led by a conspiracy of merchants and planters in the New Orleans area. And when General Alejandro O'Reilly, commanding a large Spanish army, speedily repressed that colonial rebellion, he immediately made diplomatic relations with Indigenous nations a top priority.

Some of New Orleans's most elaborate Indian ceremonies took place over the autumn months of 1769—as O'Reilly summoned emissaries after firmly establishing Spain's possession of the colony. Several communities were represented at a single council held in late September inside O'Reilly's house. Close to the noon hour, nine principal delegates arrived with their interpreters and in the company of "quite a number of Indians, singing and playing on their military instruments." O'Reilly greeted this delegation seated under a canopy alongside other military and government officials. After placing their "military implements" at the general's feet, "each one of the chiefs saluted him with his flag, which is a small pole decorated with feathers in the shape of a fan, waving it in a circle over his head, and touching him on the chest four times with it, then giving it to him." Then each guest presented O'Reilly with "his burning pipe, the chief himself holding it while he smoked, which His Excellency did as he was not ignorant of its significance." After each shook hands with the general, a Bayogoula spokesman pledged alliance to Spain on behalf of the entire party and beseeched Spanish authorities to "grant us the same favors and benefits as did the French." While the translated and recorded language found in colonial documents sounds mostly deferential and beseeching, Indian diplomats were clearly asserting themselves as sovereign allies. At the conclusion of every ceremonial visit occurring that same autumn and into the following winter, O'Reilly issued gifts of firearms, ammunition, tools, clothing, and alcohol to every nation in accordance with the size of its population. He also placed around the neck of each chief, a medal "hung from a silk ribbon of deep scarlet color."[27]

By the end of the eighteenth century, most Indian delegations visiting colonial New Orleans on a routine basis came from communities that the French
had long been calling *petites nations*—Native nations drastically depopulated
by smallpox and other epidemic diseases but still inhabiting banks of the lower
Mississippi and its distributaries. Houmas, Chitimachas, and Tunicas had occupied this land for ages, while Biloxis, Pascagoulas, Chahtos, Apalachees, and
Alabamas represented groups of people recently migrating from British Florida
to Spanish Louisiana. Altogether during the 1770s this population numbered
about a thousand people, living in at least eight villages interspersed among
spreading colonial plantations. Although their numbers continued to decline,
these communities were trying to maintain a beneficial relationship with New
Orleans as long as possible.[28]

Meanwhile, Choctaw people were forming new communities along the
north shore of Lake Pontchartrain and the adjacent Mississippi Gulf Coast. To
the dismay of British officials in West Florida, commerce with the populous
Choctaw nation from New Orleans had persisted during the 1760s and 1770s.
Merchants in Mobile and Pensacola urged the West Florida legislature "to
have a stop put to the trade that's carried on by the inhabitants of New Orleans
with the Indians on the English side . . . to the great prejudice of this Province
and particularly those concerned in the Indian trade."[29] But because Bayou
St. John and Lake Pontchartrain provided a much too convenient passage for
goods and skins, all efforts to intervene had little effect. So as Choctaws spent
more and more time hunting and traveling closer to Lakes Pontchartrain and
Maurepas, some decided to relocate there. The return of West Florida to Spain
after the American Revolution further reinforced Choctaw settlement around
New Orleans, and over the next century these so-called St. Tammany Choctaws
would exhibit a versatile public presence in the Crescent City.[30]

During the 1790s Spanish officials in New Orleans confronted the threat of
United States expansion by escalating diplomacy with the still populous and
powerful Indian nations of the interior Southeast. Competition for alliance
and trade with Choctaws, Chickasaws, Creeks, and Cherokees remained as
important as ever, driving Governor Francisco Luis Héctor de Carondelet to
encourage formation of an intertribal confederation that might protect Spanish
Louisiana and Florida against Anglo-American encroachment. Although this
grand scheme fell short—largely because the nations cautiously guarded their
respective sovereignties and territories—a flurry of diplomatic activity occurred
in and around New Orleans.

Among the more notable visits from afar was that of a Cherokee delegation led by Bloody Fellow Swan in 1793. Soon after making a trip to the U.S. capital city of Philadelphia, Bloody Fellow headed for the Gulf of Mexico and joined a large gathering of Choctaws, Chickasaws, and Shawnees in New Orleans. He made sure, through an interpreter, that Carondelet understood his anger over "the incessant usurpations" of American settlers, requesting that Spain build forts on the Tombigbee and Tennessee Rivers and demanding immediate aid against the United States. On his return journey home, Bloody Fellow's party stopped in Natchez, where he arranged for post commander Manuel Gayoso de Lemos to send his eleven-year-old son back to New Orleans in order to learn how to read, speak, and write in Spanish. "He was handing him over to me," as Gayoso reported, "on condition that I would treat him in the same way that we are accustomed to treat the sons of noblemen." Recognizing the urgent need "to cultivate the friendship of these Cherokee Chiefs," the Spanish official dispatched the boy—newly given the first name Carlos in honor of the King—with the plan for admitting him to a school in New Orleans and paying the cost of his education from his own salary if necessary. The fate of Charles Bloody Fellow Swan is not known, but whatever time he spent in New Orleans certainly marked an extraordinary attempt to form an Indigenous connection to the city and its government.[31]

Acquisition of Louisiana by the United States in 1803, of course, drastically altered the geopolitical picture and shifted the center of Indian diplomacy away from New Orleans. For the Houmas and other *petites nations* within the city's orbit, pressure to sell land to encroaching white planters and to relocate away from the Mississippi River's banks became unbearable. Biloxis and Tunicas migrated northwestward to the lower Red River, Alabamas left for the Opelousas district farther west, Houmas moved southward along Bayou Lafourche, and Chitimachas concentrated their population westward along Bayou Teche. Following a century of influence on the city's security and economy, loss of territory now quickened evaporation of their value to New Orleans. The purchase treaty with France had obliged the United States to honor Indian rights in Louisiana, but without making their own treaties directly with the federal government the Houmas, Chitimachas, and Tunicas fell into a legal limbo.[32] While these *petites nations* quickly lost diplomatic weight, the Choctaws held onto their formal relationship with the city a bit longer—when some sixty warriors participated in the Battle of New Orleans. And though this military operation marked an end to their nation's long-lasting political presence in the city, by no means did Choctaw people discontinue their intricately dynamic relationship with it.[33]

Although widening distance from the city and diminishing political influence reduced the frequency and scale of diplomatic visits by Indigenous people, a Native presence on New Orleans's urban landscape persisted nonetheless. By the dawn of the nineteenth century, Indian people were adapting and innovating different forms of public performance in order to continue their ties to the city. Stickball games played by Indians, for example, arose as a source of entertainment for non-Indian residents as well as a means of cultural self-representation by Indian participants. The earliest documentation of this Indigenous precursor to lacrosse being played for colonial onlookers there dates back to June 1764, when a delegation of Biloxis and other Indians from the Gulf Coast, as recorded by Director-General d'Abbadie, "assembled near New Orleans to play ball and for diversions, attracting there numerous spectators." Before his death in 1794, long-time city resident Guy Soniat du Fossat wrote, "The Indians are exceedingly fond of sports. It is common to see them lose all their possessions on the hazards of a game. Their favorite game is called 'Raquette,' and it is a ball game in which they display skill and bodily strength and speed in foot-racing. The contestants form sides. The winners tear off the clothes of their adversaries." At the time of Louisiana's transfer to the United States, French Prefect Pierre Clement de Laussat witnessed one Sunday "Negroes and mulattoes, in groups of four, six, eight—some from the city, others from the country"—playing "raquette des sauvages" against each other.[34]

Among Choctaw people, the game of stickball, or *ishtaboli*, had for ages encompassed a ceremonial complex known for settling conflicts and avoiding wars. It was consistent, therefore, that the calumet dance was now being replaced by what New Orleans residents began calling *raquette*, the French word roughly describing the shape and design of the ballgame sticks. Matches between clans, towns, and nations were usually preceded by ritual preparations, accompanied by conjuring and gambling, and followed by special songs and dances. As explained to anthropologist John Swanton by Mississippi Choctaw Simpson Tubby in the early twentieth century, the Choctaws valued stickball as the "peace game" and the first Choctaw to make ball sticks was named Musholeika, meaning in rough translation "'to go out' or 'to put out' like a light." Tubby credited white people with the introduction of gambling into the sport, which by the late nineteenth century became more volatile, although Swanton noted earlier and more widespread evidence of betting in American Indian games.[35] Interaction

Félix Achille Beaupoil de Saint Aulaire, *Vue d'une Rue du Faubourg Marigny, N[ouv]elle Orléans*, c. 1821. The Historic New Orleans Collection, L. Kemper and Leila Moore Williams Founders Collection.

with colonial people would have certainly introduced some new elements for adaptation and innovation, well exemplified by Choctaw incorporation of the European military snare drum into stickball ceremony. It also offered new public spaces for performance and self-representation.[36] By the end of the eighteenth and throughout the nineteenth centuries, American Indians across the Lower Mississippi Valley were holding games away from their communities as a way to both perform cultural identity and perpetuate intercultural exchange. In the city of New Orleans—where visiting Indian teams regularly played before spectators for pay—Creole residents of African and European descent even formed their own "raquette" teams, making it the Crescent City's most popular urban sport until baseball and football came along.[37]

Persistent marketing of select wares—mostly by Choctaw women—proved to be another resourceful means of displaying Indigenous identity and culture in New Orleans. While keeping the rapidly growing metropolis a part of their communities' livelihood, the sale of crafts, medicines, and foodstuffs in urban marketplaces also perpetuated their dynamic relationship with the Crescent City. Informal diplomacy, in other words, replaced formal diplomacy. One artist's watercolor of a city street depicted an Indian family in a scene that would have been common during the early nineteenth century. As New Orleans became more susceptible to outbreaks of yellow fever because of its sudden sprawl, Native visitors tended to concentrate their presence in the city during healthier winter and spring months. The banks of Bayou St. John and other spots back-of-town became campgrounds for Indians seasonally visiting the city to sell plants, game, woodcraft, and basketry still consumed by many of its residents, and a degree of performative self-representation persisted in what and how they marketed those things. Through their knowledgeable use of the wetlands around New Orleans in this way, Indigenous people were maintaining spatial rights to the city and its environs. When "a place was built on the Bayou Road to serve as a market," recalled Father Adrien Rouquette, "the Indians took possession of it as lodging place, and their claim to do so was not disputed."[38]

Behind this Native presence in the Crescent City, Lower Mississippi Valley Indians blended traditional livelihood practices with new forms of work and production. An alternative to open conflict or full retreat, a seasonal round of hunting, fishing, gathering, and trading activities—even picking cotton on plantations—secured some degree of sovereignty for American Indians. In many cases, itinerant groups of Indian people forged strong personal relationships with particular non-Indian families.[39] Many, if not most, of the Indians who developed close ties to non-Indian households and communities were people resisting pressure to leave their homeland. About Choctaws whom both he and his brother Adrien knew quite well, Dominique Rouquette wrote, "They obstinately refuse to abandon the different parishes of Louisiana, where they are grouped in small family tribes, and live in rough huts in the vicinity of planta-tions, and hunt for the planters, who trade for the game they kill." While raising poultry and planting food crops around their homes, women made baskets of various shapes, sizes, and colors "from which they derived a good profit." They also sold medicinal and culinary plants.[40]

Of course, some risk came with all of this change as white spectators began to view the lingering Indian presence in New Orleans as strictly a source of amusement and pathos. Throughout the nineteenth century, residents and visi-tors would nostalgically interpret Indigenous ball games, dances, and market-ing as the residual behavior of a nearly extinct people. As in many other places well into the next century, American Indian neighbors and local communities were only seen as "Indian" when engaged in performance.[41] With disparaging and patronizing phrases like "a ragged remnant of the once powerful Choctaw tribe," colonial settler society virtually erased Native people and their intricate ties to New Orleans from the city's history and landscape. In the faces of Indian women sitting in marketplaces, onlookers like Lafcadio Hearn saw only "the sadness that seems peculiar to dying races."[42] Such reading of hypervisible and hyperinvisible performances, as explained more broadly by Mishuana Goeman, had the effect of pathologizing mobile Native bodies and constricting their mobility. For American Indians, however, the time spent at urban markets and ballfields would comprise a strategy of persistence—continuing to utilize local resources for their livelihood while both remembering, for themselves at least, and perpetuating the dynamic role they played in the city's early development. Everyday spatial activities as well as narratives and performances of identity, in accordance with Natchee Blu Barnd's emphasis on artists and activists, became means of reclaiming Native space and resisting non-Native authority over that space.[43]

Although New Orleans stopped being a diplomatic hub for Indian emissaries after 1815, formal parties of Indigenous people did occasionally visit over the next few decades. Tragically, the largest groups to travel through the Crescent City were prisoners of war and exiles being removed from their Alabama and Florida homelands during the mid-1830s. Meanwhile, American Indians remaining in south Louisiana, especially Choctaws and Houmas living nearest New Orleans, continued to improvise their relationship with the city. For at least a half century following the Civil War, Choctaw families kept the New Orleans French Market an integral part of their income and identity—even becoming an attraction for tourists. Sassafras leaves ground into filé, the powder used to thicken and season gumbo, was a signature item sold regularly by the women. Stickball matches played between Choctaw teams before paying city spectators also became periodic opportunities for performance.

But it was rivercane basketry exquisitely woven by Choctaw and Chitimacha women, above all, that drew the kind of attention that would influence future political as well as cultural developments. At the dawn of the twentieth century, women in prominent New Orleans families began to campaign on behalf of local Indian communities in large part because of their interest in the baskets, while publicity in magazines and newspapers made them desirable objects for arts-and-crafts collecting across the country. Chitimacha weavers managed to negotiate this surge of aesthetic and ethnographic cravings for American Indian basketry into an alliance network of elite white women, anthropologists, and museum curators that would facilitate their people's acquisition of federal recognition two centuries after the founding of New Orleans. Although a far cry from that peace ceremony held by their ancestors back in 1718, this means of performing diplomacy signified a future of Indigenous adaptation and survival in urban America.[44]

A confluence of new circumstances would shape subsequent Native American relations with New Orleans. As Houma Indians in parishes adjacent to Orleans Parish grew in population, their movement into the city and its metropolitan sprawl raised the number of Indigenous people residing in the Greater New Orleans Area. Native Americans from other communities near and far also migrated to New Orleans for employment and education, leading to more than one thousand American Indians residing in the city today. With more than half of Louisiana's Indian population of thirty thousand living within a few hours' drive, their pursuits of federal recognition and environmental justice in a rapidly deteriorating coastal environment make New Orleans an essential platform for national outreach. Self-representation of their history, culture, and status relies on prominent public spaces in the city, most notably the Native American Village at the annual Jazz and Heritage Festival and at interpretive sites in the Jean Lafitte National Historical Park. Dynamic relations with New Orleans residents and visitors continue to be instrumental in today's struggles over sovereignty and territory.[45]

NOTES

1. Antoine Le Page du Pratz, *Histoire de la Louisiane*, 3 vols. (Paris: Du Bure, Delaguette, Lambert, 1758), 1:106–14; André Pénicaut, *Fleur de Lys and Calumet: Being the Pénicaut Narrative of French Adventure in Louisiana*, trans. and ed. Richebourg Gaillard McWilliams (Tuscaloosa: University of Alabama Press, 1953), 70–72, 101–2, 216–19.

2. The relationship between American Indians and colonial towns has been examined to varying degrees in Colin Calloway, ed., *After King Philip's War: Presence and Persistence in Indian New England* (Hanover, N.H.: University Press of New England, 1997); Jean M. O'Brien, *Dispossession by Degrees: Indian Land and Identity in Natick, Massachusetts, 1650–1790* (New York: Cambridge University Press, 1997); Steven C. Hahn, *The Life and Times of Mary Musgrove* (Gainesville: University Press of Florida, 2012); Dawn G. Marsh, *A Lenape among the Quakers: The Life of Hanna Freeman* (Lincoln: University of Nebraska Press, 2014); Lucy Eldersveld Murphy, *Great Lakes Creoles: A French-Indian Community on the Northern Borderlands, Prairie du Chien, 1750–1860* (New York: Cambridge University Press, 2014); Margaret Ellen Newell, *Brethren by Nature: New England Indians, Colonists, and the Origins of American Slavery* (Ithaca, N.Y.: Cornell University Press, 2015); Tiya Miles, *The Dawn of Detroit: A Chronicle of Slavery and Freedom in the City of Straits* (New York: New Press, 2017); Andrew K. Frank, *Before the*

Pioneers: Indians, Settlers, Slaves, and the Founding of Miami (Gainesville: University Press of Florida, 2017); Christine M. DeLucia, *Memory Lands: King Philip's War and the Place of Violence in the Northeast* (New Haven, Conn.: Yale University Press, 2018).

3. D. Anthony Tyeeme Clark and Malea Powell, "Resisting Exile in the 'Land of the Free': Indigenous Groundwork at Colonial Intersections," *American Indian Quarterly* 32 (Winter 2008): 1–15. There is a long and deep scholarship on how performance of Indianness by non-Indians shaped the evolution of American identity and culture, from theatrical stages and middle-class men's clubs to sports mascots and motion pictures. Performance of Indianness by American Indians in Europe has also received plenty of attention lately. When it comes to the study of Indians performing Indianness on this side of the Atlantic, however, far less has been written—with the exception of work on Wild West shows and world's fairs.

4. Richard J. Shenkel, *Oak Island Archaeology: Prehistoric Estuarine Adaptations in the Mississippi River Delta* (New Orleans: Jean Lafitte National Historical Park, 1980); Daniel H. Usner, "A Cycle of Lowland Forest Efficiency: The Late Archaic-Woodland Economy of the Lower Mississippi Valley," *Journal of Anthropological Research* 39 (Winter 1983): 433–44; Marco J. Giardino, "Documentary Evidence for the Location of Historic Indian Villages in the Mississippi Delta," *Perspectives on Gulf Coast Prehistory*, ed. Dave D. Davis (Gainesville: University Press of Florida, 1984), 232–57; Tristram R. Kidder, "Making the City Inevitable: Native Americans and the Geography of New Orleans," in *Transforming New Orleans and Its Environs: Centuries of Change*, ed. Craig E. Colton (Pittsburgh: University of Pittsburgh Press, 2000), 9–21.

5. Richebourg Gaillard McWilliams, trans. and ed., *Iberville's Gulf Journals* (Tuscaloosa: University of Alabama Press, 1981), 57.

6. Robbie Ethridge, *From Chicaza to Chickasaw: The European Invasion and the Transformation of the Mississippian World, 1540–1715* (Chapel Hill: University of North Carolina Press, 2010); Robbie Ethridge and Sheri. M. Shuck-Hall, eds., *Mapping the Mississippian Shatter Zone: The Colonial Indian Slave Trade and Regional Instability in the American South* (Lincoln: University of Nebraska Press, 2009).

7. Mary Christine Morkovsky and Patricia Galloway, eds., *La Salle, the Mississippi, and the Gulf: Three Primary Documents*, trans. Ann Linda Bell and Robert S. Weddle (College Station: Texas A&M University Press, 1987), 53–54, 57; Jean Baptiste Bernard de La Harpe, *Historical Journal of the Establishment of the French in Louisiana*, trans. from the French, presented to the American Philosophical Society, in William Darby, *Historical Collections of Louisiana*, ed. B. F. French, vol. 5 (New York: Appleton & Company, 1851), 35–36; Bienville to Pontchartrain, February 20, 1707, Bienville to Cadillac, June 23, 1716, *Mississippi Provincial Archives: French Dominion*, ed. Dunbar Rowland, Godfrey Sanders, and Patricia K. Galloway, 5 vols. (Vols. 1–3, Jackson: Mississippi Department of Archives and History, 1929–32; Vols. 4–5, Baton Rouge: Louisiana State University Press, 1984), 3:38, 214; Pénicaut, *Fleur de Lys and Calumet*, 70–72, 101–02, 159, 216–20; Le Page du Pratz, *Histoire de la Louisiane*, 1:106–14. For the widespread effects of slave-raiding for trade with British Carolina, see Christina Snyder, *Slavery in*

Indian Country: The Changing Face of Captivity in Early America (Cambridge, Mass.: Harvard University Press, 2010), 46–79.

8. May Rush Gwinn Waggoner, ed., *Le Plus Beau Païs du Monde: Completing the Picture of Proprietary Louisiana, 1699–1722* (Lafayette: Center for Louisiana Studies, 2005), 49; François Gerard Jollain, "Le Commerce que les Indiens du Mexique font avec les François au Port de Missisipi," hand-colored engraving, c. 1719–20, The Historic New Orleans Collection, New Orleans.

9. Corin C. O. Pursell, "Colored Monuments and Sensory Theater among the Mississippians," in *Making Senses of the Past: Toward a Sensory Archaeology*, ed. Jo Day (Carbondale and Edwardsville: Southern Illinois University Press, 2013), 69–89; LeAnne Howe, "Embodied Tribalography—First Installment," in *Choctalking on Other Realities* (San Francisco: Aunt Lute Books, 2013), 173–95; LeAnne Howe, "The Story of Movement: Natives and Performance Culture," in *The Oxford Handbook of Indigenous American Literature*, ed. James H. Cox and Daniel Heath Justice (New York: Oxford University Press, 2014), 250–65.

10. Le Page du Pratz, *Histoire de la Louisiane*, 1:106–14. For an ethnomusicological analysis of the Chitimacha calumet ceremony described by Le Page du Pratz, see Shane Lief, "Singing, Shaking, and Parading at the Birth of New Orleans," *Jazz Archivist* 28 (2015): 15–25. Keen insight into the identity and life of Le Page du Pratz's enslaved Chitimacha woman is provided in Patricia Galloway, "Natchez Matrilineal Kinship: Du Pratz and the Woman's Touch," in *Practicing Ethnohistory: Mining Archives, Hearing Testimony, Constructing Narratives* (Lincoln: University of Nebraska Press, 2006), 97–108.

11. For other detailed descriptions of the calumet ceremony from colonial observers, see Jean-François-Benjamin Dumont de Montigny, *The Memoire of Lieutenant Dumont, 1715–1747: A Sojourner in the French Atlantic*, trans. Gordon M. Sayre, ed. Sayre and Carla Zecher (Chapel Hill: University of North Carolina Press, 2012), 341–44. A calumet ceremony performed by Quapaw Indians for René-Robert Cavelier, Sieur de La Salle, on his journey down the Mississippi in 1682 is vividly reported in Morkovsky and Galloway, *La Salle, the Mississippi, and the Gulf*, 46–47. See also McWilliams, *Iberville's Gulf Journals*, 58–59, 66–69, for description of Bayogoula and Houma versions. The spread of the ritual among Indian nations is discussed in Ian W. Brown, "The Calumet Ceremony in the Southeast as Observed Archaeologically," in *Powhatan's Mantle: Indians in the Colonial Southeast*, ed. Gregory Waselkov, Peter H. Wood, and T. Hatley, rev. ed. (Lincoln: University of Nebraska Press, 2006), 371–419.

12. Erin M. Greenwald, *A Company Man: The Remarkable French-Atlantic Voyage of Marc-Antoine Caillot* (New Orleans: Historic New Orleans Collection, 2013), 112–13. Catherine Bell, *Ritual: Perspectives and Dimensions* (New York: Oxford University Press, 1997), 159–61, offers insightful analysis of the multiple sensory dimensions of ritual performance. See also Barbara A. Hanawalt, *Ceremony and Civility: Civic Culture in Late Medieval London* (New York: Oxford University Press, 2017) for comparative context.

13. Henri Lefebvre, *The Production of Space*, trans. Donald Nicholson-Smith (Oxford: Blackwell, 1991). The discrepancy between act and text is explored in Richard Bauman,

Verbal Art as Performance (Prospect Heights, IL: Waveland, 1993); and William M. Clements, *Native American Verbal Art: Texts and Contexts* (Tucson: University of Arizona Press, 1996).

14. Lisa Brooks, "Turning the Looking Glass on King Philip's War: Locating American Literature in Native Space," *American Literary History* 25 (Winter 2013): 718–50; Mishuana Goeman, *Mark My Words: Native Women Mapping Our Nations* (Minneapolis: University of Minnesota Press, 2013); Natchee Blu Barnd, *Native Space: Geographic Strategies to Unsettle Settler Colonialism* (Corvallis: Oregon State University Press, 2017).

15. For innovative approaches to how information networks operated among colonial and Indian peoples elsewhere, see Lisa Brooks, *The Common Pot: The Recovery of Native Space in the Northeast* (Minneapolis: University of Minnesota Press, 2008); Matt Cohen, *Networked Wilderness: Communicating in Early New England* (Minneapolis: University of Minnesota Press, 2010); Susanah Shaw Romney, *New Netherland Connections: Intimate Networks and Atlantic Ties in Seventeenth-Century America* (Chapel Hill: University of North Carolina Press, 2014), 162–72, 264–68; Katherine Grandjean, *American Passage: The Communications Frontier in Early New England* (Cambridge, Mass.: Harvard University Press, 2015); and Alejandra Dubcovsky, *Informed Power: Communication in the Early American South* (Cambridge, Mass.: Harvard University Press, 2016).

16. Cohen, *Networked Wilderness*, 21–22; Michael J. Witgen, *An Infinity of Nations: How the Native New World Shaped Early North America* (Philadelphia: University of Pennsylvania Press, 2012). See also Robert Paulett, *An Empire of Small Places: Mapping the Southeastern Anglo-Indian Trade, 1732–1795* (Athens: University of Georgia Press, 2012), an innovative study of contested metaphorical and physical spaces generated by Native-colonial trade and diplomacy extending from Charleston into Chickasaw country.

17. DeLucia, *Memory Lands*, 29–117.

18. Daniel H. Usner, "American Indians in Colonial New Orleans," in *Powhatan's Mantle*, 163–86; Daniel H. Usner, "Colonial Projects and Frontier Practices: The First Century of New Orleans History," in *Frontier Cities: Encounters at the Crossroads of Empire*, ed. Jay Gitlin, Barbara Berglund, and Adam Arenson (Philadelphia: University of Pennsylvania Press, 2013), 27–45; Daniel H. Usner, *American Indians in Early New Orleans: From Calumet to Raquette* (Baton Rouge: Louisiana State University Press, 2018), 1–41.

19. Charles R. Maduell Jr., comp. and ed., *The Census Tables for the French Colony of Louisiana from 1699 through 1732* (Baltimore: Genealogical Publishing Company, 1972), 88, 92–93; *Memoire of Lieutenant Dumont*, 208. For the dispersal of Chitimacha slaves among colonial inhabitants, see Dayna Bowker Lee, "From Captives to Kin: Indian Slavery and Changing Social Identities on the Louisiana Colonial Frontier," in *Native American Adoption, Captivity, and Slavery in Changing Contexts*, ed. Max Carocci and Stephanie Pratt (New York: Palgrave, 2012), 79–96. The exportation of enslaved Natchez people and traces of their survival are closely examined in Edward Noel Smyth, "The Natchez Diaspora: A History of Indigenous Displacement and Survival in the Atlantic World" (Ph.D. diss., University of California, Santa Cruz, 2016), 54–80.

20. Daniel H. Usner, *Indians, Settlers, and Slaves in a Frontier Exchange Economy: The Lower Mississippi Valley before 1783* (Chapel Hill: University of North Carolina Press, 1992); Shannon Lee Dawdy, "'A Wild Taste': Food and Colonialism in Eighteenth-Century Louisiana," *Ethnohistory* (Summer 2010): 389–414; Cyrus Byington, *A Dictionary of the Choctaw Language*, ed. John R. Swanton and Henry S. Halbert (Washington, D.C.: U.S. Government Printing Office, 1915), 87, 506.

21. Long after passing through New Orleans in 1725, on their way through France, the delegation of Illinois, Missouri, Osage, and Oto Indians that included Chikagou became quite a spectacle for Paris residents. Witnessing a demonstration of the calumet dance performed by these Indian celebrities, Jean-Philippe Rameau was inspired to compose *Les Sauvages* which eventually became an entrée in his opéra-ballet *Les Indes Galantes*. Frank Norall, *Bourgmont, Explorer of the Missouri, 1698–1723* (Lincoln: University of Nebraska Press, 1988); Cuthbert Morton Girdlestone, *Jean-Philippe Rameau, His Life and Work* (London: Cassell, 1957), 8–9, 320–49.

22. Father [Mathurin] le Petit, Missionary to Father d'Avaugour, Procurator of the Missions in North America, at New Orleans, July 12, 1730, in *Jesuit Relations and Allied Documents: Travels and Explorations of the Jesuit Missionaries in New France, 1610–1791*, vol. 68, ed. Reuben Gold Thwaites (Cleveland: Barrows Brothers Company, 1900), 201–3; Robert Michael Morrissey, *Empire by Collaboration: Indians, Colonists, and Governments in Colonial Illinois Country* (Philadelphia: University of Pennsylvania Press, 2015), 110–38.

23. Thwaites, *Jesuit Relations*, 68:209–11. For an outstanding study of Roman Catholicism as practiced by American Indians in French North America, see Tracy Neal Leavelle, *The Catholic Calumet: Colonial Conversions in French and Indian North America* (Philadelphia: University of Pennsylvania Press, 2012).

24. Sophie White, *Wild Frenchmen and Frenchified Indians: Material Culture and Race in Colonial Louisiana* (Philadelphia: University of Pennsylvania Press, 2012), 145–75. For glimpses into the early efforts at formal conversion of Indian people inside New Orleans, see Marcel Giraud, *A History of French Louisiana, Volume Five: The Company of the Indies, 1723–1731*, trans. Brian Pearce (Baton Rouge: Louisiana State University Press, 1987), 66–67, 306–7; and Emily Clark, *Masterless Mistresses: The New Orleans Ursulines and the Development of a New World Society, 1727–1834* (Chapel Hill: University of North Carolina Press, 2007).

25. Diron d'Artaguette to Maurepas, June 24, 1731, Jadart de Beauchamp to Maurepas, November 5, 1731, *Mississippi Provincial Archives: French Dominion*, IV, 77, 79; *A Company Man*, 146–48, and plate 6. For a detailed and deep analysis of this episode, see Sophie White, "Massacre, Mardi Gras, and Torture in Early New Orleans," *William and Mary Quarterly*, 3d ser., 70 (July 2013): 497–538, especially 518–34. See also Giraud, *History of French Louisiana*, 316–18; and George Edward Milne, *Natchez Country: Indians, Colonists, and the Landscapes of Race in French Louisiana* (Athens: University of Georgia Press, 2015), 198–99. Comprehensive and comparative investigation into how prominent public places in colonial cities became sites for torture and execution of Native prisoners of war remains to be done. During King Philip's War in New England, to cite

one case, about forty-five Indian people were either hanged or shot on Boston Common in August and September of 1676. See DeLucia, *Memory Lands*, 53–54.

26. David K. Bjork, "Documents Regarding Indian Affairs in the Lower Mississippi Valley, 1771–1772," *Mississippi Valley Historical Review* 13 (December 1926): 409; Robin F. A. Fabel, *Colonial Challenges: Britons, Native Americans and Caribs, 1759–1775* (Gainesville: University Press of Florida, 2000), 128–29.

27. Alejandro O'Reilly to Arriaga, October 17, 1769, *Spain in the Mississippi Valley, 1765–1794*, trans. and ed. Lawrence Kinnaird, 3 vols. (Washington, D.C.: U.S. Government Printing Office, 1946–49), 1:101–2, 154–55. After the American Revolution began and Spain entered the war against Britain several years later, some of these same allied Indian nations provided fighters for Governor Bernardo de Gálvez's successful campaign against British forts along the Mississippi River and Gulf Coast. Kathleen DuVal, *Independence Lost: Lives on the Edge of the American Revolution* (New York: Random House, 2015), 161–64.

28. Charles Stuart, List of the Several Tribes of Indians inhabiting the banks of the Mississippi, Between New Orleans and Red River, with their number of gun men & places of residence. January 1, 1773, Haldimand Papers, British Museum; Thomas Hutchins, *An Historical Narrative and Topographical Description of Louisiana and West Florida* (Facsimile reproduction of the 1784 edition, Gainesville: University Presses of Florida, 1968), 39–45.

29. Journal of the Commons House, Mon., March 19, 1770, *The Minutes, Journals, and Acts of the General Assembly of British West Florida*, comp. Robert R. Rea with Milo B. Howard Jr. (Tuscaloosa: University of Alabama Press, 1979), 230.

30. John Forbes to the Marquis de Casa Irujo, April 28, 1804, Panton, Leslie and Company Collection, 1739–1847, University of West Florida University Archives and West Florida History Center, Pensacola; Dayna Bowker Lee, *Choctaw Communities along the Gulf Coast: Louisiana, Mississippi, and Alabama* (Final Report Prepared for the National Park Service and the Federal Emergency Management Agency, September 2009, Contract Number P5038090018), 20–21.

31. Charles A. Weeks, *Paths to a Middle Ground: The Diplomacy of Natchez, Boukfouka, Nogales, and San Fernando de las Barrancas, 1791–1795* (Tuscaloosa: University of Alabama Press, 2005), 84–102. See also A. P. Whitaker, "Spain and the Cherokee Indians, 1783–98," *North Carolina Historical Review* 4 (July 1927): 252–69.

32. Corinne L. Saucier, *The History of Avoyelles Parish, Louisiana* (New Orleans: Pelican, 1943), 522; Mattie Austin Hatcher, "The Louisiana Background of the Colonization of Texas, 1763–1803," *Southwestern Historical Quarterly* 24 (January 1921): 187; Grant Foreman, *Indians and Pioneers: The Story of the American Southwest before 1830* (New Haven, Conn.: Yale University Press, 1930), 30; *American State Papers: Documents, Legislative and Executive, of the Congress of the United States in Relation to the Public Lands, from the First Session of the First Congress to the First Session of the Twenty-Third Congress*, vol. 3 (Washington: Duff Green, 1834), 232.

33. Arsène LaCarriere Latour, *Historical Memoir of the War in West Florida and Louisiana in 1814–15*, ed. Gene A. Smith (New Orleans: Historic New Orleans Collection

and University Press of Florida, 1999); Appendix No. 18: Copies of letters from the secretary of war to general Jackson, 209–10; Jane Lucas de Grummond, *The Baratarians and the Battle of New Orleans* (Baton Rouge: Louisiana State University Press, 1961), 55, 84–89, 106–13.

34. *Comparative View of French Louisiana*, 116; Guy Soniat du Fossat, *Synopsis of the History of Louisiana, From the Founding of the Colony to the End of the Year 1791*, trans. Charles T. Soniat (New Orleans: Louisiana Historical Society, 1903), 35; Pierre Clement de Laussat, *Memoirs of My Life to My Son During the Years 1803 and After, Which I spent in Public Service in Louisiana as Commissioner of the French Government for the Retrocession to France of That Colony and for Its Transfer to the United States*, trans. Sister Agnes-Josephine Pastwa, ed. Robert D. Bush (Baton Rouge: Louisiana State University Press, 1978), 53–54.

35. John R. Swanton, *Source Material for the Social and Ceremonial Life of the Choctaw Indians*, Smithsonian Institution Bureau of American Ethnology Bulletin 43 (Washington, D.C.: U.S. Government Printing Office, 1911), 152–55.

36. Donna L. Akers, in her *Culture and Customs of the Choctaw Indians* (Santa Barbara: Greenwood, 2013), 133–40, uses *ishtaboli* as the Choctaw word for the stickball game and explains it as "Little Brother of War"—played to settle conflict and avoid war. Marcia Haag and Henry Willis, in their *Choctaw Language and Culture: Chahta Anumpa* (Norman: University of Oklahoma Press, 2001), 338, 368, use *kapucha* for the game and *ishtaboli* for the playing field. For insight into the record of stickball among Mississippi Choctaws from colonial times to the present, see James F. Barnett Jr., "Ferocity and Finesse: American Indian Sports in Mississippi," *Southern Quarterly* 51 (Summer 2014): 9–19; Tammy Greer and Harold Comby, "Photo Essay: Stickball Fever," *Southern Quarterly* 51 (Summer 2014): 21–27.

37. Usner, *American Indians in the Lower Mississippi Valley*, 120–22. For treatment of the performative nature of Cherokee ballgames as spectator sport elsewhere in the American South, see Michael J. Zogry, *Anetso, the Cherokee Ball Game: At the Center of Ceremony and Identity* (Chapel Hill: University of North Carolina Press, 2010), especially 151–84.

38. "The Choctaws of Louisiana: Father Rouquette and His Wards in St. Tammany" *Daily Picayune*, September 22, 1882.

39. This strategy of forging personal relationships with local non-Indians through seasonal exchange and work is closely studied in Erik M. Redix, *The Murder of Joe White: Ojibwe Leadership and Colonialism in Wisconsin* (East Lansing: Michigan State University Press, 2014), 65–99. See also Marsh, *A Lenape among the Quakers*.

40. François Dominique Rouquette, "The Choctaws," translation by Olivia Blanchard from original transcript, 11–12, 50, François Dominique Rouquette Papers, Louisiana Research Collection, Howard-Tilton Library, Tulane University, New Orleans. For an insightful analysis of how American Indians utilized travel to preserve, recover, and restore their homeland spaces during the nineteenth century, see Micah A. Pawling, "*Wəlastəkwey* (Maliseet) Homeland: Waterscapes and Continuity within the Lower St. John River Valley, 1784–1900," *Acadiensis* 46 (Summer/Autumn 2017): 5–34.

41. Usner, *American Indians in the Lower Mississippi Valley*, 111–37; Patricia C. Albers and William R. James, "Tourism and the Changing Photographic Image of the Great Lakes Indians," *Annals of Tourism Research* 10, no. 1 (1983): 123–48; Laura E. Smith, *Horace Poolaw: Photographer of American Indian Modernity* (Lincoln: University of Nebraska Press, 2016), 67–68. The influence of ethnographic performance on establishing otherness is insightfully explored in Coco Fusco, "The Other History of Intercultural Performance," *TDR [The Drama Review]* 38 (Spring 1994): 143–67.

42. "The Last of the Choctaws," *Daily Picayune*, April 3, 1844; Lafcadio Hearn to H. E. Krehbiel, New Orleans, 1877, in *The Life and Letters of Lafcadio Hearn*, ed. Elizabeth Bisland, 2 vols. (Boston: Houghton, Mifflin, 1906), 1:168–69.

43. Goeman, *Mark My Words*, 5, 12; Barnd, *Native Space*, 108. Understanding how performance has filled voids created by violence, death, and dispossession—particularly in New Orleans—was significantly advanced in Joseph Roach, *Cities of the Dead: Circum-Atlantic Performance* (New York: Columbia University Press, 1996).

44. Usner, *American Indians in Early New Orleans*, 43–135. For the Chitimachas' basket diplomacy, see Daniel H. Usner, *Weaving Alliances with Other Women: Chitimacha Indian Work in the New South* (Athens: University of Georgia Press, 2015). Most Choctaws living north of Lake Pontchartrain were relocated to Indian Territory by the federal government in the first decade of the twentieth century. This left the Chitimacha Tribe of Louisiana to become the federally recognized Indian nation closest to New Orleans, although distance from their Bayou Teche reservation did not encourage any regular presence in the city.

45. Bruce Duthu, "The Houma Indians of Louisiana: The Intersection of Law and History in the Federal Acknowledgement Process," *Louisiana History* 38 (Fall 1997): 409–36; Andrew Jolivette, "Indigenous Locations Post-Katrina: Beyond Invisibility and Disaster," *American Indian Culture and Research Journal* 32, no. 2 (2008): 1–108; Denise E. Bates, *The Other Movement: Indian Rights and Civil Rights in the Deep South* (Tuscaloosa: University of Alabama Press, 2012), 11–22, 63–64, 70–98, 201; Adam Crepelle, "Standing Rock in the Swamp: Oil, the Environment, and the United Houma Nation's Struggle for Federal Recognition," *Loyola Law Review* 141 (2018): 141–86; Rachel Breunlin, ed., *Return to Yakni Chitto: Houma Migrations* (New Orleans: University of New Orleans Press, 2019).

PART II

IMPERIAL CITIES AND DISPOSSESSION
IN THE NINETEENTH CENTURY

ARI KELMAN

3

FROM MANASSAS TO MANKATO

How the Civil War Bled into the Indian Wars

As dawn broke the day after Christmas 1862, thousands of sightseers poured into the city of Mankato, Minnesota. The sea of people included some fifteen hundred soldiers from the Sixth and Seventh Minnesota Regiments, volunteer troops detailed from fighting the Civil War to maintain order in the southern part of their home state. The men were charged with pacifying bands of Native people who had killed hundreds of white settlers the previous fall. As the sun rose higher, Mankato's streets filled to bursting. Some spectators, hoping to avoid obstructed views, scaled the walls of local businesses, claiming prime real estate on the city's large, brick buildings. At 10 A.M. precisely, a company of soldiers, emblems of the federal government's power in a region that had recently flirted with anarchy, led a grim parade of thirty-eight Native American men, most of them Dakotas, into the center of town. They marched toward a structure built just between the municipal jail and the banks of the Minnesota River.[1]

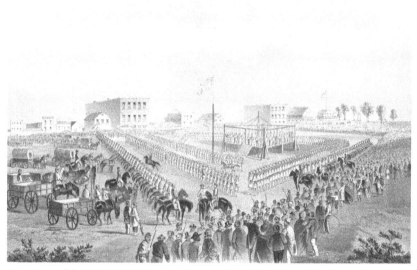

Execution of the Thirty-Eight Sioux Indians at Mankato, Minnesota, December 26, 1862. Library of Congress, Prints and Photographs Division. This widely circulated lithograph (Milwaukee Litho. & Engr. Co., c. 1883) of the execution of thirty-eight Dakota men in Mankato on December 26, 1862, emphasizes the overwhelming military force of the United States during the era of the Civil War, including throughout parts of the nation's Western territories. Rows of soldiers on foot and horseback suggest the threat of violence that faced Native peoples who resisted the consolidation of an emerging American empire in the trans–Mississippi West in the second half of the nineteenth century.

The ominous contrivance looked a bit like the bones of a circus big top stripped of flesh: a square podium, running more than twenty feet along each of its sides; massive beams rising at its four corners; and an even longer pole, with an iron pulley mounted atop it, looming higher still in the middle of the apparatus. A quartet of strong ropes connected the main floor to a huge, metal ring encircling the central "mast." The beams in each of the corners secured a second wooden frame, also square, with ten notches hewn into each of its timbers, above the main dais. The *New York Times*, which dispatched a reporter to Mankato, explained the workings of the convoluted rig. "The mechanism of the whole thing," the *Times* described, "consisted in raising the platform by means of the pulley, and then making the rope fast, when by a blow from an ax held by a man standing in the center of the square [kept safe by an aperture cut in the contraption's midsection], the platform falls." A gallows designed for mass murder, the device could kill forty people in an instant.[2]

For weeks, the thirty-eight condemned men had huddled in a nearby stockade. The correspondent from the *Times* recounted that on the morning they would die, after climbing a short flight of steps leading to the elevated platform, the warriors "filed right and left, and each one took his position as though they had rehearsed the program." They arrayed themselves beneath ropes dangling from crossbeams above. Hangmen hooded them and slipped nooses around their necks. A drumbeat started a countdown. The doomed men struggled to grasp one another's hands. A second report sounded. They shouted their names. The drum banged a third time. The axe fell—"click"—splitting the rope that suspended the platform above the ground. The men plummeted until the cords around their necks halted their progress. Most died immediately, but a few struggled. Then one of the ropes snapped, sending "its burden with a heavy, dull crash, to the platform below." Someone fetched a fresh noose. The crowd "hushed to a deathly silence by the chilling scene before them" until a small boy shouted, "hurrah, hurrah!" The soldiers' bayonets gleamed in the sun. Thirty-eight Dakotas dangled in the unseasonably warm air. So ended the largest public execution in the history of the United States.[3]

The story of the Dakota thirty-eight had urban origins. Western cities hosted concentrated populations of settlers and, as a result, represented fertile ground in which misinformation—rumors, innuendo, conspiracy theories—could take root and spread. Racial anxiety often radiated outward from cities in the trans-Mississippi regions; bloodshed escalated when urbanites believed they might fall victim to belligerent Native peoples. Such paranoia emerged out of and then amplified broader concerns about the future of the United States during the Civil War. Violent conflicts between tribal peoples, settlers, and the soldiers charged with protecting them clouded the Republican Party's vision for consolidating an American empire sprawling into the far West—expansion that hinged in part on the unfettered growth of urban centers that would serve as trade hubs and engines of dispossession. Finally, cities offered a stage upon which settlers and public officials could host morality plays, performing the sanctity of white civilization and the inviolability of federal authority and the rule of law.

The road to the gallows in Mankato ran through urbanizing Minnesota. In mid-August 1862, four Dakota men went hunting in the forests that stretched for miles north of Saint Paul, the state capital. They were frustrated by the lack of game on the Sioux Reservation—a long and narrow tract of land shadowing the southern shore of the Minnesota River, starting above its headwaters at Big Stone Lake, near the Dakota Territory line, and ending ten miles upstream of New Ulm—where their people had relocated after settlers seized the land that would become the site of Saint Paul. The Dakota hunters decided that they would leave their reservation to hunt. But on August 17, still empty-handed, they gave up and begin the long trek home. Around 11 A.M. that day, the men stopped for a rest near the village of Acton. Tired and dispirited, they argued over a small clutch of eggs they found before approaching a nearby farmhouse. Conflicting accounts shroud in mystery what happened next, but the results were clear: the hunters shot and killed three men, a woman, and a girl.[4]

Survivors of the carnage fled for a neighbor's farm. They spread tales of a "general massacre" that eventually reached panic-stricken observers of Saint Paul. By 1862, that city, which only a decade earlier had been a settlement of fewer than a thousand people, boasted nearly ten thousand residents. A bustling commercial metropolis that stretched from high ground overlooking the Mississippi to lowlands that inundated during the river's spring floods, Saint Paul featured hotels; warehouses that groaned with the region's produce during harvest seasons; a Greek Revival courthouse; a wooden bridge that, three years earlier, had for the first time spanned the Mississippi's turbid waters; and a newspaper that in good times boosted the community's prospects and in bad served up ill tidings from the ragged edge of settlement, including, later that summer and fall and into the next year, lurid tales of violence perpetrated by ostensibly vicious Native people against innocent whites.[5]

The city that settlers in the nineteenth century began calling Saint Paul also hosted one of the most important Indigenous spaces throughout the Upper Midwest: Bdote. Located just southwest of town on bluffs above the confluence of the Minnesota and Mississippi Rivers, Bdote was "the center of Dakota spirituality and history" and, like nearby Saint Paul, an entrepôt. Blessed with commanding views of the rivers that served as the region's commercial arteries, federal authorities recognized the location's strategic significance early in the nineteenth century. In 1819, troops began constructing a stone fort, a beachhead for expansion and empire, that eventually would become known as Fort Snelling. The fort remained active, a center of the fur trade and a reminder of the ambitions of a settler-colonial society through 1858, when the government decommissioned the installation and it fell briefly into private hands. But when the Civil War started, Minnesota reopened Fort Snelling, using it as a site for mustering in and training thousands of citizen soldiers who would serve the Union in its bloody conflict with the Confederacy. Even then, Bdote remained sacred to Native peoples.[6]

Returning to August 17, 1862, the four Dakota hunters fled south from Acton. Stopping only to steal a wagon and horses, the men traveled deep into the night. When they arrived at the reservation, near where the Minnesota River swallows up Rice Creek, they announced, "There is a war with the whites, and we have begun it." Red Middle Voice, their village head, understood that the United States had been sundered by rebellion, and that the federal government had withdrawn most of its troops from the region to fight in battles unfolding to the east. He wondered if the moment had arrived to drive settlers out of Minnesota. He decided to confer with other tribal leaders about such a weighty decision. He rode downriver, stopping only to share news and rally supporters, until dawn broke on August 18, when he arrived at the home of a chief named Taoyatiduta or Little Crow.[7]

As Little Crow listened to the hunters' story, he pondered everything that had brought them together in that troubled moment, including the competing histories, political economies, and settlement patterns of his people and Minnesota's settlers. Little Crow had spent much of his childhood living on the banks of the Mississippi River, in Kaposia, a village located between Bdote and Saint Paul. His childhood home had been displaced when Saint Paul's thriving economy caused the city to swell with settlers and begin expanding downriver. In fall 1837, a Dakota delegation sold approximately 5 million acres of land, their people's holdings east of the Mississippi, to federal negotiators for $1 million. A bit less than a decade later, after his father died in 1846, Little Crow became a village chief responsible for helping his people navigate increasingly fraught relations with settlers. Three years after that, the federal government, able to project power into the region because of the success of Fort Snelling and the rapid growth of Saint Paul, organized the Minnesota Territory, formalizing its designs on the region and accelerating, yet again, the pace of settlement. In that same year, Alexander Ramsey, the newly minted territorial governor, arrived in Saint Paul eager to purchase the Dakotas' remaining land and then remove the tribe entirely from Minnesota.[8]

Little Crow, whose village stood just outside the fast-expanding territorial capital, remained cagey during the ensuing negotiations. He wanted his people to have the freedom to trade with settlers while preserving their traditional ways of life: hunting rather than embracing sedentary agriculture; worshipping as they wished rather than converting to Christianity; and organizing their polities based on bands and kinship rather than by adopting a top-down system legible to the federal government. Ramsey responded to what he perceived as intransigence by employing divide-and-conquer tactics. After treaty commissioners announced a provisional compact with bands to the north, he explained that intratribal politics and urban growth had tied Little Crow's hands. The chief, Ramsey noted, had "whites along the river [the Mississippi outside Saint Paul] in front but all around you." The only solution was moving "further west." In early August 1851, Little Crow signed a new compact: the federal government would pay a bit more than $3 million for approximately 24 million acres of tribal land and create a reservation, flanking the Minnesota River, for dispossessed Dakotas.[9]

The increasing scale of development that spun off from the hub of Saint Paul—including new towns, the trade centers and outposts of empire that encouraged still more settlement—fractured the Dakotas. White newcomers platted and cleared land west of the Mississippi even before the ink on treaties dried. At the same time, the Dakotas struggled with reservation life. Crops failed; the government ignored its obligations. In fall 1854, Little Crow's people confronted the prospect of starving or leaving the reservation to hunt. Young men joined a newly formed soldier's society and sabotaged the efforts of German immigrants, who, the next year, cleared land for the village of New Ulm. Charles Flandrau, the tribes' federal Indian agent, took stock of the situation and concluded, "The advance of the whites over the frontiers has been so rapid in Minnesota that the hunting grounds of the Indians have been taken from them before they have a chance to become fully domesticated." The year after that, 1857, Dakota soldiers killed more than forty settlers living in Spirit Lake, a village near the Minnesota-Iowa border. A moment of reckoning seemed to be at hand.[10]

Expansion and urbanization advanced in lockstep after the slaughter at Spirit Lake. Federal officials responded by calling for another treaty designed, they claimed, to encourage pastoralism among the Dakotas. An observer to the ensuing negotiations suggested that the goal was a ruse, that the actual desired outcome for the government was making Minnesota more attractive to settlers: enmeshing Indigenous people in commercial networks and clearing property for speculation and agriculture. Incoming migrants, he noted, would covet reservation lands rendered more "valuable by improvement and culture." The following spring, tribal delegates met federal negotiators. Little Crow focused on the disruptive nature of recent town planning, including at Saint Paul and New Ulm, whose residents had encroached on lands ostensibly set aside in perpetuity for the Dakotas. The Commissioner of Indian Affairs rejected Little Crow's history. He suggested looking to the future instead, to a new treaty that would provide the Dakotas with permanent title to land. They would have to give up in exchange all of their remaining holdings north of the Minnesota River.[11]

Less than a month later, on May 11, 1858, Minnesota became a state, putting renewed pressure on the beleaguered Dakotas. At month's end, tribal delegates gathered again. The Commissioner of Indian Affairs warned them that they would either sign the new treaty or, as more settlers arrived, forfeit their entire reservation. Little Crow and his people, facing only bad choices, agreed to the terms. Across two decades, the Dakotas had given up roughly 30 million acres of land. Even moderates in the tribe were irate. Federal Indian agent Joseph Brown observed, "The chiefs are being accused of having spoken falsely to their young men." Brown encouraged the Dakotas to abandon tribal traditions, to begin farming reservation lands, and to embrace Minnesota's free-labor economy by hiring themselves out for work in nearby towns or more distant Saint Paul. Some Dakotas, desperate to sustain their families or hoping to register their independence, began stealing from nearby settlers. As those depredations became more common, so did regional tensions. When local traders claimed a large portion of the Dakotas' treaty annuities in 1860, violence appeared increasingly likely.[12]

The election that year exacerbated strife in Minnesota. The transition from Democratic to Republican administrations triggered secession conventions and wholesale turnover within the federal apparatus. Patronage jobs, the spoils of electoral victory, went to Republicans. Thomas Galbraith, the newly installed federal agent for the Sioux tribes, had few contacts among the people he would help govern. Nevertheless, steeped in currents of evangelical reform, Galbraith decided to reconfigure the annuity system. He wanted to serve God and President Lincoln, advancing plans for an American empire in the West. Galbraith would, he announced, only disburse money to Native people who farmed or worked for wages, enmeshing themselves in a free-labor economy rooted in Minnesota's urban network—small towns connected by trade to the metropolis of Saint Paul. Galbraith would also ignore new arrivals who were squatting on reservation lands. Then, a bitter winter in 1861–62 led to food shortages among the Dakotas. Rumors began circulating that the government had diverted treaty funds, which might have alleviated the tribe's suffering, to help finance the Civil War.[13]

During summer 1862, many Dakotas began starving. Local merchants and traders knew that, without access to federal annuity payments, they could not collect debts from Native customers. They froze credit markets. In early August, famine tightened its grip on the reservation, and members of the Dakotas' soldier's society organized resistance. They broke into a federal warehouse in the village of Lower Agency, helping themselves to sacks of flour. Agent Galbraith called a meeting with tribal leaders at which Little Crow reminded the assembly that his people's treaty funds were missing. Then he warned, "When men are hungry, they help themselves." A storekeeper named Andrew Myrick replied, "so far as I am concerned, if they are hungry, let them eat grass," before storming out of the gathering. The Dakotas erupted in anger after a translator delivered the insult. They calmed down only when John Marsh, commander of the federal garrison stationed at Upper Agency, promised to distribute what food he had available to him to the residents of the Sioux Reservation.[14]

The exchange between Myrick and Little Crow points to how settler-colonialism needed credit markets, located in cities, to oil the machinery of expansion. Without credit, the Dakotas, limited to a reservation that kept shrinking as Saint Paul and its network of outlying settlements kept growing, could not reliably stave off hunger. And without access to their treaty annuities, money meted out by the federal government, local merchants would not guarantee the Dakotas credit. Credit, then, increasingly tethered the Dakotas to a local free-labor economy and distant exchange networks that originated in Saint Paul and spread throughout the United States and beyond. Put another way, the process of transforming land into property—a kind of capitalist alchemy—was a mutually constitutive element of urbanization. And as Myrick and Little Crow both realized, violence and coercion would increasingly serve as an engine of resistance on the part of Native peoples or of further dispossession on the part of settlers. At the same time, the federal government would rely upon city building and market penetration to serve as accelerants catalyzing explosive growth in the West.[15]

All of which led back to Little Crow's home on August 17, 1862, when he wrestled with the question of whether he should lead his people into war. Little Crow worried about the unbridled aggression of the United States. He understood that while the Confederate rebellion occupied the Union's attention in that moment, the nation had an extraordinary appetite for bloodshed and would likely, if threatened by another insurrection during such a precarious moment, be eager to make an example of Native peoples who dared to challenge its imperial pretensions. Little Crow appealed to the four hunters and the other chiefs arrayed around him to be sensible. He asked them, "Do you hear the thunder of their big guns?" The younger men responded by ignoring Little Crow's appraisal of the peril they faced; they accused him of cowardice. Angry, the chief prophesied that, "You will die like rabbits when the hungry wolves hunt them." Still, he understood that expansion, often heralded by pockets of urban growth, had yet again backed his people into a corner. The Dakotas, he reckoned, had no choice but to use violence strategically to try to reclaim their ancestral lands.[16]

On August 18, 1862, word spread in the village of Lower Sioux Agency that the Dakotas' annuities had finally arrived. Merchants, whose businesses had sat idle during a credit crisis of their own making, opened their shops. But then, a throng of Native soldiers, aware of the ways that expanding networks of exchange and urbanity had pushed them off their homeland, appeared out of the surrounding forest and encircled the settlement. One of the men entered Andrew Myrick's shop, shot a clerk, and then announced, "Now I will kill the dog who would not give me credit." Myrick jumped out a second-story window and ran for cover. Troops later found his corpse riddled with bullets and arrows, his mouth stuffed with grass. The Dakotas took supplies, burned Lower Sioux Agency, and then fell upon the town of Milford, where they killed perhaps fifty people who had built their homes on Native ground. Traders, government officials, and settlers all fled in fear. Federal troops tried to restore order but were routed and had to seek safety within a nearby fort.[17]

The logic of American imperialism rested upon assumptions of geographic determinism and white supremacy. Native peoples would inevitably disappear beneath weaves of white civilization. But now the Dakotas were launching a territorial, political, and cultural counterrevolution. Little Crow dreamed of returning to Mississippi's banks, of redeeming the village of Kaposia, of reclaiming Bdote as an Indigenous place. Warriors launched raid after raid, forcing settlers off property obtained through deceit or intimidation. Little Crow eventually called for a direct attack on the center of federal power in the region: an offensive on Fort Ridgely. He hoped to drive remaining U.S. troops out of the Minnesota River Valley and then cleanse the region of settlers entirely.

Although the plan failed when the federal garrison, relying on superior firepower, thwarted onslaught after onslaught from Little Crow's soldiers, the Dakotas turned their guns on New Ulm, burning the settlement. In a terrifying inversion of expected outcomes, armed bands of Indians were surging eastward.[18]

Late in August, aware that their hold on the region had been compromised, Union officers reinforced Fort Ridgely with a fresh regiment and then withdrew to the relative safety of Saint Paul. Governor Ramsey began sending increasingly frenzied cables to Secretary of War Edwin Stanton. Casting the state's Indians as a monolithic and existential threat, Ramsey warned that even Minnesota's cities might no longer be safe. "The Sioux Indians on our western border have risen," he wrote, "and are murdering men, women, and children." Another message, this time from one of Ramsey's subordinates, suggested that confederated tribes threatened settlers throughout the Midwest: "A most frightful insurrection of Indians has broken out along our whole frontier. Men, women, and children are indiscriminately murdered; evidently the result of a deep-laid plan, the attacks being simultaneous along our whole border." Ramsey begged for federal troops and organized a militia under Col. Henry Hastings Sibley, who believed that the region's Indigenous peoples very likely had to be exterminated outright, otherwise Minnesota and the Union might fall together.[19]

On September 1, some of Sibley's green troops reconnoitered near the Minnesota River, searching the charred ruins of settlements for survivors. Dakota soldiers surrounded them and, early the next morning, began pouring relentless fire into their ranks. By mid-afternoon, the Battle of Birch Coulee was over. Some sixty men and eighty horses littered the blood-soaked ground. Two days later, Dakotas trounced militiamen near Forest City, forced more people from their homes, and then rode to Henderson, where they razed the town. What became known as the Big Woods expedition emptied another swath of Minnesota and, if only briefly, silenced discussions of manifest destiny throughout the region. Settlements that were intended as satellites of trade networks and toeholds of empire lay in ruins, their residents scattered across the countryside. Sibley, wrong-footed by his mounting losses and uncertain about Minnesota's future, sought a parley with Little Crow. The colonel asked why the Dakotas had risen up against whites. Little Crow answered that settlers and their government could not be trusted, that his people had no choice but to try to reclaim their land by force. Sibley hoped that dissension among the Dakotas would deepen; he prepared for a huge counterattack.[20]

At the end of September, a force of more than a thousand troops marched toward the Yellow Medicine River, 150 miles from the sanctuary of Saint Paul. On September 22, Little Crow's soldiers engaged with Sibley's men in what became known as the Battle of Wood Lake, a stalemate that left the already-outnumbered and internally split Dakotas battered and short on personnel. Peace chiefs, meanwhile, prepared to hand over captives that Little Crow had taken during the preceding weeks. Resigned to the reality that divisions among his people would compromise his capacity for additional fighting and squander his leverage in negotiations, Little Crow rode west with his most trusted men. He knew that Sibley wanted to "to put a rope around [his] neck" and hoped to deny the colonel the opportunity. Early September 24, Little Crow and his companions prepared to leave the Minnesota River Valley. Surveying the land, the chief announced that he would never return.[21]

The Dakota War began at an especially perilous juncture for Union officials, who were awash in bad news from the front lines of the Civil War: the Shenandoah Campaign in spring; the Seven Days' Battles late in June; and, at the end of August, the debacle at Second Bull Run. All told, casualties in those engagements skied above fifty thousand. Preserving the Union as it had been prior to secession began to seem impossible. President Lincoln shifted his war aims. He issued the Emancipation Proclamation, a document that, despite its limits, transformed the Civil War into a war of liberation. And with Southern Democrats absent from Congress, Republican lawmakers seized the chance to overhaul the nation's political economy and geography. They passed landmark legislation and created new pieces of the federal apparatus—the Morrill Act, the Homestead Act, the Pacific Railroad Act, the Department of Agriculture—underwriting the construction of vast transportation networks and providing access to land, learning, and expertise for settlers. The Republican Party was offering up the West as fair recompense for the patriotic sacrifices of soldiers who, if they served, survived, and headed overland to the trans-Mississippi territories, could create an empire for Lincoln and liberty too.[22]

The conquest and colonization of the West seemed destined to proceed at a breakneck pace, distracting from the Union's declining fortunes, mapping out a brighter future for the United States, and serving the Republican Party's political interests. But then violence engulfed Minnesota. An insurrection in the West, coupled with the rebellion already underway in the South, threatened President Lincoln's plans to restore and remake the nation. On August 25, Horace Greeley publicized the story of the Dakota War for a wider audience, writing in his *New York Tribune* of the "INDIAN MURDERS" in Minnesota. The violence, Greeley claimed, had roots among Confederate intriguers. "The Sioux," the *Tribune* insisted, "have doubtless been stimulated if not bribed to plunder and slaughter their White neighbors by White and Red villains sent among them for this purpose by the Secessionists." Agents of the South did not care about their Indian allies, because "they will have effected a temporary diversion in favor of the Confederacy, and this is all their concern." Governor Ramsey, hoping to transform regional fears into federal funds, called the violence a "national war." In this way, two distinct but related conflicts became a single fight to save the Union.[23]

With the violence in Minnesota nationalized, conflated with the struggle to crush the Confederacy, Governor Ramsey got his way: the Lincoln administration began diverting resources from the Civil War to fight the Dakota War. When Gen. John Pope bungled Second Bull Run, Lincoln reassigned him to Minnesota. In early September 1862, after Dakota soldiers thrashed Minnesota militiamen at Birch Coulee, Pope learned from his Commander in Chief and the Secretary of War that he would be tapped to oversee a new military district, the Department of the Northwest, where Native peoples were in a state of open rebellion. "The Indian hostilities," Edwin Stanton wrote, "require the attention of some military officer of high rank." Pope would go West.[24]

On September 16, Pope arrived in Saint Paul, a city gripped by collective hysteria. Although Native soldiers had not sacked any major metropolitan areas in Minnesota, Saint Paul's residents were certain they faced grave peril. Measuring the city's mood, Pope wrote to Gen. Henry Halleck: "We are likely to have a general Indian war all along the frontier." With "panic everywhere," he feared that the region "will be half depopulated before the winter begins," halting the Republican Party's project of empire building. Pope planned to reassure settlers that federal authority, though besieged by Confederates and Dakotas, remained intact in the region. Every Native man convicted by a military commission would be put to death. "The example of hanging many of the perpetrators of the late outrages is necessary," Pope insisted, "and will have a crushing effect" on the Union's enemies. Uncertain of his ability to maintain order beyond urban areas, Pope remained certain at least that a spectacle of violent retribution staged in Mankato could demonstrate government power.

The executions would be public, urban, and overseen by federal soldiers keeping the peace.[25]

The adjudication of the cases took place in Saint Paul; the results resonated throughout the United States. The process was brutally streamlined. Defendants were not allowed to enter pleas. Most trials took less than ten minutes. In just six weeks, the commission heard 392 cases, determining that 303 men should die. Military engagements, including at Birch Coulee, were treated like massacres. Native soldiers who fought against uniformed personnel thus became murderers. President Lincoln, presented with the list of the condemned for review, tried to balance competing interests. He was "anxious to not act with so much clemency as to encourage another outbreak on one hand, nor with so much severity as to be real cruelty on the other." Governor Ramsey, hoping to stiffen Lincoln's spine, warned the president to expect further erosion of the rule of law in the West if the executions did not move along expeditiously. "Private revenge would on all this border take the place of the official judgment on these Indians," Ramsey noted. General Pope suggested that "if the guilty were not all executed," settlers would perpetrate an "indiscriminate massacre of all the Indians." Lincoln eventually winnowed the list down to thirty-nine men who would die just after Christmas. Three days before the mass hanging, he pardoned an additional man, leaving thirty-eight to swing from Mankato's gibbets.[26]

At the same time, federal troops transformed Bdote into a concentration camp, imprisoning some sixteen hundred Dakota non-combatants in the shadow of Fort Snelling outside Saint Paul. Twelve-foot-high walls surrounded several acres on which Dakotas did their best to build makeshift shelters to protect their families from winter's bitter cold. As soldiers from Minnesota's Sixth, Seventh, and Tenth Volunteer Regiments looked on during that killing season, well over a hundred Dakotas—none of whom had anything to do with the violence the previous year—died of exposure, disease, and malnutrition. Then, when spring 1863 arrived, troops marched the survivors onto steamboats, which dropped the Dakotas at the Crow Creek Reservation in South Dakota. Violence had provided a pretext for still more dispossession of Minnesota's Indigenous people; federal authorities would, three years later, remove the Dakotas from Crow Creek, bringing them to the Santee Reservation in Nebraska.[27]

Governor Ramsey and General Pope insisted that the public execution of the Dakota thirty-eight and the internment of sixteen hundred other Indians would chasten the Union's enemies and buck up its allies, especially regional settlers, the shock troops of an empire that President Lincoln hoped to see flourish in the West. But violence continued. Ramsey, taking stock of the situation following the hanging in Mankato, suggested that the remaining "Sioux Indians of Minnesota must be exterminated or driven forever beyond the borders of the state." Pope agreed. "It is my purpose," he had announced earlier, "utterly to exterminate the Sioux if I have the power to do so and even if requires a campaign lasting the whole of next year. Destroy everything belonging to them and force them out onto the plains." The following summer and fall, Pope launched the so-called punitive expeditions, including slaughters at Big Mound, Whitestone Hill, and, a year later, Killdeer Mountain. In each of those cases, Minnesota volunteer soldiers attacked Native peoples who had nothing to do with the Dakota War. Yet again, violence had become an excuse for sweeping removal efforts in the state and region.[28]

As federal troops pushed Minnesota's Indigenous peoples out of their homeland, Little Crow returned to the state. Just before dusk on July 3, 1863, he and his son, Wowinape, picked berries near Hutchinson, about fifty miles outside Saint Paul. A shot rang out. A bullet struck Little Crow. He returned fire before another rifle ball caught him in the chest, killing him. Wowinape wrapped his father's body in a blanket, placed moccasins nearby, and then fled. Eleven hundred miles to the east, two armies found themselves locked in combat for a third consecutive day. The ground on which they fought, consecrated by the blood of some fifty thousand wounded men, would be hallowed four months later in a grateful president's speech. The Battle of Gettysburg is often cast as the start of the final chapter of the Civil War; the Indian Wars would not end for several decades.[29]

Over and over again, those conflicts would feature urban dimensions and callbacks to the fighting in Minnesota. In late summer 1864, opportunistic residents of Albuquerque, New Mexico, ostensibly fearing for their lives, would capitalize on the Civil War context and push government officials and Union soldiers to do what they had long sought: round up Navajo and Apache peoples, lead them on a forced march, and place them in a concentration camp. In that same year, the people of Denver, Colorado, claiming that a massive tribal alliance, including Sioux warriors supposedly still demanding revenge years after the Dakota War, stood poised to wipe out the city, would display the broken bodies of murdered settlers at a downtown intersection, a memorial and incitement to vengeance that led to the massacre at Sand Creek. In these and other conflicts between settlers and Indians, urbanization and imperialism would often be inextricably intertwined.[30]

Despite the efforts of men like Alexander Ramsey, John Pope, and the thousands of soldiers they commanded, despite federal policies crafted to foster settler-colonialism and maintain ironclad control of an American empire in the West, despite memories within their communities of dispossession and dislocation, of mass internments and executions, of epidemics and famines, the Dakotas have always maintained their ties to Minnesota. Like Little Crow in 1863, they have always returned home. In recent years, Dakota people have reclaimed landscapes at Fort Snelling and Bdote as a way of testifying to their cultural and demographic persistence. In short, as Sasha Suarez demonstrates elsewhere in this volume, the Twin Cities are still an Indigenous space.[31]

ACKNOWLEDGMENT

I would like to thank the editors of this volume, my fellow contributors, the wonderful staff at the Clements Center for Southwest Studies, and the Departments of History at Duke University, New York University, the University of Cambridge, the University of Minnesota, and Vanderbilt University, all of whom provided valuable feedback or other support as I worked on this essay. Any errors that remain are mine alone.

NOTES

1. *St. Paul Press*, December 28, 1862; *Mankato Record*, December 26, 1862; Isaac Heard, *History of the Sioux War and Massacres of 1862 and 1863* (New York: Harper and Brothers, 1864), 271–98.

2. Quotes from *New York Times*, January 11, 1863.

3. Quotes from *New York Times*, January 11, 1863. See also *Mankato Record*, December 26, 1862; and *St. Paul Press*, December 28, 1862.

4. Marion P. Satterlee, *A Detailed Account of the Massacre by the Dakota Indians of Minnesota in 1862* (Minneapolis: Marion P. Satterlee, 1923), 10–14; Heard, *History of the Sioux War and Massacres of 1862 and 1863*, 52–58; Wilhelmina B. Carrigan, *Captured by the Indians: Reminiscences of Pioneer Life in Minnesota* (Forest City, Minn.: Forest City Press, 1907), 6–8.

5. Quote from Lucius F. Hubbard and Return Ira Holcombe, *Minnesota in Three Centuries, 1655–1908*, vol. 3 (Mankato: Publishing Society of Minnesota, 1908), 311. See also Larry Millett, *AIA Guide to the Twin Cities: The Essential Source on the Architecture of Minneapolis and St. Paul* (St. Paul: Minnesota Historical Society Press, 2007), 427–35;

and John Fletcher Williams, *A History of the City of Saint Paul, and of the County of Ramsey, Minnesota* (Saint Paul: Minnesota Historical Society, 1876), 255–415.

6. Quote from *Dakota Memory Map,* http://bdotememorymap.org/. See also *The U.S.-Dakota War of 1862,* http://www.usdakotawar.org/; Return Ira Holcombe, *Minnesota in Three Centuries, 1655–1908,* vol. 2 (Mankato: Publishing Society of Minnesota, 1908), 62, 119–24; Hubbard and Holcombe, *Minnesota in Three Centuries, 1655–1908,* 3:127–215; Waziyatawin, *What Does Justice Look Like? The Struggle for Liberation in Dakota Homeland* (St. Paul: Living Justice Press, 2008), 17–41.

7. "There is a war with the whites, and we have begun it" from Charles S. Bryant and Abel B. Murch, *A History of the Great Massacre by the Sioux Indians* (Cincinnati: Rickey & Carroll, 1864), 389–91.

8. Alexander Ramsey to Joseph Brown and John Chambers, August 25, 1849, in *House Executive Document* 5, 31st Cong., 1st Sess., 980; Luke Lea to Alexander Ramsey, November 8, 1849, in National Archives, Record Group 75, Letters Received, Minnesota Superintendency; Henry Sibley to Alexander Ramsey, September 15, 1849, in Henry H. Sibley papers, Minnesota Historical Society; Asa Wilder Daniels, "Reminiscences of the Little Crow Uprising," *Collections of the Minnesota Historical Society* 12 (1908): 511–15; F. V. Lamare-Picquot, "Minnesota as Seen by Travelers: A French Naturalist in Minnesota, 1846," *Minnesota History* 6 (September 1925): 275; Gary Clayton Anderson, "The Removal of the Mdewakanton Dakota in 1837: A Case of Jacksonian Paternalism," *South Dakota History* 10 (Fall 1980): 310–33; E. S. Seymour, *Sketches of Minnesota, The New England of the West. With Incidents of Travel in that Territory during the Summer of 1849* (New York: Harper and Brothers, 1850), 90–99.

9. Quote from "Journal of the Joint Commission to Treat with the Sioux," 1851, in National Archives, Record Group 75, Documents Relating to the Negotiations of Ratified and Unratified Treaties with Various Tribes of Indians, 71–73. See also Henry Sibley to Martin McLeod, May 6, 1851, in Henry Sibley Papers, Minnesota Historical Society; "Outline of a Plan for Civilizing the Dakotas, Adopted at a Meeting of the Dakota Mission held at Kaposia," in National Archives, Record Group 75, Letters Received, Minnesota Superintendency; and Lucile M. Kane, "The Sioux Treaties and the Traders," *Minnesota History* 32 (June 1951): 65–80.

10. "The advance of the whites . . ." from Charles Flandrau to unknown, September 22, 1857, in National Archives, Record Group 75, Letters Received, Northern Superintendency. See also "Sioux Petition," December 6, 1851, in National Archives, Record Group 75, Letters Received, St. Peter's Agency; Secretary of the Interior to the President, April 5, 1854, in National Archives, Record Group 48, Letters Sent, Indian Division of the Department of the Interior; "Treaty with the Mdewakanton, Wahpekute, Sisseton, and Whapeton Sioux," National Archives, Record Group 75, Documents Relating to the Negotiations of Ratified and Unratified Treaties with Various Tribes of Indians; "Petition of New Ulm Farmers," in National Archives, Record Group 75, Letters Received, Minnesota Superintendency; Abbie Gardner Sharp, *History of the Spirit Lake Massacre and the Captivity of Miss Abbie Gardner* (Des Moines: Iowa Printing Company, 1885), 74–229.

11. "Valuable by improvement . . ." from "Pritchette Report, October 15, 1857," in National Archives, Record Group 75, Letters Received, St. Peter's Agency. See also W. J. Cullen to J. W. Denver, September 28, 1857, in *Senate Executive Document* 11, 35th Cong., 1st Sess., 339; Charles Flandrau to W. J. Cullen, September 28, 1857, in *Senate Executive Document* 11, 35th Cong., 1st Sess., 348; W. J. Cullen to J. W. Denver, November 26 and December 24, 1857, in National Archives, Record Group 75, Letters Received, St. Peter's Agency; Alfred Sully to W. J. Cullen, October 12, 1857, in National Archives, Record Group 75, Letters Sent, Northern Superintendency.

12. Quote from Joseph Brown to W. J. Cullen, September 1, 1858, in National Archives, Record Group 75, Letters Received, St. Peter's Agency. See also "Treaty with the Mdewakanton, Wahpekute, Sisseton, and Whapeton Sioux"; Joseph Brown to W.J. Cullen, September 30, 1858, in *Senate Executive Document* 1, 35th Cong., 2nd Sess., 402; Joseph Brown to W. J. Cullen, September 10, 1859, in *Senate Executive Document* 2, 36th Cong., 1st Sess., 459.

13. Thomas Galbraith to Clark Thompson, July 24 and August 27, 1861, in National Archives, Record Group 75, Letters Received, St. Peter's Agency; Clark Thompson to William Dyke, September 5, 1861, in National Archives, Record Group 393, Letters Received, Fort Ridgely, 1853–1861; Thomas Galbraith to Clark Thompson, January 27, 1863, in *House Executive Document* 1, 38th Cong., 1st Sess., 383; "Testimony of Thomas Galbraith," in Sioux Claims, in National Archives, Record Group 75, Special Files; Heard, *History of the Sioux War and Massacres of 1862 and 1863*, 47–50.

14. Quotes from Winifred Barton, *John P. Williamson: A Brother to the Sioux* (New York: Fleming H. Revell, 1919), 48–50. See also Andrew Myrick to Nathan Myrick, July 20, 1862, in "Sioux Claims," National Archives, Record Group 75, Special Files; "Testimony of Thomas Galbraith," in Sioux Claims, in National Archives, Record Group 75, Special Files; "Testimony of Timothy Sheehan," in *The Sisseton and Wahpeton Bands of Sioux Indians vs. The United States*, 1901–1907, Court of Claims docket no. 22524; Gary Clayton Anderson, "Myrick's Insult: A Fresh Look at Myth and Reality," *Minnesota History* 48 (Spring 1983): 199–204.

15. Heard, *History of the Sioux War and Massacres of 1862 and 1863*, 49–53; Anderson, "Myrick's Insult," 206–10; Bryant and Murch, *A History of the Great Massacre by the Sioux Indians, in Minnesota*, 72–77.

16. Quotes from "Little Crow's Speech," in *Through Dakota Eyes: Narrative Accounts of the Minnesota Indian War of 1862*, ed. Gary Clayton Anderson and Alan R. Woolworth (St. Paul: Minnesota Historical Society Press, 1988), 40–42. See also Return I. Holcombe, ed., "A Sioux History of the War: Chief Big Eagle's Story of the Sioux Outbreak of 1862," *Collections of the Minnesota Historical Society* 6 (1894): 384; Mr. and Mrs. Harry Lawrence, "The Indian Nations of Minnesota: The Sioux Uprising," in *Minnesota Heritage: A Panoramic Narrative of the Historical Development of the North Star State*, ed. Lawrence M. Briggs (Minneapolis: T. S. Denison, 1960), 82.

17. Quote from Heard, *History of the Sioux War and Massacres of 1862 and 1863*, 62. See also William Watts Folwell, *A History of Minnesota*, vol. 3 (St. Paul: Minnesota

Historical Society, 1924), 109–71; Bryant and Murch, *A History of the Great Massacre by the Sioux Indians*, 415–60; Sarah Wakefield, *Six Weeks in the Sioux Tepees: A Narrative of Indian Captivity* (Shakopee: Argus Books and Job Printing Office, 1864), 8–17; Carrigan, *Captured by the Indians*, 6–9.

18. "Testimony of Timothy J. Sheehan," in *The Sisseton and Wahpeton Bands of Sioux Indians vs. The United States*; Heard, *History of the Sioux War and Massacres of 1862 and 1863*, 131–157; "Report of Charles E. Flandrau, August 23, 1862," in *Minnesota in the Civil War and Indian Wars, 1861–1865*, vol. 2 (St. Paul: Pioneer Press Company, 1893), 203–7; Urinia White, "Captivity among the Sioux, August 18 to September 26, 1862," *Collections of the Minnesota Historical Society*, vol. 9 (1901): 395–426.

19. "The Sioux Indians . . ." from Alexander Ramsey to Edwin Stanton, August 21, 1862, in *The War of the Rebellion: A Compilation of the Official Records of the Union and Confederate Armies* (Washington, D.C.: Government Printing Office, 1888), Ser. I, vol. 19: 590 (hereafter *OR*). "A most frightful insurrection . . ." from "Testimony of Joseph La Framboise," in *The Sisseton and Wahpeton Bands of Sioux Indians vs. The United States*. See also: Gabriel Renville, "A Sioux Narrative of the Outbreak in 1862, and of Sibley's Expedition in 1863," *Collections of the Minnesota Historical Society* 10 (1905): 595–600; Heard, *History of the Sioux War and Massacres of 1862 and 1863*, 131–40; Hubbard and Holcombe, *Minnesota in Three Centuries, 1655–1908*, 3:335–51.

20. Henry Sibley to Innocent Indians, September 13, 1862, in National Archives, Record Group 393, Letters Sent, Sibley's Indian Expedition; Henry Sibley to Sarah Sibley, August 28, September 8 and 10, 1862 in Henry H. Sibley papers, Minnesota Historical Society; "Battle of Birch Coulee—September 2, 1862," in *Minnesota in the Civil War and Indian Wars, 1861–1865*, 2:214–19; Marion P. Satterlee, *The Story of Capt. Richard Strout and Company, Who Fought the Sioux Indians at the Battle of Kelly's Bluff, at Acton, Minn., on Wednesday, September 3rd, 1862* (Minneapolis: Marion P. Satterlee, 1909), 1–12.

21. "To put a rope around my neck . . ." quoted in Paul N. Beck, *Columns of Vengeance: Soldiers, Sioux, and the Punitive Expeditions, 1863–1864* (Norman: University of Oklahoma Press, 2014), 41. See also Henry Sibley to Alexander Ramsey, September 23, 1862, in National Archives, Record Group 393, Letters Sent, Sibley's Indian Expedition; "Testimony of Two Stars," in *The Sisseton and Wahpeton Bands of Sioux Indians vs. The United States*; Henry H. Sibley, "Battle of Wood Lake," in *Minnesota in the Civil War and Indian Wars, 1861–1865*, 2:242–51; Doane Robinson, *A History of the Dakota or Sioux Indians: From Their Earliest Traditions and First Contact with White Men to the Final Settlement of the Last of Them Upon Reservation and Consequent Abandonment of Tribal Life* (Aberdeen: News Printing Co., 1904), 294.

22. James McPherson, *Battle Cry of Freedom: The Civil War Era* (New York: Oxford University Press, 1988), 191–96, 453–62, 466–80, 528–34; Richard White, *Railroaded: The Transcontinentals and the Making of Modern America* (New York: Norton, 2011), 17–27; Harold Hyman, *American Singularity: The 1787 Northwest Ordinance, The 1862 Homestead And Morrill Acts, and the 1944 G.I. Bill* (Athens: University of Georgia Press, 2008), 35–61.

23. "National war" from Alexander Ramsey to Abraham Lincoln, September 6, 1862, in Abraham Lincoln Papers, Library of Congress. All other quotes from *New York Tribune*, August 25, 1862. See also Alexander Ramsey to Abraham Lincoln, August 26, 1862, in *OR*, I, 19:597 and *Scientific American*, September 6(1862): 147.

24. Quote from Edwin Stanton to John Pope, September 6, 1862, in *OR*, I, 19:617.

25. "We are likely to have a general Indian war . . . ," "panic everywhere," and "will be half depopulated . . ." from John Pope to Henry Halleck, September 16, 1862, in *OR*, I, 19:642. All other quotes from John Pope to Henry Halleck, October 10, 1862, in *OR*, I, 19:724.

26. "Anxious to not act . . ." from Abraham Lincoln to Senate, December 11, 1862, in Roy P. Baisler, *The Collected Works of Abraham Lincoln*, vol. 5 (New Brunswick, N.J.: Rutgers University Press, 1953), 551. "Private revenge . . ." from Alexander Ramsey to Abraham Lincoln, November 10, 1862, in *OR* I, 19:787. "If the guilty were not all executed . . ." from John Pope to Abraham Lincoln, November 11, 1862, in *OR*, I, 19:788.

27. Corrine L. Monjeau-Marz, *The Dakota Indian Internment at Fort Snelling, 1862–1864* (Saint Paul: Prairie Smoke Press, 2005), 13–47, 55–84; Gary Clayton Anderson and Alan R. Woolworth, *Through Dakota Eyes: Narrative Accounts of the Minnesota Indian War of 1862* (Saint Paul: Minnesota Historical Society Press, 1988), 219–67; *St. Paul Union*, November 22, 1862; *St. Paul Pioneer*, November 19, 1862.

28. "The Sioux Indians . . ." from *Executive Documents for the State of Minnesota for the Year 1862* (St. Paul: William R. Marshall, State Printer, 1863), 12. "It is my purpose . . ." from John Pope to Henry Sibley, September 28, 1862, in *OR*, I, 19:685. See also: Testimony of Iron Hoop," in *The Sisseton and Wahpeton Bands of Sioux Indians vs. The United States*; "Report of Brigadier General Alfred Sully," September 11, 1863, in *OR*, I, 32:555–62; John Pope to Henry Halleck, August 20, 1863, in *OR*, I, 33:463–64; "Report of Brigadier General Alfred Sully," July 31, 1864, in *OR*, I, 83:141–44; "Report of Brigadier General Alfred Sully," August 13, 1864, in *OR*, I, 83:144–48; "Report of Brigadier General Alfred Sully," August 18, 1864, in *OR*, I, 83:148–49; Scott W. Berg, *38 Nooses: Lincoln, Little Crow, and the Beginning of the Frontier's End* (New York: Pantheon Books, 2012), 283–83; J. C. Luse, "The Battle of Whitestone Hill," *South Dakota Historical Collections* 5 (1910): 415–20.

29. *St. Paul Daily Press*, August 4, 13, and 21, 1863; *St. Paul Pioneer Press*, August 13, 1863, and October 24, 1897; Marion P. Satterlee, "Narratives of the Sioux War: The Killing of Little Crow," *Collections of the Minnesota Historical Society* 15 (1905): 367–70; Loren W. Collins, *The Expeditions Against the Sioux Indians in 1863* (St. Cloud: Journal-Press Print, 1895), 20.

30. Gary L. Roberts, *Massacre at Sand Creek: How Methodists Were Involved in an American Tragedy* (Nashville: Abingdon Press, 2016), 95–158; Ari Kelman, *A Misplaced Massacre: Struggling Over the Memory of Sand Creek* (Cambridge: Harvard University Press, 2013), 1–43; David F. Halaas and Andrew E. Masich, *Halfbreed: The Remarkable True Story of George Bent—Caught between the Worlds of the Indian and the White Man* (Cambridge, Mass.: Da Capo Press, 2004), 113–54; Lynn R. Bailey, *Bosque Redondo:*

The Navajo Internment at Fort Sumner, New Mexico, 1893–1868 (Tucson: Westernlore Press, 1998), 127–66; Jennifer Denetdale, *The Long Walk: The Forced Navajo Exile* (New York: Chelsea House Publishers, 2008), 69–120; Clifford E. Trafzer, *The Kit Carson Campaign: The Last Great Navajo War* (Norman: University of Oklahoma Press, 1982), 169–246; Gerald Thompson, *The Army and the Navajo: The Bosque Redondo Experiment, 1863–1868* (Tucson: University of Arizona Press, 1976), 10–159.

31. *Dakota 38 Memorial Ride—Dakota Wicohan Sunktanka Program*, http:// sunktanka.weebly.com/dakota-38-plus-2-memorial-ride.html; Mark Fischenich, "New Sculpture Planned for Reconciliation Park," *Free Press*, April 7, 2019; Sheila M. Eldred, "Walker Center's Reckoning with 'Scaffold' Isn't Over Yet," *New York Times*, September 13, 2017; Alicia Eler, "'Scaffold' Sculpture to be Dismantled, Then Burned in a Dakota-Led Ceremony," *Star Tribune*, June 1, 2017; Rachel Hutton, "4 Dakota Landmarks Hide in Plain Sight along the Mississippi River," *Star Tribune*, August 17, 2018; *Dakota Memory Map*, http://bdotememorymap.org/; *The U.S.-Dakota War of 1862*, http://www.usdakotawar.org/.

MISHUANA R. GOEMAN

4

ELECTRIC LIGHTS, TOURIST SIGHTS

Gendering Dispossession and Colonial
Infrastructure at Niagara Falls

Unlike all other North American cities, Niagara Falls gave birth to the electric
grid that would power urban skylines across the globe; like all North American
cities, it also starkly highlights settler colonial methods of dispossession. It is a
simultaneously a monument to humanity's ability to harness nature and a thing
of natural sublime wonder: it is a place occupied by humans who twist and turn
the natural world, the courses of its rivers, in order to possess and dispossess
others. Niagara Falls holds multiple histories. Native mappings precede and
perhaps also aid the mainstream, familiar histories of the place. Yet the co-
option of Native presence at Niagara Falls is important to consider, as it reveals
Niagara Fall's importance as a place that gave rise to American middle-class
social and familial practices (especially involving tourist honeymoons) and as
the site of the invention of the hydroelectric power grid that devoured Native
lands on a much broader spectrum.[1] Although the logics of capitalism operated
plainly here, Native dispossession, affective mapping, and biopolitics are rarely

understood as central to the story of Niagara Falls. Drawing on the methods of critical geography and Indigenous studies, this essay offers a meditation on how these elements intertwine at Niagara Falls.

For Haudenosaunee people, the Falls have been a historical fishing and trading place. They also are a place of significant social and cultural importance. It is a storied place, one where the powerful Thunder Beings reside. Ancient battles between the Thunder Beings and Horned Serpents take place at the Falls, marking the connections between the human and nonhuman.[2] It is also a place where the battle between wind, water, and rock took place, carving out the Falls through time well before human beings arrived.[3]

The Haudenosaunee Confederacy (which Americans called the Iroquois Confederacy) is composed of Five Nations: the Mohawks, Oneidas, Onondagas, Cayugas, and Seneca. The political structure is structured by the longhouse and kinship relations. During the eighteenth century, a Sixth Nation, the Tuscarora, had been displaced by the Indian wars in the Southeast, and migrated north; the Seneca provided them with sovereign land at the Falls, extending the Haudenosaunee rafters to what are now Six Nations. The nations of the Confederacy were later split by the boundary of the United States' northern border and Canada's southern border after the American Revolution and in 1818. Later treaties confined them and shrunk their land base to reservations with boundaries outlined by old-growth forest, diminishing tribal sovereignty and a different way of living than that practiced by settlers in rural upstate New York.[4]

For the United States and Canada, the Niagara Falls site ideologically marks the recognition of co-constitutive settler powers, where might over right wins out in the extraction of resources. This fact was especially clear at the turn of the twentieth century, when hydroelectric power from the Niagara Falls generating station drove the development of power grids and enriched the industrial class in Buffalo, New York—a technological feat celebrated at the 1901 Buffalo World's Fair. Ostentatious displays of settler technology contrasted with a dire lack of resources and the neglect of treaty rights on reservations in both New York State and elsewhere in Indian Country. Moreover, Niagara Falls reveals a pattern: the placement of hydroelectric dams and other energy generation plants on Native lands throughout the twentieth century.[5]

The completion of the Erie Canal in 1825 connected Buffalo and Albany in what commentators celebrated as "the Wedding of the Waters." It also set off a flood of tourists to Niagara Falls, suddenly much more accessible.[6] As industry and tourist opportunities arose, Native peoples were pushed to the edges of

Niagara. Many Seneca and Tuscarora people worked in the new industries as wage laborers as Buffalo expanded. While the area no longer looks like rich tree-filled traditional lands, the Tonawanda Band of Seneca Reservation remains, Niagara Falls still flows, and the Great Lakes continue to mark the boundary between the United States and Canada. The border is also ideological, enforced through settler military power. Yet Buffalo and its surrounding lands were and still are the homeland of the Haudenosaunee people from the Tuscarora and Seneca Reservations, a people distinct from those who live in white working-class neighborhoods in close proximity. The streets of Buffalo grew along with the new technologies that would make possible a century of industrialization and the settlement of Native lands.

The Falls mark the struggle for power—both literally and figuratively, the latter through the telling of stories that helped constitute the national identities of the United States and Canada. Beginning with the earliest Europeans to see the Falls—the explorer and profitier René-Robert Cavelier, Sieur de La Salle, and his men in 1679—European explorers and settlers continually disparaged the political, cultural, and organizational elements of the Haudenosaunee Confederacy. This continued into the early nineteenth century, when the Falls were built up as a tourist site and then later when it was marketed as a honeymoon destination. Then, entrepreneurs created and marketed the fable of the "Maid of the Mist," a fictional creation that purported to be a real "Indian" story. It involves an "Indian Maiden" sacrificed to the Falls by her uncaring father. The story depicted Haudenosaunee people as inhumane and inhuman, justifying their dispossession while also helping to constitute American middle-class norms, a patriarchal institution that stood in stark contrast to Haudenosaunee matrifocal formations.

The stories and monuments perpetuated by the tourist industry at Niagara Falls and the Buffalo area marked Indian deaths as part of a pre-industrial past while trumpeting the rising technological wonders of the future. In other words, Indian deaths opened up room for a budding American property-owning citizenship. Yet the story of the "Maid of the Mist" was in tension with the experiences of real Native women who remained in that place. Monument making at the turn of the nineteenth century was a common practice meant to convey the message of a united peoples; it does memory work, as Jean O'Brien and Lisa Blee make clear in their discussion of a statue of the Wampanoag leader Massasoit in *Monumental Mobility*. As O'Brien and Blee argue, the Massasoit statue "otherwise reveals obscure dimensions of American Memorial culture: a certain elasticity of historical imagination; a tight-knit relationship between consumption, experience, and commemoration; and the twinned urge to sanitize and grapple with the meaning of settler colonialism."[7] The circulation of stories and souvenirs (many made by Tuscarora and other Haudenosaunee women) from Niagara Falls did similar work. But like much monument making, it not only conveyed the message of the state but also produced an affective mapping of nation-states, genders, and technologies.

My analysis of the Falls as geopolitics and ideology builds on scholarship on state-produced space (especially on the making of monuments and creating jurisdictions) and Indigenous placemaking (especially on intergenerational stories on specific sites that are indicative of entire value systems). Violent stories of Indian men and sacrificed maidens abound across the landscapes of the United States, while personal stories of colonizing non-native violence against Native women is the reality passed down through generational stories. If we consider Scott Morgensen's argument that "the terrorizing sexual colonization of Native peoples was a historical root of the biopolitics of modern sexuality in the United States,"[8] we can see the Falls as an important site of such biopolitical practice. The natural wonder of Niagara Falls is now considered a must-see for tourists from all over the world. It is a place of stories—not just Indigenous stories, of the Thunder Beings, but settler stories too, of movies, plays, novels, and political propaganda. Settler stories include those who tightrope over the cataracts or float over the Falls in a barrel, making them resonate as a place of spectacle and American bravery. Tourist interpretations that read Indians through what Renato Rosaldo calls "imperialist nostalgia'"—which "makes racial domination appear innocent and pure" by making the colonizers think that they respect what they have tried to destroy—provide a foundation for these gender formations.[9] With the Americanizing of Indian lands into city spaces, white Americans solidified their class position by participating in the middle-class practices of the tourist industry and the consumption of natural resources that would give rise to industrialization and cities across the globe. Moreover, the modern concept of honeymooning relies on heteronormative notions of coupling.

SETTLER FICTIONS

The settler project of the first half of the nineteenth century was about the harnessing of Haudenosaunee lands and waterways; part and parcel of this was creating a visual and narrative apparatus that would *see* Native peoples as collectible souvenirs in burgeoning settler states. Tourist magazines and newspapers gave pride of place to Niagara Falls in the American imaginary: they proclaimed that Niagara Falls "was to be the focus of the future."[10] That future, the settler treatment of Native peoples, and the rising middle-class family all required a colonial nostalgia. Or as Rosaldo argues, white settlers had "to remain essentially different from the people they colonize, thus allowing the colonizers to justify their conquest."[11] As a monumental site, Niagara Falls was at once configured as a bold allegory of Native "sacrifice" and as a monument to capitalism and settler masculinity. As the Niagara Falls Commission report of 1903 stated, the Falls was "a glory in which even the redman saw an expression of his manitou and which evoked from him his heathen sacrifices and invocations."[12]

The death of an Indian women was a story that became "fact" in 1846, by the promotion of "Maid of the Mist Tours." This story served not only to draw tourists near and far to view the sublime landscape but also to perpetuate depictions of the Haudenosaunee as cruel and savage. It promotes a romantic vision of an Indian woman who is never named: she is simply presented as a "chief's daughter." Sue Wilson compactly relates the commodified and oft-repeated story, widely contested by Haudenosaunee people, in her following statement: such stories "demonize Native culture by inventing a narrative that has the maiden being the victim of an annual human sacrifice ritual [that] is part of traditional Iroquois custom." The melodramatic story portrays a "beautiful Indian maiden sacrificed against her will in [an attempt to] appease the gods now[,] or pay in spades later."[13] This story was swiftly adopted into popular culture and became part and parcel of a network of tales that attempt to disempower Haudenosaunee people by telling accounts of savagery and brutal violence— tales still celebrated even in literature touted as Native American (such as the 2013 novel *The Orenda* by non-Native author Joseph Boyden) or in mythologies perpetuated by the Canadian government where stands for sovereignty and protection of land are considered militant and hostile acts.[14] The social, cultural, and political work in these economies of dispossession are active mechanisms of state power that serve to "power" notions of the sanctity of settler life and of death to the Native who must die as pristine nature gives way to technological civilization. The geographic site was also a place where white settlers could mourn the passing of the imagined harmony of Native people and "untouched nature" while they welcomed the future of hydroelectric power and industry.

Niagara Falls and the Buffalo area were rich in stories and monuments marking Indian deaths as part of a pastoral past while celebrating the rising technological wonders of the future. In mainstream society the story of Maid of the

The Indian Sacrifice, Niagara Falls, N.Y. Postcard. Detroit Publishing Company, 1903–4. Courtesy Wikimedia Commons. This early twentieth-century postcard from Niagara Falls replicated the older stories and titillated tourists by portraying a naked "Maid of the Mist" rowing herself to sacrifice.

Mist is perhaps the most popular, coinciding and reiterating values regarding virginity, purity, and sacrifice. An epitome of paternalism and maternalism, the story affectively maps settler placemaking. Jonathan Flatley writes that an affective map "is a map less in the sense that it establishes a territory than that it is about providing a feeling of orientation and facilitating mobility."[15] For Flatley, affective attachment is an active doing, a kind of energy that mobilizes subjects and enables them to imagine and cohere as a community.

This decontextualizing of Native stories of place and presence and the concomitant recreating of new, false narratives are necessary to the colonial project. Niagara becomes a honeymoon destination by building on the idea of dying for true love. The death of the Indian maiden is a celebration of the moment where the nation's inheritance is affirmed through sexual reproduction. The effect affirms Euro-placemaking, claiming a racialized heteronormative futurity. Yet the American Indian becomes a touchstone that the state inherits, granting it a privileged role in American folklore. Avery Gordon defines haunting as "an animated state in which a repressed or unresolved social violence is making itself known."[16] The imaginative focus of the death of Indian women is, I believe, such a haunting. The specter (or ghost, so defined), and actual presence of Seneca and Tuscarora peoples, remains to haunt Niagara Falls as such, because there can be no reconciliation as land is lost under diverted river pathways, pollutions of the water continue, and colonial structures are still in place. The Indian *Maid of the Mist* is a ghost or "the sign, or empirical evidence, if you like, [of] things . . . not [being] in their assigned places."[17] In the origin stories of Canada and United States, the fabricated monument of sacrificing Native women legitimates the settler state. Native women's actual, continued presence at the Falls is testament to the "unsettled" nature of the United States and Canada as settler states. Although speaking in relation to slavery, Avery Gordon reminds us that "the ghost is not simply a dead or missing person, but a social figure, and investigating it can lead to that dense site where history and subjectivity make social life."[18] Furthermore, Coll Thrush and Colleen Boyd relate the haunting to a form of settler shame or ghosts who become "animated" through the retelling of the story. These histories are "first and foremost . . . a technique of removal,"[19] and, also, as I suggest, a form of affective mapping.

Historian and geographer of the Falls, Patrick McGreevy writes about the interplay between technology and the romanticization of the falls, stating: "Niagara remained inaccessible even to North American centers of population until the opening of the Erie Canal in 1825. But even with the beginning of tourism on a large scale, the image of a fabulous remote waterfall did not entirely perish: people simply found new ways of imagining it as if it were remote. One of these ways, often expressed in travelers' accounts and poetry, was to see Niagara as a symbol of death."[20] And at the heart of this symbol was the death of a nameless but pure Native maid, killed by the cruelty of her savage father supported by the rituals of her ancestors. Achille Mbembe argues (in a different context) that colonialism "helped produce an imaginary capacity," or what is settler affective mapping, or "converting the founding violence into authorizing authority." Deciphering the historical roots of honeymooning and the foundations of hydroelectric power at this site are key for combatting the epistemic violence that these seemingly innocent and romantic stories and visuals depict.

SETTLER SITES AND HETERONORMATIVITY

Niagara Falls' symbolism is also imbued with compulsory heterosexuality. Colonial practices at the Falls were bound up in gender normativity, which were formative at a point in time that did not coincidentally occur with the domestication of Indian lands in the post–reservation era. The power of story was routinely operationalized to get the financial backing necessary for these exploratory hydroelectric operations. By disparaging the political, cultural, and organizational elements of the Haudenosaunee Confederacy, as well as depicting Indigenous character and morality as inhuman, the explorer and profitier René-Robert Cavelier, Sieur de La Salle, sought to gain control at the Falls. Unable to do so, he inspired others to conduct a smear campaign that lies at the very roots of the Maid of the Mist fabrication.[21] As early as 1906, Peter Porter recognized the lie: "It has so much the appearance of a made-to-order story, such a specially-prepared-to-fit-the-locality aspect, it savors so strongly an attempt to make the early Indian Mythology conform."[22] If we visit the site of the creation of hydroelectric power and ponder the death of an Indian Maiden and Indian "savagery," we might wonder, What is it telling us about social life of settler Americans and Canadians? Why have these stories of Haudenosaunee violence and primitivism continued into the present? Why is the Maid of the Mist story, known to have originated in 1669 from early explorer La Salle, still retold and accepted? La Salle, like many of the men who travelled into our territories, was clearly seeking to dispossess Haudenosaunee Nations from our land and natural resources.

In order to answer these questions, we also need to address the epistemic violence of naturalizing of Native male violence and Native women's deaths, a

Maid of the Mist below Horseshoe Falls, 1909. Library of Congress, Prints and
Photographs Division. This image from a 1909 tourist booklet emphasizes the thrill of
danger—and safety—of the *The Maid of the Mist* boat tour. From *Niagara* (Portland,
Maine: L. H. Nelson, 1909), 7.

reiteration of settler narratives that normalize whose bodies matter and whose
are relegated to death. Mark Rifkin deftly demonstrates the "queering" of Native
coupling through the credulity and savagism presented in the story. The recip-
rocal family and natural kinship systems of Haudenosaunee people that pivot
around reciprocity and accountability are undermined in this narrative. The
lynchpin of the myth of the maid, however, originates in the social circuit of
European patriarchal control; the story and its resonant power demonstrates
the links that Judith Butler, Sara Ahmed, and Jasbir Puar illustrate in addressing
the epistemological and ontological resonances between masculinity and the
nation-state (through heterosexuality as a biopolitical technology of power).[23]
In biblical language that places "savages" in the past, James C. Carter declared
at the 1885 Dedication of the Niagara Reservation: "Niagara is an awful symbol
of infinite power—a vision of infinite beauty—a shrine, a temple erected by the
hand of the Almighty for all the children of men."[24] These logics of heteronor-
mativity and heteropatriarchy are mechanisms of Indigenous elimination and

erasure. As Niagara Falls grows as an urban site, with Buffalo as its industrial counterpart, the violence against Native people in urban places becomes all the more important to address. Settler colonial structures at the Falls speak to the power dynamics that give life to settler priorities that become storied through the death of Native women, savagery, Indian masculinity, and communities, all wrapped in a campaign of promoting Niagara Falls as the ultimate symbol of heterosexual coupling.

Although a trading site that far preceded colonialism, Niagara Falls became a site in which the Canadian and U.S. governments first combined their efforts to harness hydroelectric energy and promote cross-border tourism. As early as 1827, with the first opening of a curiosity shop, the tourist industry absorbed Indians into the market economy and touted them as a major part of the landscape. Tuscarora were particularly well known for their bead work and often sold bags, pouches, jewelry, and other crafts to those visiting from east coast cities. Purchasing such crafts became a priority for many, with the nearby Tuscarora village becoming an important tourist destination in its own right. The link between collecting Native objects at Niagara Falls and erasing an unsettled national consciousness through the collecting of objects deemed "past" coincided with the ongoing economies of dispossession in relation to Native lands. As textile historian Beverly Gordon makes clear about the relationship between object and audience, "When tourists purchased an actual Indian made object and took it home as a souvenir, they were in effect taking home a 'piece' of the Indian—and by association, a 'piece' of the Falls themselves. The whimsy or related Indian souvenirs, then, a symbol, an object that could capture and make tangible something ephemeral and wild: the power and majesty of Niagara."[25] The countless hours of beading labor, largely done by women in Haudenosaunee communities, produced gorgeous multicolor purses and totes. The craft in these souvenirs was remarkable and today many are museum pieces.

The amount of money spent on these items far exceeded a tourist's cost on hotels and food at the Falls. Capitalism and Native dispossession supported the burgeoning tourist shops that quite literally arose with the fabricated story of the Indian women's deaths and with the exploitation of Indian women's labor. Tuscarora artist and scholar, Jolene Rickard, writes:

The bark booths . . . have become for me a classic projection of Indian people's place in the economy. Everyone knows that Indian handicrafts are harmless. But what is really negotiated in this trade of money for what we create? The people from Ska ru re and most other Indian nations developed specific items for exchange . . . What we create, tourist items or not, serves as a reminder of our spiritual, economic, and cultural survival. The strongest remaining symbols among the Ska ru re are the beadwork and the white corn.[26]

This artistic practice of beading and the Falls as a trading spot was—and still is—an element of the economic, political and cultural Indigenous survival. Beadwork continues among the Tuscarora along with knowledge of the Falls and their meanings to the Haudenosaunee.

There is also much evidence that hucksters came to dominate and sell fake "Indian goods," which spurred the need for tourists to actually see the making of goods at the site in order to feel they had made contact with authentic Indigeneity. These Native performances feed and sustained the Tuscarora through much economic hardships. Beadwork and other crafts were economic conduits for Haudenosaunee communities experiencing new capitalist markets, and they enabled them to survive through difficult financial hardships. Jenny Tone-Pah-Hote eloquently lays out the importance of women's skilled work, even that deemed kitsch tourist art, in her book *Crafting an Indigenous Nation.* Tone-Pah-Hote explores the role of Kiowa women's expressive art in nurturing communities and bolstering sovereign practices during upheaval.[27]

In 1874 curiosity shops, hotels, and street hustlers became so problematic at the sites that councilmen began to transfer private property to the state for an establishment of a great park modeled after New York City's Central Park and Chicago's Hyde Park. A joint resolution passed in 1879 to continue with a commission to design the tourist area. The Niagara Commission was particularly worried about hucksters and the "transient character of the visiting [which] was attributed chiefly to the constant annoyances to which the traveler was subjected—the pestering demands and solicitations with which he met and the exasperating exactions and impositions to which he was subjected."[28] The Commission hired landscape architect Frederick Law Olmstead, who presented a report along with developer James T. Gardner to the state legislature. Now considered the "father" of American landscape architecture, Olmstead also previously designed New York's great "civilized" parks—Central Park and Prospect Park—and later the landscaping for the "White City" of Chicago's 1893

World's Fair, named as such because of the massive amount of street lighting and stucco. Even in his time, Olmstead was viewed as a landscape architect par excellence, and such prestige further cemented Niagara Falls' iconic status.

The Niagara Falls Commission remained concerned that this push to American middle-class excellence would not be spoiled by the lower classes. The Commission proclaimed at the time that state control was "the only prospect of such relief," necessary to enable the "higher emotional and native faculties" that were necessary in this case, as "whatever prevented or interrupted a contemplative and receptive frame of mind caused a deeper irritation than elsewhere amid other surroundings."[29] Olmstead believed that landscape design could bring out the best in improving the average American. Previously a journalist, he had been commissioned to do a series of works on the American South and slavery. In those works, he laid out the perils to America of not having a middle class and the importance of creating arenas of improvement through the designing of property. "The truth has been overlooked that the accumulation of wealth and the power of a nation are contingent not merely upon the primary value of the surplus of productions of which it has to dispose, but very largely upon the way in which the income from its surplus is distributed and reinvested," he wrote.[30] In designing Niagara Falls, these early reflections on class clearly came into play with the push to construct unencumbered middle-class leisure at the Falls and the surrounding areas of Buffalo. That city continues to reverberate with his name, and his life's work still resonates in Buffalo, which boasts the first system of parks in America.

Wealthy and powerful landowners Peter and Augustus Porter, who had a close relationship with tribal members in the adjacent Tuscarora Reservation, made the point in their negotiations that the sale and transition of land include a caveat to maintain the rights of Tuscarora women to sell their goods at the Falls' sites. This cleaning up and regulating of the space through settler laws was further perpetuated when later Haudenosaunee women, including from those reserves in what is now known as Canada, needed to obtain a license from the U.S. government, of all places, to sell at the site of the Falls. As stated earlier, the Haudenosaunee Confederacy preceded the territories of the United States and Canada, and the Jay Treaty (1794) ensured the rights of the Six Nations to travel freely as sovereign nations across the border. The Niagara Falls had long been a traditional trading site before European settlers set foot on these shores. The political efficacy of the newly budding settler states knew they needed to ensure the maintenance of sovereign rights to continue to trade at the site.[31]

The attempted incorporation of Native women into the state through licensing is a continuation of the colonial logics of elimination, specifically through the restriction of the licensing and regulating of the tourist industry at the park. In speaking of Kahnawá:ke Mohawks who travelled across the border to sell their wares, a local paper in 1900 states that:

> [They sat up] in the park close beside the faithful Tuscarora women. Of course the latter object, but they have so far said little. The Canadian squaws, it is said, brought five big trunks of work with them this season, and they have already announced that next year, Pan-American year, they intend to be on deck May first. The Tuscarora squaws cannot see why the white man's law does not protect them, as well as the products of the whites. Furthermore the Tuscaroras point out that years ago Tuscarora were *faithful to the Stars and Stripes* and [today send their sons to fight] . . . . People who learned of the situation in the park yesterday plainly stated that they thought the Montreal squaws should be asked to retire to Victoria Park. . . . Public sentiment is that the Tuscaroras should be *undisturbed by foreign competition* [original emphasis].[32]

In this newspaper article, we see the perspective of a settler view of incorporation: notions of "our Indians" and the language of settler nationalism are at work. The article ignores treaty rights and the living relationships between the Six Nations while promoting a theme of "commercial well-being and good understanding among the American Republics."[33] The incorporation of Native women and lands into the tourist industry was further perpetuated by the obtaining of licenses to sell goods at the "reserved sites," named as such because they reserved land from the ever-increasing industry at the site. There was also pressure to present a pastoral environment, as the 1901 location of the Pan-American Exposition was hotly debated. Eventually, Buffalo won the bid to host, not Niagara, but Thomas Edison still lit up the exposition using the energy the Falls generated from twenty-five miles away.

Although a historian notes that the 1870 and 80s were "the height of nefarious practices," in regard to treatment of Native peoples at the site of the Falls, this is far from the actual case. Such settler "nefarious" practices and swindling were just beginning. Even more than Niagara Falls as a tourist site, the infrastructures of electrical power in the modern nation-state enabled economies of dispossession. While the harnessing of water began in 1748 at the Falls, it was in 1875 that engineers utilized the natural right angle of the river and its curve: this amounted to the second phase of the harnessing of energy to sustain growth and development in the area. The installation of a small generator would make Niagara Falls a birthplace of the hydroelectric development that would create settler colonial infrastructures throughout North America, indeed the world. The repercussions are felt today and reach well beyond Haudenosaunee lands, giving rise to Aluminum Company of America, the Union Carbide and Carbon Corporation, and the Carborundum Company. These companies located their manufacturing in the area (releasing pollutants that are still in the St. Lawrence Seaway). Hydroelectric, electrochemical and electrometallurgical industries would have a profound economic, political, and social impact on this contested area. In a very real sense, this birth of industry coincided with the rise of, and need for, the story of a sacrificial Indian maiden and the licensing of authentic Indians at the site. Anxiety produced by the destruction of natural habitats was mediated by the story of authentic Indians. So even while resource extraction drove the politics of the day, many protested the destruction of the "pristine" site. Parks—or what were then-unironically called reservations— were established on both sides of the river in 1883 and 1885. Historians note how manufacturing changed the experience of tourists: "As the setting of the falls became more and more humanized, many visitors found that they could no longer feel that peculiar combination of rapture and terror they associated with the sublime."[34] Niagara Falls' sublime power was not simply restricted to its awesome natural majesty. The death of one Native woman, told again and again, stood out as a tragic moment from the past and as a resonant connection to the thundering cataracts.

Avery Gordon's idea of haunting is applicable here: "abusive systems of power make themselves known and their impacts felt on everyday life, especially when they are supposedly over and done with" and they make themselves present precisely because of "the reality of certain obvious things."[35] The seemingly superior rights of settler nation-states to absorb lands and abandon bodies,[36] blind us to the process of how the Falls come to situate and produce settler power; it buries the violence and "ways in which those things are expressly produced and fundamentally enabled by a history of loss and repression."[37] That is, the monument of Niagara Falls comes to stand in for the loss of the primordial. Or to quote from McGreevy, who examines the travel literature of the time, "Niagara seemed a survivor and hence a representative of the distant past where nature reigned, undisturbed by human will. There are numerous descriptions of this primordial world in the poetry and travel literature of Niagara." The states of

Canada and the United States were less concerned about the survival of actual Native people and, in fact, through repression of Indigenous economies and heavy-handed state tactics, worked to ensure death through its urban planning.

ELECTRIC LIGHTS AND DISPOSSESSION

The intertwining of the pastoral with the fabricated story was used to also promote the inventive electrical wonders that occurred at Niagara Falls. In portraying those innovations and the Falls, the pastoral and the future are affectively mapped as if they occurred in different temporalities. The Falls is a monument to ridding the past of the primitive and harnessing and domesticating the land and water for the future of settler nations. In pop-culture depictions of Maid of the Mist, in magazines, movies, books and tourist items, the artistic renditions of the story start with dark and mutated figures that eventually become lightened subjects resembling Greek figures. These depictions of the sacrificial maid coincide with infrastructure development along the riverbanks and grounds a narrative of progress from savagery to civilization, from wilderness to industry, from past to present. Examining how the story makes affective maps of belonging moves us toward rethinking settlement at the core, as it exposes the work that must be done to create settler cities.

I now choose to directly talk about the origin of damming projects that proceed from the hydroelectric inventions and harnessing of the Falls' power as engines of dispossession because such foregrounds Native dispossession. The mourning of land loss, without considering dispossession, paints a picture that there was not an active part played by the U.S. and Canadian settler states that acted in concert.[38]

In 1890, the Niagara Falls Power Company attempted to generate power from a central source for industries in the area. The competitive industry sent their best scientists to Europe to learn more about hydraulics in order to learn how to use the immense power of the Falls. The United States and Canada made multiple treaties regarding the distribution of hydroelectric power. Both Thomas Edison and Nikola Tesla were involved in trying to harness hydroelectric power. Previously, electricity was scarcely used in industrial projects and thus the work undertaken at this time was revolutionary. These water treaties, as well as complicit settler tourism, became key to the development of both nations. The Adams power station that allowed for the successful harnessing of the power of water at Niagara Falls, a sacred place of the Haudenosaunee, was "so successful . . . that today all central power stations and transmissions systems are modeled after the original Falls project."[39] The domestication of Indian land led to large engineering projects and the harnessing of lands to create infrastructures that continue to this day. People at the time knew that this was unprecedented, as William Andrews stated in June 1901: "One of the boldest engineering and commercial feats of the past century, the successful development of the water-power of Niagara Falls, was the signal for the utilization of water powers all over the world. This masterpiece of nature remains to-day with its beauty and grandeur unmarred, its 8,000,000 horse-power inappreciably affected by the petty thefts of man, and its usefulness enhanced a thousand-fold."[40]

If one considers Native people as humans, and as a living people who are part of the lands, what begins to become evident is not only the ongoing colonial dispossession and bad environmental practices but also how Niagara Falls serves as a flash point for damming and controlling of the environment at the expense of Native peoples' lifeways and future generations. When conceiving of the dam that would flood Cornplanter and Seneca lands in 1960 under President John F. Kennedy, the pattern were the same as that at Niagara Falls, with the very same priorities: namely, to generate as much power as possible, and to save the Falls as a pristine site for the tourist economy. The plans to flood, like so many during the New Deal and later infrastructure changes in the 1950 and 60s, would largely take place "out of sight"—on Indian land. Here we can return to the important metaphor of the haunting death of the Indian maiden, the one who sacrifices for love but must always die. The purposeful telling of her death by her inhumane and immoral father, who just happens to be chief of the tribe and political symbol of sovereignty, creates a moral justification for the destruction of tribal lifeways. Her death is just an unfortunate consequence of progress in the imagination of the white settler. Native people are denied personhood and thus rights to the land. Native occupancy and relationships to these flooded spaces are rarely considered and the idea of *terra nullius* manifests itself in the colonial mind as much as it does in law. Nefarious practices, indeed.

CONCLUSIONS

Economies of dispossession require the active dispossession of land, legacies, and personhood. When we talk about the damming projects of the early nineteenth century, the New Deal, the post–World War II order, and the harnessing of hydroelectric power, we must return to the start. That start is Niagara Falls in which Haudenosaunee land and lifeways became national sacrifice zones as the "logics of elimination" produced and circulated myths of the Maid of the Mist. The circulation of maid-of-the-mist imagery enacts a white settler "necropolitics." It is important to remember that settler colonialism is an ongoing process[41] whereby occupation is a never-ending condition. As Achille Mbembe explains, "Late-modern colonial occupation is a concatenation of multiple powers: disciplinary, biopolitical, and necropolitical."[42] Such "occupation" constitutes a particular formation of terror.[43] The ongoing absorption of Native lands into state-run and state-owned territory at the will of bureaucracy advocating for the greater good remains an ongoing terror. Mbembe refers to part of this formation as a state of siege: "itself a military institution [which] allows a modality of killing that does not distinguish between an internal and an external enemy."[44] Consequently, the value of those marked as excess expresses itself through their targeting for death in a settler colonial system of sovereign power where "invisible killing is added to outright execution."[45] As Seneca lands were subsumed for Canadian and U.S. industrialization, so were their community and kinship relations. The heteronormative promotion of Niagara as a honeymoon destination and family vacation spot is most apparent in the phallic symbolism of the Electric Tower building, first put up for the Pan-American exposition in 1901 and then later replicated. Standing 294 feet high with a bright white opalescent prominence in the Buffalo skyline, it maps American innovation while obscuring Indigenous land sacrifices and breaking of treaties.

Whether working hard at the site to sell goods to survive or protesting the dam, the Haudenosaunee have always fought against dispossession. In exploring the tourist economies and the visual postcards and other romanticized propaganda, the fissures and contradictions in settler colonial placemaking become clear. The United States and Canada continue as colonial formations while perpetuating the myth and carrying out the actions of making dead Indians. As Angie Morrill and others argue, "Settler colonial societies are haunted by the host of gone peoples—they pulse at the center. I have said before that I am a future ghost . . . Precarity is politically induced."[46] There remains a haunting of the Falls today at this area where water connects places and generations. Again, Gordon states that haunting is a "mediation," which is a "process that links an institution and an individual, a social structure and a subject, and history and a biography." [47] It is the center of Native life—seen as the peripheries from the settler perspective—that feeds the growing urban city. As the cities of Niagara and Buffalo grew to late nineteenth-century industrial wealth and prominence, we must also remember the Haudenosaunee places devoured in their wake.

Rather than Native women being invisible at Niagara Falls, their presence continues to haunt and occupy the place, as does the strength of Haudenosaunee politics. In many ways when you walk and visit the various paths and monuments of Niagara Reserve, there is little acknowledgement of it as Seneca Land or part of the Haudenosaunee Confederacy or of the vast time period in which Indigenous people from all over meet at the waterways. The story of what powers the city is obscured through the narrative of American exceptionalism and ongoing emphasis on the sublime. More recently however, the Seneca Nation of Indians has harnessed tourist money and the Seneca Casino, the latter now in the brightest of neon lights. The casino has become a local landmark, an expression of Indigenous sovereignty that shines as one of Niagara Falls' largest attractions. By turning casino profits into important revitalization efforts in the form of language revitalization, land education efforts, and community support, the Seneca Nation of Indians continues a long tradition of using the resources at Niagara Falls to create healthy communities. The omission of Haudenosaunee deep relationship to place is nothing new to settler structures that necessitate the erasure of histories, political practices, and ongoing Native relationships to land. Yet the power of the Thunder Beings remains and the Falls will always be a Haudenosaunee place.

NOTES

1. For an example of the electric grid's tendency to devour Native lands in a different context, see Andrew Needham, *Power Lines: Phoenix and the Making of the American Southwest* (Princeton, N.J.: Princeton University Press, 2014).

2. J. N. B. Hewitt, "Iroquois Cosmology, Part I," in *Bureau of American Ethnology*, ed. J. W. Powell (Washington, D.C.: Government Printing Office, 1903).

3. This was a story told to me in a personal communication by Stonehorse Lone Goeman, July 15, 2013.

4. Susan M. Hill, *The Clay We Are Made Of: Haudenosaunee Land Tenure on the Grand River* (Winnipeg: University of Manitoba Press, 2017); and Audra Simpson, *Mohawk Interruptus: Political Life across the Borders of Settler States* (Durham, N.C.: Duke University Press, 2014).

5. For an in-depth history of dam projects' effect on Seneca people, see Laurence M. Hauptman, *In the Shadow of Kinzua: The Seneca Nation of Indians since World War II* (Syracuse, N.Y.: Syracuse University Press, 2016).

6. Carol Sheriff, *The Artificial River: The Erie Canal and the Paradox of Progress, 1817–1862* (New York: Hill & Wang, 1996), 58.

7. Lisa Blee and Jean O'Brien, *Monumental Mobility: The Memory Work of Massasoit* (Chapel Hill: University of North Carolina Press, 2019), 6.

8. Scott Lauria Morgensen, "Settler Homonationalism: Theorizing Settler Colonialism within Queer Modernities," *Journal of Lesbian and Gay Studies: Sexuality, Nationality, Indigeneity* 16, no. 1–2 (2010): 105, 106.

9. Renato Rosaldo, *Culture and Truth: The Remaking of Social Analysis* (Boston: Beacon Press, 1993), 68.

10. Patrick McGreevy, *Imagining Niagara: The Meaning and Making of Niagara Falls* (Amherst: University of Massachusetts Press, 2009), 48.

11. Rosaldo, *Culture and Truth*, 285.

12. Commissioners of the State Reservation at Niagara, *Nineteenth Annual Report* (Albany: N.Y.: Argus Company, 1903), 17.

13. Sue Wilson, "White Myths, Indian Maidens, Haudenosaunee Controversy: 'Maid of the Mist' More Than a Legend," *Amerinda: Empowering Native American Artists*, accessed October 10, 2020, http://www.amerinda.org/newsletter/5-1/whitemyths.html.

14. For more information on the Canadians' treatment of Haudenosaunee people during land protection struggles, see *Kanehsatake: 270 Years of Resistance*, directed by Alanis Obamsawin (Montreal: National Film Board of Canada, 1993); Gerald R. Alfred, *Heeding the Voices of Our Ancestors: Kahnawake Mohawk Politics and the Rise of Native Nationalism* (Toronto: Oxford University Press, 1995); and Audra Simpson, *Mohawk Interruptus: Political Life across the Borders of Settler States* (Durham, N.C.: Duke University Press, 2014).

15. Jonathan Flatley, *Affective Mapping: Melancholia and the Politics of Modernism* (Cambridge, Mass.: Harvard University Press, 2008), 7.

16. Avery Gordon, *Ghostly Matters: Haunting and the Sociological Imagination* (Minneapolis: University of Minnesota Press, 2008), xvi.

17. Gordon, *Ghostly Matters*, xvi.

18. Gordon, *Ghostly Matters*, 8.

19. Colleen E. Boyd and Coll Thrush, "Introduction," in *Phantom Past, Indigenous Presence: Native Ghosts in North American Culture and History*, ed. Colleen E. Boyd and Coll Thrush (Lincoln: University of Nebraska Press, 2011), ix.

20. McGreevy, *Imagining Niagara*, 49.

21. Isaac Joslin Cox, ed., *The Journeys of René Robert Cavelier, Sieur de La Salle*, 2 vols. (New York: Barnes, 1905), 7.

22. Peter A. Porter, *Niagara, an Aboriginal Center of Trade* (Niagara Falls: Wentworth Press, 1906).

23. Sara Ahmed, *Queer Phenomenology* (Durham, N.C.: Duke University Press, 2006), 65–107; Judith Butler, *Gender Trouble* (New York: Routledge, 2006), 22–24.; Jasbir Puar, *Terrorist Assemblages: Homonationalism in Queer Times* (Durham, N.C.: Duke University Press, 2007), 13–15, 32.

24. Commissioners of the State Reservation at Niagara, *Nineteenth Annual Report*, 17.

25. Beverly Gordon, "The Niagara Falls Whimsey: The Object as a Symbol of Cultural Interface" (Ph.D. diss., University of Wisconsin–Madison, 1984), 22.

26. Jolene Rickard, "Cew Ete Haw I Tih: The Bird That Carries Language back to Another," in *Partial Recall*, ed. Lucy R. Lippard. (New York: New Press 1992), 108.

27. Jenny Tone-Pah-Hote, *Crafting an Indigenous Nation: Kiowa Expressive Culture in the Progressive Era* (Chapel Hill: University of North Carolina Press, 2019).

28. Commissioners of the State Reservation at Niagara, *Nineteenth Annual Report*, 25.

29. Commissioners of the State Reservation at Niagara, *Nineteenth Annual Report*, 25.

30. Frederick Law Olmstead, *The Cotton Kingdom; A traveller's observations on cotton and slavery in the American slave States. Based upon three former volumes of journeys and investigations by the same author* (New York: Mason Brothers, 1861), 25.

31. This fact is documented and noted in the very title of Porter's 1906 history of the Falls; see Porter, *Niagara, an Aboriginal Center of Trade*.

32. *Niagara Falls Gazette*, July 28, 1900, 6.

33. After the Spanish-American War, which began in 1898, this slogan of the Pan-American Exposition suggested that the direct interests of the United States were central to its imperial ambitions.

34. McGreevy, *Imagining Niagara*, 48

35. Gordon, *Ghostly Matters*, xvi and ix.

36. Gabriel Piterberg, *The Returns of Zionism: Myths, Politics, and Scholarship in Israel* (London: Verso, 2008), 246.

37. Gordon, *Ghostly Matters*, ix.

38. Here I would like to thank Alyosha Goldstein and Robin Kelly for this discussion on May 20, 2014, at the University of California, Los Angeles.

39. Wallace McIntyre, "Niagara Falls Power Redevelopment," *Economic Geography* 28, no. 3 (1952): 261–73, 263.

40. William Andrews, "How Niagara Has Been Harnessed," *American Monthly Review of Reviews* 23 (June 1901): 694–97, 697.

41. Patrick Wolfe, "Settler Colonialism and the Elimination of the Native," *Journal of Genocide Research* 8, no. 4 (2006): 387–409.

42. Achille Mbembe, "Necropolitics," *Public Culture* 15, no. 1 (2003): 29–30.

43. Mbembe, "Necropolitics," 22.

44. Mbembe, "Necropolitics," 30.

45. Mbembe, "Necropolitics," 30.

46. Angie Morrill, Eve Tuck, and the Super Futures Haunt Collective, "Before Dispossession, or Surviving It," *Liminalities: A Journal of Performance Studies* 12, no. 1 (2016): 7.

47. Gordon, *Ghostly Matters*, 19.

NATIVE WASHINGTON

Indigenous Histories, a Federal Landscape,
and the Making of the U.S. Capital

On Saturday, September 29, 1837, a group of Lakota, Iowa, Sauk, and Fox men and women from the Missouri River sat in the National Theater in Washington, D.C., watching the romantic opera *The Mountain Sylph*. They found themselves, as many of the other audience members likely did, mesmerized by the prima donna, a soprano named Annette Nelson portraying "Aeolia, the sylph," the opera's lead character. So impressed by her agility and beauty—"appearing and vanishing with a rapidity that reminded them of the fleetness of the deer in their native hunting grounds," wrote one newspaper—the men saluted her, right in the middle of the performance. In a show of respect, Palaneapapi, a Yankton man, threw an eagle-feathered cap at her feet; Pokona, a Sauk chief offered his cap as well; while Tokaca, another Yankton, gave her his white wolf skin robe. Although their collective appreciation was completely unplanned, the actress, displaying poise and grace, thanked the men, saying she would "ever regard them as friends and brethren." She then gifted each man an ostrich plume from her costume.[1] To a modern audience, this scene appears entirely unexpected and not just as a breach of theater etiquette; the presence of Native men and women in an 1830s Washington, D.C., theater enjoying opera seems unbelievable.

How unexpected was it, though? Despite how we might think about the capital today, across the nineteenth and early twentieth centuries, hundreds and thousands of Native people traveled to and from and lived in the federal city. In reality, scenes like this one happened all the time. Yet it seems a settler colonial "veil" has descended to obscure our ability to see and understand Indigenous presences in the urban spaces of the capital; we've been trained to ignore, overlook, or even hide them. Coll Thrush has written most eloquently about this idea, calling it "the narrative estrangement of urban and Indigenous histories," and he elaborates on it as "the deeply held notion that urban and Indigenous histories, like urban places and Indigenous peoples, have little to do with each other except as mutually exclusive opposites."[2]

While every Indian nation has its own unique and rich history; one thing that unites all of them is their relationship with the federal government and, as the government "incarnate," Washington, D.C. As historian Donald Fixico writes, "tribal experiences have been diverse, but they can usually be viewed in common through the lens of the federal government."[3] And these experiences often overlapped, from Washington's earliest day. Consider British diplomat Sir Augustus John Foster, who lived in the city before the War of 1812 and wrote a travel narrative filled with interesting anecdotes on multitribal experiences there. He describes escorting a group of Mandan leaders to the theater, where they were seated next to five Osage men, one Delaware diplomat, and several Native women and children from various nations.[4] Foster also writes about meeting a group of Osage men and women lodging with several Sauk, Dakota, Mississauga, and Missouri leaders across the street from a boarding house where a large Cherokee delegation stayed.[5] By the mid-nineteenth century, though perhaps surprising today, cultural representations of life in the capital featured Native people as prominent figures. The 1857 play *Fashions and Follies of Washington Life*, meant "to exhibit a panoramic view of characters and events, illustrative of Metropolitan life and society," featured among its clerks, politicians, and debutantes, "a live Indian Chief" named Tonawaha.[6]

These episodes appear unexpected to us today because of a perceived incongruity of Native people in urban spaces. And this unexpectedness is especially rooted in Washington, D.C., due to the creation of a commemorative landscape—centered in the art and architecture of federal buildings, but dispersed around the city as well—that disseminated notions of pacification, of conquest as a fait accompli , and of vanishing Indians.[7] This essay argues that—unlike these stylized Native subjects of capital art and architecture—Indigenous visitors and inhabitants engaged with non-Native individuals and the symbols of settler society in Washington City, carved out their own spaces within it, and claimed or reclaimed symbolic ownership of the place. In doing so, Indigenous people shaped how the capital came to be understood as an imperial center. Washington was, after all, a local place first and foremost, and especially so in the nineteenth century; it had yet to become the nation's city and imperial capital and, later, global metropolis. It's in that "becoming" that Native people played a significant role.[8]

The following sections offer three collections of stories about the capital. Each collection addresses non-Native cultural expectation—or the ways in which white Americans have imagined Indians—as well as the "hidden" Native histories of the city. In an effort to accurately portray the diversity of these experiences in the capital, the stories here are each grounded in particular spaces within the city and move fluidly back-and-forth through time. This is a deliberate strategy that also seeks—as many Indigenous studies scholars have encouraged—to destabilize chronology as a narrative foundation and instead anchor our stories in place.

The first collection focuses on the development of expectations of Indian violence and pacification expressed through art and culture, also speaking to actual Indigenous presences in the city; the second demonstrates how Native people engaged directly with those expressions resisting and reshaping them while laying claims to physical space; while the final set of stories describes deep layers of expectation, revealing how recognizing the "hidden" Indigenous histories of Washington provides us with a much different sense of the city.

COLLECTION 1: TONAWAHA'S RAGE

In a scene in the fourth act of *Fashions and Follies*, Tonawaha accosts Emma, the female protagonist.[9] Tonawaha exclaims his love for her, crying, "Oh! Pretty! Pretty! Indian like Squaw." He then quickly laments, "squaw no love Indian . . . Indian ugly man. Squaw love great white chief." Moments later, Noall, who is described as a gentleman who quite literally "knows all about it," enters and insults Tonawaha, calling him an "ill-bred savage." Tonawaha responds by choking him. Only at the last second is he spared at Emma's urging.[10] While

Tonawaha is represented among the clerks and debutantes as part of the fabric of the city, he is also unpredictable, violent, and dangerous.

The theme of potential Indian violence had deep roots in the capital and can be seen in other, earlier expressions of public discourse. In 1828, for example, Margaret Bayard Smith, a chronicler of social life in the early capital, declared herself the "self constituted delegate from the young ladies of Washington" and she begged Secretary of War Peter Porter to "use his authority and forbid the ferocious Winebagos from assaulting the girls in the manner they did." Lewis Cass, then-Governor of Michigan Territory, overheard the discussion and defended the Indians, but to little avail. Although Smith had not witnessed or experienced this treatment first-hand, the threat of sexual violence loomed large in her expectations. In a letter to her husband she exclaimed, "You have no idea, what a general dread [these Indians] inspired."[11]

Washington newspapers often commented upon the Indigenous diplomats that visited the city; many of their columns lent credence to the notion that those diplomats were ill prepared for existence in an urban space and that violence by Native men was a constant possibility. In 1828, the *Daily National Journal* warned that the Ho-Chunk delegation in D.C. "will no doubt be much annoyed by the countless number of idle boys who will follow them." The reporter imagined potential violence, stating that the boys should feel "a sense of personal danger" because these Indians would not abide their pranks like other D.C. visitors. Later in the same article, the columnist warned—playing upon expectations of Indian drunkenness—that no one give the Indians "ardent spirits . . . [because they were] already sufficiently ungovernable, and when excited cannot be controlled."[12]

Closely related to their fears of potential Indian violence, newspaper commentators frequently imagined how overwhelming the experience of visiting the capital must have been for Indian men and women. An 1858 letter to the editor at the *Daily National Intelligencer* detailed an account of a sightseeing tour by a delegation of Pawnee, Ponca, Dakota, and Potawatomi representatives. At the end of the article, the author speculated that "there can be no doubt the events of the day will be long impressed on their memories." The writer read the moment as one in which the Indian visitors, once again, were clearly ill prepared, when he noted that the Pawnee, who saw fit to honor their hosts with a dance, had to be "informed that, owing to the difference in taste, they must, in deference to the white ladies present," remain fully dressed. Hinting at Indigenous sexuality, he further suggested that this exchange affected the

Native men, as they were "hampered at not being permitted on the occasion to dance themselves 'out of their clothes.'"[13]

Under the headline, "Arrival of Distinguished Scalp-Hunters" (suggesting yet again the potential for violence) another writer recounted the first evening tour of the 1870 Lakota delegation that included, among others, Spotted Tail, Swift Bear, and Red Cloud. The reporter described with amusement how these "bewildered sons of the forest" wandered about Pennsylvania Avenue before retiring to their hotel rooms. Once there though, the mysteries of urban life continued to confuse them: "not knowing the comfort of mattresses and sheets," he suggested, the Indians clung "to their primitive notions of luxury by sleeping on the floor."[14] Another reporter concluded, after several days of meetings and sightseeing tours, that the Indians were "rather astonished at the sights which have met their visions in the civilized regions they have passed through" and that Spotted Tail had "already more to tell his people than twelve months time will allow."[15]

The theme of Indian violence is expressed clearly in artwork within and surrounding the U.S. Capitol Building. Yet it shares space with depictions of pacification or North American continental conquest nearing completion. Carved between 1825 and 1827, a large relief adorns each of the four directional doors in the Capitol Rotunda. They are entitled, respectively, *Preservation of Captain Smith by Pocahontas* (by Antonio Capellano, 1825); *Landing of the Pilgrims* (Enrico Causici, 1825); *William Penn's Treaty with the Indians* (Nicholas Gevelot, 1825); and *Conflict of Daniel Boone and the Indians* (Enrico Causici, 1827). This final relief depicts a mortal struggle between Boone and an anonymous Indian warrior, both of whom are standing atop a second, already defeated Indian man. Taken together, these reliefs portray moments of initial contact within a colonial world, and the overall message is one of inevitable subjugation or assimilation for Native people.

Countless Native visitors viewed the rotunda reliefs, but the tale most often told in nineteenth-century tourist guidebooks involved the Ho-Chunk delegation of 1837. The story originated in William Force's *Picture of Washington and its Vicinity*. The Indians, whose "faces were painted of various colors, . . . [with] their scalping knives and tomahawks, and . . . their long iron looking bows and arrows," examined the first three reliefs, but stopped in front of the Boone image. They "looked intently . . . scrutinizing and recognizing every part of the scene . . . [and then] suddenly, as of one impulse, they raised their dreadful war-cry and ran hurriedly from the hall."[16] Force offered no further

Conflict of Daniel Boone and the Indians. Courtesy Architect of the Capitol.

explanation and left his readers to wonder if perhaps the Ho-Chunk ran out to avenge the deaths of the depicted Indians, his message was clear however—these men were not suited to life in the city and the potential for violence always bubbled just below the surface.

"Violence and American nationhood . . . [has] progressed hand in hand," wrote historian Ned Blackhawk, and both the commemorative landscape of the capital, as well as the perceptions of non-Native journalists and guidebook authors seemed to reflect that.[17] Of course, a focus on the lived Indigenous landscape of the capital suggests otherwise.

COLLECTION 2: ELY PARKER'S CHALLENGE

In 1847, visiting Washington on behalf of the Tonawanda Seneca, Ely Parker stood in the Capitol Rotunda and challenged the legacy of moments depicted in sandstone. In his diary, he wrote about seeing the rotunda reliefs I described in the first collection of stories. I quote from the full entry for that day:

Saturday, January 2nd, 1847: Went up to the Capitol and listened to some nonsensical speeches made by some nobody member of Congress. In entering the rotunda of the Capitol, the object first meeting my vision is the representation of the landing of the Pilgrims in 1620 upon the barren shores of New England. They are represented as in a starving condition, and being about to land, an Indian has come forward offering them provision of his bounty—Who now of the descendants of those illustrious Pilgrims will give one morsel to the dying and starving Indian . . . Turning around we are met by another representation in plaster of paris, of William Penn and the Indians entering an alliance. What virtue is there now in Indian treaties? . . . Turning round a little more, we observe another representation, that of the young and beautiful Pocahontas saving Captain Smith at the risk of her own life. Who now among the descendants of those whom she saved will risk his or her life for an Indian. No sooner would they see him hanged like a Mexican traitor then risk one hair on their heads to save him. How ungrateful is man to his fellow man? Turning still more around we find another and final representation, intended no doubt as a climax to the whole scene, that of Col[.] Boone, the hero of Kentucky in a mortal combat with an Indian. Both are struggling for life. But Boone has already killed one Indian and has trampled upon his mangled body. Such is the fate of the poor Red Man. His contest with the whites is hopeless, yet he is not permitted to live even in peace, nor are his last moments given him by his insulting foe to make his peace with his God. Humbly we ask whether justice will always sleep and will not the oppressed go free?[18]

Far from screaming and running from the Capitol building as guidebook authors suggested of the earlier Ho-Chunk delegation, Parker engaged with the imagery and narrative of conquest and critiqued the settler hypocrisy. His very presence, let alone his cultured comments, marks a dramatic response to expectations about the capital, where Indians are supposed to be bewildered, violent, or simply absent.

One hundred and sixty-seven years later, and a mere two miles away, Pyramid Lake Paiute artist-activist Gregg Deal, a longtime capital resident stood in the center of a dilapidated corner store at 1511 Seventh St. in the Shaw neighborhood of Washington, D.C. It was September 27, 2014, and there fans of the Washington NFL team "the Redskins" hurled insults and racial epithets at him. He was called "Chief Hashtag," because of his presence on social media; he was told to get over the past, to worry about more important issues; he was told that his opinion did not matter because he did not belong in the city anyway. In short, he stood (or rather "sat") and saw how the city viewed him. But, that night, Deal spoke back and challenged the legacies and ongoing persistence of settler colonialism in the capital.[19]

In truth, this "event" was actually a piece of performance art that Deal called "Redskin," conceived and performed as part of D.C.'s annual "Art All Night" event. He was protesting the team mascot by subjecting himself to an intense bout of microaggressions, in a confined space, to demonstrate the cumulative effect of this kind of trauma for Native people in Washington and elsewhere. And he was also surrounded by his own murals, paintings, and prints that made claims to the space and Native peoples' continual and ongoing presence there. In fact, Deal is probably most well known as a street artist; marking walls and claiming spaces within the city with stickers, wheat-paste, and paint is a big part of his work, and he's been doing it in D.C. for many years.

Marking walls, claiming spaces as Indigenous, and challenging settler narratives in public art has a long history in Washington. Remarkably, for a twenty-year period in the early nineteenth century, Charles Bird King, a Washington artist whose studio was located just down the street from the War Department, painted visiting Indian delegates. Thomas L. McKenney, the longtime

Performance artist Gregg Deal at *Art All Night*, September 27, 2014. Photograph by
Dave Cooper. Courtesy Gregg Deal.

commissioner of Indian Affairs used government funds to purchase King's
nearly one hundred and fifty portraits and arrayed them on the walls of the
Indian Office. Indian leaders from John Ross to Keokuk, and Black Hawk to
Pushmataha, graced the portrait gallery. For more than three decades, dis-
tinguished visitors, international and domestic, made their way to the Indian
Office to visit them.[20]

Despite most of the collection being lost in a fire at the Smithsonian, we
can gauge the public response to the portraits, and the overall message of the
gallery, by examining the words of a few of its visitors. In his 1830 guidebook,
Jonathan Elliot encouraged his readers to stop at the Indian Office. It "possesses
much interest," he stated, "perhaps more than any other in the Government."
The paintings, he wrote, were "not only fine specimens of the art, but [bear] . . .
close resemblance to the originals, they are *perfect*." His following sentences,
though, read almost like a phrenological assessment. He described the clarity
with which the Indians' heads had been portrayed, paying special attention to
the "central hemispheres," because it is there that the "governing powers that
lift man so far above the lower order of beings, and . . . distinguish his relative
grade, and characteristics of mind and intellect" reside. Special care, he noted,

had also been "taken to preserve the costume of each tribe." The social-scientific tone to his description was complemented by his invocation of the Vanishing Indian trope, ever popular in the nineteenth century. Imagining that Indians would eventually cease to exist, Elliot stated, "our posterity would ask in vain—'*what sort of a looking being was the red man of this country?*'" Seemingly unaware of the irony in this statement, he reminded readers that Indians "must be *seen* to be known."[21]

In her response to McKenney's Indian portrait gallery, British travelogue author Francis Trollope focused upon the emotions she imagined on the subjects' faces. "The countenances are full of expression," she wrote, "but the expression in most of them is extremely similar." She continued, "I should say that they have but two sorts of expression; the one is that of very noble and warlike daring, the other of a gentle and naive simplicity, that has no mixture of folly in it."[22] The noble savage, in other words, in its various permutations. The daring warrior. The childlike innocent of the wilderness. The vanishing Indian.

The portrait gallery came to hold different meanings for Native men and women, though. In 1828 a group of Ho-Chunk who visited the gallery became the subject of a lengthy correspondence between Commissioner McKenney and Secretary of War Peter Porter. They delighted in "seeing so many who were known to them," but complained, "*We see no Winnebagos here.*" The government had, for a time, refused to pay for the portraits, but the visitors, McKenney wrote, made "almost daily visits," and "evince so much anxiety to have a similar respect paid to them." They offered to sell "their bells, & ornaments, & caps, & . . . their war clubs" to defray the costs of the portraits, or barring that, asked at least that these items be hung in the gallery as memorials. In the end, five of them sat for Charles Bird King to commemorate the visit. Caleb Atwater, a government agent at Prairie Du Chien, later recalled that "nothing pleased [the men] so much as . . . that their likenesses were in the War Department."[23]

Seeing the paintings and being a part of the group meant something. The visitors looked for portraits of members of their communities who visited the city previously; it became a way to connect across time with people who had similar experiences. There are two other significant explanations for why having one's portrait in the collection was so meaningful for Indigenous people: first, the men were depicted wearing symbols of power and prestige that represented their accomplishments and status (feathers, ribbons, peace medals); second, and more importantly, it became a way to mark the landscape as Indigenous and commemorate the experience of being in that place. It's not unlike scrawling "Red Jacket was here, 1828" on the wall.

By the late twentieth century the Indian Office had moved across the city and had been transferred from the War Department to the Department of the Interior. And, in late 1972, Native activists laid claim to the building and challenged the colonial bureaucracy's legitimacy. That, however, had not been the plan initially. On November 1, 1972, activists from the American Indian Movement (AIM) began arriving in Washington, D.C., from across the continent as part of a demonstration called the Trail of Broken Treaties. The activists intended to erect symbolic tipis and sweat lodges in West Potomac Park; hold demonstrations and entertainment at the Sylvan Theater on the grounds of the Washington Monument; conduct a spiritual service at Arlington National Cemetery; commemorate Pima World War II hero Ira Hayes at the Iwo Jima Memorial; and present and discuss a document drafted by Hank Adams, an AIM leader from Fort Peck, that became known as the Twenty Points Proposal.[24] Upon arriving in the capital, the AIM activists quickly saw their plans fall apart. Lodging and meal arrangements fell through—the result of poor planning and execution—and, weary from the cross-country trip, the activists converged the next day on the Bureau of Indian Affairs (BIA), where tensions quickly erupted resulting in a seven-day occupation of the building. In their book, *Like a Hurricane*, Robert Warrior and Paul Chaat Smith argue that "the BIA takeover was less a revolution than a conference planners['] nightmare. It was a case of incompetent planning and appalling manners, a trifling event of no consequence; yet it somehow captured the essence of the BIA's failure to work with and for Indian tribes."[25] They are making a national-level argument, which makes sense, but from the prospective of Indigenous histories of Washington, D.C., it's difficult to think of this as simply a trifling event.

As they saw their lodging and accommodation arrangements fall apart, AIM activists also learned that the National Park Service had denied their permits to conduct ceremonies at Arlington and the Iwo Jima Memorial. The context here is important, because by the end of 1972, demonstrations in Washington—anti-war, student, women's liberation, and civil rights—had become commonplace and one can easily imagine the resentment these young and passionate (and exhausted) AIM men and women felt. At this point they could have chosen among a wide variety of different actions: they could have left the city; they could have tried to come up with alternate plans for housing and meals; or they could have selected other locations for ceremonies, vigils, demonstrations, and protests. And yet they chose the Bureau of Indian Affairs as their destination, a place their original plans had not included at all. Sid Mills, a twenty-one-year-old Yakima activist, expressed important sentiment worth pondering. He said, "Where are we going to go? We're going down to our building. We're going down to the Bureau of Indian Affairs. We own that son of a bitch."[26] These words could be dismissed simply as an emotional reaction by a passionate, young activist, especially if one fails to recognize the significance that Washington, D.C., more specifically, the Indian Office, held for tribal nations. Indeed, one need only recall the Ho-Chunk, for whom claiming space on Indian Office walls mattered in significant ways.

More than a thousand AIM activists ended up at the BIA on November 2, 1972, and the uncertain situation turned into an occupation when DC police in riot gear tried to forcibly remove them. For federal officials, this looked like a disaster, it was only five days before a presidential election; Native revolutionaries, who vowed to die before they would surrender, held the building. The next day, after another botched federal removal attempt, the AIM occupiers unfurled a banner across the front of the BIA building claiming it as the "NATIVE AMERICAN EMBASSY." They erected a tipi on the front lawn.[27]

Federal negotiators worked with AIM leaders, especially Hank Adams, to end the occupation, but a series of events over the weekend, on November 5 and 6, led to a rash of vandalism inside the building. Paul Chaat Smith and Robert Warrior describe the experience for AIM activists as one of "psychological torture," the result of "the nearly constant threat of attack and . . . [involving] roller-coaster mood swings." The result was "a ferocious wave of violence against the building," as activists destroyed documents, desks, chairs, and cabinets, and other furniture, and graffitied the walls with spray paint.[28] Scholars disagree on how to interpret this vandalism and the occupation more generally. Ward Churchill argues that it "did more to bring Indians into the BIA than all the petitions and letters of 'more responsible' and 'legitimate' tribal officials over the preceding fifty years."[29] Historian George Castile, however, asserts that Churchill's point was "demonstrably untrue" and that, in fact, the occupation resulted in the dismissal of Mohawk Commissioner of Indian Affairs Louis Bruce and his staff of young, Native activists.[30] Smith and Warrior argue that for the activists the looting and trashing represented a feeling that the records had to be "destroyed because of what they and the building that housed them

American Genocide, Reconciled through Football, by Gregg Deal. Photograph by
Dave Cooper. Courtesy Gregg Deal.

represented."[31] Yet when the actions of the AIM activists are paired with earlier
visitors to Washington and the Indian Office, a different interpretation emerges.

The actions of the AIM activists—renaming the BIA the "Native American
Embassy," erecting a teepee in front of it, and spray painting the walls—strangely
echo the actions and experiences of the men and women whose portraits hung
on the walls of the War Department in the early nineteenth century. These AIM
men and women were making a claim to this space and did so in ways that would
likely have resonated with all of their "forebears" or predecessors visiting the
capital and capitol. When they painted the walls, they could've presumably
written anything, but they chose to write "AIM," and tribal names: "Sioux,"
"Ponca," "Ute," "Shoshone," "Nez Perce," "Bannock," and "Blackfoot." And,
provocatively, in one photo, it looks like someone wrote "Mike was . . ."; the
final word is indistinguishable; maybe it said "here." They were commemorating this moment and marking this space as Indigenous.

Although Gregg Deal's performance piece (described above) was staged,
all of the insults and microaggressions he faced came from actual experience,
including the Washington football team's fan message boards. And it was fleeting, for one night only. In northeast Washington, however, as part of a public art

and mural event on Rhode Island Avenue, Deal painted a mural that endured and contains many of the same elements addressed throughout this collection of stories.

There, in his painting, Deal challenged the notion that the Washington team honors anything other than the legacy and pervasiveness of the culture of settler colonialism. He did so by using an iconic image of the Nez Perce leader, Hinmatóowyalahtq'it or Chief Joseph. And most viewers would probably see the image simply as a generic Plains Native, or recall Chief Joseph as a resistance leader who famously (and apocryphally) uttered the words, "I will fight no more forever." Yet it is worth also recalling that Joseph was also known in Washington, D.C., as a savvy diplomat who traveled to and through the city as a guest of several presidents, including Rutherford B. Hayes and Theodore Roosevelt. In fact, despite his less than enlightened attitude toward Native people more generally, President Roosevelt once noted that Joseph "had some genuine ground of serious complaint against our government and people."[32] Deal's mural illustrates how Native claims to place using paint and stone continue on in earnest.

The final story in this collection moves to the middle of the twentieth century. Two groups of statues that stood on the cheek-blocks of the Capitol building's east front for over one hundred years were curiously removed in 1958. Horatio Greenough's *Rescue* and Luigi Persico's *Discovery of America* were commissioned, carved, and placed there from the 1830s to the 1950s. Although there were initial critiques of them (as there were for every piece of art placed in or around the Capitol), the statues served as fixtures at every presidential inauguration from the 1850s onward.

Then-senator James Buchanan said that Persico's group represented "the great discoverer when he first bounded with ecstasy upon the shore, all his toils and perils past, presenting a hemisphere to the astonished world, with the name America inscribed on it."[33] Of course, it's worth noting that Senator Charles Sumner, a consistent critic of Capitol art demanded, "What is Columbus going to do, play a game of nine pins?"[34] Secretary of State John Forsyth said of the statue on the other side of the staircase, "I know of no single fact in profane history that can balance the one so wisely chosen by Mr. Persico as the subject of [Greenough's] group . . . which shall commemorate the dangers and difficulty of peopling our continent" (ignoring, of course, the fact that the continent had already been long "peopled").[35] In these initial critiques, those most vocally antagonistic to Greenough's effort focused on the dog (its placement, demeanor, attitude, facial expression, and imagined breed). Little was said about the more dramatic and violent aspects of the group.

In the 1950s, though, a campaign led by Leta Myers Smart (Omaha) and the California Indian Rights Association resulted in the removal of the statues for good (they are currently held in a remote Smithsonian storage facility at Fort Meade). Smart wrote dozens of letters in the 1950s, including one that was published in *Harper's* and which ultimately garnered the support of several congressmen and senators, as well as the long-serving Architect of the Capitol David Lynn. In her *Harper's* piece, Smart wrote that the message of the statues is "unflattering and unjust."[36]

Smart shrewdly deployed the language of Cold War internationalism, moreover, which contributed significantly to her success. For example, in a 1953 letter to the National Sculpture Society—from whom she was seeking support in her campaign—she wrote, "The American Indian is no longer,—if he ever was, the blood-thirsty savage Greenough made him out to be in this group of sculpture . . . we feel we ought to *rescue the Indians* from these deplorable straits, not forgetting to mention the other reasons why this should be done or because these statues are bad propaganda for America and would make excellent fodder for our enemies."[37] In another letter she wrote that removing the pieces would be "in better keeping for the right kind of propaganda for Americanism."[38] In yet another she argued that replacing the statues would demonstrate that the United States deserved to be "in that enviable position of being a good example to the rest of the world."[39] In yet a fourth, she stated that "Rescue" and "Discovery" were "not only a disgrace to the Indians . . . but something that is not good for our country,—something that could be made much of and in the wrong way by our enemies if they were wont to make something of them."[40] By framing her critiques in terms of the international politics of the Cold War and by using patriotic rhetoric, Smart infused her campaign with a certain amount of urgency, and it's worth noting that she never missed an opportunity to infuse some humor, too. In a letter to Lynn, she threatened "to take a stick of dynamite (no, two sticks!), and blow up the 'Rescue Group' (laugh)." But then feigning fear over having just incriminated herself, she suggested that perhaps she'd just "have to get the communists to do the job!"[41]

Although several other factors contributed to the removal of the statues, Smart's campaign played the decisive role. In a letter to George Stewart, Lynn's replacement as Architect of the Capitol, on the subject of what should happen to the statues, Republican congressman from Michigan August Johansen opined that "maybe this is a good time to make peace with the Indians."[42] Smart's campaign is important because removing these statues represents a refusal to succumb to non-Native expectations. It demonstrates how Native visitors and inhabitants continued, and continue today, to carve out a place, commemorate, and engage with the city and its symbols.

COLLECTION 3: KICKING BEAR'S PRESENCE

This collection contains only one story, and it begins with a personal anecdote. In 2010, a fellow historian and I were in Washington, D.C., on research. One day I went to the archives and he went for a run. When I returned to our room later that evening, he asked if I knew anything about a bridge with four gigantic buffaloes. I had only just begun the research for this project and knew nothing about the bridge. I went back to the archives the next day and he took a walk around the city with his camera. When I returned the second evening, he showed me pictures of the buffaloes as well as the fifty-six "Indian head" reliefs that adorn the bridge. "Native people are everywhere in this city," he said. I had to learn more.

Georgetown was founded in 1751, many years prior to the District of Columbia or the even city of Washington. For most of the nineteenth century, Georgetown remained a separate legal entity from the capital, but in 1871 it was merged with Washington. Rapid growth and residential sprawl over the next few decades encouraged city leaders to provide a connecting artery between north Georgetown and Dupont Circle. There was only one problem: Rock Creek and the surrounding heights separated the two. Although the initial plan involved filling the gorge, the McMillan Commission, a Senate committee whose report guides capital development to this day, rejected it, opting instead for a bridge. They selected Q Street as the location for the new bridge, despite the fact that Q Street in Georgetown is 185 feet south of Q Street in Dupont Circle. The bridge would need a curve. Also, it came to a dead-end at the historic Dumbarton Mansion, which would have to be moved about a hundred feet.[43]

Glenn Brown, a proponent of the McMillan Commission and the City Beautiful movement, designed the bridge, while famous animal sculptor Alexander Phimister Proctor made the buffaloes. The bridge features several City Beautiful design elements: its neoclassical arches, corbel arches, piers, and pillars are reminiscent of Roman aqueducts. More obviously, its scale and style were typical of the City Beautiful aesthetic; after all, they could have simply built a functional and utilitarian structure. The use of the buffalo and Indian head iconography, the most distinctive elements of the bridge, expressly connect its design to the City Beautiful movement. The movement got its start in 1893 at Chicago's Columbian Exposition and, like the World's Fair itself, the bridge reflects a certain nostalgia for a vanishing frontier. In fact, in an interview, Glenn Brown noted, "we naturally determined to give the carving in other portions of the structure an American character." In this formulation, it makes sense that the designers chose what seems to be a generic Plains motif: these images are mobile and serve as free-floating stand-ins for a constellation of ideas that simultaneously express and excuse settler anxieties and guilt.[44] The problem, of course, is that these images are not free-floating, and these histories are not metaphors.

There is yet another way to understand this bridge and its iconography, one that focuses on the history of non-Native expectations, alongside looking to the deep Indigenous history of the city. The busts that sit below each pillar were actually modeled from a life mask of Mato Wa-na-day-ka or Kicking Bear, a Miniconjou Lakota leader who played a significant role in bringing the Ghost Dance movement to the Plains. In the 1890s, Kicking Bear traveled to Washington, D.C., to advocate on behalf of the Lakota to the Office of Indian Affairs. As an anticolonial leader of the Ghost Dance movement, critic of white settlement, and outspoken leader, Kicking Bear is not unlike the Ho-Chunk delegates in the first collections of stories and Leta Myers Smart in the second.

In the 1890s archaeologist William Henry Holmes, who worked for the Smithsonian Bureau of Ethnology and then served as head curator of anthropology at the U.S. National Museum, conducted significant excavations around Washington, D.C., including digging up Connecticut Avenue at one point. One of the sites his team investigated thoroughly was the Dumbarton Heights—an area just north of where the bridge was ultimately built. There Holmes and his team found an important stone-quarry site where Piscataway peoples, for generations upon generations, excavated materials and made tools.[45]

Non-Native ways of seeing, and more importantly, Native ways of seeing and Native challenges to place and the progressive narratives of settler colonialism within the U.S. capital, are all implicated in this one site: a bridge built in the 1910s, using cutting edge architectural technology and trendy design elements, that is meant to memorialize and celebrate a generic and supposedly bygone American past is, in actuality, undermined by the fact that the bust commemorates a Native leader who challenged U.S. colonialism spiritually and militarily on the Plains, as well as politically, in the city itself. That and the fact that the bridge and this artwork was built atop land that has been significant to Indigenous inhabitants since time immemorial.

EPILOGUE: HENRY OLD COYOTE'S WORDS

On April 26, 1978, the director of the Smithsonian's National Anthropological Archive, Herman Viola, interviewed Henry Old Coyote, member of the Crow Nation and advisor to the Senate on legislation involving Indigenous communities. In the 1970s Viola created a program at the Smithsonian called the American Indian Cultural Resources Program, designed to provide opportunities for Native people interested in pursuing careers as archivists, curators, and historians. In the course of this far-reaching conversation, Old Coyote talked about the reasons a visit to Washington, D.C., was meaningful for many Native people. "It's the nation's capital," he said, "[but] it's more like a shrine to the Indians." He continued, laying out a paradox, "It's . . . undesirable to the Indian . . . [but there's] a sacredness of the city." Perhaps sensing the complexity in Old Coyote's response, Viola pressed further, asking what was "important symbolically" about Washington. Old Coyote answered, Indigenous people "love their country and [Washington is] the seat of the government . . . as such [they] . . . feel that a certain reverence should be extended to the place."[46]

Old Coyote's words were laden with significance. He was speaking not only for Native visitors and inhabitants of the capital in the late twentieth century but also for Indigenous people in general and their historical experiences. The complexity of his thoughts on placemaking—that the city is simultaneously "sacred" and "undesirable"—points to a fundamental uneasiness in Native Washington. The stories rehearsed herein focus on the Indigenous presence in the city. But it's important to honor the Indigenous present as well. The kinds of experiences and cultural work these stories invoke and evoke, occurring over the past two hundred years or so, by no means exist only in the past. Native scholars, artists, museum curators, attorneys, and others continue today in their acts of creative, imaginative resistance to the art and architecture of the capital. It's heartening that they do; it's appalling that they have to. To give (almost) the last word to Henry Old Coyote, the situation is both "sacred" and "undesirable."

In these stories, place matters—although Washington, D.C., was not the sort of place where most people come from but only where they end up (aside, of course, from the Piscataway Conoy). As for the commemorative landscape of the capital, the portrayals of Native violence and of a conquest completed came from the minds of European artists and U.S. policymakers who commissioned them. These portrayals are historically significant as moral justifications for past federal policies. But they are also significant for what they came to represent in terms of an emerging and burgeoning imperial cultural mythology. Here, white men claimed ownership of the city (and the nation) and decorated it with images of conquest. Yet, as these stories suggest, they were never successful in commanding the city (or the nation) in a way that precluded the claims of others. Commemorative expressions also hid a much more complex and more interesting lived landscape in which Native people engaged with non-Native individuals and the symbols of settler society in the heart of an imperial metropole. The telling of some of these stories belie claims that "Indians and cities— cannot coexist, [or that] one must necessarily be eclipsed by the other."[47] Such certainty has certainly not been reflected the history of Washington, D.C., nor its monumental art and architecture.

These stories also demonstrate how Native actions have all too often been interpreted through Euro-American expectations and help point to how we came to certain kinds of narratives and not others. One of the most important elements of Native Washington is its ability to suggest the possibilities of hidden Indian histories, though perhaps they are not actually all that hidden if we but take the time to look.[48] After all, they are written in stone and paint, plastered all over the walls, and lived out on the streets.

NOTES

1. "The Indians Seeing the Play," *Daily National Intelligencer*, October 4, 1837.

2. Coll Thrush, *Indigenous London: Native Travelers at the Heart of Empire* (New Haven, Conn.: Yale University Press, 2016), 13.

3. Donald Fixico, "Federal and State Policies and American Indians," in *A Companion to American Indian History*, ed. Philip J. Deloria and Neal Salisbury (New York: Blackwell, 2002), 379.

4. Richard B. Davis, ed., *Jeffersonian America: Notes on the United States of America, Collected in the Years 1805–6–7 and 11–12 by Sir Augustus John Foster, Bart.* (San Marino, Calif.: Huntington Library, 1954), 28.

5. Davis, ed., *Jeffersonian America*, 32.

6. Henry Clay Preuss, *Fashions and Follies of Washington Life: A Play in Five Acts* (Washington D.C.: Published by the Author, 1857), introduction.

7. Although there is a significant literature on the art and architecture of Washington, D.C., much of it focused on the Capitol building itself, books focusing specifically on Indian imagery are limited. The best example is Vivien Green Fryd's *Art and Empire:*

The Politics of Ethnicity in the United States Capitol, 1815–1860 (1992; repr., Athens: Ohio University Press, 2001). For other works on Washington art and architecture, see Charles E. Fairman, *Art and Artists of the Capitol of the United States of America* (Washington, D.C.: Government Printing Office, 1927); Ellwood Parry, *The Images of the Indian and the Black Man in American Art, 1590–1900* (New York: George Braziller, 1974); Angela Miller, *The Empire of the Eye: Landscape Representation and American Cultural Politics, 1825–1875* (Ithaca, N.Y.: Cornell University Press, 1993); Donald Kennon, ed., *The United States Capitol: Designing and Decorating a National Icon* (Athens: Ohio University Press, 2000); William Dickinson, Dean Herrin, and Donald Kennon, eds., *Montgomery C. Meigs and the Building of the Nation's Capital* (Athens: Ohio University Press, 2001); Donald Kennon and Thomas Somma, eds., *American Pantheon: Sculptural and Artistic Decoration of the United States Capitol* (Athens: Ohio University Press, 2004); Cynthia Field, Isabelle Gournay, and Thomas Somma, eds., *Paris on the Potomac: The French Influence on the Architecture and Art of Washington, D.C.* (Athens: Ohio University Press, 2007); Sarah Luria, *Capital Speculations: Writing and Building Washington, D.C.* (Durham.: University of New Hampshire, 2006); C. M. Harris, "Washington's Gamble, L'Enfant's Dream: Politics, Design, and the Founding of the National Capital," *William and Mary Quarterly*, 3rd ser., 56, no. 3 (July 1999): 527–64; and Kirk Savage, *Monument Wars: Washington, D.C., the National Mall, and the Transformation of the Memorial Landscape* (Berkeley: University of California Press, 2011).

8. In theory and method, Philip Deloria's book *Indians in Unexpected Places* and Coll Thrush's *Native Seattle*, have been profoundly important in helping me conceptualize urban Indigeneity and the ways that cultural expectations cloud our historical vision. More directly, anyone doing work on Native histories of Washington, D.C., or the Native delegation experience owes a debt of gratitude to Herman Viola's *Diplomats in Buckskins*, the go-to volume on Indigenous diplomatic travel to Washington (personally, he has also generously provided guidance and support to me). Additionally, art historian Vivien Green Fryd's *Art and Empire*, which examines much of the artwork in and around the Capitol Building, has been extremely useful in understanding the commemorative landscape of the city. I don't seek to refute or revise any of their arguments—I find them overwhelmingly persuasive—but rather to tie them together and build from there. See Philip J. Deloria, *Indians in Unexpected Places* (Lawrence: University of Kansas Press, 2004); Coll Thrush, *Native Seattle: Histories from the Crossing-Over Place* (Seattle: University of Washington Press, 2007); Herman Viola, *Diplomats in Buckskins: A History of Indian Delegations in Washington City*, 2nd ed. (Bluffton, S.C.: Rivilo Books, 1995).

9. Preuss, *Fashions and Follies of Washington Life*, persons of the drama.

10. Preuss, *Fashions and Follies of Washington Life*, 58–61.

11. Gaillard Hunt, ed., *The First Forty Years of Washington Society, in the Family Letters of Margaret Bayard Smith* (1906; repr., New York: Frederick Ungar Publishing, 1965), 245. This episode is fully recounted in the letter from Margaret Smith to her husband, dated November 30, 1828, and reprinted in this collection.

12. "The Winnebago Visitors," *Daily National Journal* (Washington, D.C.), October 24, 1828. In *Diplomats in Buckskins*, historian Herman Viola explained that the

many Indian delegations who travelled to Washington "generally underwent the same experiences—sightseeing, a round of social and diplomatic appointments, and interviews with high state officials." This pattern, he argued, was designed to intimidate potentially hostile Indian leaders or to introduce them to the "superiority of civilized life compared to theirs." The delegations, both authorized and unauthorized (or invited by the federal government and of their own volition) came to D.C. to negotiate treaties when negotiations in the field had failed; to quell intertribal warfare through mediation, or to declare peaceful intentions or friendship, or loyalty; and to receive gifts from the federal government, many visiting again and again. See Viola, *Diplomats in Buckskins*, 20, 28.

    13. "Indians at Washington," *National Daily Intelligencer*, March 1, 1858.

    14. "Arrival of Distinguished Scalp-Hunters," *New York Herald*, May 25, 1870. Article reprinted from Washington, D.C.

    15. "Disadvantage of Civilization," *New York Herald*, May 26, 1870. Article reprinted from Washington, D.C.

    16. William Q. Force, *Picture of Washington and its Vicinity, for 1848, with twenty embellishments on wood, by Gilbert & Gihon, and eighteen on steel, and an introduction by Rev. R. R. Gurley* (Washington, D.C.: William Q. Force, 1848), 57–61. This was a reprint edition that was remarkably similar to the 1845 edition. It was reprinted annually as new buildings and art installations were completed. In her Pulitzer Prize-winning book on Washington, Constance Green retold this story, noting "Negroes as well as whites doubtless relished telling of the fierce Winnebagos who were persuaded to enter the 'Rotundo' of the Capitol and, upon seeing the frieze of Daniel Boone slaying a savage, suddenly uttered a dreadful war whoop and fled the building" (147). See Constance Green, *Washington: Village and Capital, 1800–1878* (Princeton, N.J.: Princeton University Press, 1962).

    17. Blackhawk, *Violence over the Land: Indians and Empires in the Early American West* (Cambridge, Mass.: Harvard University Press, 2006), 9.

    18. Ely S. Parker, "Twenty-two pages of a diary with comments on . . . ," January 1–13, 1847, Box 2, 1846–1848, Ely S. Parker Papers, American Philosophical Society, Philadelphia, Pa.

    19. On the culture of colonialism, I'm especially influenced by Nicholas Thomas, *Colonialism's Culture: Anthropology, Travel, and Government* (Princeton, N.J.: Princeton University Press, 1994).

    20. Viola, *Diplomats in Buckskins*, 174–78.

    21. Jonathan Elliot, *Historical Sketches of the Ten Miles Square Forming the District of Columbia; with a Picture of Washington, Describing Objects of General Interest or Curiosity at the Metropolis of the Union* (Washington, D.C.: J. Elliot Jr., 1830), 165–67.

    22. Francis Trollope, *Domestic Manners of the Americans*, vol. 1 (London: Gilbert and Rivington Printers, 1832), 314–15.

    23. McKenney to Peter Porter, Nov. 3, 1828, Office of Indian Affairs, Letters Sent, vol. 5, p. 169, Record Group 75, NARA, Washington D.C.; McKenney to Porter, Dec. 9, 1828, Office of Indian Affairs, Letters Sent, miscellaneous, Record Group 75, NARA, Washington D.C.; Caleb Atwater, *The Indians of the Northwest, Their Manners, Customs,*

&c. &c. or Remarks Made on a Tour to Prairie du Chien and Thence to Washington City in 1829 (Columbus, Ohio, 1850), 119. For the best account of Charles Bird King and the portrait gallery, see Herman Viola, *The Indian Legacy of Charles Bird King* (New York: Doubleday, 1976).

24. For a reprint of the Twenty Points Proposal, see Alvin Josephy, Joane Nagel, and Troy Johnson, eds., *Red Power: The American Indians' Fight for Freedom*, 2nd ed. (Lincoln: University of Nebraska Press, 1999), 44–47.

25. Robert Warrior and Paul Chaat Smith, *Like a Hurricane: The Indian Movement from Alcatraz to Wounded Knee* (New York: New Press, 1996), 158. For more on the FBI investigation into the AIM activists who carried out the BIA takeover, see Steve Hendricks, *The Unquiet Grave: The FBI and the Struggle for the Soul of Indian Country* (New York: Thunder's Mouth Press, 2006).

26. Quoted in Warrior and Smith, *Like a Hurricane*, 153.

27. Warrior and Smith, *Like a Hurricane*, 156–57.

28. Warrior and Smith, *Like a Hurricane*, 161–62.

29. Quoted in Sherry L. Smith, *Hippies, Indians, and the Fight for Red Power* (New York: Oxford University Press, 2012), 249, n 56.

30. George P. Castile, *To Show Heart: Native American Self-Determination and Federal Indian Policy, 1960–1975* (Tucson: University of Arizona Press, 1999), 124–25.

31. Warrior and Smith, *Like a Hurricane*, 162.

32. Viola, *Diplomats in Buckskins*, 112.

33. *Register of Debates*, Senate, 24th Cong., 1st Sess., April 28, 1836, 1316.

34. Handwritten note attributing the quote to *"The Story of the Capitol* by Feeley (Congressional Record 1844)," File: 19/2 STATUES: CAPITOL & GROUNDS, Folder: Discovery Group—Description, Curator's Office, Architect of the Capitol, Washington, D.C.

35. Greenough to Forsyth, July 1, 1837, *Letters*, ed. Wright, 214.

36. Leta Myers Smart, "The Last Rescue," *Harper's* 219, no. 1313 (October 1959), 92.

37. Smart to Joseph Morris, Managing Editor, The National Sculpture Society, September 9, 1953, File: 19/2 STATUES: CAPITOL & GROUNDS, Folder: Rescue Group—Indian Protests, Curator's Office, Architect of the Capitol, Washington, D.C.

38. Leta Myers Smart to David Lynn, Architect of the Capitol, November 3, 1952, File: 19/2 STATUES: CAPITOL & GROUNDS.

39. Smart to Joseph Morris, Managing Editor, The National Sculpture Society, September 9, 1953, File: 19/2 STATUES: CAPITOL & GROUNDS.

40. Smart to J. George Stewart, Architect of the Capitol, January 24, 1955, File: 19/2 STATUES: CAPITOL & GROUNDS.

41. Leta Myers Smart to David Lynn, Architect of the Capitol, November 1, 1953, File: 19/2 STATUES: CAPITOL & GROUNDS.

42. Johansen to Stewart, October 5, 1959, File: 19/2 STATUES: CAPITOL & GROUNDS.

43. There is little written about the history of this bridge. My information is derived from the Georgetown Metropolitan, a self-described neighborhood blog, available at https://georgetownmetropolitan.com/2010/08/11/the-interesting-story-of-dumbarton

-bridge/, and from personal interviews and correspondence with Jeff Nelson, formerly of the band *Minor Threat*, who has long been researching the bridge for a coffee table book.

44. For more on this concept of free-floating histories, see Jean O'Brien and Lisa Blee, "What Is a Monument to Massasoit Doing in Kansas City? The Memory Work of Monuments and Place in Public Displays of History," *Ethnohistory* 61, no. 4 (Fall 2014): 635–53. They argue that the image of Massasoit has come to serve as a potent symbol for a certain kind of nostalgic and romanticized telling of the American founding myth of Plymouth Rock and the welcoming Native diplomat. For more, see James J. Buss, *Winning the West with Words: Language and Conquest in the Lower Great Lakes* (Norman: University of Oklahoma Press, 2011); Jean O'Brien, *Firsting and Lasting: Writing Indians Out of Existence in New England* (Minneapolis: University of Minnesota Press, 2010); and Philip J. Deloria, *Indians in Unexpected Places*.

45. For more on this dig and Holmes' career in general, see David Meltzer and Robert Dunnell eds., *The Archaeology of William H. Holmes* (Washington, D.C.: Smithsonian Press, 1992).

46. Interview with Henry Old Coyote, transcript, Herman J. Viola Papers, Box 26, Folder-Transcripts, Interviews, National Museum of Natural History, National Anthropological Archive, Suitland, Md.

47. Coll Thrush, *Native Seattle*, 8.

48. Deloria, *Indians in Unexpected Places*, 6–7.

6

WHEN THE CITY COMES TO THE INDIAN

Yavapai-Apache Exodus and Return to
Urban Indian Homelands, 1870s–1920s

On the side of an old one-story building on the corner of N. Main St. and W. Pinal St. in Cottonwood, Arizona, a mural attempts to depict the life and history of central Arizona's Verde Valley. The tropes are familiar: pioneers in covered wagons, white cowboys and Mexican-American *vaqueros*, trains, "primitive" Indians, and Indian ruins. An Indian woman in the foreground wearing a camp dress holds a burden basket while a bald eagle flies overhead, the ruins of Tuzi-goot behind her. Two Indian men in buckskin stand behind a larger-than-life basket and petroglyph-laden rock face, with the ruins of Montezuma Castle to their rear.[1] A white family of four sits happily in front of a camping tent. They are, not surprisingly, the only "modern" people in the mural. The young daughter contentedly reads a book, whose cover depicts two Apache ga'an.[2] The message is clear: Indians in the Verde Valley are historical relics; we figure only in the imagination and landscape: in books, ruins, and rock carvings.[3]

The mural inadvertently tells a much more important story, however. In the last decades of the nineteenth century and first decades of the twentieth, settlers and the U.S. Army pursued successive—and often simultaneous—policies of conquest and extermination, forced congregation, removal, and halting tolerance vis-à-vis our people, the Yavapais (People of the Sun) and Dilzhe'e (The Hunters, often referred to as "Tonto") Apaches. After our removal and twenty-five years of confinement, we found our homelands dotted with boomtowns such as Cottonwood, Camp Verde, Rimrock, Lake Montezuma, Clarkdale, and Jerome, as well as the farms, ranches, churches, stores, schools, and the infrastructure to support this bustling settler population.[4] We began scraping out a marginal existence in the Verde Valley. Our tribal history tells we were "living in the nooks and crannies of the old home country,"[5] often invisible to our non-Indian neighbors. Unlike the experiences of those who participated in the Bureau of Indian Affairs' relocation and termination programs of the mid-twentieth century, the history of our people in the Verde Valley amounted to the city "coming" to the Indian. At every step of this decades-long process, we confronted the forces of urbanization. We were critical and mobile participants in Arizona's urbanizing landscape and growing industrial wage economy, working in Globe and Miami, in Jerome's mines, on the roadways of the "Apache Trail," and on hydraulic projects at Fossil Creek and the Roosevelt Dam.[6]

Historian Daniel J. Herman has argued that Yavapai-Apache labor "transformed Arizona into a modern state, with railroads, highways, schools, courthouses, telegraph and telephone lines, monumental dams, and hydroelectricity," and that Yavapai-Apaches and settlers "became part of one another's lives. They learned peaceful ways to interact. They began to change one another in subtle ways," with settlers learning "toleration" and even "friendship."[7] But stories of increasing coexistence belie the ways that the emerging urban ordering of space served as an ongoing structure of confinement, one that continues to shape our ability to live in our homeland. It's no small wonder that, a century later, our reservation consists of five non-contiguous parcels of ancestral lands totaling some two thousand acres, surrounded by urban centers that grow and prosper unabated from our land, water, resources, and labor.

YAVAPAI-APACHE HISTORY TO 1875

Today's Yavapai-Apache Nation, headquartered on the Middle Verde Reservation, is comprised of two distinct cultural groups: Yavapais and Dilzhe'e Apaches.[8]

Yavapais are Upland Yumans, linguistically and culturally related to Hualapais and Havasupais. They once ranged over some twenty thousand square miles of central Arizona.[9] Dilzhe'e Apaches are Athabaskan-speakers who controlled a large area east of the Verde River that included much of the Mogollon Rim and Tonto Basin. They are linguistically and culturally related to other Western Apache groups. Collectively, we have survived for centuries gathering saguaro, ocotillo, prickly pear, yucca, agave, mesquite beans, acorns, and piñon, planting corn, beans, and squash along the waterways, and hunting deer, antelope, squirrels, rabbits, and field rats.[10] For both Yavapais and Dilzhe'es, the Verde Valley and Red Rock Country are our "spiritual heartland."[11] Montezuma Well is the place where our ancestors emerged from the underworld.

With the Verde River serving as an informal boundary, our people commonly intermingled and intermixed with each other. Grenville Goodwin goes so far as to assert that some Dilzhe'e Apaches lived "permanently intermixed" with Yavapais, and "very definitely considered several of their clans to be identical with Yavapai clans."[12] The areas of greatest interaction were along the drainages of the Upper Verde: Fossil Creek, Oak Creek, Dry and Wet Beaver Creeks, and the East Verde River.[13] But Yavapais and Apaches retained their own territory, identity, and connections to sacred places independent of each other. Yavapai elder Frieda Eswonia maintains that Yavapais "were known to associate a lot with the Apache; but that did not mean that we were the same." "Although some intermarriage occurred . . . the Yavapai and Apache remained separate and distinct from each other."[14] The ties and similarities were close enough, though, that Anglo-Americans often mistook Yavapais for Apaches, referring to Yavapais as Mohave-Apaches or Yuma-Apaches.[15]

Beginning in the late sixteenth century, successive groups of non-Indian invaders came to our territory. In 1583 and 1598, Hopis guided Antonio de Espejo and Marcos Farfán de los Godos, to the Tonto Basin and Verde Valley, respectively, with both parties reaching the rich copper mines on Mingus Mountain,[16] the site of present-day Jerome. We had mined turquoise and copper ore there for centuries, having dug a mine shaft deep into the mountain. While Espejo characterized the Yavapai-Apaches he met as simple and generous, both he and Farfán were disappointed to find only copper.[17] Such seemingly inauspicious beginnings foreshadowed later settler demands for Yavapai-Apache mineral wealth, and land would help spur new urban spaces, with disastrous results.

We remained relatively undisturbed through the Spanish and Mexican periods,[18] and even the U.S. conquest during the U.S.-Mexico War. Life began to change in the 1860s. In 1863, Joseph Walker's[19] party first panned gold in Lynx Creek near present-day Prescott. Pauline Weaver's party struck gold later that year, while Henry Wickenburg's group made the third strike before the year was out. By 1865 there were more than three thousand placer mines just in the vicinity of Prescott,[20] which were followed by farmers, ranchers, merchants, towns, and, most of all, violence. Yavapais were the first affected, being "hunted down like animals in their own country" within two years of the Lynx Creek strike.[21] A short time later, Dilzhe'es, who had had little or no contact with whites prior to the establishment of Camp Verde,[22] would also be subjected to terrible violence. Prescott, Arizona's first territorial capital,[23] thus became the organizing space for genocidal violence.

One 1874 visitor described Prescott as "mountainous and fertile," and "very attractive."[24] But it lacked a large, permanent river. This lack of reliable water left the surrounding area simply unable to supply the livestock, produce, and fodder necessary for the city. Settlers quickly cast their eyes on our homelands in the Verde Valley. The Verde flows through the most fertile portion of Arizona, with wide floodplains and three perennial tributaries: Oak Creek, Beaver Creek, and West Clear Creek. Its lower elevation, milder winters, and ample farm and range land made it an ideal place for producing the necessary items.[25]

Settlers came to the Camp Verde area—where West Clear Creek meets the Verde—in 1865, and quickly requested, and received, military assistance.[26] This initiated our time of terror. Between 1860 and 1874, Yavapais alone suffered sixteen massacres at the hands of settlers, vigilante militias, and the U.S. Army.[27] In the mid-1860s, a Prescott vigilante gang of some one hundred men under King Woolsey terrorized and murdered Yavapais and Dilzhe'es. Arizona Superintendent of Indian Affairs Charles D. Poston justified Woolsey's murders. "[Woolsey] had been ruined by the Apaches," Poston wrote, "and adopted [their] method of retaliation."[28] An 1864 report characterized us as a "mongrel race of Indians living between the Verde . . . and the Colorado . . . composed of renegades." We led a "nomadic and pilfering life, and although not bad Indians, [we] occupy such an equivocal position that [we] are in continual danger of slaughter from the miners and the frontiersmen."[29]

Official reports contended that in order for mining, agriculture, and settlement to succeed in the Verde Valley and environs, Yavapai-Apaches would need to be removed. Outright murder would do as well. An 1865 report recommended that Dilzhe'es and Yavapais be removed from central Arizona. James Carleton, of Diné Long Walk infamy, proposed transplanting us to the Pecos River in

Texas.[30] The hysteria was so severe that Lt. Col. Roger Jones wrote in 1869 that Yavapais were "for a long time the greatest foe to civilization of all Indians inhabiting Arizona." Gen. Thomas Devin called Dilzhe'es "the most cowardly of the Apache tribes, [but] as murderous as any, and [they] have caused the death of more of the pioneers of northern Arizona than, perhaps, any other tribe."[31] To individuals like Devin, we were "cowardly" because we utilized guerilla warfare tactics and only engaged in battles we were sure we could win. In the end, the demands of proto-urban settlements such as Prescott and Camp Verde served as the engine of our dispossession.

After several episodes of unspeakable violence, including the Camp Grant Massacre of April 1871, President Ulysses S. Grant sent a peace commission headed by Quaker Vincent Colyer (and including Gen. Oliver O. Howard) to establish peace in Arizona. The federal government eventually decided to establish a number of "Military Reserves" across Arizona Territory. In October 1871, Grant signed an Executive Order creating the Rio Verde Reserve. It set aside eight hundred square miles of reservation land for Yavapais and Dilzhe'es.[32] Gen. George Crook, a veteran Indian fighter, was also sent to Arizona to "finally iron out the wrinkles," taking command of the Department of Arizona in June 1871.[33] Crook's mission was simple: subdue "renegade" Yavapais and Apaches. Crook perfected the art of hunting Yavapais and Apaches, pursuing us relentlessly in our mountain hideouts while making expert use of pack mules and Indian scouts. Crook enlisted many Yavapais and Apaches (and even some Hualapais and other Indians) to scout in his campaigns, and it was their help that most enabled him to conquer our people.[34]

After 1871, we congregated on the Rio Verde Reserve in increasing numbers (Yavapais from Date Creek would also be moved to Rio Verde) while Crook relentlessly hunted down and massacred Yavapai and Dilzhe'e "resisters" throughout central Arizona. His winter campaign of 1872–73 was particularly brutal.[35] For example, the army captured a Yavapai boy named Hoomothya (Wet Nose) and forced him to divulge the location of his camp. On December 28, 1872, Crook's men surprised the Yavapais at Skeleton Cave in Salt River Canyon. The young boy, later named Mike Burns after the army officer who captured him, was forced to watch as his entire family was murdered. As he lamented, "No more hope, no more kinfolk in all the world. What would I do? . . . In all history no civilized race has murdered another as American soldiers did my people in the year 1872. They slaughtered men, women, and children without mercy, as if they were not human. I am the only one living to tell what happened to my people."[36] John Williams, another Yavapai, similarly concluded, "When the White people come around, they kill all of my people. They kill all of my relatives. I don't know why. I guess, they just like to kill. They must feel good when they kill. The soldiers kill my people, kill them, kill them and kill them again."[37]

This relentless season of slaughter changed somewhat with developments on the Rio Verde Reserve. Hoomothya remembered many Yavapais and Dilzhe'es going to Camp Verde in the early 1870s to meet with Crook, who was "friendly" to the Indians. Crook "told them they could make their homes in the Verde Valley for as long as they lived." The general also promised us that if we "were tamed," we could remain in our homelands. We earnestly planted crops and dug a large irrigation ditch. We cut wood for the army and settlers and volunteered for scouting work—both for wages.[38] By 1873, the Rio Verde agent reported a population of some two thousand. While our people set about fulfilling the conditions we believed would allow us to remain in our homelands, which included settlement into more dense communities, life was neither easy nor pleasant at Rio Verde. Col. William Henry Corbusier, an army doctor posted there, wrote that we were "half starved . . . and subject to dysentery and malaria." "Deaths were so frequent that the bodies were left in their oowas [dwellings] which were burned over them or they were left to mummify in the dry air, as there were not enough well Indians to cut and carry the wood with which to burn the dead, as was their custom."[39] Relocating our community from the river to the foothills of nearby Mingus Mountain at Haskell Springs mitigated conditions somewhat.[40] By 1874, we had built a dam, dug ditches—including a four-mile ditch capable of irrigating two hundred and fifty acres of land—and planted corn, pumpkins, melons, potatoes, and beans.[41]

The population at Rio Verde fluctuated, as many came in for rations, wage work, or to escape violence, and then left the reserve. The figure came to hover around 1,500 between 1873 and 1875. Hoomothya asserted that Dilzhe'es outnumbered Yavapais at Rio Verde, "but some were married to Apache Mojave [Yavapai] women, and some of the Apache Mojave men had married Tonto [Dilzhe'e] women. They were all different people, and they spoke different languages, with the same trouble that a white man meeting a Mexican has."[42] Rio Verde actually marked the largest single concentration of Yavapais and Dilzhe'es to date, much larger than that of any of our pre-invasion communities, even in times of summer encampments, which saw several bands combine. In addition to farming, ditch-digging, and wage work, we held jury trials, took English classes, and interacted with white soldiers and settlers. In some ways,

we coexisted. But we also watched helplessly as the first steps in the urbanization of the Verde Valley proceeded in earnest.

By late 1874, we believed our stay at Rio Verde would be permanent.[43] Despite
the frustrations and difficulties, we had persevered as a group, at least residing
on a small portion of our homelands. While we approached self-sufficiency at
Rio Verde, we ran up against the deep public corruption that infused the Office
of Indian Affairs. The prospect of self-sufficiency alarmed a powerful group
of Tucson contractors who delivered food, tools, blankets, and other supplies
to Rio Verde and the other reserves. This group, known as the Tucson Ring,
wanted Rio Verde closed, since it represented a potentially significant loss to
their business. The Office of Indian Affairs was also intent on reducing the
number of reservations in Arizona, and cutting the number of soldiers, Indian
agents, and provisions needed for the territory's administration.[44]

The decision was made in late 1874 to move all Yavapais and Dilzhe'es from
Rio Verde to the San Carlos Reservation. Our tribal history explains that "the
government . . . used the contractor issue as an excuse to remove [us] from the
valley."[45] San Carlos Indian Agent John Clum tricked us into agreeing to the
move before we actually knew what we had agreed to. When we realized what
was happening, we were furious. Women wailed while men painted themselves
for war.[46] Crook opposed the move, as many Yavapais and Dilzhe'es had agreed
to settle at Rio Verde due to his explicit promise that it would be a permanent
home. He eventually supported relocation, but he also made another promise.
According to Hoomothya, Crook "wanted [Yavapais and Dilzhe'es] to move
over to San Carlos to set an example to the wilder class of Indians over there,
saying that they could return to their homes within seven years, possibly even
five. His fine promises, however, were never carried out."[47]

The forced march began on February 27, 1875. Officials refused to let us use
established roads and trails to avoid mountainous terrain and dangerous creek
and river crossings, instead insisting we cover the one hundred and eighty
miles as the crow flies, and demanded we travel entirely on foot. According
to Corbusier, who accompanied our people, we traveled "by rough trails, over
high mountains and across numerous streams that were liable at any hour to
rise many feet and become impassable."[48] Our exodus caused immense suffering. Yavapai elder Lucy Satala recalled: "Little children and old people, they
can't make it. They just die on the way. They didn't have time to bury them I
guess." Soldiers did not allow us to stop for proper care of the living or dead.
"They had to leave the dead people behind. Mostly young people made it. This

The *Exodus* monument. Photograph by Maurice Crandall.

is how they lost lots of our tribe."[49] Vincent Randall remembers elders telling him that many drowned when they were unable to hold ropes strewn across swollen creeks and rivers, although the soldiers did carry some of the children across flooded waterways on horseback.[50] Corbusier recorded an episode that is commonly shared in our oral history: "One old man placed his aged and decrepit wife in [a burden basket], with her feet hanging out, and carried her on his back supported by a band around his head, an average of eight and a half miles a day" for upwards of ten days.[51] Many died along the way, especially the young, old, and infirm.

The stress of the march, coupled with freezing temperatures and lack of supplies, led to tensions and even bloodshed between Dilzhe'es and Yavapais. The grueling three-week affair is ever present in our collective memory. The official report—so matter-of-fact in its language—captured none of the trauma: "The removal of the Verde Indians, in March last, brought about one thousand four hundred more [Indians to San Carlos]. These were composed of Tontos, Mojaves, and Yumas."[52] Agent Clum even expressed pride in his handling of the removal, thereby "opening to ranchmen and miners . . . important tracts of agricultural and mineral lands." He had the nerve to report that the removal had been accomplished "without the loss of a single [Anglo] life and without destroying the property of [white] citizens."[53] On April 24, 1875, President Grant officially abolished the Rio Verde Reserve by executive order. The order "restor[ed] said reservation to the public domain."[54] During this time of violent conquest, the city "came to us" through practices of dispossession and exile, and the process would continue for several more decades.

SAN CARLOS AND THE GROWTH OF THE VERDE VALLEY

Not surprisingly, the pace of settlement in our homelands accelerated after 1875. Hiram Hodge, who traveled around Arizona in the 1870s, wrote, "There has been a large increase in the population of Yavapai County in the past two years [which includes the Verde Valley], and its increase in wealth and productiveness has kept pace with the increase in the population." He was effusive in his praise of the "early pioneers of Arizona," referring to those in Yavapai County as "almost wholly of white people of the better class," who "continued their exertions towards developing the Territory of Arizona." But Hodge also noted that Crook had "gathered [Yavapais and Dilzhe'es] on a Reservation on the Verde River, promising them that the Reservation should be their home so long as they remained good Indians." He felt that neither "the Government nor its agents should ever make promises to Indians" unless they were prepared to keep them.[55]

In addition to the growth of Prescott and Camp Verde, more white communities sprang up after 1875, building on our previous labors. For example, in 1876 John James Thompson became the first white settler in Sedona. Thompson found a Yavapai-Apache garden in Oak Creek Canyon, still bearing crops, which came to be called "Indian Gardens." He literally moved onto one of our abandoned agricultural sites that was still bearing fruit thanks to our violent removal. More settlers arrived, and by the end of the 1880s, several families had put scores of acres under irrigation, using Oak Creek for water. Surveyors from the General Land Office designated the township and range lines in 1889.[56] With the "Indian menace" safely removed from the Verde Valley, miners descended on Mingus Mountain and established Jerome. The first white miners filed claims there in June 1876. Al Sieber, chief of Yavapai and Apache scouts for Crook, filed the first claim.[57]

Charles Douglas Willard's family typified those settlers who took advantage of our removal. In 1879, his family settled a ranch across the Verde River from what became Cottonwood. He described the area as "a hunter and stockman's paradise. Wild game was everywhere and the grass was knee high and plentiful." He also commented that most settlers brought cattle, horses, or sheep, which trampled and destroyed the riverine ecosystem and altered the river course. Fortunately for Willard and others like him, "there were very few Indians left in that part of the country, most of them had been transported to the San Carlos Reservation." Free from Indians, settler farming, ranching, mining, and urbanization could proceed apace in the valley.[58]

While white settlements in the Verde Valley grew, we struggled to adjust to San Carlos. Farming there was difficult due to the drier climate. For several years agricultural output was inconsistent and unpredictable. The Gila River, which passes through the reservation, flooded repeatedly. There were also years of severe drought.[59] Perhaps to offset the unpredictable nature of agriculture there, we increasingly participated in the regional cash economy, particularly in the towns of Globe and Miami. Dilzhe'e elder Vincent Randall tells how Yavapais and Dilzhe'es obtained passes from reservation officials to work in Globe:

Globe was becoming a thriving mining town. And there were two commodities that were really needed by the people that were moving into Globe, and that was wood and hay. And so, what the agent down there [did was] . . . issue these little copies of paper saying, "these are good Indians. You can trust them." And they gave [us] the permit . . . to cut wild hay, and [we] sold it in Globe. And [we] also sold wood in Globe.[60]

We also found whatever unskilled work we could. The San Carlos agent reported in 1877, "Numbers of these Indians are constantly employed in the towns of Globe and McMillans [McMillenville] and are in different mining camps and ranches. . . . They are engaged in bringing in hay and wood, making adobes, herding cattle, &c., and thereby manage to clothe and help support themselves and their families."[61] Some also found work on the railroad construction crews of the Gila Valley, Globe and Northern Railway.[62]

Yavapai and Dilzhe'e men also continued to enlist as scouts for army campaigns. According to Vincent Randall, "A lot of our guys served as scouts. And the old timers always said that they served as scouts because Crook told them that if they served as scouts and brought in Geronimo and any other renegades, that they could come home; that they could come home. And I always heard that."[63] Maggie Hayes, a Yavapai who recalled that her father was "pressed into service," remembered that scouting brought desperately needed economic benefits. Scouting was "compensated for in part when each year they would give [my father] a pony or a sow. Also, his meals and clothing were furnished. As a scout, he was able to relocate to an area near Globe, Arizona, called Coyote Springs."[64] For their part, women did domestic work such as laundering and cleaning houses, and a small number turned to prostitution in desperation.[65] A few of our people found work in Wild West shows.[66]

Even with increased economic integration, largely fueled by the growth of nearby Globe, we refused to accept San Carlos as a permanent home. We also refused to cease traditional practices, in spite of severe pressure to do so. Vincent Randall's grandmother told him how our people would sneak off the reservation to gather acorns during full moons. We would pick under the moonlight and then "steal back" onto San Carlos.[67] Maggie Hayes, who was sent to the federal boarding school at Grand Junction, Colorado, fondly remembered, "Mother would send me a package of acorns or other wild food, that she remembered I had enjoyed so very much as a little girl."[68] Traditional food gathering was done at great risk; those off-reservation without a pass risked being "hunted down" and punished.[69] The agent reported in 1894 that he had to send after "acorn hunters on the west side of the reserve on one or two occasions" during the year.[70]

We incorporated some elements from whites that proved useful, but only on our terms. One agent reported that while Indians seemed more and more inclined to avail themselves of white doctors, the "Indian doctor still holds his sway."[71] Agent John Bullis wrote with frustration in 1888 that not enough Indians lived in proper "dwelling-houses," instead preferring "brush houses or wick-ups [sic]." He also lamented persistent Yavapai crematory practices, which included burning the body, possessions, and dwelling, as the "prevailing superstition that [the] spirit [of the deceased] will forever afterward haunt it" if cremation was not performed. We continued to manufacture tiswin and tulpai, traditional alcoholic beverages, and gamble for recreation. Agent Bullis referred to tiswin consumption as the "greatest drawback at the present time to the improvement of these people."[72]

We also refused to let officials forget Crook's promise that we could return home within a short time. Agent Bullis wrote in 1888, "Though industriously disposed and desirous of making the best of their present situation, the [Yavapai and Dilzhe'e] tribes of Indians are greatly dissatisfied with their location. From the date of their arrival, over fourteen years ago, they have never been contented, and have always been anxious to return to the Verde country, from which they were removed." He added, "In my opinion the causes of their dissatisfaction are just."[73] Bullis similarly reported in 1890 that he was in favor of our return to the Verde Valley, with one key addendum: "provided there be sufficient land for them at the place mentioned."[74] In 1899, Agent W. J. Nicholson wrote that Yavapai-Apaches were "most anxious to return to their old homes in the Verde country. . . . I would recommend that something be done for them toward their settlement in their old home."[75]

The Indian Bureau's change of heart made sense in the context of Geronimo's final surrender in 1886. Absent the twin fears of Apache "renegades" and reservation "breakouts," the federal government significantly relaxed its hold on San Carlos. The government understood the "Indian Wars" as essentially over after 1890. While places like San Carlos remained official reservations, "there was no longer military authority to enforce who came and went. When people realized that they would leave, a lot of them did just that."[76]

The biggest unknown was what we would find when we returned to the Verde Valley. Twenty-five years of settlement, ranching, farming, mining, and urbanization had significantly altered our homelands, just as our imprisonment at San Carlos had changed us. We had embraced the cash economy, working both for and alongside whites, and even in their homes. But we had doggedly held officials to past promises of a return home. Furthermore, some Yavapai-Apaches had never left the Verde Valley, taking refuge in places like Fossil Creek. They would emerge from hiding in the years around 1900 to take their place alongside their returning relatives. Not least of all, those at San Carlos had learned a new way of life that, in the context of nineteenth-century Arizona, we might call "urban." While not a city in the traditional sense, we had been congregated on a reservation that was one of the most populous places in Arizona Territory. Capt. Adna R. Chaffee of the Sixth Cavalry, Acting Indian Agent at San Carlos, counted a total population in 1879 of 4,552. Alphonse Pinart, a Frenchman who traveled to Arizona in 1876, put the population of San Carlos at 4,133. By comparison, Pinart reported a population of 1,800 in Prescott that year, while Phoenix was a "little town of 300 inhabitants, about half Mexican."[77]

RETURN TO THE VERDE VALLEY

Our homecoming is generally placed at 1900. In actuality, small groups had been returning throughout the 1890s, and some as early as the 1880s. As restrictions for leaving San Carlos became more lax, we "drifted back into the Verde Valley."[78] The first official acknowledgment of our return in an *Annual Report to the Commissioner of Indian Affairs* dates to 1904, when Agent Luther S. Kelly wrote, "Nine families, numbering 38 souls . . . have established themselves permanently at Angora, Ariz., and a few families are at Camp Verde; all, I understand, are in a prosperous condition."[79] While the march to San Carlos was officially regulated, extraordinarily violent, and relatively brief, our return home was piecemeal and dragged on, sometimes for years. Our tribal history explains, "Families and individuals began the long walks back to their home country in Payson, Camp Verde, Red Rock Country, from Prescott downhill to Wickenburg and even westward towards Bagdad (Arizona)." We would stop at one location "to work on a road or dam project," then stop again, "because of a new baby being born or an old person being sick."[80]

The experiences of Billy Smith, a Dilzhe'e born at San Carlos in 1882, are exemplary. Smith was part of a family that had lived and worked in Globe for a time before returning north. Departing in 1898 with official papers in hand, the Smiths first went to Payson, staying with other Dilzhe'es for several months. While there, Billy worked for a white family. His multigenerational group eventually made it to the Verde Valley, camping at various locations including Camp Verde, and ultimately settled at Rimrock.[81] Yavapai Gertrude Smith similarly recalled her great-grandparents' journey home. They traveled from San Carlos to Fossil Creek, and then to Clear Creek, where her grandmother was born "somewhere around 1900–1901." The family stayed at Clear Creek "for a minute," with members working on dam and road projects. They eventually resided in Camp Verde and Middle Verde. Many of those who returned to Camp Verde lived on the Wingfields' property—local store owners—and worked for the family.[82]

Unsurprisingly, during our absence "the old places had filled up with settlers—farmers, ranchers, merchants, teamsters, teachers, and government workers were everywhere." Whites claimed the best lands, waterways, and springs. We were "pushed to the margins and treated as second-class citizens." We barely scraped by, "living in the nooks and crannies of the old home country." Everywhere we lived, from Camp Verde to Jerome, we were squatters.[83] We had witnessed the growth of boomtowns such as Globe and Miami, but these were not in our territory. It was something altogether different to find swirling towns at Camp Verde, Cottonwood, Clarkdale, Sedona, Cornville, and elsewhere. The growing white communities of the Verde Valley were what sociologist Harvey Molotch describes as growth machines; places where the settler desire for growth (through appropriating Indigenous land and resources, and through Indigenous labor) is the "very essence of a locality."[84] After decades of displacement and exile, we now faced marginalization at home through the forces of urban growth.

Some of our people congregated around the abandoned barracks of Fort Verde. Many Yavapais lived near the Camp Verde salt mine, while Dilzhe'es lived around Beaver Creek. After our people lobbied Governor of Arizona Territory Joseph Kibbey for schools to be built for our children, the federal government sent Taylor Gabbard to Camp Verde in 1906 to oversee Yavapais and Dilzhe'es spread across the Verde Valley and beyond. Gabbard opened a day school for Indian children at Camp Verde on September 1, 1907, and served as superintendent.[85] In 1910, the government set up an eighteen-acre "postage-stamp" agency at the old barracks.[86] Gabbard initiated a furious letter-writing campaign to officials in Washington, D.C., calling for more land for our people squatting at Camp Verde, Cottonwood, Fossil Creek, Jerome, Mayer, Prescott, and in the Tonto Basin: "None of these Indians own land, neither do they receive aid from the Government."[87] In 1910, he asserted, "If these people are permitted to continue living as they are at present [e.g., without land], they must gradually waste away and finally perish."[88]

With many of our people facing starvation, Gabbard asked in 1911 that "two tracts of land . . . be purchased, one at Camp Verde and the other at Jerome, about twenty-five miles northwest of Camp Verde. The number of acres in each tract should be determined by the number of Indians who would be expected to live on them."[89] Gabbard's lobbying eventually paid off, when in 1914 and 1916, two tracts of land were set aside for Yavapai-Apaches at Camp Verde and Middle Verde, respectively. Around four hundred people settled on the two non-contiguous tracts totaling some 476 acres.[90] This official reservation represented only the most miniscule portion of our original homelands.

Nevertheless, many white settlers feared our presence, even insisting we return to San Carlos. To them, we seemed an impediment to future growth. While Molotch points out that "parochial" local businessmen—boosters of the growth machine—are generally not out to save or destroy the environment, enslave or liberate blacks, or eliminate or enhance civil rights,[91] a number of Camp Verde residents wanted our elimination. Problems seem to have begun around 1910 when the federal government purchased a one-fortieth interest in the New Verde Ditch from George W. Hance and his wife, Partheny H. Hance, for $750, "for the benefit of the Camp Verde Indians day school and the Indians living adjacent thereto."[92] Perhaps experiencing seller's remorse, Hance and his compatriot, James D. Sellers, who were virulent Indian-haters, wrote for several years to territorial delegates and senators, complaining about Yavapai-Apaches around Camp Verde. Hance wrote to Senator Henry Ashurst in 1913, "The sentimental plea of allowing them to return to their old stomping ground should be a thing of the past." There was simply no room for us, he argued. The old Indians who had previously lived in the Verde Valley were nearly all dead, there was not enough game left to hunt, and the only work for us was "at manual labor." The valley had land and water, but our presence degraded white labor. Yavapai-Apaches worked for "less than the wage that should be paid a white laborer." Employers offered "no inducements for desireable [*sic*] people to settle here." The pair also characterized us as diseased carriers of trachoma, complaining that the white school and the Indian school playgrounds "adjoin," and if "intermingling of white and Indian children be allowed in the stores and the post office the disease is bound to spread."[93] Such statements were in line with the global "segregation mania" of the late nineteenth century, fueled by public health concerns in Africa and the so-called colonial world, where blacks were blamed for the spread of malaria plasmodia carried by mosquitos that killed white colonizers.[94] American cities similarly blamed ethnic populations, including Native Americans, for the spread of communicable diseases that they believed endangered whites living in close proximity.

It would have been no surprise if such unabashed racism had carried the day, but the removal scheme ultimately failed. In 1913 Sellers and Hance had secured over two hundred signatures from white Camp Verde settlers in favor of removal. The government sent Otis B. Goodall, Supervisor of Indian Schools at Las Vegas, Nevada, to question those who had signed the petition. He found many of those interviewed expressing ambivalence: The Indians were not a "nuisance," although they did fear the spread of disease. They were reliable workers, but they worked for lower pay. Most settlers did want them removed but felt that a few miles from Camp Verde would be sufficient to keep a proper distance between whites and Indians. Jacob Webber of Camp Verde, for one, stated, "When I signed the petition I was under the impression that the Indians had a reservation, but in the meantime I am informed that these Indians have no reservation rights, which I can't understand." He referred to us as "shiftless and irresponsible, immoral and pilfering," but felt that the language of the petition was "too strong." He asked that the Indians "be removed to a tract of land sufficiently large to make them self supporting and not be in such close contact with the Whites as they are at present."[95] In short, they sought a system of racial segregation similar to those that structured rapidly growing cities in the East and Midwest at that time. It is important to note, however, that while segregation allowed white residents in the Verde Valley to hoard resources and power, and make us available for menial labor (yet still remaining distant from their daily lives), we were unlike other racial and ethnic communities in the urbanizing, Progressive-Era United States. We were not newcomers trying to gain access to resources and power; we were original inhabitants trying to reclaim at least a small portion of what was already ours.

Somewhat surprisingly, a group of white settlers sent a counterpetition to Senator Ashurst in March 1913. The petitioners "protest against the proposed removal of the Indians now residing in this locality." They characterized such an action as "wholly unnecessary and undesirable." They called such treatment of "a helpless and neglected people . . . unworthy and un-American." Those who signed included white settlers of Camp Verde and the valley from many occupations: W. G. Wingfield (farmer); R. W. Wingfield (postmaster); Dennis S. Hibben (mail contractor); W. C. Miller (store clerk); D. V. Snowgoose (miner); Ralph E. King (forest ranger); A. S. Fain (stockman); and D. W. Wingfield (merchant).[96] All told, thirty-seven individuals signed the petition. The competing petitions seemed to cancel each other out in the eyes of authorities and removal efforts faded. By the mid-1910s, Yavapai-Apaches closed the book on the possibility of removal from Camp Verde.

More so than at Camp Verde, which was never a site of industrial activity, our most important confrontations with urbanization and industrialization came at Jerome and Clarkdale.[97] Mining camps sprang up in both locations after our exodus, with Jerome emerging as a major center of copper extraction. Following incorporation of the United Verde Copper Company (UVCC) in 1883, industrialist William Andrews Clark developed railroads to carry the copper to market, making the Jerome mining operation profitable. Clark also bought a number of nearby ranches in 1910, planning to build a smelter and model town.[98] But Yavapais and Dilzhe'es squatting on the site of the proposed smelter posed a problem. They would need to be moved. Vincent Randall recalls his mother's account of what happened: "She said [Clark] told them to leave, and so what happened was . . . the Yavapai contingent moved over to where the res is today [to the north] . . . and that was known as . . . 'Yavapai Camp' . . . . And the Apaches moved west of town," near the present turnoff to Tuzigoot National Monument.[99]

The industrial portion of Clarkdale with old smelter buildings, a railroad depot, and a slag heap from the smelter. Photograph by Maurice Crandall.

The growth of mining and industry in Jerome/Clarkdale was incredibly destructive to the ecology of our homelands. The vast pine forests that covered the mountains surrounding Jerome were quickly cut for mine timber and housing. Acid fumes from the smelter and ore roasting pyres killed undergrowth. The area around Jerome remains mostly deforested to this day.[100]

Near Jerome, we established a camp at a place called "Hogback," which, like our communities in Camp Verde, served as a source of menial labor. Glenellen Ewell of Jerome told how an "Apache Indian woman" by the name of Susie, and her niece, Maggie, worked for her family. Susie was the wife of Jim Ketchum, one of Crook's scouts. Ewell commented that Susie, who had been educated at Carlisle, was a "beautiful pianist." This did not stop her from having to scrub floors, and Ewell characterized Susie as a "good worker," for whom the "floors weren't cleaned unless scrubbed."[101] Yavapai-Apache women also did considerable domestic work in Clarkdale. Maggie Hayes recalled, "Through the years I . . . worked for many white families in their homes."[102] Jim Byrkit, whose parents came to Clarkdale in 1924 and hired Maggie Hayes to work in their home, stated that she was "beloved by everyone who knew her."[103] Such quaint recollections of harmonious coexistence belie the fact that Yavapai-Apache women were forced to perform backbreaking labor for white families on stolen land in Clarkdale and Jerome.

In the 1910s, while the mines in Jerome thrived, Clarkdale became the industrial center of the Verde Valley. On the land he had purchased there, Clark built his company town (which he naturally named after himself). An admirer of the

City Beautiful movement, Clark hoped that an attractive, planned town would lure better quality workers for the smelter.[104] The smelter began operation in May 1915, and Clark succeeded in constructing a model segregated town. Clarkdale had more electric ranges per capita than any town in America at the time, along with broad streets, a central park with a gazebo, and a clubhouse with a pool and bowling alley. But it also had "Patio Town" for Mexican American workers, and Yavapai and Dilzhe'e camps on the fringes of the planned community.[105] We were not allowed to swim in the pool or bowl in the clubhouse. My grandfather worked as a pinsetter in the bowling alley; our labor was welcome, if not our patronage. Our camps around Clarkdale numbered some four hundred people, with many working at the smelter, performing much of the dangerous work, exposed to toxic fumes resulting from the smelting process.[106] Clarkdale was a monument to American industrial might in the first half of the twentieth century, built on the backs of Yavapai-Apache workers and on Yavapai-Apache land. The Indian camps throughout the Verde Valley demonstrate that the racialization of space and subordination of communities of color were as much at work in smaller, industrializing urban centers as they were in industrial powers like Detroit.

CONCLUSION

By the 1930s, our presence in the Verde Valley was no longer in question. Our communities at Camp Verde, Middle Verde, Rimrock, Clarkdale, and elsewhere spoke to a persistence in the face of urbanization and industrialization. After the passage of the Indian Reorganization Act in 1934, we adopted a tribal constitution and formally organized under the IRA in 1937. As the Yavapai-Apache Tribe—later Nation—of Camp Verde, Arizona, our status as a sovereign Indigenous nation was secured. This nation, however, has existed in a homeland under almost constant transformation by forces of urbanization for some 160 years. From the 1860s to the present, Yavapai-Apaches have confronted an unending stream of settlement, urban growth, and industrialization. The challenges posed by the numerous and growing settler communities in the Verde Valley persist to the present. While in the nineteenth century Yavapai-Apaches suffered murder and removal, in the latter part of the twentieth century we endured Custard's Last Stand, a custard store in Camp Verde, and settler commemorations such as a parade float in the "Fort Verde Days" celebration of 1965 titled "Blood, Sweat, Tears, 1865–1965." The float depicted a minister speaking at the grave of a settler killed by Indians, while a cavalryman stood triumphantly over the body of a dead Indian.[107]

Boynton Canyon. Photograph by Maurice Crandall.

The challenges to our land and sovereignty posed by urbanization persist to the present. Where once industrialization presented the most pressing challenge, increasingly, tourism infringes upon our homelands. In 1902, the federal government established the precursor of Coconino National Forest, which included the Sedona Red Rock Country.[108] Coconino encompasses Boynton Canyon, the place where the log carrying Kamalapukwia (Old Lady White Stone) came to rest after the Great Flood. It is one of our most sacred sites, but it is set aside as a playground for the tourists who flock to Sedona, as well as the city's wealthy residents, many of them second-home owners. Enchantment Resort blocks the most direct route to the canyon. The last weekend of each February, during our Exodus Day commemoration, we remember our removal and return. Enchantment is fairly accommodating, providing an easement to our ceremonial grounds, but the fact remains that we do not exclusively control access to the site.

Similarly, while the Clarkdale smelter closed years ago, a cement plant now abuts the Clarkdale Reservation. Our community cemetery, begun while we were still squatters on UVCC land, actually falls on the cement plant grounds. There is no easement to reach the cemetery, and we must secure permission at the cement plant's guarded entrance to visit our ancestors. Tribal members are sometimes made to wait inordinate amounts of time while our IDs are checked, and we are subjected to the everyday slights of sighs and rolled eyes.[109]

In the final case, Montezuma Well, the place of our emergence, is part of the greater Montezuma Castle National Monument. The site has a long history of settler occupation and desecration. As early as 1870, white ranchers grazed their animals around the well. It became a popular picnicking site for army officers and their families, and in 1883 a squatter living there claimed ownership through squatter's rights. William Back bought the Well in 1888, giving ten cent tours of the ancestral dwellings, with rowboat rides on the water. It was not until 1947 that Congress paid $25,000 for its purchase,[110] and now the National Park Service controls access to the popular tourist site. These kinds of new regulations of space have also come to be the major structures shaping our lives. They, along with growing settler cities, ensure that we retain only small slivers of our traditional territory, and we are barred from exclusive control of important ancestral and ceremonial sites. As other essays in this volume suggest, "Indigenous urbanism" has been a project that we have creatively and resiliently pursued but seldom on our own terms. When the city came to the Indian, it was a violent process that altered the fundamental ways in which we could live and work in our homelands. Yet we have ensured that the city that has come to us remains Indian.

NOTES

1. Archaeologists designate Tuzigoot and Montezuma Castle, located near Camp Verde, Arizona, as coming from the Sinagua people. According to their narrative, Sinaguan people "departed" or disappeared some six hundred years ago; see "History and Culture," Montezuma Castle National Monument, https://www.nps.gov/moca/learn /historyculture/index.htm, accessed September 5, 2019. This narrative erases Yavapai-Apache presence in the Verde Valley. For us, Montezuma Castle and Tuzigoot are important ancestral sites occupied by our ancestors who neither departed nor disappeared.

2. In Apache culture, the ga'an are powerful and sacred spirits who live in the mountains and caves. Ga'an are benevolent spirits, but non-Indians often deemed them evil, even going so far as to call them "devil dancers," and many have been fascinated by them because of their striking appearance. We believe that the ga'an bring gifts, knowledge, and healing to our people through song, ceremony, and dance.

3. This is one of at least three murals depicting the history and culture of the Verde Valley. The other two, one in Cottonwood and the other in Camp Verde, similarly portray the valley's Indigenous peoples as archaic and peripheral.

4. Yavapai population estimates (not including Dilzhe'e Apaches) on the eve of Anglo-American invasion in the 1860s are between two thousand and twenty-five hundred scattered over thousands of square miles. By 1920, the total population of Yavapai County, which includes the Verde Valley and Prescott, was 24,016. Such a figure may seem small, but it represented a significant transformation of our homelands; see Timothy Braatz, *Surviving Conquest: A History of the Yavapai People* (Lincoln: University of Nebraska Press, 2003), 67–68; and "Population of Arizona Counties by Decennial Census: 1900 to 1990," United States Census Bureau, https://www.census.gov/population/cencounts /az190090.txt, accessed July 3, 2018.

5. *A Short History of the Yavapai-Apache Nation* (Camp Verde, Ariz.: Yavapai-Apache Nation Cultural Resource Center, 2007), 23.

6. Vincent Randall (Apache Culture Director, Yavapai-Apache Nation), interviewed by the author, Camp Verde, Ariz., March 21, 2018.

7. Daniel J. Herman, *Rim Country Exodus: A Story of Conquest, Renewal, and Race in the Making* (Tucson: University of Arizona Press, 2012), 7, 9.

8. For the label "Tonto" Apaches, some scholars have argued that "tonto," meaning foolish or stupid in Spanish, was in reference to the dialect of Apache spoken by this band, which other Apaches and Spaniards found more difficult to understand than other Western Apache dialects; see Herman, *Rim Country Exodus*, 32.

9. Mike Harrison and John Williams, *The Oral History of the Yavapai*, ed. Sigrid Khera and Carolina C. Butler (Gilbert, Ariz.: Acacia Publishing, 2012), 3. Yavapais subdivide into four regional groups: Kwevkapayas to the southeast, Yavapés to the northwest, Tolkepayas to the south and west, and Wipukepas in the Verde Valley and Red Rock Country; see Braatz, *Surviving Conquest*, 38. Today most Yavapais are citizens of three nations: the Fort McDowell Yavapai Nation; the Yavapai Prescott Tribe; and the Yavapai-Apache Nation.

10. Maurice Crandall, "Wassaja Comes Home: A Yavapai Perspective on Carlos Montezuma's Search for Identity," *Journal of Arizona History* 55, no. 1 (Spring 2014): 3. My grandfather Ned Russell recalled being sent out by his mother with a slingshot to kill the rats from which she made rat stew. Several elders have told me that it is delicious, but rat preparation seems to be a lost art.

11. Herman, *Rim Country Exodus*, 27.

12. Grenville Goodwin, *The Social Organization of the Western Apache* (Tucson: University of Arizona Press, 1969), 89, 107.

13. Goodwin, *The Social Organization of the Western Apache*, 46–47; Herman, *Rim Country Exodus*, 32.

14. Frieda Ann Eswonia, *Survival of the Yavapai* (Sedona, Ariz.: Sedona Heritage Publishing, Sedona Historical Society, 2015), 11, 18. Even with intermarriage, tribal identities remained strong thanks to matrilineal ties. In both Apache and Yavapai cultures, we owe allegiance to our mother's clan and consider ourselves Yavapai or Apache because of our mother.

15. "The Yavapai-Apache in the Verde Valley," in the "History" section of the official website of the Yavapai-Apache Nation, http://www.yavapai-apache.org/history/, accessed June 28, 2018. Eswonia commented that when outsiders asked Yavapais who they were, they replied, "Abaja," the Yavapai word for *people*. It sounded similar to "Apache," and so Yavapais were mistaken for them; see Eswonia, *Survival of the Yavapai,* 23.

16. Mingus Mountain got its name from the Mingus brothers, who established a camp and sawmill on its slopes in the latter part of the nineteenth century; see Herbert V. Young, *They Came to Jerome: The Billion Dollar Copper Camp* (Jerome, Ariz.: The Jerome Historical Society, 1972), 5.

17. Braatz, *Surviving Conquest,* 54, 57–58; Herman, *Rim Country Exodus,* 37; "The Yavapai-Apache in the Verde Valley." Vincent Randall, Dilzhe'e Apache elder and Apache

Culture Director for the Yavapai-Apache Nation, points out that the turquoise deposits at Mingus Mountain were much more important to Hopis, Dilzhe'es, and Yavapais than copper, even if we did utilize the copper ore. Since copper sulfate indicates the presence of turquoise, he believes Hopis were guiding Spaniards to turquoise deposits, not the shiny yellow metal Spaniards sought. Vincent Randall, interviewed by the author, phone interview, December 14, 2020.

18. Ewing Young and others, including Kit Carson and Bill Williams (from whom the northern Arizona city and mountain take their name), trapped along the Verde in the 1820s.

19. Walker had also been involved in the capture and murder of Mimbreño Apache leader Mangas Coloradas in 1863.

20. Herman, *Rim Country Exodus*, 42.

21. "A Short History of the Yavapai-Apache Nation," 12.

22. Goodwin, *Social Organization,* 49.

23. Fort Whipple, the army base near what would become Prescott, was technically the first territorial capital, designated as such by Congress in 1853. It would be moved to nearby Prescott in 1864.

24. Martha Summerhayes, *Vanished Arizona: Recollections of My Army Life*, ed. Milo Milton Quaife (Chicago: Lakeside Press, 1939), 74–75.

25. Mary A. McCarthy, "Reading Arizona's Valley: Agri-ecology, Industry, Landscape Change, and Public History, 1864–2014" (MA thesis, Northern Arizona University, 2014), 1–3, 39–40.

26. Steve Ayers and the Camp Verde Historical Society, *Images of America: Camp Verde* (Charleston, S.C.: Arcadia Publishing, 2010), 7. Ayers was a longtime journalist in the Verde Valley and is presently the Economic Development Director for the Town of Camp Verde.

27. Harrison and Williams, *The Oral History of the Yavapai*, 80–82.

28. Charles D. Poston to William P. Dole, Commissioner of Indian Affairs, September 30, 1864, *Annual Report of the Commissioner of Indian Affairs, for the Year 1864*, United States, Office of Indian Affairs (Washington, D.C.: Government Printing Office, 1864), 155 [hereafter cited as *Annual Report, year*]. King Woolsey was one of the most infamous Indian-killers in Arizona history. It must also be noted that Woolsey had a Yaqui mistress with whom he fathered a daughter; see Katrina Jagodinsky, *Legal Codes and Talking Trees: Indigenous Women's Sovereignty in the Sonoran and Puget Sound Borderlands, 1854–1946* (New Haven, Conn.: Yale University Press, 2016).

29. Charles D. Poston to William P. Dole, Commissioner of Indian Affairs, September 30, 1864; *Annual Report, 1864*, 156.

30. Herman Ehrenberg to William P. Dole, Commissioner of Indian Affairs, September 25, 1865; *Annual Report, 1865*, 139.

31. Roger Jones, Lt. Col., Assistant Inspector General to Brevet Maj. Gen. R. B. Marcy, Inspector General U.S.A., Washington, July 21, 1869, and General Thomas Devin; quoted by Jones, in *Annual Report, 1869*, 217–18, 221.

32. *A Short History of the Yavapai-Apache Nation*, 13. The army's headquarters at Rio Verde were located at present-day Cottonwood. Those Yavapai-Apaches who surrendered east of the Verde were sent to Rio Verde, while a separate "temporary" reserve was set up at Camp Date Creek near Prescott for those who surrendered on the other side of the mountains that separate the Verde Valley and Prescott. According to Vincent Randall, there were initially more Dilzhe'es at Rio Verde, but more Yavapais arrived after 1873. Camp Date Creek was closed and reverted to public domain in 1874. Vincent Randall interview, December 14, 2020.

33. Thomas E. Sheridan, *Arizona: A History*, rev. ed. (Tucson: University of Arizona Press, 2012), 89.

34. It is difficult to understand why Yavapais and Apaches would agree to scout in campaigns against other Yavapais and Apaches, but it was not a simple matter of being a "race traitor." Yavapais and Apaches scouted for various reasons, including a promise that they would be able to retain some portion of their homelands. Our people often scouted against Yavapais and Apaches from other bands, who were not, technically, "our people." For example, Lucy Satala, a Yavapai-Apache whose father scouted in campaigns against Geronimo's band, recalled, "My father said it was the best time he ever had. He got to run around on the hills looking for him. . . . They found him. They caught Geronimo"; see Pamela Williams, "Lucy Satala: Oldest Living Yavapai in Verde," *Verde Independent*, special issue, "The Story of a People," March 1999, 6.

35. Herman characterized Crook's military tactics as "prolonged massacre"; see *Rim Country Exodus*, 74–75. Thomas Sheridan stated that in the fall of 1872, "the federal government finally unleashed General Crook and his troops"; see Sheridan, *Arizona: A History*, 90.

36. Mike Burns, *The Only One Living to Tell: The Autobiography of a Yavapai Indian*, ed. Gregory McNamee (Tucson: University of Arizona Press, 2012), 6. Hoomothya's first cousin, Wassaja, was also captured during this time and later attained national fame as Carlos Montezuma.

37. John Williams, in Harrison and Williams, *The Oral History of the Yavapai*, 116.

38. Harrison and Williams, *The Oral History of the Yavapai*, 3, 61, 70.

39. William Henry Corbusier, *Record of William Henry Corbusier, Colonel, U.S. Army, Retired*, 1924, AZ 116, University of Arizona Library Special Collections, 18. Yavapais burned the bodies of the deceased; Dilzhe'es did not.

40. In actuality, as Vincent Randall tells me, the headquarters were moved several times. The Rio Verde Agency was first headquartered at Pecks Lake near present-day Clarkdale, was then moved to the site at present-day Cottonwood, and finally moved to Haskell Springs in the foothills of Mingus Mountain; Vincent Randall interview, December 14, 2020.

41. W. S. Schuyler, 2nd Lt., Fifth Cavalry to the Assistant Adjutant-General, Department of Arizona, July 28 1874, in *Annual Report, 1874*, 299; Herman, *Rim Country Exodus*, 97. Our settlement at present-day Cottonwood sat at roughly the same spot as the mural mentioned in the introduction to this chapter. As Vincent Randall explains, Yavapais favored the location at Haskell Springs, while Dilzhe'es preferred a site on the east side of

the Verde near present-day Dead Horse Ranch State Park. Vincent Randall interview, 14 December 2020.

42. Burns, *The Only One Living to Tell*, 67–68.

43. Braatz, *Surviving Conquest*, 161.

44. Braatz, *Surviving Conquest*, 170.

45. *A Short History of the Yavapai-Apache Nation*, 16.

46. Herman, *Rim Country Exodus*, 97–98.

47. Burns, *The Only One Living to Tell*, 70.

48. Corbusier, *Record of William Henry Corbusier*, 31. The trails used were Yavapai-Apache trails, but they were rough and more suited to the healthiest travelers. Vincent Randall relates that some of our people were transported by wagon south through Phoenix first, but the vast majority were made to travel on foot; Vincent Randall interview, December 14, 2020.

49. Williams, "Lucy Satala: Oldest Living Yavapai in Verde," 6.

50. Vincent Randall interview, December 14, 2020.

51. Corbusier, *Record of William Henry Corbusier*, 31.

52. John P. Clum, United States Indian Agent at San Carlos, to Commissioner of Indian Affairs, September 1, 1875, in *Annual Report, 1875*, 215.

53. John P. Clum to Commissioner of Indian Affairs, September 18, 1877, in *Annual Report, 1877*, 34.

54. Order Rescinding the Rio Verde Reserve, Office of Indian Affairs, Department of the Interior, Submitted April 24, 1875, National Archives and Records Administration Documents, Yavapai-Apache Nation Cultural Resource Center Archives, Camp Verde, Arizona (hereafter, YAN-NARA). The Yavapai-Apache Nation is in possession of a series of documents copied from the National Archives and Records Administration in Washington, D.C. and Laguna Niguel. These documents were collected by Tribal Archaeologist Chris Coder and deal with many aspects of our history in the nineteenth and twentieth centuries.

55. Hiram C. Hodge, *Arizona as It Was, 1877* (Chicago: Rio Grande Press, 1962), 150, 148, 114, 175–76. Hodge entered Arizona in 1874, spending several years there.

56. "History of Sedona," City of Sedona official website, http://www.sedonaaz.gov/home/showdocument?id=34040, accessed June 30, 2018.

57. Jeanette Rodda, "Hizzoner, Baking Powder Bill and Rawhide Jimmy: Jerome's Mining History to the Great Depression," in *Experience Jerome and the Verde Valley: Legends and Legacies*, ed. Aliza Cailou (Sedona, Ariz.: Thorne Enterprises, 1990), 122.

58. "Charles Douglas Willard," in *Pioneer Stories of Arizona's Verde Valley*, ed. Bonnie Peplow and Ed Peplow (Camp Verde, Ariz.: Camp Verde Historical Society, 2019), 149–50.

59. Braatz, *Surviving Conquest*, 179–80; Herman, *Rim Country Exodus*, 156–57.

60. Vincent Randall interview, March 21, 2018.

61. H. L. Hart, United States Indian Agent to Commissioner of Indian Affairs, August 1,1878, in *Annual Report, 1878*, 7.

62. Sedgwick Rice, 1st Lt., Seventh Cavalry, Acting Agent to the Commissioner of Indian Affairs, August 24, 1898, in *Annual Report, 1898*, 130.

63. Vincent Randall interview, March 21, 2018. It is noteworthy that Randall repeats the line, "that they could come home." Scouting could be an exciting activity, but it also likely involved some feelings of ambivalence on the part of the Indians. The prospect of being able to return home to the Verde Valley was an even stronger motivator.

64. Maggie Hayes, quoted in Eswonia, *Survival of the Yavapai*, 30.

65. Herman, *Rim Country Exodus*, 157–58.

66. Braatz, *Surviving Conquest*, 186–87.

67. Vincent Randall interview, March 21, 2018.

68. Maggie Hayes, in Eswonia, *Survival of the Yavapai*, 37.

69. Vincent Randall interview, March 21, 2018.

70. Albert L. Myer, Capt., Eleventh Cavalry, Acting Agent to the Commissioner of Indian Affairs, August 25, 1894. Vincent Randall has related to me that acorn gathering has become increasingly difficult in recent decades with the destruction of Emory oak (our preferred acorn source) habitat due to increased settlement and other causes.

71. J. C. Tiffany, United States Indian Agent to the Commissioner of Indian Affairs, September 6, 1881, in *Annual Report, 1881*, 9.

72. John L. Bullis, Capt., Twenty-Fourth Infantry, Acting Indian Agent to the Commissioner of Indian Affairs, August 24, 1888, in *Annual Report, 1888*, 7; Bullis to Commissioner, August 26, 1889, in *Annual Report, 1889*, 122. My great-grandmother Daisy Quesada Russell was born at Cibecue in 1897. She was renowned for her Tulpai-making abilities until her death in 1984.

73. Bullis, *Annual Report, 1888*, 8.

74. John L. Bullis, Capt., Twenty-Fourth Infantry, Acting Indian Agent to the Commissioner of Indian Affairs, October 29, 1890, in *Annual Report, 1890*, 11.

75. W. J. Nicholson, Capt., Seventh Cavalry, Acting Agent to the Commissioner of Indian Affairs, September 12, 1899, in *Annual Report, 1899*, 168. Many Dilzhe'es who would eventually leave San Carlos to return home did not come from the Verde Valley but from other points in the Mogollon Rim country. Many returned to areas around Payson and Gisela, for example.

76. *A Short History of the Yavapai-Apache Nation*, 21.

77. Annual Report for the San Carlos Agency, Adna R. Chaffee, Capt., Sixth Cavalry, Acting Indian Agent, to Commissioner of Indian Affairs, August 11, 1879, in *Annual Report, 1879*, 7; Alphonse Pinart, *Journey to Arizona in 1876* (Los Angeles: Zamoro Club, 1962), 43, 31, 33.

78. "Insights into Yavapai and Apache Culture: Modern Land," interview of Vincent Randall by Judie Piner (manuscript, March 2014), Yavapai-Apache Nation Archives, 1.

79. Luther S. Kelly, United States Indian Agent to the Commissioner of Indian Affairs, August 10, 1904, in *Annual Report, 1904*, 151.

80. *A Short History of the Yavapai-Apache Nation*, 21.

81. Rebecca Smith, "Apache History: Billy Smith," Yavapai-Apache Nation Archives, no date.

82. Gertrude Smith (Yavapai Culture Director, Yavapai-Apache Nation), interviewed by the author, Camp Verde, Ariz., March 19, 2018.

83. *A Short History of the Yavapai-Apache Nation*, 22–23.

84. Harvey Molotch "The City as a Growth Machine: Toward a Political Economy of Place," in *American Journal of Sociology* 82, no. 2 (September 1976): 310.

85. Taylor Gabbard, Superintendent of Camp Verde School to Commissioner of Indian Affairs, July 28, 1911, YAN-NARA, 1. Gabbard gave that date as the "beginning of the Indian day schools at this place."

86. Herman, *Rim Country Exodus*, 182–83.

87. Taylor Gabbard to Commissioner of Indian Affairs, July 24, 1909, YAN-NARA, 2.

88. Taylor Gabbard to the Commissioner of Indian Affairs, September 17, 1910, YAN-NARA, 2.

89. Taylor Gabbard to Commissioner of Indian Affairs, July 28, 1911, YAN-NARA, 3.

90. Herman, *Rim Country Exodus*, 183–84.

91. Molotch, "The City as a Growth Machine," 314–15, 317.

92. Annual Report of the Camp Verde Indian School, fiscal year 1911, August 15, 1911. Submitted by Taylor Gabbard, YAN-NARA, 13.

93. George Hance to Senator Henry Ashurst, May 10, 1913, YAN-NARA, 6–7, 9.

94. Carl Nightingale, "Spatial Segregation and Neighborhoods," in *Oxford Research Encyclopedia of American History* (March 2, 2015), 6, accessed May 23, 2021, https://doi .org/10.1093/acrefore/9780199329175.013.62

95. Statement of Mr. Jacob Webber, of Camp Verde, Arizona, March 16, 1914, YAN-NARA, 1.

96. "Letter to Hon. Henry F. Ashurst, Washington, D.C., from petitioners from Camp Verde, Arizona, against the proposed removal of Indians from the locality," March 17, 1913, YAN-NARA.

97. While we had always lived in both places, the Clarkdale Yavapai-Apache Reservation was not officially established until 1969.

98. Jeanette Rodda, "Hizzoner, Baking Powder Bill and Rawhide Jimmy," 124–34.

99. Vincent Randall interview, March 21, 2018.

100. Young, *They Came to Jerome*, 7.

101. Nancy R. Smith, "Jerome's Billion Dollar Boom, Bustle and Bust: 1898 to the Present," in Cailou, *Experience Jerome and the Verde Valley*, 240. Vincent Randall says that Jim Ketchum, who became an Indian policeman for our people after his scouting days, was adept at catching criminals. He was so good that people would say that he could always "catch 'em," thereby receiving the name "Ketchum"; Vincent Randall interview, December 14, 2020.

102. Maggie Hayes in Eswonia, *Survival of the Yavapai*, 54.

103. Jim Byrkit, "Remembering Clarkdale: The Story of an Arizona Smelter Town, 1910 to 1950" (manuscript), Clarkdale Historical Society and Museum Archives, 15.

104. "City Beautiful Movement," exhibit at Clarkdale Historical Society and Museum.

105. Rodda, "Hizzoner, Baking Powder Bill and Rawhide Jimmy," 132–34.

106. Jim Byrkit, "Remembering Clarkdale," 14. This was not our only experience with large-scale industrial works. Many of our people worked on Roosevelt Dam, completed in 1911. Originally called Tonto Dam, it was the largest artificial dam in the world at

that time, costing over $10 million. President Theodore Roosevelt considered it one of his administration's two great accomplishments, the other being the Panama Canal. Yavapais and Apaches "made up many of the work crews who would build this monument to Anglo progress"; see Sheridan, *Arizona: A History*, 215–17. We also worked on the flume at Fossil Creek, and on various road projects. My great-grandfather, Henry Russell, worked on the road from Flagstaff to Lee's Ferry on the Colorado River. He was a mule skinner. The entire family went with him, and my grandfather recalled wandering the countryside as a boy, living in a tent, and the family cooking their meals on fires as Henry worked on the road; see Crandall, "The Early Life of Ned Russell," 10–11. Clarkdale's racial and economic segregation also affected Mexican Americans, who primarily lived in the portions of Clarkdale known as Centerville and Patio Town.

107. Ayers and the Camp Verde Historical Society, *Images of America: Camp Verde*, 79, 122.

108. "History of Sedona," City of Sedona, http://www.sedonaaz.gov/home/showdocument?id=34040, accessed June 30, 2018. The change to Coconino came in 1908.

109. The cement plant is operated by Salt River Materials Group, an enterprise of the Salt River Pima Maricopa Indian Community. This instance of the urbanization and industrialization in Clarkdale is made all the more bitter since a fellow tribal nation operates the cement plant.

110. Rod Timanus, *Images of America: Montezuma Castle National Monument* (Charleston, S.C.: Arcadia Publishing, 2014), 97–98.

PART III

BUILDING COMMUNITY IN TWENTIETH-CENTURY INDIAN CITIES

ELAINE MARIE NELSON

7

MNI LUZAHAN AND "OUR BEAUTIFUL CITY"

Indigenous Resistance in the Black Hills up to 1937

In the summer of 1904 hundreds of Lakota, Cheyenne, and Crow men, women, and children gathered for the heralded "Council of Nations" in Rapid City on grounds not far from the U.S. Indian Boarding School. Months earlier tribal leaders announced they would hold an intertribal meeting in the South Dakota town on July 4 to discuss "the Indian in his present condition and his needs for the future." Local newspapers quoted Native peoples who lived in Rapid City on their immediate concerns about citizenship and education: "What is the use of our sending children to school and giving them a literary education," Native leaders asked, if they do not become "equal to the whites" for the purposes of gaining the rights of American citizenship?[1]

Native American men and women strategically used the timing of a summer holiday and the platform of the city to deliver their protestations against continued federal and state land theft, lack of employment opportunities and citizenship, and poor economic conditions. Some Lakotas also used the event to

meet with lawyers to discuss ongoing treaty inquiries against the illegal settlement of the Black Hills. Immediately following the opening events on July 4,
Yellow Owl, a respected leader from Cheyenne River Reservation, delivered
a forceful speech laced with a scathing review of how the federal government
and white citizens treated Indians. "In the early day—the Indians were all over
the country, but have been pushed back until now they are on reservations,"
he said. Yellow Owl was pleased to see so many Indians joined together in that
moment "to tell the white people" that "they have given up the fish ponds and
game lands. . . . You white people have all the coal, timber, minerals, etc.—
while the Indians have nothing left except what is on reservations." Yellow Owl
also accused the federal government of forcing Native children to attend the
boarding school in Rapid City without providing them with adequate training
for employment upon graduation: "Whites have not done what they promised
and that is why Indians are now poor."[2]

Unfortunately, Indigenous calls for change and resilience fell upon the deaf
ears of Rapid City's majority white population. Energized by the opportunity to
boost tourism, the Rapid City Board of Trade instead exploited the intertribal
event as an economic opportunity for the city. They agreed that the "Council
of Nations," as it was then called, would draw a large crowd and they tried to
co-opt the event as a tourist attraction through aggressive advertising, fundraising, and planning for a grand "Independence Day." White organizers admitted
that a concentrated presence of American Indian nations for the event would
benefit the town. The Council of Nations, they boasted, "made it possible to
secure the best of speakers of the west on this occasion," and reported that local
grocery stores and suppliers would make a lot of money from the event. They
also knew visitors were particularly drawn to the fabricated "wild west" experience that dominated white views of defeated or vanished Native Americans
and resulted in the expansion of tourism as a major pillar of settler colonialism
in the Black Hills.[3] This response reflected both the tumultuous history and
controversial future of the mistreatment of Native peoples in Rapid City and
throughout South Dakota.[4]

Despite clear attempts to hijack the Council of Nations, this 1904 event
was the first of many small and large-scale intertribal gatherings organized by
Indians in Rapid City in the twentieth century. It is symbolic of the ways that
Indigenous people used urban spaces to form coalitions and to resist the erasure
of their continual presence and the structural legacy of settler colonialism that
seeped into the Black Hills. While they represented different tribal nations, each

with their own unique treaties, their struggles to survive were the same. Faced with the trauma of land dispossession, child removal, warfare, disease, cultural suppression, incarceration, and inadequate housing, health, and living conditions, Indigenous people in and around Rapid City ultimately devised multiple strategies to utilize metropolitan communities, push for reform, and claim their rights to the land. Rapid City's Indian population proved they could be effective in protesting these conditions through their connections to the tourism industry and alliances with non-Native institutions. Their insistence on remaining on their treaty lands while the city formed all around them was one mechanism through which they built access to the media, legal services, employment, and their children at the boarding school. Although Rapid City's Native American population is often viewed through the lens of post–World War II migrations, the Red Power Movement of the 1960s–70s, and the Rapid City Flood of 1972, this essay examines their enduring legacy to combat removal, marginalization, and racial discrimination up to the 1930s.[5]

INDIGENOUS BLACK HILLS

More than sixty Indigenous tribes trace their people to travels or homes in the Black Hills. This includes (but is not limited to) the Mandan, Cheyenne, Crow, Kiowa, Na'isha Apache, Arapaho, Hidatsa, Lakota, Dakota, Nakota, Sutaio, Arikara, Ponca, Shoshone, Padouca Apache, and Comanche nations. The Black Hills are known as Pahésabe ("Black Hills" in the Omaha and Ponca language), Xó-kó-qòp ("Black Rocks Mountains" in the Kiowa language), Moxtavhohona ("Black Hills" in the Cheyenne language), and He Sapa ("Black Mountains" or "Black Hills" in the Lakota language). The Black Hills is an intertribal meeting place where multiple nations gathered for trade, councils, ceremonies, hunting, and prayer. It remains one of many landmarks that connects the plains surrounding the Rocky Mountains and Missouri River.[6]

Research conducted in the late 1880s concludes that this place once hosted a reportedly sprawling "Indian City" with carefully lined streetways that housed a population larger than 15,000 people. More research on this finding, published in 1915, estimated that "if standing today" this Indian city "would outnumber in population the largest municipality in either of the Dakotas" (South Dakota's largest municipal population in 1910 was 14,000 and in 1920 was 25,000).[7]

For centuries Indigenous tribes met, camped, and traveled the creek known in the Lakota language as Mni Luzahan. Named for its "fast water," Mni Luzahan stretches over eighty miles and connects the flat plains of the Cheyenne River with the lush valleys and towering canyon walls of the interior Black Hills. The rapid waters of the creek were said to never freeze over, and the interior canyon walls blocked blistering winds to offer shelter to Lakotas and other tribes during the harsh winter months. Mni Luzahan holds cultural and sacred significance to Lakota peoples and became a well-known tributary in the region's vast trade networks between tribes. By the late eighteenth century white trappers permanently altered these economic ties in the plains and Rocky Mountains. Structural changes transfigured the Black Hills when missionaries, explorers, and scientists traveled there more frequently in the 1850s. These outsiders referred to the fresh-water trail into the Black Hills as "Rapid Creek."[8]

Violations to the Fort Laramie Treaties of 1851 and 1868, which resulted in the Black Hills settler rush of 1874–79, occasioned war and dispossession of ancestral lands. White, African American, and Chinese populations poured illegally into the Hills. Despite their status as trespassers on Native land, settlers and laborers formed mining and agricultural enclaves and established townsites that steadily grew. To prevent further incursion, Lakotas—sometimes with the reluctant support of the U.S. military, compelled by federal obligations—defended the borders of their land. But settler numbers only increased.

In February of 1876, a group of settlers drew lots near Mni Luzahan and identified their community as "Rapid City," taking the name of the nearby creek.[9] Within three weeks, Lakota warriors attacked the illegal encampment and protested the U.S. encroachment in the Black Hills through the summer and fall months. Their attempts to thwart the U.S. invasion of the Black Hills became futile, especially after their stirring defeat of Lt. Col. George Armstrong Custer and the Seventh Calvary in June 1876. The aftermath of this intertribal victory resulted in widespread anger among military personnel, politicians, and Anglo citizens seeking revenge. U.S. Congressmen devised a once-and-for-all strategy to take the Black Hills and remove Indians from the land, threatening tribal leaders with removal and starvation. Surrounded by military forces and placed under extreme duress, 230 representatives from the Arikara, Cheyenne, Yanktonai, Santee, and Lakota signed the Agreement of 1876. Congress promptly passed this agreement as the Act of 1877 and, in a stunning act of imperial aggression and criminality, stripped 7.7 million acres of land away from the Oceti Sakowin. This included the Black Hills and Mni Luzahan. Leo Weasel Bear (Hunkpapa Sioux), recalled, "We signed this treaty against our wishes, being treated like little children" with threats.[10]

THE CITY COMES TO THE CREEK

Despite hostile treatment and attitudes toward the tribes in Dakota Territory, Lakotas migrated in and out of the Hills, with and without permission from reservation agents. On their way to hunt, hold ceremonies, and cut lodgepoles, they continued to seasonally migrate along Mni Luzahan. The "Rapid City" camp settlement grew quickly and became the seat of Pennington County, Dakota Territory's newest county in 1877. Two years later white settlers in the town claimed it as the "New Denver" of the West that boasted a post office, coach service, newspaper, and school. The three hundred townspeople held a July Fourth parade, with businesses and organizations displaying floats with statements directed at Indians living along Mni Luzahan. Banners chillingly read, "We Conquer to Save," "By Industry We Thrive," "God and Country," and "We Are Here to Stay." White Rapid City settlers "tolerated" their proximity to Native families that resided on the creek. This is likely because the U.S. military troops at nearby Fort Meade served as cover, as they were trained to "protect Black Hills settlements from hostile Indians" and target any of their attempts to make "unauthorized" visits to the Black Hills.[11] Eventually, military and political leaders in Dakota Territory used Rapid City as a hub to establish "home guards" to control, intimidate, and even attack Native tribes in the area. Known as "part cowboy militia," the armed group of men ambushed a village of Native men and women at Cuny Table, killed a hunting group at Buffalo Gap (on and near the Pine Ridge Reservation, respectively), and spread terror across the land.[12]

Rapid City struggled to develop, largely because it lacked a steady economic infrastructure early on. Businesses and investors were attracted to other Black Hills towns like Deadwood, Lead, Spearfish, Buffalo Gap, and Hot Springs, which had booming mining, farming, and warm water springs. Rapid City also lacked a direct railroad line, due to its peripheral location that bordered Indigenous reservation land. But the town benefitted from its prosperous neighboring communities and served to support the exploitation of gold, tin, and lumber. The Rapid City Light and Gas Company and George Hearst's Homestake Mining Corporation were the first of many businesses to dam Mni Luzahan on separate banks of the creek, powering both a steam plant and an ore-reduction mill. The dams created Canyon Lake, which town boosters promoted as a resort-like setting to compete with tourism businesses in Hot Springs and Sylvan Lake. The Lamphere-Henrichs Lumber Company (which became the Warren-Lamb

Mni Luzahan (Rapid Creek) in the Dark Canyon interior of the Black Hills, west of Rapid City, South Dakota. South Dakota State Historical Society, South Dakota Digital Archives (2008-07-22-011).

Lumber Company in 1914) purchased land on the north banks of Mni Luzahan to build sawmills and cut timber for the growing demands of gold mining and serviced the "multiple use" method adopted by the Black Hills National Forest in 1897. This ultimately turned Rapid City into a major conveyer of resources in and out of the Black Hills, through railways and roads that crisscrossed Mni Luzahan over one hundred times.[13]

The Sioux Agreement of 1889 divided Lakota agencies into separate reservations, stole more Native land, and brashly cleared the path for South Dakota statehood, homestead filings, and railroad expansion. In the earliest stages of this land seizure, U.S. commissioners met unified resistance from Lakotas. In the 1880s they visited the Pine Ridge agency to discuss another round of land concessions. One Lakota leader spoke directly to a commissioner present at the previous land negotiations: "We all know you," he said. "You are the old thief that stole the Black Hills from us in 1877. You are the biggest liar in America."[14]

Looking west toward the Rapid City Indian School from the elevated "Hangman's Hill" in Rapid City, South Dakota, c. 1905. Mni Luzahan (Rapid Creek) is visible in the foreground. South Dakota State Historical Society, South Dakota Digital Archives (2009-02-03-001).

RAPID CITY BOARDING SCHOOL AND THE ECONOMICS OF CHILD SEPARATION

Even after this so-called "land rush," Rapid City's white population did not grow. So they looked at other ways to bring people (and money) to their settlement. In 1893 influential town leaders, reservation superintendents, and South Dakota politicians lobbied the Commissioner of Indian Affairs to establish a federal Indian Boarding School in the Black Hills. The proposal had an economic incentive for Rapid City's white residents, who knew a government-funded school would bring employment and development to their now-sagging community. Rapid City's mayor believed the school would force large enrollments of Native children from plains reservations. He was "confident that the Indians at Pine Ridge and Rosebud agencies would much prefer to have their children attend school at Rapid City" instead of sending them further away east or south.[15] The Office of Indian Affairs initially denied the request but approved it three years later. The government purchased 1,200 acres of land for $3,000 on the western bank of Mni Luzahan just outside of Rapid City. Construction began in 1897 and the Rapid City Indian Boarding School opened in 1898 with fifty Native children from Pine Ridge, Cheyenne River, and Wind River Reservations. The first two students were siblings Nora and Oscar Ammiott from Pine Ridge. One decade after they arrived, Rapid City's non-Native population more than doubled. In the early twentieth century the boarding school expanded with new buildings to accommodate increased enrollment, and by 1910 it housed 250 Indian children. Rapid City locals, which included whites and African Americans, celebrated the new school, upholding the child separations as just the remedy for the town's dwindling settlement.[16]

Young Native children at the school pulled a larger American Indian population into Rapid City. Native families from South Dakota, Montana, and Wyoming reservations migrated to the town to be physically closer to their children. Some moved there permanently. Others, like the grandparents of Dakota intellectual and novelist Dr. Elizabeth Cook-Lynn from the Crow Creek Sioux Tribe, migrated there only during the spring, summer, and fall months. Cook-Lynn, whose father was taken to the Rapid City Indian School when he was four, was born and raised in Fort Thompson, South Dakota, on the Crow Creek Reservation. She recalls how her grandparents traveled over 200 miles to be closer to him: "My grandparents would get in their wagon, come way out there from Fort Thompson to Rapid City, and camp there from the time school started until the snow came to get a glimpse of their children. They weren't allowed to go into the school and see them. But they would get a glimpse of their children. Then, when the snow came, they would go back to Fort Thompson."[17]

At the school Native girls and boys faced verbal abuse and corporal punishment, which included draconian discipline (forced marching while chained), spanking, and hitting. Employees who deployed these crude means were often fired or replaced. Yet such sanctions on the part of school administrators did little to discourage homesick and abused children from running away. The children had a set summer break from the school. In June, many of their families waited eagerly for the youth to complete their end of the year program, which was a formal event open to all Rapid City residents—Indian, African American, and white. During their break, some moved into the Black Hills (for ceremonies), some remained in their camp along Mni Luzahan, and others returned to their reservations. Even their break from school was threatened by disciplinary strategies, a tactic school administrators used to deter the children from running away. There was very little evidence that this worked, as runaways persisted, even at the risk of exposure to the elements, bodily harm, and death.[18]

Families that followed their children to Rapid City continued their tradition of residing along Mni Luzahan. In the spring, summer, and fall they found seasonal employment with local and area businesses, ranchers, and farmers, and in the railroad and mining industries. Even Native people who did not have connections to the boarding school moved to Rapid City for access to steady, seasonal employment. Several graduates from the boarding school, who found themselves grappling with the trauma of separation from their tribes, stayed in Rapid City for work or enrolled in the local business college. While a younger generation of adults took up residency in the city, they maintained strong connections to their reservation communities. Their family ties brought additional migrations of Indians from reservations to Rapid City. The American Indian population in the city grew steadily in the early twentieth century because of the multiple challenges that plagued South Dakota's reservations. In 1905 the superintendent of the boarding school observed that "there is usually a considerable Indian population at or near Rapid City" who worked for two or two and a half dollars a day, which was "better than they can do on the reservation." Lack of employment, reductions in rations, disease, poverty, struggles with land ownership and allotment, and constant scrutiny from reservation agents who restricted dancing, giveaways, and other ceremonies vital to their lives, were among their many challenges.[19]

NATIVE AMERICANS IN RAPID CITY TOURISM

White residents and visitors from Rapid City and other Black Hills towns did not hesitate to exploit American Indians if it boosted tourism. They did not want to create a town that offered inclusivity to Rapid City's Native population, but they did view them as vital to the town's competition in the growing Black Hills tourism market. In 1893, on the heels of the killing of hundreds of Lakota men, women, and children at the Wounded Knee Massacre in 1890, Rapid City boosters convinced Indian families living along Mni Luzahan to dance for the town's visitors in the commercial district and outside of hotels. In 1894 the manager of the public library hired a group of Native dancers and musicians to perform in the library hall. This event was so popular that they repeated their performance for large audiences and received "a small profit" (likely food or other provisions) for their work.[20] Through the 1890s multiple "Indian curio shops" opened in Rapid City and other Black Hills communities. Townspeople and visitors perused the inventory of these businesses, which prominently displayed and sold beads, belts, headdresses, clothing, arrowheads, baskets, and other items that white settlers stole off Native bodies while scavenging massacre sites and battlegrounds.[21]

These demands for entertainment and relics continued for decades, as whites continued to find ways to profit from the emerging myth of Western conquest. The Western South Dakota Stock Growers' Association meeting, held intermittently in Rapid City, hired Native peoples from the town and reservations to perform in their annual show. In 1903 the event drew thousands of people to Rapid City. Indians participated in (segregated) rodeo competitions and horse races as well as sham wagon and stagecoach hold-ups. The planners of the event were pleased and touted the participation of Native men and women: "The events were all interesting, and were witnessed by thousands. . . . Eastern people who were here were much pleased with the Indian war dances and parades." The town also held a large Fourth of July celebration that summer. Five hundred Indians from Cheyenne River, Pine Ridge, and other reservations participated in the races, parade, and dances. They held their own dances at their camp and collected donations to help defray their living and travel expenses.[22]

While Rapid City's boosters strove to cast American Indians as carnival and carnivalesque characters for crowds of tourists, tribes across South Dakota and Montana focused on defending their land and rights as citizens. In the early twentieth century Indigenous resistance increased as they continued to combat the theft of the Black Hills and watched homesteaders take more and more of their land. In 1903 a delegation of Oglalas, led by American Horse, traveled to Washington, D.C., to "make a protest about a lot of things and incidentally demand their rights" of President Roosevelt. More specifically, they presented a petition that addressed the issue of the loss of the Black Hills and the price that the federal government paid for it. Washington officials called it the "very best treaty ever made with the Indians." They returned President Roosevelt's remarks with a "look of disgust." Immediately following their visit, a delegation from the Yankton Nation visited to protest boarding schools, lack of employment, and corruption of land leases. They left after receiving a similar lecture from elected officials. In 1904, a mere three weeks before tribes in South Dakota announced the Council of Nations to take place in Rapid City, Roosevelt announced he would sign the "Rosebud Bill." This law confiscated 416,000 acres of land from the Rosebud Reservation, without taking a care for obtaining the legal requirement of three-fourths adult male signatures from the tribe. Again,

Rapid City residents wrongly believed claims that the law would spark "one of the largest land rushes in years."[23]

Rapid City's Native population used the town to create their own gatherings and circumvent federal interference. But they orchestrated such events under the guise of entertainment for white residents and tourists. The town's proximity to plains and mountain tribes and the existence of the boarding school made it an ideal location and central hub for intertribal meetings throughout the twentieth century. Tribes from across the region were not, of course, eager to perform sham battles and dances on command for white tourists. But they *were* motivated to gather, converse, and strategize over the issues that directly impacted their nations, on and off their reservations. Tribal organizers knew that scheduling these meetings around summer holidays (such as the Fourth of July) would appeal to tourists' desires to see "real live Indians" and town leaders who sought a seasonal boost to their economy. One of the most important benefits for Native organizers is that by performing in these events, Indian families could make extra money to cover travel and living costs and attend important intertribal councils.[24]

The 1904 Council of Nations marked their first attempt at organizing such a gathering within the confining limits of Rapid City's exploitative tourism industry. In the week leading up to the meeting, thousands of Indians from Montana, Wyoming, North Dakota, and South Dakota arrived in Rapid City and resided along a nearly two-mile stretch of Mni Luzahan. They, along with the Indian population that lived in the city, delivered a resolution: "Shortly before the Fourth of July of each year the three hundred children who attend the government school at this place are given three months vacation, which brings the parents from the various agencies here to Rapid City in order that they may take their children home for vacation time. As a result there is of necessity a large number of Indians here." In the early planning stages of the event, the Indians "ask and insist that they be accorded a reception worthy the day and occasion."[25]

Over the next two decades Rapid City did not concentrate on job creation for American Indians, and instead poured energy into fine-tuning its tourism attractions, civic infrastructure, and economy. Indians sought more employment than the Black Hills tourism industry could offer, but very few businesses in Rapid City would hire Indians. Farrar & Jepsen (a real estate company), the Warren-Lamb Lumber Company, the Missouri River and Northwestern Railroad, and the Rapid City Indian School were some of the few places where

Native Americans employed to perform in front of the International Hotel in Rapid City on the corner of Main and Sixth Streets, 1893. William J. Collins Collection, Leland D. Case Library for Western Historical Studies, Black Hills State University, Spearfish, South Dakota (#881).

Representatives from Pine Ridge, Rosebud, and Cheyenne River meet in 1911 with federal and local leaders south of the U.S. Indian School in Rapid City to outline their protests to the 1876 and 1889 agreements, which violated the 1868 Fort Laramie Treaty. Minnilusa Historical Association, Rapid City, South Dakota (#P02064).

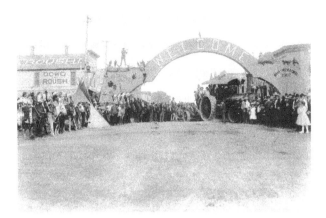

Native Americans, to the left of the archway, were employed to perform in Rapid City's Railroad Jubilee in 1907. The "Welcome Arch," built in the early 1900s, was a tourist symbol to brand Rapid City as the "Gate City" or "Gateway" to the Black Hills. On the left, where Native Americans posed, the arch reads, "As We Found It, 1876." On the right, where settlers posed, the arch reads, "What We Made It, 1907." William J. Collins Collection, Leland D. Case Library for Western Historical Studies, Black Hills State University, Spearfish, South Dakota (#495).

Native Americans employed to perform in a Rapid City parade on the north side of Main Street between Sixth and Seventh Streets for the 1907 Western Stock Growers' Association Meeting. William J. Collins Collection, Leland D. Case Library for Western Historical Studies, Black Hills State University, Spearfish, South Dakota (#367).

Indians living in the city found stable employment. Some local retail and shop employers sought to hire the young women graduates from the Indian School because of their reputation for cleanliness and order.[26]

Some Native people who lived in Rapid City both seasonally and permanently agreed to labor for the tourism industry as performers in sham battles, horse races, and parades held for the town's growing tourist market (at the Stock Grower's and Stockmen's celebrations, Rapid City Railroad Jubilee, Alfalfa Palace rodeo and fairs, and other events). They did this on the condition that they receive wages, supplies, provisions, grazing lands, access to water, and campgrounds where they could meet. Some said they were eager to return to Mni Luzahan for work and gatherings. In 1907 Yellow Owl wrote Mayor Emrick to offer work for pay in the tourism venue: "I want to let you know the Cherry Creek peoples are ready to pick up their children at the school . . . about 50 wagons will arrive in Rapid City where they will have a celebration."[27]

During the city's events American Indians, and particularly Lakota leaders, met formally and informally to discuss the issues they faced both on and off their reservations, including the Black Hills claim. To this effect, reservation officials started to discourage future gatherings—big or small—of nations who wished to discuss their grievances toward the federal government. Major John R. Brennan, agent at Pine Ridge Reservation and self-proclaimed founder of Rapid City, warned Washington officials that "there is danger of an Indian war if the councils being held throughout the Sioux nation . . . are allowed to continue." Brennan was compelled to contact his superiors because "three thousand desperate, hungry Indians with a grievance real or fancied, are a host to be reckoned with."[28] But Lakotas remained bold in the face of reservation-wide restrictions on meetings and called upon white lawmakers to assist their pursuit of legal recourse.

URBAN INDIAN CONDITIONS IN RAPID CITY

Rapid City grew slowly and by 1920 still had fewer than six thousand residents.[29] Unfortunately, it is unlikely that American Indians were represented in this number despite the hundreds (and later thousands) who lived there year-round. In the 1910s Native peoples created permanent homes for themselves in clustered camps along the Mni Luzahan. Rapid City's white residents complained about Indians' disorderly misconduct and other inconveniences, such as the destruction that Indian ponies brought to residential lawns. As their community grew along the creek's path, Indians concentrated near Osh Kosh Street.[30]

Problems of disease also took place in the camps, especially with reliance on Mni Luzahan as the main water source. The creek supplied drinking water for the boarding school, but it also powered mills and factories for the Black Hills Light and Power Company and Homestake Mine. Both corporations were known for polluting waterways throughout the Black Hills. The Indian camps along Mni Luzahan were often plagued by diseases, including smallpox and tuberculosis. In 1918 Cyril Weazel, a baby less than two years old, died at the Indian camp, likely of the Spanish flu.[31] With the entire city on lockdown amidst the Spanish flu epidemic, the *Rapid City Journal* reported the disease was "in worse form" at the Indian School "than it has been at any other place" as it invaded the population of children boarding at the school. Even with over a hundred cases, as the paper assured its readers, "time will make everything all right there." Despite this, Jennie Pretends Eagle (Standing Rock), Nicholas Eaglehorn (Rosebud), and Adolph Bissonette (Pine Ridge) are some of the children who died from the disease in October 1918.[32]

Other issues of injustice at the Indian Camp, later known more formally as the Osh Kosh Camp, emerged. In 1924 the Rapid City police targeted it for illegal gambling. The town also created cruel jokes that centered on the stereotypes of Native Americans and dog meat. One citizen commented on the city's need to round up stray dogs. "After that," he said, "we'll dispose of them by shooting, killing, or giving them to the Indians." The dogs "might find their way into the Indian camp on Rapid Creek with the suggestion that the canines would make juicy soup bones." Despite the obvious racism that targeted the Osh Kosh Camp (which was located on land later owned by the Warren-Lamb Lumber Co.) it grew as more Native people unsuccessfully sought housing in Rapid City.[33]

Despite the horrific conditions they faced on reservations and in Rapid City, Lakotas continued to work through legal channels to challenge the Black Hills land case. In the 1910s they drafted their list of grievances against the federal government. They worked with the Society of American Indians (organized in 1911 by Native leaders across the country, including Chauncey Yellow Robe and Henry Standing Bear, who resided in Rapid City) to lobby politicians "for legislation allowing the Court of Claims jurisdiction over Indians claims." They repeatedly pursued these efforts through active lobbying and commissions until, finally, the Office of Indian Affairs agreed to their requests. In 1920, Congress allowed the Lakota nation to seek and hire an attorney in order to properly file with the Court of Claims. In June 1923 their lawyer, Ralph Case, submitted their claim.[34] Quietly the following year, and through the careful persuasions of a

U.S. Representative from Rapid City, Congress passed legislation that allowed for the sale of 3.95 acres of Rapid City land to private land owners. This was the first of three laws that would appropriate land from the Rapid City Indian School, property that should have been distributed to tribes according to later federal policies.[35]

In the 1920s and 1930s Rapid City emerged as an active hub of Indigenous activity connected to the growth of tourism venues throughout the Black Hills. Native men, women, and children from Rapid City and nearby reservations performed as employees in pageants, rodeos, and parades in the towns of Custer, Lead, Belle Fourche, and Hot Springs, as well as the nearby Dark Canyon Resort. In 1926, Rapid City resident Rosebud Yellow Robe traveled to Deadwood to write the first draft of a pageant later known as the "Deadwood Days of '76 Pageant."[36] As the eldest daughter of Chauncey Yellow Robe, the Indian School Superintendent, she attended Rapid City's public schools throughout her life before becoming involved in performance art and music as a teenager and young adult. In 1927 she became famous overnight for bestowing President Calvin Coolidge with a feather headdress at the Deadwood Days of '76 tourist event, during the summer when Coolidge made Rapid City his summer White House.[37] (Her father, once a staunch opponent of Native people performing in wild west shows, stood at her side for the duration of the event.) In the 1930s a group of Rapid City Indians who danced in front of Duhamel's supply store formed an enclave to write and perform the "Sioux Indian Pageant" at Duhamel's Sitting Bull Crystal Caverns (located not far from Rapid City). As tourism continued to boom, Custer State Park, Mount Rushmore National Monument, and Wind Cave National Park hired Native peoples to perform in various encampments at popular Black Hills sites. Like Yellow Owl's in 1904, many of these performances asserted the Lakota Nation's rights to their land. While locals exploited them as a boon to their bottom lines, the strong Native presence disrupted settler notions of their disappearance or irrelevance in the Black Hills.[38]

RESISTANCE AND REFORM IN THE CITY

In the spring of 1929 Henry Standing Bear, Oglala Lakota leader and founding member of the Society of American Indians, announced that the "Council of American Indians" would take place in Rapid City. In April and May Standing Bear, along with representatives from a dozen tribes, met with the Chamber of Commerce to plan the event. They all emphasized that the "general council of American Indians is to be a serious event, not one which the Indians are used for show purposes." They planned to discuss several "matters of importance" including the Black Hills claims and conditions facing Indian populations on and off reservations. Standing Bear proclaimed, "The time is at hand that such a council, or conference should be held by the Indians themselves to discuss the most important questions"—of education, health conditions, employment, and agriculture. Robert High Eagle, Hunkpapa Lakota teacher and consultant, was elected chairman of the meeting. He also pushed for the council to consider the issue of the Black Hills claim as an important discussion point for the gathering. "If anyone thinks the Sioux Indians, who conquered six tribes and drove them out of the Black Hills after years of bloody warfare, have approved the government's consideration of the Black Hills treaty," High Eagle countered, "they are mistaken."[39]

The selection of Rapid City as the location for the gathering was strategic. High Eagle explained, "Everyone knows the Black Hills is the most beautiful region . . . with thousands of persons gathered here for the council and rodeo, they will see the Hills and then the value of such a wonderful region will be brought home to them, aiding in directing public opinion to the Indian's cause." In the last week of June wagon trains and carloads from dozens of tribal nations around the country arrived to form an "Indian City" in the Black Hills. Groups of Hopi, Diné, Ute, Osage, Kiowa, Crow, Arapaho, Cheyenne, and Anishinaabe arrived in full force for the meeting. They set up camps in the city's Alfalfa Palace and spread outside of the facility along Mni Luzahan and near the Osh Kosh Camp. Organizers invited federal delegates including vice president Charles Curtis, Office of Indian Affairs representatives, and South Dakota's state and national delegates. The tribes also invited President Coolidge. Ultimately, only two U.S. Senators and three Congressmen attended. Holding their event in Rapid City required negotiations with the Chamber of Commerce. In exchange for free campgrounds, supplies, and provisions, the meeting organizers agreed to hold a parade and participate in horse racing for prize money. They also lobbied Custer State Park to donate elk and buffalo from the park's herd. The Chamber of Commerce requested that whites be allowed to "tour" their campgrounds. Tribal leaders agreed, but they insisted that reporters and attendees understood that the council meetings were real, and not to be treated as a show.[40]

This request fell on deaf ears and tensions with Black Hills tourism operators once again sparked. With an economic boost on the horizon, Rapid City tourism officials bounced into action to profit from the gathering. They ordered five hundred spare tire covers that advertised the summer event with a "picture of an Indian chief in warpath regalia." They circulated seventy-five thousand one-of-a-kind colored advertising folders to central and eastern states to promote the event and placed "Indian signs" as trail markers on highways to guide tourists in the direction of the city. The advertising was patently racist, with one local white resident suggesting residents all lock up their dogs, for fear they would be eaten by Indians who arrived for the gathering.[41] Rapid City business owners and boosters claimed the event would "bring more crowds to the Hills than anything else at the time, and everyone will benefit directly from the celebration." Regardless of their anticipation, Native leaders like High Eagle reminded them: the council is serious and "for the Indians," but the rodeo will "be for the white people."[42]

As the council met, they immediately prioritized the issues at hand. There was plenty of passionate discussion of the Black Hills treaty and other land claims, as some spokesmen "prepared protests against the government's part in treaties signed when the west was being settled."[43] But this was tabled in favor of issues of more pressing concern. One was education and the subject of the Rapid City Indian School. The council vehemently objected to reports that suggested the school's closure and transition to a sanitarium (for tuberculosis patients, mainly). "If the government wants a sanitarium," High Eagle said, "let it build one here. There is plenty of room, but the Indian School is a necessity for Rapid City's Indians who lived there." Many viewed the school as "something" in the city "which they can be part of." The council's strong protests were successful, as they overturned the government's decision and kept the school open for an additional four years. The gathering made many Native peoples conclude that they should hold an annual assembly where "they may make forceful resolutions" regarding the multiple factors that determined their lives both on and off reservations. Grateful for the gathering "in our beautiful City," council leaders stated: "We hope, through the help of the Great Spirit to spare us so as to see many more of these gatherings."[44]

After the 1929 council, Indians in Rapid City grew more determined to continue the momentum for positive change. For them, this meant education, health care, and employment. The conditions of communities along Mni Luzahan and in the Osh Kosh Camp grew considerably worse in the 1930s as the Great Depression closed in on the northern plains. In 1928 a group of Native women living in Rapid City formed the Rapid City Indian Welfare Association. They shared membership with white women and held meetings that, in the early years, consisted of music, songs, and educational discussions about Indians over tea. In 1930 the group became the Winona Women's Club with membership of Native women whose purpose was to "assist local Indian families." They met at the local YWCA or at members' homes to sew, mend clothing, and organize fundraising efforts to help local Indians in need. American Indian women from several tribes were involved in helping "reservation Indians adjust to urban living" and "bring cheer" to Indians struggling with health problems or who lived in the Sioux Sanitarium. They sewed layettes for new Indian babies in Rapid City, helped "destitute" families with food and clothing, encouraged youth to attend school, and raised money by selling their quilting, beadwork, and other works of art. Overall, the women aimed to give "material and spiritual aid to their own people."[45]

Native men in Rapid City also met in an Indian Welfare Association. While the women organized the Winona Club, men organized the Black Hills Peace Pipe Council in 1931. It also included mixed membership of "Indians and their white friends," but Native men held the elected positions. While the Winona Club was limited to women, the men who joined the Peace Pipe Council often brought their wives to business meetings and social gatherings.[46] The two groups— Winona Club and Black Hills Peace Pipe Council—often held joint meetings as their mission and mutual interests overlapped. Their combined efforts were especially important over the holidays and winter months. Beginning in 1931 they planned a Christmas event which included dinner, a tree, and a program with Christmas carols (many translated into Lakota), for Rapid City's Indian families. They raised donations from Indian School employees, the Rapid City Chamber of Commerce, and Custer State Park (which provided buffalo and elk meat for their dinners), and organized the distribution of children's gifts. The program outgrew its original location in 1931 as it drew between two hundred and fifty to three hundred Indians from the city each year.[47]

Despite years of protests from Rapid City's Indian community (including the Winona Club and Peace Pipe Council), the Indian School closed in 1933. In 1932 Congress reallocated some of the Indian School land to the National Guard for a training center that became known as "Camp Rapid."[48] Six years after it closed, the school's buildings reopened as the "Sioux Sanitarium" and treated only American Indian patients who contracted tuberculosis (TB). "Sioux San" tells its own story of the growth of segregation in the Black Hills between whites and Indians. Native people were forced to enter Rapid City's facility and were turned down when they sought treatment at the "white" sanitarium in the town of Custer. Beginning at the age of sixteen, Madonna Swan from Cheyenne River endured Sioux San for seven years and recalled being surrounded by death every day. She was admitted to the Custer Sanitarium only after her father insisted to South Dakota's governor that she be transferred to receive better treatment. There she noticed a massive difference in the quality of care afforded to white patients. Hundreds of Native men, women, and children perished from TB at Sioux San until the distribution of antibiotics in the 1940s and 1950s curbed the death rate. Sioux San's patient number also dropped because Indians in the city lobbied the hospital to set up at least one TB vaccination clinic near the large population of American Indians living in the Osh Kosh Camp (to attract the Indian communities living along the banks of Mni Luzahan). After the TB death rate among American Indians dropped, the old buildings of the Rapid City Indian School transitioned once again. This time, in 1966, they formed the Rapid City Indian Health Service (IHS) clinic.[49]

The Black Hills Peace Pipe Council maintained strong relationships with the reservation. In 1935 four members (three men and one woman) served as delegates to represent Rapid City Indians at an all-Indian council meeting at Pine Ridge to discuss the policies proposed by the 1934 Indian Reorganization Act.[50] Unexpectedly the same year, members terminated the Peace Pipe Council for reasons that remain unclear. In 1936, however, the city's Native population announced their intention to form a permanent organization for Indians, "so that they may be able to function on a collective basis." They met at the 4-L (Timber Union) Club House, close to the Osh Kosh Camp. This was a convenient location to draw a larger crowd. "Everybody Welcome," advertisements read, with "Plenty to Eat." After food and business commenced, the group formed the "Black Hills Tribal Council" with all-Native leadership that represented the diversity of Rapid City's Indian population. With over 250 members, it was intertribal, inclusive of gender, and represented several generations drawn to Rapid City for multiple reasons.[51]

Within three months of their first meeting, the Black Hills Tribal Council announced their plans for a rehabilitation center for Rapid City's homeless Indian population and a series of resolutions that attacked the Black Hills tourism industry. First, the Council stated, more employment should be available for Indians at the Sioux Sanitarium: "The jobs in an Indian institution in an Indian country should be held by Indians." Next, they addressed the issue of what they believed to be "surplus" land west and south of the former Rapid City Indian School. Paul Dion, the President of the Council, declared the group's proposal that this land be "set aside for rehabilitation of Indian families in this section."[52]

The group also announced formal resolutions for the "hiring and use of Indi-ans in celebrations and shows" connected to the Black Hills tourism industry (especially for proprietors and vendors in Rapid City). By this point, the leaders recognized the important role Native peoples played in the lucrative growth of regional tourism. These included four major points of recognition. First, they announced that Indians in tourism are often misled in their expectations regarding wages and work conditions. Second, the entertainment they labor for perpetuates "untruthful habits and customs . . . that are . . . unfair to the Indian and misleading to the public." This results in discrimination, "race hatred" and "race prejudice." Third, the Council called for a solution to the unreasonable wages of Indians who worked in shows and celebrations. Along with a pay scale for Native men, women, and children, the group urged contractors to also provide per diems and rations. Finally, the employment contracts should include the time (often days) it takes for Indians to travel from their homes—both on reservations and in towns or cities—to the locations of shows. "To this end," the Council wrote, "we ask all Indians for their support and co-operation, not to take part in any celebration or show unless they be contracted and the contract approved."[53]

The sudden closure of the Rapid City Indian Boarding School, the passage of the Indian Reorganization Act, and the continued development of tourism spurred a major transition in the chapter of urban Native Americans in Rapid City. Their growing population aimed to focus on reform for their people as they faced continued exploitation, housing and public health discrimination, and limited educational and economic opportunities in the 1930s. They forged strong intertribal partnerships to force the city to acknowledge the hardships their people faced. Despite the hardships placed on Native populations in the early decades of the twentieth century by the Rapid City Indian School, local and regional tourism, and dire urban conditions, Indigenous people established effective forms of survival and resistance that resulted in a permanent, vibrant community. Following on the heels of earlier demands for land rights and reform, Indigenous populations in the Black Hills refused to accept the erasure that accompanied settler narratives in their lands. The presence of Native peoples in the city strengthened through their consistent use of Rapid City's land and resources. They also continued to use the city's obsession with the tourism industry to assert an intertribal platform for resistance against federal policies and state and local injustices against tribal nations. In echoing Yellow Owl's sentiments and actions from 1904, Native residents in Rapid City remained strong in their resolve to "tell people what the Indians were, are today, and what they hope to be."[54]

NOTES

About the title: The phrase "our beautiful city" was part of the Council of American Indians welcoming statement, quoted in *Rapid City Journal*, August 2, 1929.

1. *Black Hills Weekly Journal*, May 20, 1894; *Rapid City Journal*, May 17, 1904; and *Rapid City Journal*, May 18, 1904. South Dakota tribes tried to organize an "Indian congress" in 1902 with the intention of discussing Indian citizenship and voting rights in the United States, but area superintendents prevented them from gathering for that purpose. The 1904 "Council of Nations," organized as a "July Fourth" event, was likely their solution to circumvent federal intervention in a large intertribal gathering; see *Argus-Leader*, November 10, 1902. The articles refer to the tribes as "Sioux, Cheyenne, and Crow," but the people involved in the Council were from Lakota tribes. The "Sioux" was a federally designated label that does not fully describe the Oceti Sakowin or the "Seven Council Fires" (listed as the "Great Sioux Nation" in treaties and other rhetoric). According to oral tradition, the Oceti Sakowin includes three major nations: Lakota, Dakota, Nakota. The Lakota comprised of one of the seven council fires making up the "Oceti Sakowin" and further divided into seven tribes: Oglala, Sicangu, Hunkpapa, Mnikowoju, Itzipco, Oohenunpa, and Sihasapa. See Craig Howe, Lydia Whirlwind Soldier, and Lanniko L. Lee, *He Sapa Woihanble: Black Hills Dream* (St. Paul, Minn.: Living Justice Press, 2011), 3–4, Vine Deloria Jr., "Spirits and South Dakota Land," in *A New South Dakota History*, ed. Harry F. Thompson (Sioux Falls, S. Dak.: Center for Western Studies, 2005), 1–2; and Jeffrey Ostler, *The Lakotas and the Black Hills: The Struggle for Sacred Ground* (New York: Penguin, 2011), 7.

2. The Black Hills claim is a landmark case concerning Native American treaty rights, which the people of the Oceti Sakowin protested throughout the nineteenth and twentieth centuries. *Rapid City Journal*, July 6, 1904. On July 6 the *Rapid City Journal* reported that Congressman Eben W. Martin, who met with tribes in 1902 and 1903 in a legal capacity to discuss the Black Hills land theft, spent the entire day of July 5 at the Indian camp; *Rapid City Journal*, July 6, 1904. Martin assisted South Dakota's tribes in their efforts to make legal challenges to the treaties and land commissions that set compensation values for their land loss; Ostler, *The Lakotas and the Black Hills*, 130. Newspapers also covered the movement of Native peoples in the week leading up to the event, which included a gift-giving ceremony between Indians and local businesses where Native peoples shopped for provisions; see *Rapid City Journal*, June 16, 1904 and July 8, 1904; and *Black Hills Union and Western Stock Review*, June 24, 1904.

3. Unlike agriculture, tourism does not attract permanent populations to expand land-based settlement; yet it's an industry that sustains permanent populations with its seasonal boost to local economies. In truth, tourism drew larger (albeit temporary) populations than agriculture, and it contributes to the continued encroachment of Indigenous

lands and erasure of Indigenous people. See Patrick Wolfe, "Settler Colonialism and the Elimination of the Native," *Journal of Genocide Research* 8, no. 4 (December 2006): 395; Lorenzo Veracini, "Introducing *Settler Colonial Studies*," *Settler Colonial Studies* 1, no. 1 (2011): 1–12; and John Mack Faragher, "Settler Colonial Studies and the North American Frontier," *Settler Colonial Studies* 4, no. 2 (2014): 1–6.

4. *Rapid City Journal*, May 20, 1904, and June 29, 1904. Other speakers included the aforementioned congressman Eben W. Martin, and the mayor of Rapid City.

5. Included here is a brief list of the secondary sources that inform my argument and framework for this essay. On racism in Rapid City, see Thomas Biolsi, *Deadliest Enemies: Law and Race Relations on and off the Reservation*, 2nd ed. (Minneapolis: University of Minnesota Press, 2007), 4–5. For how urban Indians avoided "administrative technologies" (including surveyance), see Thomas Biolsi, *Organizing the Lakota: The Political Economy of the New Deal on the Pine Ridge and Rosebud Reservations* (Tucson: University of Arizona Press, 1992). New ideas of the complex overlays of tourism, settler colonialism, and urban America in the early twentieth century come from Penelope Edmonds, *Urbanizing Frontiers: Indigenous Peoples and Settlers in Nineteenth-Century Pacific Rim Cities* (Seattle: University of Washington Press, 2010); Rosalyn R. LaPier and David R. M. Beck, *City Indian: Native American Activism in Chicago, 1893–1934* (Lincoln: University of Nebraska Press, 2015); Catherine Cocks, *Doing the Town: The Rise of Urban Tourism in the United States, 1850–1915* (Berkeley: University of California Press, 2001); Sherene H. Razack, ed., *Race, Space, and the Law: Unmapping a White Settler Society* (Toronto: Between the Lines, 2002); and Stephanie Nohelani Teves, *Defiant Indigeneity: The Politics of Hawaiian Performance* (Chapel Hill: University of North Carolina Press, 2018).

6. I do not italicize Indigenous languages as they are not foreign to North America. For the Omaha Tribe, see Alice C. Fletcher and Francis La Flesche, *The Omaha Tribe* (Washington, D.C.: Bureau of American Ethnology, 1911), 102; for "Moxtavhohona," see John H. Moore, *The Cheyennes in Moxtavhohona: Evidence Supporting Cheyenne Claims in the Black Hills Area* (Lame Deer, Mo.: Northern Cheyenne Tribe, 1981), 14; for "Xó-kó-qòp," see William C. Meadows, *Kiowa Ethnogeography* (Austin: University of Texas Press, 2008), 263. The Lakota know the Black Hills as variations of He Sápa, or Paha Sápa (with and without accents). These translate to mean "Black Mountains" and "Black Hills," respectively. They are also referred to as "Wamakaognaka E'cante"—the "heart of everything that is"; translations from Frank Fools Crow, "Introduction," in Tom Charging Eagle and Ron Zeilinger, *Black Hills, Sacred Hills* (Chamberlain: Tipi Press, St. Joseph's Indian School, 2004), n.p. "Wamákognaka" also means "Creation, the contents of the world, the whole of creation," while "icáŋte" means "in or at the heart"; Eugene Buechel and Paul Manhart, eds., *Lakota Dictionary: Lakota-English/English-Lakota*, New Comprehensive Edition (Lincoln: University of Nebraska Press, 2002), 340 and 102.

7. Evidence of large Native occupancies, referred to as "Ruins of an Indian City," was discovered in stone foundations and teepee imprints along several miles of Mni Luzahan; *Rapid City Journal*, October 23, 1889, and *Lead Daily Call*, April 23, 1915.

8. Like most words and phrases in American Indian languages, "Mni Luzahan" has been recorded with various spellings. Amos Bad Heart Bull (Oglala Lakota) identified "Miniluzahan" on his infamous Black Hills map of sacred sites; see Amos Bad Heart Bull and Helen Heather Blish, *A Pictographic History of the Oglala Sioux* (Lincoln: University of Nebraska Press, 1967), 289–90. For the significance of Mni Luzahan, see James LaPointe, *Legends of the Lakota* (San Francisco: Indian Historian Press, 1976), 74; and Linea Sundstrom, "The Sacred Black Hills: An Ethnohistorical Review," *Great Plains Quarterly* 17 (Summer/Fall 1997): 187, 194–95. In his work on resistance movements and the Oceti Sakowin, Nick Estes traces the history of Mni Sose (Missouri River) and the white trade networks that forced decades of exploitation and the "devastation inflicted by white traders, emigrants traversing the land, and the increasing U.S. military presence. Each was a foreboding sign of white encroachment"; Nick Estes, *Our History Is the Future: Standing Rock versus the Dakota Access Pipeline, and the Long Tradition of Indigenous Resistance* (New York: Verso, 2019), 9 and 87. More recent scholarship on Indigenous people and Mni Luzahan includes Nick Estes, "Anti-Indian Common Sense: Border Town Violence and Resistance in Mni Luzahan," in *Settler City Limits: Indigenous Resurgence and Colonial Violence in the Urban Prairie West*, ed. Heather Dorries, Robert Henry, David Hugill, Tyler McCreary, and Julie Tomiak (East Lansing: Michigan State University Press, 2019); and Stephen Hausmann, *Urban Indian Country: Race and Environment in Twentieth-Century Rapid City* (forthcoming, University of Nebraska Press).

9. On white settlers' "founding" of Rapid City, see David B. Miller, *Gateway to the Hills: An Illustrated History of Rapid City* (Northridge, Calif.: Windsor Publications, 1985), 15–16.

10. After 1871, "Agreements" (as opposed to treaties) were signed by representatives and then passed through Congress as legal statutes ("Acts") for the United States regarding land appropriations of, or transactions with, federally recognized tribes. The low number of signatures in the Act of 1877 did not fulfill the stipulations outlined in the Fort Laramie Treaty of 1868, which required that future land seizures be approved and signed by three-fourths of the population of Native adult men; Ostler, *The Lakotas and the Black Hills*, 98–101. Their signatures, "x-marks," reveal the duality of consent and coercion in the transference of space and land in Indian country during the nineteenth-century "frontier"; Scott Richard Lyons, *X-marks: Native Signatures of Assent* (Minneapolis: University of Minnesota Press, 2010), 16–19, 122–26. See also Patricia C. Albers, "The Home of the Bison: An Ethnographic and Ethnohistorical Study of Traditional Cultural Affiliation to Wind Cave National Park," (Cooperative Agreement #CA606899103 between the U.S. National Park Service and The Department of American Indian Studies, University of Minnesota, 2003), 252. On November 13, 1911, nine reservations gathered at the Lower Brule Reservation and drafted a resolution to declare the U.S. taking of the Black Hills illegal. During this time several men from the "Great Sioux Nation" who signed the "Agreement of 1876" swore official affidavits about their recollection of the commission's negotiations and threats to tribes. For Leo Weasel Bear's recollections, see "No. 52: 1911, Indian affidavits regarding ceding of the Black Hills,"

in the Welch Dakota Papers, "Oral History of the Dakota Tribes, 1800s–1945, as told to Colonel A. B. Welch, the First White Man Adopted by the Sioux Nation," http://www .welch-dakotapapers.com. For the specific statute of the Act of 1877, see *An act to ratify an agreement with certain bands of the Sioux nation of Indians and also with the Northern Arapaho and Cheyenne Indians*, in *U.S. Statutes at Large*, vol. 19 (Washington, D.C.: Government Printing Office, 1877), chap. 72, 254–64.

11. Miller, *Gateway to the Hills*, 15–16. Between 1890 and 1900, Fort Meade was "one of the largest cavalry posts in the United States"; see "Fort Meade," Fort Meade Vertical File, South Dakota State Historical Society, Pierre, South Dakota. For the 1879 Rapid City Fourth of July parade, see *Rapid City Journal*, July 10, 1904.

12. The "home guard" is well documented in the testimony of Renée Sansom Flood in the U.S. Congress, Senate Select Committee on Indian Affairs, *Wounded Knee Memorial and Historic Site; Little Big Horn National Monument Battlefield* (Washington, D.C.: Government Printing Office, 1991), 113–16. Flood also cites Nellie Snyder Yost, ed., *Boss Cowman: The Recollections of Ed Lemmon, 1857–1946* (Lincoln: University of Nebraska Press, 1969), 151. The use of "Home Guards" on the Great Plains was also evident in the early 1860s, when military leaders enlisted volunteers to occupy rural areas around forts for "protection" in the "event that regular troops were withdrawn for service elsewhere"; see Brenda K. Jackson, "Holding Down the Fort: A History of Dakota Territory's Fort Randall," *South Dakota History* 32, no.1 (Spring 2002): 9.

13. Eric John Abrahamson, *Improving Life with Energy: The First 125 Years of Black Hills Corporation* (Rapid City, S.Dak.: Black Hills Corporation, 2008), 15; *Rapid City Journal*, March 24, 1892, and June 12, 1891; for the milling companies, see *Daily Deadwood Pioneer-Times*, January 16, 1914, and *Lead Daily Call*, March 25, 1914. Established in 1897, the Black Hills National Forest was one of the first national forests in the country. It was the first large-scale national forest sale of timber ("Case No. 1") which was a direct result of Homestake Mining Corporation's request of one thousand acres of timber. (The prior limit had been set at 160 acres.) By the early 1900s, "more timber is logged in the Black Hills than any other national forest in the Rocky Mountain region"; *Rapid City Journal*, February 12, 1989.

14. On February 10, 1890, President Benjamin Harrison announced that nine million acres of the "Great Sioux Nation" were open for homestead filings; *Black Hills Weekly Journal*, September 13, 1889, and *Daily Deadwood Pioneer-Times*, November 30, 1882. "An act to divide a portion of the reservation of the Sioux Nation of Indians in Dakota into separate reservations and to secure the relinquishment of the Indian title to the remainder, and for other purposes," in *U.S. Statutes at Large*, vol. 25 (Washington, D.C.: Government Printing Office, 1889), chap. 405, 888–99. For more details on the complex events surrounding the "Sioux Bill," see Herbert T. Hoover, "The Sioux Agreement of 1889 and Its Aftermath," *South Dakota History* 19, no. 1 (1989): 56–94. Frances Paul Prucha, *The Great Father: The United States Government and the American Indians* (Lincoln: University of Nebraska Press, 1995), 633–40; Jeffrey Ostler, *The Plains Sioux and U.S. Colonialism from Lewis and Clark to Wounded Knee* (Cambridge: Cambridge University Press, 2004), 218–39.

15. "Report of Superintendent of Indian Schools," *Annual Report of Commissioner of Indian Affairs, 1893* (Washington, D.C.: Government Printing Office, 1893), 371 [hereafter cited as ARCIA]; *Rapid City Journal*, May 23, 1893, and March 1, 1893. In 1890 the Episcopal Church built a mission school on the northern edge of Rapid City to educate American Indian children. It remained empty and unused until some suggested that the government turn it into a federal Indian boarding school. The Rapid City Indian School land did not assume this property and instead built west of the town; *Rapid City Journal*, October 2, 1890, and January 5, 1893.

16. Scott Riney, *The Rapid City Indian School, 1898–1933* (Norman: University of Oklahoma Press, 1933); and Scott Riney, "Life at the Rapid City Indian Boarding School," in *An Inconvenient Truth: The History behind Sioux San (Rapid City Indian Boarding School) Lands and West Rapid City*, ed. Heather Dawn Thompson, Kibbe Conti, Scott Riney, and Karin Eagle (Rapid City: Mniluzahan Okalakiciyapi Ambassadors, 2017), 3–4.

17. Howe, Whirlwind Soldier, and Lee, *He Sapa Woihanble*, 12.

18. Riney, *Rapid City Indian School*, 144–66. In 1909 two young boys running away, Paul Loves War and Henry Bull, lost both their lower legs to frostbite, and in 1910 James Means and Mark Sherman were struck and killed; Riney, 151–52.

19. J. F. House, "Report of School at Rapid City," in ARCIA, 1904–5, 434.

20. Alvin M. Josephy Jr., ed., *Black Hills, White Sky: Photographs from the Collection of the Arvada Center Foundation, Inc.* (New York: Times Books, 1978), 156–57. The library hall performance identifies the musicians as the "Pine Ridge orchestra," but does not specify if they traveled from Pine Ridge for the event; *Rapid City Journal*, September 1894.

21. Immediately following the Wounded Knee Massacre, dozens of settlers scavenged miles of land surrounding the massacre site and took jewelry, clothing, supplies, and other items off the dead frozen bodies of Lakota men, women, and children. Two men, Riley Miller and Frank Lockhart, brought seven loads of items to Rapid City and distributed their findings to various shop owners. W. J. Collins, a Rapid City photographer, captured the hundreds of items in a photograph of Riley Miller that was displayed in a shop window on Main Street; see *Rapid City Journal*, February 4, 1891. Lockhart remained in Rapid City where he bought land, owned and operated a quarry, and established himself as a liaison between the city and Indian performers for tourist attractions. Miller opened exhibits on the stolen Wounded Knee items in museums across the country and became wealthy in his exploitative ventures; see Pete Lemley interview, South Dakota Oral History Project, 1959, and *Rapid City Journal*, March 25, 1891. Curio shops existed throughout the Black Hills. The popular "curio" businesses in Rapid City were White-Indians on Lake and Bump Street, McNamara's Bookstore on Main Street, Duhamel's on Main Street, and Ye Old Curiosity Shop on Main Street (each store sold a combination of books, gifts, supplies, and home goods to both locals and tourists).

22. *The Weekly Livestock Report* 13, no. 17 (April 24, 1903): 1, 5; *Rapid City Journal*, July 7, 1903; *Rapid City Journal*, July 1, 1903.

23. *Lead Daily Call*, March 28, 1904; *Black Hills Weekly Journal*, April 29, 1904; and *Daily Deadwood Pioneer-Times*, April 23, 1904. It was reported that in "opening surplus Indian lands without submitting the question to the Indians, congress is following a precedent established by the United States supreme court in what is known as the Lone Wolf case, to the effect that as the Indians were wards of the government, congress has the right, if it wishes, to open to white settlement the surplus lands of the red men without their consent"; *Rapid City Journal*, April 22, 1904. This report references *Lone Wolf v. Hitchcock* (1903). The Rosebud Bill opened a lottery for 2,412 homesteads to encourage a strong land rush. There is additional evidence of intertribal gathering in other areas of the country. In 1904 the Gros Ventres, Blackfeet, Crow, and Assiniboine Nations gathered at the Fort Belknap agency on July 4. They likely met to discuss the thousands of acres of land from the Flathead Reservation that opened to settlers earlier that year; *Great Falls Tribune*, July 2, 1904.

24. Quoting a tourist who attended the 1904 Western Stock Growers' meeting; *Daily Deadwood Pioneer-Times*, April 22, 1904. Words such as "real" or "authentic" are complicated terms often used to define one's degree of "Indianness" or measure Native identity. It is not my intention to reveal how non-Indians (in this case, white tourists) identified what an American Indian looked like or how he/she/they acted. Rather, these quotes from tourists provide an overview of the challenges that Indigenous people faced while working within the exploitative structures of Black Hills tourism. For more discussions on authenticity, Indigenous populations, tourism, and colonial systems, see Paige Raibmon, *Authentic Indians: Episodes of Encounter from the Late Nineteenth-Century Northwest Coast* (Durham, N.C.: Duke University Press, 2005). Raibmon's study claims authenticity is "a powerful and shifting set of ideas that worked in a variety of ways toward a variety of ends," and was "not a stable yardstick against which to measure 'the real thing,'" 3. Furthermore, these performances were purely "mock" ceremonies, not a full representation of the complexity and sacredness of Indigenous cultures and spiritual beliefs. This might be historicized as a version of what Mary Louise Pratt terms "authoethnographic expression" or "autoethnography" which refers to the ways that "colonized subjects . . . represent themselves in ways that engage with the colonizer's own terms." In this instance, the tourist, or the tourism industry as a whole, serves as the colonizer or the agent of colonization. Autoethnographic representations on the tourist stage are *not*, then, "authentic" representations of culture; see Pratt, *Imperial Eyes: Travel Writing and Transculturation* (London: Routledge, 1992), 7.

25. *Black Hills Weekly Journal*, May 20, 1894; *Rapid City Journal*, May 17, 1904; and *Rapid City Journal*, May 18, 1904. American Indians on reservations used national holidays as an excuse to bring their dances out of the shadows because BIA agents did not think events like the Fourth of July were "dangerous occasions"; see Severt Young Bear and R. D. Theisz, *Standing in the Light: A Lakota Way of Seeing* (Lincoln: University of Nebraska Press, 1994), 55 and 86–87, 98–99. John Troutman discusses similar ideas in the form of Lakota dance and music in the early 1920s: "A consideration of cultural performance as an everyday form of resistance reveals the simultaneous expression of overt political action and hidden transcripts." However, his work assesses their actions

while confined to the space of their reservations, and not in connection to employment outside reservation boundaries; see Troutman, "The Citizenship of Dance: Politics of Music among the Lakota, 1900–1924," in *Beyond Red Power: American Indian Politics and Activism since 1900*, ed. Daniel M. Cobb and Loretta Fowler (Santa Fe, N. Mex.: School for Advanced Research Press, 2007), 104. See also James C. Scott, *Domination and the Forms of Resistance: Hidden Transcripts* (New Haven: Conn., Yale University Press, 1990), xii–xiii. Part of the draw of Native peoples to the Black Hills for tourism events coincided with the rising popularity of tribal fairs in the 1910s. Tribal fairs offered Indians from Wyoming, Montana, South Dakota, and North Dakota the opportunity to travel across reservation and state lines with very little scrutiny—until federal officials learned of council gatherings and the presence of the Sun Dance at some of the fairs. This prompted the Commissioner of Indian Affairs to outlaw dancing and schedule all tribal affairs during the same week/weekend to circumvent Native peoples from holding intertribal meetings.

26. *Rapid City Journal*, October 7, 1905, and August 18, 1914. Some reservation officials called on the railroads, irrigation companies, and ranches to hire Indians as laborers. See also *Weekly Pioneer-Times*, April 27, 1905; and Riney, *Rapid City Indian School*, 217.

27. *Black Hills Weekly Journal*, June 28, 1907.

28. *Black Hills Weekly Journal*, June 28, 1907. During the next two decades, Rapid City repeated grand Independence Day celebrations, held an extravagant "Railroad Jubilee" affair, and hosted the Stock Growers' Association meetings. They employed American Indians to perform in these events; see Brennan's report in *Daily Deadwood Pioneer-Times*, October 5, 1904. Interestingly, for two years newspapers printed monthly ads promoting Rapid City boosterism and mentioning the Indian boarding school as a benefit to the community. In a clever bit of marketing, Rapid City rebranded itself "Gate City" or "Gateway to the Black Hills." It also built a new events arena, the Alfalfa Palace, which opened in 1912 at Seventh and St. Joe Streets; see *Rapid City Journal*, January 30, 1919; and Miller, *Gateway to the Hills*.

29. Through an examination of urban settlement in the Great Plains, geographers and historians have identified how both timing and migration created unique development patterns. While the Great Plains remains largely rural, the majority of the population in the region's states live in urbanized villages or areas such as Sioux Falls, Fargo, Omaha, Kansas City, Wichita, Tulsa, Billings, and Rapid City. See James R. Shortridge, *Cities on the Plains: The Evolution of Urban Kansas* (Lawrence: University Press of Kansas, 2004); Michael P. Conzen, "Cities and Towns," in *Encyclopedia of the Great Plains*, ed. David J. Wishart (Lincoln: University of Nebraska Press, 2004), 151–57; Andrew Becker, "The Urban Fabric of the Great Plains" (Undergraduate thesis, University of Nebraska–Lincoln, 2011), https://digitalcommons.unl.edu/envstudtheses/74/; and Kurt E. Kinbacher, *Urban Villages and Local Identities: Germans from Russia, Omaha Indians, and Vietnamese in Lincoln, Nebraska* (Lubbock: Texas Tech University Press, 2015). This short list reveals the need for the "urban history" field to expand into this understudied region of urban migration and living, especially in regard to Indigenous peoples.

30. In 1910 the "Indian police" arrived in the city to try and curb the selling of alcohol to Indians but said their "jurisdiction does not extend off the reservation." When one Indian policeman tried to solve a situation using the Rapid City police, they refused to get involved; *Rapid City Journal*, October 1, 1910, and October 3, 1914.

31. *Rapid City Journal*, May 12, 1901, and October 19, 1918.

32. Because the concerns of other Rapid City hot spots (including the School of Mines) were reported, conditions there and elsewhere improved; the Indian School's situation, however, worsened; see *Rapid City Journal*, October 8, 9, 13, and 17, 1918, for a chronicle of the city's efforts to shut down the epidemic's spread. Through examination of federal records, oral histories, and independent sources, it's clear that at least fifty children perished at the Rapid City Indian School during its existence as a boarding school. The intertribal organization Remembering the Children, 1898–1933 located several unmarked graves near the old school and plans a memorial to honor all the children and "be a place of prayer, gathering, and remembrance"; see https://rememberingthechildren.org.

33. *Rapid City Journal*, April 8, 1924, and May 27, 1924. Other Black Hills communities made some effort to accommodate Native residents. Hot Springs supported an Indian camp which "has gradually been incorporated into a residence district and the white men's bungalows have taken the place of tepees." To resolve the issue the commercial club sought to "secure ground near Hot Springs for an Indian campground . . . free to pitch their tents and remain as long as they like . . . The Indians are fond of Hot Springs and come in considerable numbers during the summer. It is proposed to make it possible for them to have their bead work and other articles on display for sale and to give an opportunity to tourists to observe the Indians' native customs"; *Rapid City Journal*, February 1, 1928.

34. The tribe and Ralph Case believed their land claim issue would be settled by the end of the decade. But the Court of Claims instead took nineteen years to make the decision to ultimately dismiss the case; Ostler, *The Lakotas and the Black Hills*, 131–32. By comparison, it took Congress less than four years to approve a new national monument in the Black Hills and after sixteen years (and nearly one million dollars) Mount Rushmore was completed on October 31, 1941.

35. Riney, "Life at the Rapid City Indian Boarding School," 6–9. Riney's essay in Thompson et al's *An Inconvenient Truth* refers to this legislation as the "Act of April 12, 1924." In 1924 Congress passed House Resolution 2812 to authorize the sale of Rapid City Indian School lands no longer "needed." *An Act to authorize the sale of lands and plants not longer needed for Indian administrative or allotment purposes*, Public Law 77, U.S. Statutes at Large, 93 (1924).

36. *Lead Daily Call*, July 14, 1926.

37. "Days of '76 Program 1927," Days of '76 Papers, Centennial Archives, Deadwood City Library; *Rapid City Journal*, 9 July 1927; Marjorie Weinberg, *The Real Rosebud: The Triumph of a Lakota Woman* (Lincoln: University of Nebraska Press, 2004).

38. Chauncey Yellow Robe, "The Menace of the Wild West Show," *Quarterly Journal of the Society of American Indians* 2 (July–September 1914): 224–25.

39. *Rapid City Journal*, April 15, 1929; May 13, 1929; and July 27, 1929.

40. *Rapid City Journal*, July 26, 1929, and July 30, 1929. No stranger to South Dakota, President Coolidge spent his 1927 summer vacation in the Black Hills with his summer White House headquartered in Rapid City. During this tourist season, he met twice with Native leaders—once at the Deadwood Days of '76 and once at the Pine Ridge Reservation; *Rapid City Journal*, July 29, 1929.

41. City boosters also exaggerated that the gathering would attract seventy-five thousand visitors; *Rapid City Journal*, February 21, 1929; April 3, 1929; May 3, 1929; and July 22, 1929. Various businesses promoted the event that summer, including Cordes Motor for gas and oil and Rapid City Cleaners, the latter posting an advertisement that read "Making Whopee . . . Makes clothes soiled. Let us clean and press them"; *Rapid City Journal*, July 25, 1929.

42. *Argus-Leader*, July 27, 1929. Locals and tourists stated what they hoped and expected to see: an "Indian sun dance," the "Indian rodeo," and "thousands of Indians dressed in regalia and war paint"; *Rapid City Journal*, July 26, 1929. Despite their insistence of the gravity of the event for their people's survivance, Rapid City residents viewed the Council of American Indians as a "show." They hoped it would be held each year as a community event and get "bigger and better and draw larger crowds," like other Black Hills events, including the Deadwood Days of '76, Custer Gold Discovery Days, and Hot Springs Water Carnival. Of the thirteen special events held in Rapid City in the 1929 tourist season, the Council of American Indians was by far the largest; *Rapid City Journal*, July 29, 1929, and September 9, 1929. Highways into the Black Hills from the south, west, and north "make it possible for tourists to visit the Black Hills without coming to Rapid City." But the Council of American Indians contributed "largely" to the city's increase in tourism traffic. The *Rapid City Journal* also reported that more than a half a million tourists visited the Black Hills in the 1929 season; *Rapid City Journal*, July 30, 1929.

43. *Daily Plainsman*, July 30, 1929. Reporting was inconsistent regarding the inclusion of a discussion focused on the Black Hills claim during the meeting. Standing Bear reportedly said the Black Hills land claim would not be part of their meeting while High Eagle insisted that a discussion about the claim would take place. In the end, the Black Hills claim was reportedly not included in the meeting; *Rapid City Journal*, June 27, 1929.

44. *Rapid City Journal*, July 25, 1929, and August 3, 1929. On August 1, the council wrote a resolution asking that the Indian School remain a school. On August 2, the Department of the Interior sent a notice that it would be turned into a sanitarium in the fall. This prompted the council to respond with another resolution, asking that "the school be allowed to continue as an educational institution as requested in the resolution adopted yesterday by the council, a copy of which was telegraphed to you today"; *Rapid City Journal*, August 2, 1929.

45. "Winona" (or "Winúŋna") translates to "first-born daughter" in Lakota and Dakota languages. This stood for the club's status as the first "recognized" Indian women's club in the state (meaning that it was admitted to the state federation of women's clubs in 1931). Some claim it was the first recognized Indian women's club in the nation. While Mrs. Frank Huss, the wife of a white missionary in Rapid City and the chairwoman of

South Dakota's Indian Welfare Program, is credited with establishing the Rapid City Indian Welfare Association for women, the leadership and officers were Native women over several generations, including Julia McGaa, one of the early "anchors" of the group; *Rapid City Journal*, January 6, 1951, May 24, 1964, and November 16, 1975.

46. *Rapid City Journal*, April 13, 1931, and September 22, 1931. In 1931 the group invited Gutzon Borglum, known associate of the Ku Klux Klan, white supremacist, and lead sculptor of Mount Rushmore, to attend one of their meetings, but he declined; *Rapid City Journal*, November 16, 1931. Although widely accepted as fact, no one has ever been able to prove Borglum was an official member of the KKK.

47. *Rapid City Journal*, December 16, 24, and 26, 1931, and December 19 and 27, 1932.

48. "Camp Rapid" emerged through the passage of the Act of June 6, 1932, which took 84.4 acres of land from the Rapid City Indian School; see Heather Dawn Thompson, "Rapid City Indian Boarding School Lands: Where Did It All Go?" in Thompson et al., *An Inconvenient Truth*, 6.

49. Kibbe Conti, "History of Sioux San as a Segregated Tuberculosis Clinic," in Thompson et al., *An Inconvenient Truth*, 5; Mark St. Pierre, *Madonna Swan: A Lakota Woman's Story* (Norman: University of Oklahoma Press, 1994); and *Rapid City Journal*, June 9, 1949.

50. *Rapid City Journal*, January 2, 1935. The representation of "Rapid City Indians" was unique in that most delegates represented the interests of specific Native nations—not an intertribal, urban concentration of Native peoples with several tribal affiliations. In the year prior, delegates from sixteen tribes from the northern Great Plains began meetings with government officials, including BIA Commissioner John Collier, at the Rapid City Indian School to discuss the Indian Reorganization Act. Meetings between tribal delegates and federal officials continued in Rapid City in 1934–36; *Rapid City Journal*, March 1 and 6, 1934. For full minutes of the 1934 meeting see Vine Deloria Jr., ed., *The Indian Reorganization Act: Congresses and Bills* (Norman: University of Oklahoma Press, 2002), 24–101.

51. *Rapid City Journal*, March 26 and 28, 1936. The Winona Club maintained its existence as an Indian Women's club throughout the twentieth century and into the present day.

52. *Rapid City Journal*, June 23, 1936. Also noteworthy is the amount of revenue the state tracked through Black Hills tourism venues which, by 1938, amounted to over nine million dollars; *Rapid City Journal*, October 22, 1938.

53. *Rapid City Journal*, June 23, 1936.

54. *Rapid City Journal*, July 6, 1904.

8

INDIGENIZING MINNEAPOLIS

Building American Indian Community Infrastructure
in the Mid-Twentieth Century

As Franklin Avenue extends through South Minneapolis in the northeast corner
of the Phillips neighborhood, a curious thing happens. The expected exteriors
of inner-city space give way to something at once urban and Indigenous. Urban
tribal offices sit in brick buildings displaying woodland floral designs. Sidewalks
are carved with totemic representations of eagles, bears, and other animals.
Green bike racks curve into flowers. Colorful murals with Indigenous faces
adorn buildings. For roughly five city blocks, green banners hang from light
posts declaring this stretch of main Minneapolis throughway as the American
Indian Cultural Corridor (hereafter the "Cultural Corridor"). Franklin Avenue,
affectionately known as "The Avenue" for decades by Phillips residents, has
had a long, storied history of Indigenous presence.[1] During the 1960s and '70s,
American Indians of various tribal nations could be found shopping in Gray's
Drugstore or socializing in bars and restaurants.[2] Indeed, it's on Franklin that
the Minneapolis Indian community birthed the American Indian Movement

(AIM) in 1968, and it's where in 1975 the community opened the doors of the Minneapolis American Indian Center, which recently celebrated its forty-fifth year of operation. The history of Franklin marks this space as clearly inhabited by Indigenous people, and with the 2010 commemoration of the Cultural Corridor, the urban Indian community continued a long process of (re)indigenizing the space of the city.[3]

This process of (re)indigenizing began in the early twentieth century when Indian women, particularly those from the White Earth Ojibwe Reservation in northern Minnesota, began gathering in social groups that acted as adaptive social networks from home. These women moved to Minneapolis–Saint Paul because of dispossession and severe unemployment on the reservation and built a foundation upon which larger, transformative projects would grow. In what follows, I demonstrate how the White Earth Ojibwe community persisted and thrived in the urban landscape. In particular, I examine how two White Earth Ojibwe women, Winnifred "Winnie" Jourdain and Emily Peake, worked to create social programs from the 1940s to the 1960s, and I demonstrate how this work led to their founding of the Minneapolis Indian Center. Their work, in effect, indigenized the landscape of an urban environment that was supposed to hasten their assimilation. With other Indian people in the city, these women transformed the urban spaces they inhabited into ones that accounted for Indigenous presence.

I interpret the (re)indigenizing process of Minneapolis–Saint Paul as twofold, requiring distinctly different conversations about Indigenous placemaking in the city and the larger metropolitan area. The first requires an immediate emphasis on Minneapolis as Dakota homeland and the Twin Cities as encompassing Bdote, the place of Dakota origin at the confluence of the Minnesota and Mississippi Rivers.[4] For Dakota people, the Twin Cities have always been an Indigenous place. Settler colonial claims on the Twin Cities involve the disregarding of Dakota rights to their homeland, as well as the dispossession and violent state-enforced exile of Dakota people in 1863, not only from the Twin Cities but also from what is now the state of Minnesota. Dakota call Minneapolis Bde Óta Othúŋwe, a city of lakes, and the Dakota community work to reinscribe the cityscape with their history, culture, and language, all of which make manifest Dakota resilience and refusal to be erased from their homelands. Community members launched the *Bdote Memory Map* online, which features virtual mapping with place names, histories, and videos of community members. Dakota worked tirelessly for years to legally change the name of former Lake Calhoun back to Bde Maka Ska, thereby demanding Minneapolitans recognize Dakota history and their ongoing right to be in their homelands.[5] Their practices and relationships to the city as homeland should be read as a confrontation with, and dismantling of, settler placemaking by returning Dakota meaning to the geography of a city stolen from their ancestors by the State of Minnesota and the United States.

The other conversation about indigenizing urban space involves accounting for mobile Indigenous people who belong to tribal nations other than Dakota. This chapter engages with this second examination of indigenizing urban space by centering on White Earth Ojibwe and our cultural practices of social infrastructure and community organizing that propelled Ojibwe placemaking in Minneapolis. I want to make clear that by examining Ojibwe placemaking I acknowledge that the land upon which the city sits is *not* Ojibwe homeland. Within this acknowledgment is room for larger conversations about urban Indigeneity and what it means to claim urban space in the homeland of other Indigenous nations. The experiences of non-Dakota Indigenous peoples are notably different. Movement to Minneapolis, while also involving dispossession, isn't a return, but, rather, a series of arrivals that requires a different method of placemaking, or indigenizing, of space.

While intertribal relationships brought non-Dakota Indigenous peoples to the area prior to the founding of Minneapolis as a city, their relationship to this space is one that is inherently different. For Dakota people this area is the center of the world and the location of their birth as a people. But for other Indigenous nations, including Ojibwe people, the land of Minneapolis does not carry this specific significance, and so non-Dakota Indigenous engagement with this space in the twentieth century was markedly different. For Ojibwe who make up a significant portion of the Minneapolis Indian community, indigenizing space is primarily about claiming space physically and socially for the continuity of Ojibwe identity and community. I write this study from the position of an urban White Earth Ojibwe woman. I have chosen to focus on White Earth networks for two reasons: first, because these are most familiar to me and my relationship to this place is inherently different; second, because widespread dispossession around the end of the nineteenth century led to migration and the transportation of our social networks from White Earth to Minneapolis. This migration is the foundation upon which the Minneapolis Indian community continued to build during the twentieth century.

For Indigenous peoples in Minneapolis, having a *physical* infrastructure to support the community is an essential part of our self-determinative practices that defy settler colonial expectations of assimilation. When I speak of infrastructure, I am writing about buildings that visibly promote Indigeneity through design, signage, and murals. I am speaking of physical manifestations of the city's Indigenous population, "signs" of belonging on roads, parks, and other urban infrastructure. The American Indian community within the city began erecting these physical signs decades before establishment of the Cultural Corridor. In the late 1960s, Minneapolis's Indian community made their presence known and Indian organizations and businesses have existed along Franklin ever since. The Indian community, under the leadership of AIM, was particularly important in shutting down bars and liquor stores that dotted the small stretch of city the Indian community frequented, resulting in new kinds of communal public space.[6]

Yet the community had to utilize preexisting structures to house schools, organizations, and services in the 1950s and 1960s, and they dreamed of building Indigenous-designed infrastructure.[7] In the 1970s the city's two most relevant examples of Indian-designed infrastructure were opened: the Little Earth of All Tribes housing development (1973) and the Minneapolis American Indian Center (1975), forever changing the landscape of Minneapolis. The physical creation of these places is a strong reminder that Indigenous presence—indeed, urban Indigenous existence—wouldn't have been possible without the tireless efforts of community members who fought for such visibility. I argue that the work to actualize Indigenous infrastructure began before the Second World War, with the transportation of White Earth Ojibwe community practices, relationships, and adaptive organizing methods. White Earth Ojibwe transported practices that provided for the community and built up a supportive social infrastructure that was the groundwork for contemporary indigenized placemaking.[8]

By examining White Earth connections to the foundation of Minneapolis's Indigenous community, I also highlight how Ojibwe cultural practices informed their indigenizing processes. Through tracing White Earth migration to Minneapolis in the 1920s, I discuss the mobile flexibility of Ojibwe community practices as they existed within women's sewing clubs, Indian organizations, and fledgling Indian centers. By detailing the lifelong work of Winnie Jourdain and Emily Peake, I explain how their work, understood from an Ojibwe perspective, provided other Indigenous peoples with space in the city, non-discriminatory services, and a vibrant intertribal network that continues to shape the ways we work and live.

WHITE EARTH OJIBWE AND TWENTIETH-CENTURY MIGRATION

The presence of Indigenous peoples in Minneapolis precedes the city itself. Despite violent removal from their lands following the Dakota-U.S. War of 1862, Dakota people have found ways to remain within the Minneapolis area. Yet the growth of the city hinged upon their removal, and while they remained numbers were small and easily overlooked. Such was the process of settlers' claiming of Dakota land. It wasn't until the twentieth century that Minneapolis began to see an increase in Indian peoples. Even then the population was small. The 1928 Meriam Report noted that the Indian population in Minneapolis was three hundred, with another three hundred across the Mississippi River in Saint Paul.[9] The trouble with census data is the ease with which census takers summarily decided citizens' racial makeup (as many public officials and scholars have noted, American Indian populations in urban areas have always been vastly underreported). In any case, there was a growing core of White Earth Ojibwe that would only increase in the 1930s.

White Earth Ojibwe visibility is the result of policies of dispossession and fraud starting in the 1890s and continuing through the first quarter of the twentieth century. White Earth has a well-documented history of land dispossession. From its inception, the reservation was designed to open up Ojibwe lands to white settlers. Established in 1867, the White Earth Reservation was created for the purpose of removing all Ojibwe to the northwestern swath of land in Minnesota. While federal attempts at removal ultimately failed, there was enough movement to make the reservation a reality.[10] Yet the threat of dispossession and displacement persisted across Minnesota. For White Earth Ojibwe, the land would remain threatened by settler interests well into the twentieth century.

White Earth also perfectly illustrates how Ojibwe people used mobility to maintain and structure community. Those who moved to White Earth brought with them all manner of Ojibwe social kinship networks and economic practices—in a word, Ojibwe ways of being. For Ojibwe people, seasonal economies made mobility essential: ricing, berrying, sugarbush camps, and winter villages varied in location and were governed by Ojibwe kinship rules. Through these seasonal rounds, families and clans reaffirmed relationships and alliances across and outside of Ojibwe political entities. Importantly, responsibility for community organizing during many of these labors often resided with Ojibwe women.[11] While movement to White Earth required some modification of Ojibwe economic systems, the core of such systems, and thus Ojibwe community, remained the same.[12] And while White Earth was different than previous homes farther east, Ojibwe people continued to perform cultural labor to uphold Ojibwe identity. Thus through the continuation of core cultural practices, those who moved to White Earth during the nineteenth century preserved Ojibwe identities by transposing land-based practices within White Earth. White Earth Ojibwe would adapt these same practices in urban spaces through social infrastructural networks in a similar fashion in the twentieth century following dispossession.

The passage of multiple federal Indian policies had devastating impacts on Ojibwe land bases and thus on the abilities of Ojibwe people to maintain land-based practices.[13] In 1889 Congress passed the Nelson Act, which worked in tandem with the General Allotment Act of 1887 and attempted to force Ojibwe to accept their allotments in White Earth, thereby relinquishing their claims to lands throughout Minnesota. The Nelson Act also set the legislative stage for further dispossession as White Earth's population rose over the next decade. Greed for timber left White Earth particularly vulnerable after the passage of the 1904 Steenerson Act, the 1906 Burke Act, and the Clapp Rider attached to the 1906 Indian Appropriation Act. These three pieces of legislation all engaged in eugenicist language of mixed-blood competency to argue for the permittance of selling timber and allotments.[14] Finally, the 1920 establishment of a White Earth "blood roll" marked a tremendous number of White Earth citizens as mixed and thus "competent" enough to sell off their allotments under existing laws.[15] Ensuing fraudulent land transfers meant that by the mid-1920s many Ojibwe families were landless.[16] Without land upon which to continue self-sustaining practices, many turned to waged labor to make ends meet. Families moved to bordertowns and nearby locales that offered steady work. Even more people moved to cities such as Duluth, Milwaukee, and Chicago.[17] Naturally, because of its proximity, White Earth Ojibwe also moved to Minneapolis, the regional hub of industry, in search of employment. In the city one could find work in clothing factories, laundries, homes and other businesses (doing domestic work), as well as performing manual labor and various forms of white-collar and skilled blue-collar work.[18]

By the late 1920s, White Earth Ojibwe were joining other Indigenous peoples who had moved before them. These newcomers were welcomed by an Indian population that the 1928 Meriam Report considered "middle-class" and "well-established wage earners."[19] While small in comparison to Minneapolis's largely

Euro-American population, this community was by all accounts tightknit and unwilling to cast off their Indigenous identities and social networks. While the Meriam Report preferred to focus on the economic transformation of poverty-stricken Indians into comfortable urban, middle-class "whites," it also had to reckon with "great insistence . . . [on] the right to be designated 'Indian'" by persons they deemed as white "with a dash of Indian blood."[20] Given the large number of families bonded by ties of sociality and tribal affiliation (the former especially noted in the Meriam Report), Indigenous assimilation into Minneapolis society was far from a sure thing in the 1920s and 30s.[21] Determined to retain their Indigenous identities, they built on their preexisiting social networks, which allowed them to meet, engage with, and support one another. A number of organizations, both political and social, appeared in Minneapolis in the 1930s and 1940s, including the Sah-Kah-Tay (Sunshine) Club, and the Na-gu-aub (Rainbow) Club.[22]

SOCIAL CLUBS, SOCIAL INFRASTRUCTURE, AND MOVING TOWARD A CENTER

Winnie Jourdain was twenty-six when, after the death of her first husband, she moved to Minneapolis in 1926. A widow, Jourdain's decision was primarily one of economic necessity; the search for work led her to the city in the hopes of being able to support herself and her young son. The general response to her move was not enthusiastic, as she would recall: "'Everyone told me I would starve to death down there but what could I do? There was no work on the reservation."[23] And she continued, "'I told them I wouldn't starve as long as my knees could bend and there were floors to scrub.'"[24] The employment situation in Minneapolis was far better than at home, and Jourdain and her son moved to the city where her sister, Clara, was already employed as a maid. For nearly twelve years from the time she arrived, Jourdain worked at Minneapolis Custom Laundry as part of their mailing operations.

During this time she enjoyed a mobility that allowed her to visit White Earth regularly. It's unclear exactly how she traveled, but it's likely that she went by train. With a station in Mahnomen, rail had a great effect on transportation to and from the reservation. Jourdain's mobility allowed for the maintenance of ties to family and home while living in Minneapolis. Indeed, it was on a trip back to White Earth that she met her second husband, Sonny Jourdain. Her social network encompassed the journey from city to reservation, and while her life was certainly different than it had been before 1926, there's little evidence that she wavered in her Ojibwe identity. The fact that living in Minneapolis did not preclude her from visiting White Earth is precisely the kind of continued mobility that Ojibwe have long folded into our collective understandings of self, community, and the multiple places we call home.

Indian Minneapolis was small, yet Jourdain's early years there introduced her to a community of other Indian women. Jourdain's role as an organizer was minimal in the 1930s. Most of her memories were of working and raising her children. Still, it was at this time that she most likely met the Peakes, another White Earth Ojibwe family who had been active in the community for years. The Peakes represent multigenerational Ojibwe work in the Minneapolis Indian community. Frederick and Louise Peake moved to Minneapolis from White Earth around 1914, with their young daughter Natalie. By all accounts, the Peakes have typically been identified as part of the "middle-class" Minneapolis Indians discussed in the Meriam Report. Fred's training as a lawyer as well as his previous practice in White Earth should have secured some financial stability. Yet Fred struggled to break into the legal profession in the Twin Cities, with some suggesting that it was primarily because he was Indian. When their youngest daughter, Emily, was born in 1920, the family was making do with Fred's wages as a laborer with General Mills, but the circumstances of the Peakes' lives in the city hinged entirely upon his ability to work.[25]

After 1929, Fred was no longer a part of the family's day-to-day life, as his struggles with employment, combined with a chronic battle with depression, resulted in an attempted suicide. He was hospitalized and would remain there until his death in 1935.[26] This loss had a profound effect on the family. Despite her sorrow, Louise, now raising her children alone, continued to focus her energies on the community. The Peake house had operated for years as a safe place for traveling family and friends who were in need of shelter. Louise was an earnest host, always facilitating the networking that the growing Indian community relied upon. Reflecting on Louise's well-known hospitality years later, former director of the Upper Midwest American Indian Center Jim Longie (Cree) recalled, "Louise's house was always open to anyone and everyone. We would all go over . . . to visit Louise. [She] would feed anyone who came by. She helped everyone and fed people in need."[27] Under her mother's care, Emily grew up in Ojibwe and intertribal social networks. These experiences would have a great influence over Emily's own future role within Indian Minneapolis.

By the 1930s, Louise was an active participant in a variety of non-Indian women's church groups and in the late 1930s she would begin hosting the Sah-Kah-Tay Club, which sometimes met at the Peake house on Fifth Avenue, four blocks south of Franklin. Involving both Indian and non-Indian women, Sah-Kah-Tay operated as a space where women socialized around food, sewed or planned dinners, and held other fundraisers for the Indian community. While its membership was mixed, the leadership of women such as Louise made it an Indian-driven club. Following the Second World War, Louise sponsored the Na-gu-aub Club, an affiliate club of Sah-Kah-Tay made up entirely of young Ojibwe women.[28] Like its forerunner, Na-gu-aub was a space for socializing, learning, practicing Ojibwe cultural skills, and discussing important Indian issues. The intergenerational engagement shown between the two clubs represents the continuation of cultural practices in urban settings. Among Sah-Kah-Tay's public outreach efforts, the club also made baskets, rugs, beadwork, and moccasins, often around someone's dining room table. The skills associated with creating these cultural products were "taught . . . to the younger girls so that there are now some experts among them, too."[29] Through Na-gu-aub, young women who had moved to the city for work were able to develop urban Ojibwe networks that acted as "a comfortable refuge in a strange city."[30] These clubs rooted the Peake women within the growing Minneapolis Indian community. By leading and participating in these clubs, the Peakes engaged with existing Ojibwe social networks and created new ones in the bargain. Through their involvement, they worked to reimagine an urban landscape that accounted for Indigenous presence.

By the time Emily Peake reached adulthood at the beginning of the Second World War, the family's presence was cemented within the social landscape of Indian Minneapolis. After a period serving in the Coast Guard, Emily returned home in 1953 to support her mother and niece.[31] Once there, she continued the community-oriented work she had witnessed throughout her childhood. She organized children's recreational events and joined a small group hosting Indian powwows, dinners, and other programs in non-Indian spaces like the Edward F. Waite Neighborhood House. Like her mother, Emily would maintain her home as a place of refuge, particularly for youth, for the rest of her life.[32] As federal relocation encouraged more Indigenous movement to the city in the 1950s, Emily Peake became a grassroots organizer for the Upper Midwest American Indian Center (UMAIC), the city's first Indian center. By the 1960s, she was a central figure in the growth of Indigenous infrastructure in Minneapolis, maintaining her family's longstanding role as determined supporters of an urban Indian future.[33]

Meanwhile, during the war years, Winnie Jourdain "became active in the many problems that began to present themselves" and "was drawn into more and more activities" centered around creating physical spaces and resources for the community.[34] She quickly became engaged with Sah-Kah-Tay, serving as treasurer for a number of years. Her involvement with Indian women's clubs would continue until she moved back to White Earth in the 1980s. Alongside her membership in these home-based community spaces, she provided support on an individual level. Like the Peakes, the Jourdain family acted as a point of entrance for Indian people as they adjusted to the city. Whether it was people passing through to a final destination or young women straight out of boarding school, many, as Jourdain quickly realized, shared a familiar story of moving for work only to come up empty-handed. Jourdain felt it was her responsibility to help newly arrived Indians get on their feet. Her house on Franklin and Portland Avenues also served as a temporary home for migrant Natives, particularly young women. Years later Jourdain recalled,

The city was full of prejudice. I think it still is. I helped Indian people get jobs. It was hard for them, they were the last ones hired and first to be fired. I helped 19 girls from Flandreau get work. I told them 'Never stay at a job if you don't like it. Quit! I'll take you in until you get a new job.' I did this for many years . . . because my people needed help, not because I wanted recognition.[35]

Winnie's support for the community was vital to many Indians moving to the city at this time. In the postwar years she became a pivotal figure within other social organizations such as the Broken Arrow Service Guild, believing they were of great importance to the community.

Broken Arrow followed in the spirit of previous sewing clubs, particularly Sah-Kah-Tay, and its members first met in the late 1940s in private homes to sew, plan fundraisers, and socialize. The group was well known for its work hosting quilting luncheons and fundraising dinners for scholarships. Most importantly, Broken Arrow served as a social hub for Indian women in a manner similar to earlier sewing clubs. Winnie Jourdain, one of its cofounders and longtime members, saw how the group lessened the "loneliness and frustration" of life in the city, especially for grandmothers who stayed home to "[babysit] for their grown children."[36] The Guild, Jourdain said, "got them out of the house and involved.'"[37]

During its first decade, Broken Arrow developed relationships with non-Indian religious and civic organizations, which propelled their abilities to host events, secure social and financial support, and increase their public visibility. In the early 1950s, the group secured sponsorship through the United Church Women and moved their operations into the larger space of the Gethsemane Episcopal Church. Such a move meant more visibility within the non-Indian religious space of United Church programming. Under this umbrella, Jourdain and other members asked that non-Indian women offer rides and join them in friendship while listening and learning about urban Indian experiences. By the mid-1950s, Broken Arrow was meeting at the Waite House and was included in their Indian programs. It was at this time that Jourdain, along with other Indigenous Waite House organizers, started to design Indian organizations that would bring attention to urban Indian issues and secure necessary support for Indian-specific services.[38]

By the 1960s, both Jourdain and Peake were deeply invested in creating Indian organizations that appropriately served the community. Their years of work prior to their involvement in the founding and operation of a number of flourishing Indian organizations bound them closely with other Indigenous people, many newly arrived to the city. Peake's and Jourdain's organizational work within the Indian community was intimately tied to Ojibwe cultural practices that position women as decision makers and influencers within Ojibwe nations. As Brenda Child articulates, Ojibwe nations have historically valued women's roles within the community as such. When Ojibwe people transitioned to urban living, women adapted their communal roles for a city environment. These responsibilities come with being part of the collective and, as organizers of key community endeavors (whether in a seasonal economy or the city), this responsibility translated into work on "behalf of their communities."[39]

These women sought little praise for their efforts, performing this crucial work because it was needed and because they had something to offer. That was how Ojibwe social networks operated regardless of where they were transplanted, their work being an extension of Ojibwe social infrastructure. Movement itself didn't sever connections to family, friends, or homeland; rather, it required an adaptive understanding of what Ojibwe life would look like in the city. For these women, ties with family and community facilitated their leadership within an urban Indian community that would expand rapidly in the 1950s and 1960s.

THE PROBLEM OF THE CENTER: ACTUALIZING INDIGENOUS INFRASTRUCTURE

By the 1960s, the Indigenous population of Minneapolis had started to rise dramatically. By 1963 the over five thousand Indians living there struggled to find decent housing, stable employment, and adequate social services support.[40] The city's social services structures required permanent residence in the city, which newly arrived Indians could not prove, and attempts to seek help with finances, employment, and housing often resulted in an endless chain of referrals that bounced people from community centers to social service agencies and back. The city itself was aware of Indian struggles, at least to the extent that numerous research committees at the city, county, and state levels were formed throughout the 1960s. Despite civic and religious organizations attempting to "solve the Indian problem," non-Indian Minneapolitans were no closer to creating solutions to the problems facing the city's Indigenous population.

Indigenous organizations, however, formed throughout the city to attempt to provide desperately needed services, recreational space, and cultural programming. As noted, Indian women's sewing groups acted as spaces for Indigenous women to socialize and strategize, and these groups would begin moving into non-Indian community centers in the 1950s and 1960s. There White Earth Ojibwe women like Winnie Jourdain and Emily Peake were able to garner financial support for preexisting programs to integrate Indigenous needs into non-Indian community centers' missions. Indeed, Peake's work at Edward F. Waite Neighborhood House allowed her to act as a pivotal point of entrance for newly arrived Indians. Her volunteer shifts placed her directly in the path of those looking for community and assistance. It's little surprise that Indian organizations and early Indian centers were born in these non-Indian spaces and that relationships with community centers allowed them to access some funds and to develop institutional strategies to ask for more support from the city's range of non-Indian community organizations.

Yet by the late 1960s, Indian organizations were still struggling to secure monetary support to realize the kinds of Indian-run employment, housing, education, and recreational programs they envisioned. Even more importantly, the community's dream of a centrally located, large Indian center that could serve as the core point of Indian gathering was no closer to being realized than it had been at the beginning of the decade. Multiple research committees throughout the 1960s published reports that found there was need for such an Indian center, yet little was done beyond this declaration. Small Indian centers renting out minimal space from other organizations like the Waite House, the Division of Indian Work, and Unity House in north Minneapolis were left to find ways to expand beyond their current circumstances.[41]

When the Community Health and Welfare Council (CHWC) of Hennepin County established the American Indian Centers Committee in 1968 to evaluate existing Indian centers and their struggles, Indigenous women quickly became involved. The committee itself was created with the input of the Indian community and included individuals "considered representative of the Indian community, the non-Indian community," and the CHWC.[42] Among those serving on the committee were Winnie Jourdain, Pearl Bisson (White Earth Ojibwe), and Ada Deer (Menominee). Their presence on this research committee was part of a decade of Indigenous women's participation on predominantly non-Indian committees on Indian issues. Just a year prior, six Indian women—including Jourdain and Peake—actively steered the League of Women Voters to conduct more thoughtful research on urban Indian issues and to engage with organizations like Broken Arrow and UMAIC.[43] Jourdain, Bisson, and Deer—joined by a number of Indigenous men—steered the CHWC committee, which was more than unusual. What made the 1969 CHWC *American Indian Centers Review* unique in terms of previous research was its examination of seven different Indian centers in the Twin Cities. These centers "all provid[ed] some services to some Indian people," but "none of the centers provid[ed] the amount and kinds of programming needed to meet the total needs of the Indian population in the urban area."[44] The hope was that by examining these seven centers and comparing offered services and pinpointing their struggles with programming, staffing, funding, and physical location, the Indian Centers Committee would be better able to provide clear recommendations toward the creation of a single, large Indian center.

The seven centers spanned the Twin Cities but were mostly clustered in south Minneapolis, especially in the densely populated Indian community in the Phillips neighborhood just south of downtown. The report included the Division of Indian Work (DIW), the Episcopal Neighborhood Center (not specifically Indian), the Indian American Youth Center, the American Indian Citizens Community Center (AICCC), and UMAIC.[45] Of these south Minneapolis centers, only DIW and UMAIC were located some distance from Franklin Avenue. Many of these centers had shared histories, Indigenous community members having moved between them as volunteers and staff, and some centers had previously been linked through funding. The interlocked history of Indian centers in Minneapolis is particularly apparent when discussing the AICCC and UMAIC.

UMAIC's role in the development of other Indian centers, including the Minneapolis American Indian Center, is the result of its early development and the collaborative efforts of the center's staff and board members—including Emily Peake—which connected Indian and non-Indian organizational spaces. Following decades' old practices of using private homes to organize, UMAIC was founded in the late 1950s when a small group of Indians gathered in a "private home . . . to discuss the establishment of an Indian Center" and then proceeded to develop this hypothetical center by asking for support from non-Indian individuals and community centers.[46] UMAIC's founding was also inherently linked to non-Indian organizations like the Waite House, where Peake and fellow Ojibwe Larry Martin networked and developed the community center's Indian programming with Jourdain and other Indigenous women and men. In fact, in 1961, prior to UMAIC's incorporation, Peake, along with James Longie, met with a group of non-Indians to discuss securing a location in north Minneapolis for the new center.[47]

Between 1961 and 1969, UMAIC struggled to obtain funding for a permanent home, salaried staff, and enough financial resources to actively help the community on issues such as employment, housing, and childcare.[48] UMAIC's instability speaks to the dilemma that Indian organizations often found themselves in: the need they were seeking to meet was acknowledged as important by the non-Indian community, but often actual fiscal support was long in arriving, which limited their ability to succeed. Aware of their own shortcomings, UMAIC's larger projects were limited primarily to "various activities, most of them being social in nature," including suppers and monthly powwows organized by a small committee of women including Peake and Jourdain.[49] By the late 1960s, UMAIC had started to apply for federal funding through the Office of Economic Opportunity (OEO), which would have a profound effect on the Minneapolis Indian community.

By the time of the CHWC report, UMAIC and the AICCC were becoming distinct entities with dissenting opinions on providing for the community, but their tumultuous relationship hinged upon the fact that UMAIC played a large part in creating the AICCC. In 1966, UMAIC submitted an OEO grant proposal for an Indian center and, when it was selected under the OEO's Citizens Community Center program, UMAIC was positioned to manage its development, programming, and finances.[50] Thus for roughly three years, the AICCC and

UMAIC operated under the same programming missions and shared staff. Throughout this period Emily Peake worked with both centers, distinct only in name, and by 1968 she was serving as director of the AICCC. In time, however, Peake's method of community organizing within institutional systems and in collaboration with non-Indian organizations would come into direct conflict with a different approach to Indian organizing derived out of radical action and Red Power.

The divergence of Indian organizational practices played out within the AICCC, as Peake and AIM members sought to direct the center's programming and future. A number of factors propelled AIM's founding in the summer of 1968. When AIM was founded, relocation had been in full swing for years and thousands of American Indians across the country had traveled to cities in the hopes of securing work, good housing, and some level of upward socioeconomic mobility as promised by the Bureau of Indian Affairs.[51] Minneapolis was not an official relocation city, yet its proximity to an incredible number of reservations meant that thousands of Indians moved to the Twin Cities regardless. Once there, the city's social service system and stretched-thin community center structures offered little support for newly arrived Indians. Still people found each other in non-Indian centers, in bars, in neighborhoods where rent was affordable, and through preexisting social networks. As the size of the community grew, so did the visibility of anti-Indian discrimination. Years of police brutality and a lack of decent, secure employment and housing, among other issues, culminated in AIM's creation. AIM's high-profile leaders harnessed a different kind of politics than Peake's generation and AIM used confrontation protest and portrayed militancy. These differing tactics resulted in a split between the AICCC and UMAIC in 1969, when AIM leaders charged that the AICCC under Peake didn't serve the Indian community, that its leadership was predominantly white, and that it was unable to provide for the community.[52]

The messiness of Indian organizing is often portrayed as "fracturing," divisive, and full of escalating tension, but I want to make clear that I am not interested in those narratives. Rather, I see Peake's 1969 resignation from the AICCC, and UMAIC's split from that center, as evidence of a multigenerational, fast-growing community navigating a shifting social landscape impacted by urban deterioration, Indian relocation, and larger radical social movements. UMAIC, which had been founded by older members of the Minneapolis Indian community, was without doubt more conservative than Red Power and AIM's militancy. The two centers that shared financial resources and staff were, also, miles apart over issues of method, non-Indian involvement, and programming for the Indian community. The realities of Indian Minneapolis were that incredible growth in the 1960s, along with rising radical politics and activist organizing of the era, operated alongside older generations of Indian Minneapolitans who had been working within non-Indian systems since the 1920s.

While the public relationships between Peake and UMAIC and between AIM and the AICCC had been severed by the time of the CHWC report, both UMAIC and AIM continued to work with other Indian organizations on the creation of a larger Indian center. Despite UMAIC's struggles, the CHWC report recommended that the city's oldest Indian center represent the community in its bid to achieve what would become the Minneapolis American Indian Center (MAIC).[53] The steps forward were also promoted by the year-old American Indian Urban Federation, a representative organization designed to "[unify] all American Indian organizations" in the city while acting as a negotiator for the Indian community's needs and wishes.[54] The Federation was not the first multiorganizational structure in Minneapolis. Nearly twenty years prior, Winnie Jourdain joined a small contingent of postwar Indian leaders to found American Indians, Inc., which also sought to act as a representative voice for various organizations and community members.[55] The Federation, however, was unique in its ability to mediate between the city and the various Indian centers and organizations, particularly in relation to securing property and funding for the MAIC.

With UMAIC at the helm and various organizations involved, including Broken Arrow and AIM, the Federation began the process of securing property for the MAIC. The way forward was not always clear. Though the Federation and UMAIC were able to secure a 1971 grant through the OEO's Community Action Program for a Model Urban Indian Center project, the city of Minneapolis was clearly intent on deciding where such a center would be built. It was at this juncture that Winnie Jourdain, who had been working for decades to indigenize spaces for the Minneapolis Indian community, became the main voice of the fight for the MAIC. The oft-repeated story involves an elderly Jourdain, who stood up alongside other Indian women organizers and publicly shamed the city council, saying, "'You took this whole country from us. . . . All we want are a couple of acres.'"[56] With those words ringing in their ears, the city of Minneapolis approved the use of the lot immediately beside the Adams Elementary lot at Franklin and Bloomington Avenues. The MAIC was now fully under development at the heart of the Indian community in Phillips.

It would be another four years before MAIC opened its doors at 1530 East Franklin, the literal center of the Indian community along Franklin Avenue. The process of founding the center was long and arduous, exposing diverse strategies that Indigenous people in Minneapolis pursued to indigenize city space. Indian community members had to find common ground among themselves, apply for a plethora of grants, and work within and alongside municipal, state, and federal institutions and governments. The center was intended to serve a wide variety of purposes. It was meant to be a central space for housing, employment, educational, and social services support, as well as for social and ceremonial gatherings. It would house cultural programming, clubs, afterschool programs, and arts displays and hold a library and archives. In essence MAIC was designed to be "a place where [the community] could come to live as Indians and more fully understand what being Indian means."[57]

Peake and Jourdain are just two of the women who worked to actualize an Indian center in Minneapolis. Their skills as organizers, researchers, and staffers meant they had amassed a deep knowledge of how to work within state and federal systems to obtain the necessary financial support to implement Indigenous-driven programs. Furthermore, their involvement with numerous Indian organizations meant that these women were instrumental in the behind-the-scenes planning that made this dream a reality. MAIC was groundbreaking not only locally but also nationally. It was one of the first Indian centers of "its kind in the country [to be] planned, funded and run entirely by urban Indians."[58] Its physical design was also unique. Its architecture was intended to "proclaim to the Indian community and the rest of the city an emerging pride in the Indian heritage," while existing as part of an urban space.[59] The design, including exteriors and landscaping, was undertaken by Hodne-Stageberg Partners in collaboration with Dennis Sun Rhodes (Arapaho) in 1970, with a ground-breaking ceremony two years later.[60]

The building's design included substantial Indigenous elements and natural materials. Glass walls open onto large high-ceilinged gathering spaces and athletic courts to create a spacious, airy feel. Wood was used throughout, including on the south-facing façade designed by Ojibwe artist George Morrison. Architectural plans for the building followed Indigenous requests to reflect cultural knowledge about east and west as cardinal directions, and circles were so fully incorporated into the building's design that one would be hard pressed to count them all.[61] The fact that the entire design was influenced by community members cannot be overlooked. Their involvement signifies the building's reflection of the community and their values, hopes, and dreams that are now rooted in an urban landscape. MAIC's continual presence on Franklin is not only a focal point of the area but also a point of pride. Although MAIC has been joined by other organizations that have left their mark upon the Minneapolis cityscape, the Indian Center's presence as one of the first creations of Indigenous landscape mean its history is bound up in how Minneapolis Indian community members understood themselves in relation to one another, to other Minneapolitans, and to the space of the city itself.

The Ojibwe women chronicled within this chapter by no means did this work alone, yet Indian women's community organizing work deserves far more attention than it has received. Their efforts extend back into Minneapolis history and were based upon understandings of community and the work needed to support their people in a variety of spaces. Their experiences led to the successes of UMAIC and the founding of the MAIC. Their work was vital. As Jourdain said decades after MAIC had opened, "We were there."[62] Their presence is an extension and continuation of not only Ojibwe practice but also the intertribal community that Minneapolis was and continues to be. Their work has shaped the community and the very landscape of the city itself. In the process Jourdain and Peake have influenced urban Indian understandings of what belonging to this place means, and that legacy continues into the future.

NOTES

1. A terminological note: I use Indigenous, American Indian, and Indian interchangeably, maintaining tribal affiliation where possible. My choices stem from the communities I write about and their respective usages.

2. Kay Erickson, "The Ojibwe Project," accessed April 10, 2018, https://www .ojibweproject.com/.

3. Native American Community Development Initiative, "Franklin Avenue Past, Present, and Future," YouTube video, 9:30, posted by nativespotlight, January 7, 2010, www.youtube.com/watch?v=mymMxqrY_CR4.

4. Gwen Westerman and Bruce White, *Mni Sota Makoce: The Land of the Dakota* (St. Paul: Minnesota Historical Society Press, 2012), 15.

5. Minnesota Humanities Center, *Bdote Memory Map*, accessed April 20, 2019, https: /bdotememorymap.org/.

6. Literature on AIM includes Paul Chaat Smith and Robert Allen Warrior, *Like a Hurricane: The Indian Movement from Alcatraz to Wounded Knee* (New York: New Press, 1997); and Clyde Bellecourt, *The Thunder before the Storm: The Autobiography of Clyde Bellecourt* (St. Paul: Minnesota Historical Society Press, 2018).

7. Native American Community Development Initiative, "Franklin Avenue Past, Present, and Future."

8. Influential work that discusses similar urban Indigenous social infrastructural practices includes Coll Thrush, *Native Seattle: Histories from the Crossing-Over Place* (Seattle: University of Washington Press, 2007); Renya K. Ramirez, *Native Hubs: Culture, Community, and Belonging in Silicon Valley and Beyond* (Durham, N.C.: Duke University Press, 2007); Nicholas Rosenthal, *Reimagining Indian Country: Native American Migration and Identity in Twentieth-Century Los Angeles* (Chapel Hill: University of North Carolina Press, 2012); Susan Applegate Krouse and Heather A. Howard, eds., *Keeping the Campfires Going: Native Women's Activism in Urban Communities* (Lincoln: University of Nebraska Press, 2009); and Evelyn Peters and Chris Andersen, eds., *Indigenous in the City: Contemporary Identities and Cultural Innovation* (Vancouver: University of British Columbia Press, 2013).

9. Institute of Government Research, *The Problem with Indian Administration* (Baltimore: Johns Hopkins University Press, 1928), 727. Hereafter cited as the Meriam Report.

10. Gerald Vizenor and Jill Doerfler, *The White Earth Nation: Ratification of a Native Democratic Constitution* (Lincoln: University of Nebraska Press, 2012), 39. See also Jill Doerfler, *Those Who Belong: Identity, Family, Blood, and Citizenship among White Earth Anishinaabeg* (East Lansing: Michigan State University Press, 2015); and Melissa Meyer, *The White Earth Tragedy: Ethnicity and Dispossession at a Minnesota Anishinaabe Reservation, 1889–1920* (Lincoln: University of Nebraska Press, 1999).

11. For more on Ojibwe seasonal economic practices, consult Brenda J. Child's work.

12. Winona LaDuke, "The White Earth Anishinaabeg Economy: From Self-Reliance to Dependence and Back Again" (MA thesis: Antioch University, 1988), 50.

13. Red Lake is the exception.

14. Meyer, *White Earth Tragedy*, 142–43, 153.

15. Meyer, *White Earth Tragedy*, 166–71.

16. This history needs to balance individuals' choices to sell allotments with fraudulent deed transfers. The federal government was aware that the White Earth situation, like allotment in general, had been a failure by the late 1920s. The extent of fraudulent land sales was further exposed by a 1980s investigation, which contributed to the creation of the White Earth Land Settlement Act of 1986.

17. Information derived from an analysis of 1930s White Earth rolls.

18. Meriam Report, 730–31.

19. Meriam Report.

20. Meriam Report, 729.

21. Meriam Report, 732. The report maintains that "most Indians hold to old friendships with the Indian associates of their childhood and youth"; that they make effort to socialize with friends in disparate urban and reservation locations; and that while there weren't large pockets of Indian people in the early twentieth century, connections were maintained among Indians in the city and on reservations.

22. Nancy Shoemaker, "Urban Indians and Ethnic Choices: American Indian Organizations in Minneapolis, 1920–1950," *Western Historical Quarterly* 19 (1988): 431–47.

23. Pauline Brunette, "Winnifred Jourdain: A Profile of Courage," *Indigenous Woman* (Spring 1991): 22.

24. Emily Peake, " Winnie," Research File on Minnesota Ojibwe Women, Minnesota Historical Society.

25. Notes from meeting with Jackie Heine, May 25, 2001, Jane Pejsa Collection on Emily Peake, Box 2, Folder 13, James K. Hosmer Special Collections, Hennepin County Public Library, Minneapolis, Minn.

26. Jane Pejsa, *The Life of Emily Peake: One Dedicated Ojibwe* (Minneapolis, Minn.: Nodin Press, 2003), 70–74, 77.

27. James Longie, Interview with Jane Pejsa, April 30, 2001. Jane Pejsa Collection on Emily Peake.

28. Jackie Heine, Interview with Jane Pejsa, Apr. 19, 2001. Jane Pejsa Collection on Emily Peake.

29. "Indian Women Are Active in the Federation," *Minneapolis Star*, October 24, 1940, 28.

30. Pejsa, *The Life of Emily Peake*, 80, 90–91.

31. Emily's sister Natalie was hospitalized in the early 1940s and would remain so for the rest of her life.

32. Joyce Yellowhammer, phone interview notes by Jane Pejsa, March 20, 2002, Jane Pejsa Collection on Emily Peake, Box 2, Folder 13.

33. Pejsa, *The Life of Emily Peake*, 136–44.

34. Peake, "Winnie," 9–10.

35. Brunette, "Winnifred Jourdain."

36. George Grimm, "I Like It Here," *Minneapolis Tribune*, January 18, 1965, 20; Brunette, "Winnifred Jourdain," 23.

37. Brunette, "Winnifred Jourdain, "23.

38. Edward F. Waite House Records, Minnesota Historical Society, St. Paul, Minn.; Greater Minneapolis Council of Churches Records, Minnesota Historical Society, St. Paul, Minn.

39. Brenda J. Child, *Holding Our World Together: Ojibwe Women and the Survival of Community* (New York: Viking, 2012), xvi.

40. "Chapter 7: An Inventory of Present Day Indian Life in Cities and on Reservations," *Draft of The Indian in Minnesota, c. 1963*, Indian Subject Files, 1947–1964, Governor's Human Rights Commission Records, Folder 18, Box 1, Minnesota Historical Society, St. Paul, Minn.

41. Edward F. Waite House Records; Greater Minneapolis Council of Churches Records; Upper Midwest American Indian Center Records, 1961–1968, Minnesota Historical Society, St. Paul, Minn.

42. American Indian Centers Committee, *American Indian Centers Review* (Minneapolis, Minn.: Community Health and Welfare Council of Hennepin County, 1969), 3.

43. Dottie Speidel to Fran Paulu, Nancy Wita, and Marguerite Bensen, undated, League of Women Voters Minneapolis Records, 1919–1991, Box 19, Folder 2, Manuscripts Collection, Minnesota Historical Society, St. Paul, Minn.

44. American Indian Centers Committee, *American Indian Centers Review*, 3.

45. American Indian Centers Committee, *American Indian Centers Review*. The North-Side American Indian Teen Center and the St. Paul American Indian Center were also included.

46. "History of Upper Midwest American Indian Center," Upper Midwest American Indian Center Records, 1961–1968, Box 1, Folder 1, Manuscripts Collections, Minnesota Historical Society, St, Paul, Minn.

47. Al Rosen, interview notes by Jane Pejsa, June 6, 2001, Jane Pejsa Collection on Emily Peake, Box 2, Folder 14.

48. UMAIC moved to at least four locations in eight years.

49. Handwritten UMAIC History from Joyce Yellowhammer, Jane Pejsa Collection on Emily Peake, Box 1, Folder 12; Larry Martin, interview notes with Jane Pejsa, November 8, 2001, Jane Pejsa Collection on Emily Peake, Box 2, Folder 14.

50. American Indian Centers Committee, *American Indian Centers Review*, 5.

51. There's an extensive literature on the BIA's relocation program and its repercussions. For detailed histories, consult the work of Donald Fixico, Douglas K. Miller, Troy Johnson, Susan Lobo, Kurt Peters, and James B. LaGrand.

52. "Indian Center Aides Reply to Grievances," *Minneapolis Tribune*, June 29, 1969, 2B; Upper Midwest American Indian Center Records, Box 1.

53. American Indian Centers Committee, *American Indian Centers Review*, 28.

54. American Indian [Urban] Federation of the Twin Cities, Constitution and By Laws, c. 1968, Minnesota Indian Affairs Council Records, Box 4, Folder 16.

55. American Indians, Inc., *The Peace Pipe* 1, no. 1 (1956), 3, in Minnesota Department of Human Rights, Records, Box 127.L.13.1B, Folder 8.

56. Paul Levy, "Spirit of White Earth: City Life," *Star Tribune*, April 29, 1999, E14. Jourdain's grandson, Andy Favorite, attributed this quote to Emily Peake in an interview with Jane Pejsa in 2001.

57. Betty Binkard and Ilga Eglitis, "Urban Indian Center: New Focus for the Indian Community," in *Closing the Circle: The Indian in Minneapolis, A New Era*, ed. Betty Binkard (Minneapolis: University of Minnesota School of Journalism and Mass Communications, 1975).

58. Mike Steele, "Indian Center Will Shatter Stereotypes," *Minneapolis Tribune*, February 16, 1975, 9D.

59. Carol Herselle Krinsky, *Contemporary Native American Architecture* (New York: Oxford University Press, 1996), 162.

60. Krinsky, *Contemporary Native American Architecture*, 162–64.

61. Krinsky, *Contemporary Native American Architecture*, 163.

62. Brunette, "Winnifred Jourdain."

DOUGLAS K. MILLER

9

THERE IS NO SUCH THING AS AN URBAN INDIAN

Native American People Living in Dallas

"The urban Indian is a joke to us," Dallas Indian Center Executive Director Mary Williams told a reporter in 1971. This was one year prior to the Bureau of Indian Affairs' (BIA) termination of its urban relocation program. Beginning in 1952, the relocation program provided limited support for the one-way movement of Native American peoples from ancestral homelands and reservation lands to major metropolises mostly west of the Mississippi, including Dallas, which became a relocation center in 1957. In the context of Cold War cultural consensus, city living, the program promised, would deliver new and better work, education, and social opportunities. Meanwhile, Native and non-Native critics of the program argued that relocation was a false promise—a new strategy in the United States' old effort at detribalizing Indigenous peoples and destroying Indigenous cultures. Mary Williams, however, shared a different assessment, one that transcended binary thinking. From her perspective, Indigenous peoples practiced Native nationalism in urban space: they imagined the city as a resource while remaining connected to home. Intertribal urban communities reflected creative Indigenous survival strategies, but the formation of urban communities was not an initial or primary concern. "Indians go to the city for jobs and education and work skills to take back home," she elaborated. "Detribalized Indians are scarce. Even when they mix here at the center, they're tribe first and Indian second." They found the city exhausting and home rejuvenating, she explained. "We have to go home to get built back up, so that we can come back and keep going, but Dallas is an interlude and home is home."[1]

To Angela Young, a Choctaw citizen and Indian center director at Dallas's Inter-Tribal Center almost fifty years later, the idea of an urban Indian remains a joke. "What is an *urban* Indian?" she asked me during an interview in 2018. "We're Indian, no matter where we live. You're Choctaw, no matter if you're in Alaska. You're Choctaw, no matter if you're in Hawaii." "Yeah, you're not *Alaska* Choctaw," fellow Choctaw citizen and center behavioral health counselor Mike Frazier agreed. "Right," they laughed together. "You're still Indian, no matter where you're at." "There is an urban definition," Young continued, "and it's from [the] urban relocation [program]. That's how 'urban Indians' got their identity. It's because of the relocation."[2]

In Dallas, urban intertribalism has been an important story, but for many it is not most important. With Choctaw people such as Angela Young and Mike Frazier comprising the highest proportional number of Native people, it is tempting to discern a distinct band of Dallas Choctaw. Yet Indigenous Dallas and all its complicated referents are just as much a product of restorative connections to homes in Oklahoma, New Mexico, Arizona, and elsewhere as they are a reflection of intertribalism. Because of these persistent connections to tribal nations, communities, clans, and families, many Native people in Dallas refuse to be defined by the city, even when they have spent most of their lives there. "Urban," then, amounts less to an essential and discrete social and political identity and more to a geographic and demographic reference point. As Young and Frazier concluded in our interview, there are no urban Indians. There are only Indians living in urban places.[3] There is great power in their assertion. To reject the designation of "urban Indian" is to reject the central political economy of settler colonialism, and to reject settler assumptions about whom or what Native people exercising their right to live and thrive in Dallas were supposed to become.

This thematically organized chapter explores how and why Indigenous people have made and remade communities in Dallas, how connections to ancestral homes have shaped that ongoing experience, and how Native people, through a self-determined and shifting sense of citizenship, defied federal officials' conditional and correctional plans for how and where they can belong in cities. Beginning in the 1950s, thousands of Native American people coming from nearby Oklahoma to faraway Alaska realized their own vision of what life in Dallas could mean not only for their chances at "success," but also for kin who remained "home." They built a community that has transformed across space and time, and transgressed boundaries, while remaining grounded in concrete and terrestrial intertribal institutions, including churches, Indian centers, bars, and a radio program. With that, this chapter builds on recent scholarship, including that by fellow *Indian Cities* contributors Sasha Suarez and David Hugill, that explores how Indigenous peoples ensured visibility and audibility in major cities, used cities for their own purposes, established themselves as important members of urban communities, and unmade cities' settler-colonial potentials from within, all while strengthening ancestral communities and establishing Indigenous presence and presents at increasingly global crossroads.[4]

Native Americans may not have become "urban Indians," but they made Dallas an Indian city, and something more. In addition to functioning as a "hub," as Renya K. Ramirez brilliantly characterizes San Silicon Valley's relationship to Indian communities, Dallas has functioned as a virtual suburb for Native peoples from Oklahoma. While they certainly made culture in Dallas, the city was not necessarily their cultural center. Many went somewhere else for that. In Dallas, Indigenous people have promoted and enhanced tribal economies and sovereignty, concerned just as much with Native nationalism, to borrow Kent Blansett's term, as urban intertribalism. Many Indigenous people in this chapter tended to prioritize their Indigenous nationality over an intertribal Dallas identity. Importantly, this trend corresponded with Native peoples' larger movements for self-determination and sovereignty during this era. Sovereignty and Indigeneity did not disappear as a consequence of geographic and social mobility. Rather, Indigenous people practiced it from within cities, in a sort of physical but unbounded third space.[5]

Finally, this chapter foregrounds important features of Indigenous Dallas that distinguished it from other destinations within the BIA's blend of relocation and vocational training programs. It considers not just movement to Dallas, and its Metroplex partner Fort Worth, but also generations of movement within the Dallas–Fort Worth (DFW) area. In doing so, it demonstrates some ways in which Native peoples remained connected to Indigenous nations, cultures, and communities from new urban positions.[6] Among the federal relocation program's protean official destinations, only Chicago, with its relative proximity to numerous reservations in Wisconsin and Michigan, came close to rivaling Dallas's accessibility to the substantial Indian population in Oklahoma.[7]

This is more than a story of geographic mobility to the city, as a singular and terminal event. It is a story of social, class, and political mobility both throughout and through the city, as ongoing events. Movement did not terminate at the bus terminal. Across decades and cityscapes, Native people maneuvered and improvised, navigated intersections of opportunity and crisis, explored new avenues to belonging, mined urban resources to strengthen tribal communities, and contributed to the culture and identity of postwar Dallas.

From Chicago to Wichita to Galveston, The Texas Chief cut right through the heart of Indian Country. A Pullman streamliner in the Santa Fe Railway's feature Chief fleet, the Texas Chief lacked transcontinental latitude and survived on scrap material from its parent engines. Averaging fifty miles per hour, it could make Dallas from Ponca City, Oklahoma, in seven hours, and from Oklahoma City in five. It was not as fast as the flagship Super Chief, but fast enough. For the thousands of Native American people who caught the Number 15 southbound to Dallas, life would only get faster.[8]

Most Native people rode trains or buses to Dallas. Others drove their own cars, and some hitchhiked. Those who began moving in September 1957 as part of the BIA's federal urban relocation program first had to register at the local BIA office at 912 Commerce Street in downtown Dallas. From there a program official booked them into temporary lodging, prepared to move them into public housing, and shared tips on jobs and job-training programs. If this went according to plan, the BIA promised, American Indian people it characterized as impoverished and marginalized would achieve a middle-class dream in "mainstream" America. In reality, this often translated to apartment living and vocational jobs vulnerable to economic downturns in a still-maturing industrial metropolis. This was the best-case scenario. Many never experienced this ideal, while others exceeded it. In any case, the possible outcomes transcended an assimilation-dislocation "two-worlds" binary, in which decisions made by Native Americans in cities necessarily reflected a choice between being American and being Indian, or being Indian and being Chickasaw, for example.[9]

Indeed, Native American people were much more experienced and adaptable then federal officials understood. As recently as the 1930s, federal policymakers were unsure whether Indian people could actually live in houses, whether urban or rural. And this was in the context of the supposedly enlightened "Indian New Deal"—a reorientation of the United States' relationship to Indian nations in response to both the Great Depression and the alarm the 1928 Meriam Report sounded on socioeconomic conditions in Indian Country. But then, in American history, housing has always illuminated the nation's color line. In a 1933 BIA documentary film titled *Rebuilding Indian Country*, the narrator claimed, "Formal houses and Indians are not basically compatible. Before house building can be undertaken, the Indian must be convinced of the superior advantages of the white man's home, over the shelters he has found to his liking for so many generations, but the transformation of thought is underway." Thought transformation? Who decided which housing was "formal" (a discursive term, to be sure)? In fact, not only did numerous Indian people already live in "formal housing," but many decried the terrible "crackerbox" housing on reservations. Dirt blew right through some Rosebud Sioux people's homes in South Dakota. "They should have been condemned earlier," one Rosebud person protested. When the houses predictably and prematurely declined, federal officials and bordertown "deadliest enemies" blamed it on some lingering colonial fantasy of Indian savagery.[10]

By the 1950s, not only did BIA personnel remain uncertain about Native people's potential for domestication, they wondered too if Indian people could understand the concept of time. "Time is something that Indian people generally don't know anything about," Dallas relocation director Ola Beckett surmised. With that, the very person in charge of helping relocated Indians in Dallas advanced a stereotype of Indian people who do not understand capitalism, routine work schedules, or the industrial clock. But Native American peoples were not timeless. A majority of the first wave of relocation program participants were World War II and Korean War veterans who probably knew more than something about time and accountability.[11]

The false notion that American Indians needed to learn the concept of time reflects the degree to which the Voluntary Relocation Program was the logical conclusion of ongoing assimilation programs rooted in late-nineteenth-century land allotments and boarding schools. The goals behind the 1952 Voluntary Relocation Program and the 1956 Adult Vocational Training Program were decades old. Some Native people expressed great skepticism. "The government put us on reservations in the first place to get rid of us entirely and terminate the whole Indian nation, so they put us in the most desolate places where no one could survive, and we did[,] so they had to think up a new system," suggested one Rosebud Lakota woman living in Dallas.[12] The BIA underestimated the durability and portability of Indigeneity. Unsure whether Indian people could even live in houses, the BIA did not anticipate Indian people surviving city life on their own terms.[13]

The BIA considered designating Dallas an official destination during the program's inception in 1952, and actually began relocating some people there that year, with no local office to greet them. Program officials liked Dallas because its postwar boom featured rapidly expanding industry, an active housing market, and relatively weak unions that could not prevent an influx of cheap labor. The BIA ultimately balked at relocation to Dallas, however, because the city's economy was at that time suffering cyclical seasonal layoffs. Moreover, those same weak unions meant low wages for prospective Native workers, many of whom were already coming from poverty and lacked leverage. Meanwhile, Wichita, to the north of 39 Indian nations in Oklahoma, called for industrial workers to solve its labor shortage. Although Wichita featured a military base and a vibrant Native community that relocated there for World War II–era jobs, the BIA would not move in that direction either, because Wichita lacked adequate housing. Dallas had housing but no jobs; Wichita had jobs but no housing. Until 1957, Native people from Oklahoma would have to look farther afield to Denver as their nearest program option.[14]

Prior to program expansion to Dallas, the area offices at Anadarko and Muskogee, Oklahoma, routinely beat the "success" rates of seven other area offices. However, the initial statistics on relocation to Dallas from Anadarko, which housed the Cheyenne-Arapaho, Kiowa, and Pawnee agencies, did not match that office's national reputation. In 1958, the Anadarko office sent 78 people to Dallas but received 88 returnees. By contrast, the Muskogee area office, which oversaw the Choctaw and Five Civilized Tribes agencies, fared much better. The Muskogee office sent a total of 156 people to Dallas and received only 27 returnees. In sum, Dallas received a total of 448 new relocatees from across all area offices nationally, while losing 302 returnees. At the national program level, only Cincinnati featured worse rates of "success" than Dallas. This indicates how the 1958 "Eisenhower Recession" hit these two cities particularly hard. But it is also likely that Dallas featured such high return rates because it was so much easier for people from there seeking temporary economic refuge to return home, as a significant majority of the Dallas Indigenous community came from only a few hours away in Oklahoma. At the same time, the fact that people from Choctaw Country fared better suggests that their majority population in the Metroplex made it easier for people to stay and cope with the capricious job market. Across the next two years, relocation rates from Anadarko stabilized and then darted upward for net gains. Between 1957 and 1970, roughly ten thousand Indian people relocated to Dallas through the BIA program. While roughly one-third of them returned home, roughly one person self-relocated for every two people who relocated through the BIA, thereby offsetting the number of returnees. All told, between the opening of the Dallas office in 1957 and the termination of the program in 1972, roughly twelve thousand Native peoples relocated to Dallas through the BIA's program.[15]

Relocation to Dallas coincided with an expansion of the initial Voluntary Relocation Program to include the Adult Vocational Training program, which offered vocational training prior to departure, or on-the-job training upon arrival. Roughly one-third of the first wave of migrants to Dallas chose the latter path. Job training programs included X-ray technology, typing, cosmetology, business, bricklaying, welding, electronics assembly, plumbing, and printing, among other skills. Some Native people took night classes in order to earn their high school diploma or improve upon their English-language skills.[16]

Once arrived, single individuals often temporarily stayed at the YMCA, YWCA, Salvation Army Club, or private homes. Reflecting old settler stereotypes of wild Indian men and obedient Indian women, the BIA sometimes provided apartment living, but only for single women, believing that single men could not be trusted in unchaperoned settings. Initially, the BIA also rented rooms at area boarding houses, but it discontinued this approach because very few met minimum sanitation standards. This is rather ironic, given that BIA officials were unsure whether Indian people could keep house.[17]

Stereotypes about domestic habits notwithstanding, neither the BIA nor Dallas business leaders doubted Native people's labor value, but this is because they believed other stereotypes, about Indian deftness and passivity. Employers extolled Indian workers' "excellent finger dexterity," commended an employee who "works at his job and is less talkative than the average worker," and generally praised the way an Indian worker "can stand the monotony of mass production better than the non Indian" and "awaits his turn for promotion and is appreciative of advancement." Job leaders believed Indian employees, absent "the academic background," possessed the "native intelligence to complete a training program." Using Native Americans as a prop in their claims for progress in race relations, condescending DFW employers congratulated themselves for contributing to Indian uplift.[18]

Amid these settler fantasies, Indigenous peoples embraced opportunities to improve their standards of living. Herbert Brown Otter (Dakota) expressed optimism for what he perceived as an inevitable transition: "We're in the middle of the stream. We can't change horses now . . . we're products of civilization. Ours is not to degrade, but to contribute to that civilization." This would not be easy. As one Native navy veteran cautioned, "If you haven't got job training, you're just about out the door." The majority of vocational training dropouts were single males who, according to the BIA, never intended to stay and did not like working. But the BIA often did a terrible job of screening applicants for relocation. Mistakes included the recruitment of a seventeen-year-old girl who failed to meet the minimum eighteen-years age requirement, two women later diagnosed as "psychotic," several individuals battling alcoholism, and a woman from Alaska suffering a brain tumor. Often the obstacles to "successful adjustments" began back home in Indigenous communities and not as an effect of urban relocation. Still, the BIA clearly did a poor job of preventing the relocation of people whose problems would only be exacerbated in the city.[19]

From Raven Hail's perspective, the BIA fostered a system of paternalism within a program that promised to liberate Native Americans from reservation poverty. A Cherokee person born in Washington County, Oklahoma, in 1925, Hail studied for two years at Oklahoma State University before finishing her education at Southern Methodist University, and then staying in Dallas. The BIA did not liberate her. She made her own relocation program and trained herself. "[T]he first problem is everyone comes to the Indian and *tells* him what the facts are and what he thinks, and tells him how he should feel and what the answers are, and expects him to parrot them back," she argued. In Dallas, the BIA pressured Native women to avoid single motherhood and warned young people about alcohol. The local office also taught program participants to be afraid: get receipts; lock your doors; avoid talking to strangers; hide your money. Among the general warnings, one is especially unsettling: "always tell the truth on lie detector tests." At the program's departure point, federal agents sold a future of economic stability and social belonging. At the urban arrival point, by contrast, federal agents revealed how new life in the city would be difficult and frightening. It was in program participants' best interest, the BIA suggested, to embrace austerity, maybe rewarded by occasional trips to the bowling alley. "Remember—It is not our needs that get us in trouble," an orientation packet advised. "It is our wants."[20]

In reality, many Native people in Dallas did not enjoy the luxury of worrying about their wants. City living, on a tight budget, and far from extended family, could quickly devolve from mere survival to sheer tragedy. In 1962, an O'odham family that relocated from Arizona to Dallas was getting by until the father lost three fingers (during machinist training) and descended into alcoholism and domestic abuse. A few years later he died from a hit-and-run accident, while the mother sustained serious injuries. The eldest daughter returned home from Job Corps—a vocational and academic training program for teenagers and young adults coming from poverty—to fill in, while the oldest son, at sixteen, functioned as a father to his numerous siblings, providing food on the meager income he earned from a fried chicken stand. Over the next couple of years, the younger siblings struggled between scrapes with the law and staying in school. The eldest daughter frequently woke from terrifying nightmares in which her father lurked near her bed. "It's scary," she said.[21]

Indeed, life could be quite dreary for Indian families trying to make it in Dallas. The BIA claimed it never put families with more than one child in one-bedroom units. Yet a Pueblo family occupied an East Dallas apartment so cramped that one of their two children slept on a loveseat in the living room. They did not recall ever having any choice in their living arrangement. Their building boasted a central air-conditioning system, but it did not work. With no parks nearby, the children played on a concrete driveway where the apartment manager often harassed them. Inside their apartment, only a tape recorder and tape of Pueblo music offered an obvious connection to home.[22]

Still, not all Indigenous people experienced tragedy, discrimination, and isolation in Dallas. Some experienced a much warmer reception. The BIA literally staged a red-carpet welcome for the first Indian family to go on relocation to Dallas. Richard Lester and his Choctaw family arrived on September 17, 1957—not from rural Choctaw Country but urban Oklahoma City, where Richard had been an ironworker. In a second amusing twist, among the people on hand to greet the "Indian 'Settlers'" were Indian people who were already living in Dallas and had already established an Indian club. "We're simply overwhelmed at the wonderful reception Dallas has given us," Richard said. "We've never seen anything like it."[23]

For the BIA, a typical relocation success story resembled that of the Beartracks—a Kiowa family from Oklahoma. "We just couldn't have had any-thing nicer happen to us," father Edmund wrote to the family's relocation agent back in Anadarko. "I have been very fortunate in getting a job that I know I will never be dissatisfied with." Edmund landed steady work making $200 per month as a surgical technician at the Parkland Memorial Hospital, a position that earned him the nickname "Dr. Beartrack" among friends. His wife Nellie took classes at an adult educational center while his two daughters attended public school. The Beartracks enjoyed listening to records, watching television, going to the movies, square dancing, and competing in a softball league. One highlight of their first year in Dallas came with a visit by their church leader from Oklahoma. The only real problem they faced was the children's bout with chicken pox. Still, as much as the Beartracks seemed to like Dallas, they eventually returned home to Oklahoma, where in 1999 Edmund died among his people.[24]

In a different example, Greenwood McCurtain (Choctaw) expressed no great emotional anguish over city living, although he did suffer physically: "They say to me, 'Greenwood walks the white man's way,' but I did what I needed. I learned punctuality, made a success. It took long hard work. I developed ulcers, had open-heart surgery and two heart attacks. I learned to walk the white man's street during the week, and on weekends I still go to powwows and religious ceremonies in Oklahoma." McCurtain focused on the importance of "home" in more ways than one. In 1979, he was busy working with the Fort Worth City Council to secure Housing and Urban Development funding for a 400-home Indian housing program. His attitude toward urban relocation signaled a reckoning with the past and pragmatism toward the future. "They can't give up their traditions. But the buffalo is not coming back," he reasoned. "They say the red man will inherit the earth. Who knows? The world travels in circles, and it may happen."[25]

The Western and Sunbelt cities that boomed during the Second World War mostly adhered to a decentralization impulse. In the sprawling cities access to "modernity" depended on automobile ownership, leisure time, and dispos-able income—luxuries many Indian people both desired and lacked. Many found themselves isolated within impoverished neighborhoods—where they became both subjects of and participants in America's enduring and evolving anti-urban critique.[26]

At first, the BIA sent relocated people to the West Dallas public housing project. Construction on the 3,500-unit project finished in 1956 (two years after Dallas annexed West Dallas), at which point new tenants moved into segregated units: white, black, and Hispanic. Native people were only allowed to occupy the Hispanic-designated Elmer Scott complex, or "Little Mexico."[27] Not surprisingly, West Dallas was not exactly an idyllic part of town. Legendary outlaws Bonnie and Clyde grew up there in the 1920s. Its reputation had hardly improved thirty years later. When Indian tenants complained about roach infestations, Elmer Scott landlords objected: "Those are Texas boll weevils."[28] The BIA prepaid the $40 monthly rent, with families paying a sliding percentage of wages earned. Previous scholarship has claimed that the BIA intentionally tried to scatter relocatees throughout various cities to expedite cultural assimilation. But in Dallas hundreds of families resided together at Elmer Scott. The BIA liked this, because it made it easier to surveil the relative "progress" of the community and to conduct unannounced home visits.[29]

The presence of the manmade and notoriously neglected Fishtrap Lake notwithstanding, locals called the West Dallas area "Cement City," as it provided home for numerous industrial factories. Most notoriously, the RSR Corporation's northern boundary lay a mere fifty feet from the housing project. During the 1980s, through a series of lawsuits, it finally came to light that since the 1930s RSR's lead car-battery smelting facility had been dispersing up to *two tons* of lead-waste particles into the ground and air annually, assaulting the health of poor area residents who could not afford air-conditioning and had to leave windows open for ventilation during summer.[30]

In 1965, after the BIA convinced Beatrice McLean that relocation was the only way to make any money, she moved from South Dakota's Rosebud Reservation to Dallas. "You get so tired," she recalled about the 36-hour journey. When their BIA chaperone tried to take her and her husband to the West Dallas housing project, they protested. They had already heard about this place. The deplorable Elmer Scott housing project's reputation had spread 36 hours north to South Dakota. When a BIA housing agent finally took them to a fourth place in East Dallas, Beatrice, so tired, surrendered, "Let's just stay here." Seven blocks from the notorious Peak Avenue and Bryan Street "Corner," where Dallas police often targeted and arrested Native American bar patrons on weekends, it was not much better. As a parting sentiment, the BIA agent warned the McLeans to lock their door and not open it to strangers. So frightened, Beatrice "stayed in that apartment for two weeks straight without ever coming out."[31]

230 DOUGLAS K. MILLER

By the end of the 1960s, no longer willing to tolerate such conditions, most Native people had left the Elmer Scott complex and were living in Oak Cliff and East Dallas, with older families gravitating toward the former and young people leaning toward the latter. Others had scattered into the suburbs. Baptist minister James Goodner, who previously worked with Indigenous peoples in Albuquerque, Oakland, and Wichita, suggested that the movement within Dallas–Fort Worth reflected Indigenous cultures rooted in histories of dispersed living arrangements, long distance travel for meetings, and large gatherings of extended kin.[32] The successes Native peoples achieved in homeowning did not come easily, however. "It is so hard for an Indian to get a loan to buy a home," one Indigenous person from Dallas told a federal panel. "A lot of these Indians don't really have good-paying jobs to qualify for these loans and the BIA doesn't help you one bit."[33]

While West Dallas is experiencing gradual renewal today, it hardly sits in proximity to Dallas's elite neighborhoods or even the area's middle-class cultural districts. The "mainstream" did not run through West Dallas. Strangely, or perhaps not, today's West Dallas offers no discernible indication that Indigenous people ever lived there.[34]

Native peoples who escaped the terrible public housing conditions did so through self-relocations within DFW and a system of mutual institution building and rebuilding to satisfy their changing needs. Through this process, intertribalism sustained Native nationalism. Most prominent in modeling this strategy were Juanita and Vernon Ahtone, who moved from Kiowa Country in Oklahoma to Dallas in 1952, five years prior to the latter becoming a program destination. A Haskell Institute graduate, great-granddaughter of Kiowa Chief Lone Wolf, and daughter of founding National Congress of American Indians member James Dahgomah, Juanita began serving as the assistant director of the Dallas American Indian Center in the early 1970s. By then she had accumulated almost twenty years of experience in Indigenous community organizing in Dallas. This activism grew out of Vernon's appointment as the first Native person employed by the Dallas Police Department, which challenged a history of prejudice in Dallas law enforcement. Vernon often met fellow Indians at the bus station on his patrol route. Juanita embraced them as extended family from Oklahoma. Vernon regularly extended invitations to dominoes and dessert on the weekends. These regular gatherings of roughly fifteen families visiting in each other's homes organically developed into the first Dallas Indian Social Club, founded in 1953. Three years later, a second Indian club opened in Fort Worth to accommodate people living there who lacked reliable transportation to Dallas.[35]

In October 1969, Juanita Ahtone led the establishment of Dallas's first Indian center in a house located at 722 N. Beacon Street. All board members were Indian, though that was not required. The Indian Center became a place for income tax assistance, legal services, GED classes, job tips, a housewives club, medical referrals, emergency food and clothing, recreation, and a place for kids to watch Sesame Street. "We don't have our hands out," Ahtone said, characterizing the center's self-sufficient attitude. Significantly, the center sponsored a youth council and chartered a bus to send young Indians from Dallas to Oklahoma so they could connect with Indian culture.[36]

By 1972, the center had become a place run by and for Indian people, as non-Indians who participated in center operations realized that patrons preferred Indian people in leadership roles. Moreover, many Native members resented non-Indian members' tendency toward paternalism, especially when BIA officials invited themselves to meetings. "If you want to help us, fine. Advise us, but keep your mouth shut otherwise," Ahtone admonished. Tensions over the role of non-Indians in center activities soon erupted and non-Indians withdrew their support, resulting in the temporary collapse of some programs, including the Sesame Street Club. Relationships became strained between Native members, too. Ahtone was not sentimental about intertribalism: "I ask this question always: Why must *we* be the ones who are united when you're not—the Republicans, the Democrats, George Wallace . . . ?" Some Indian youths complained that the center was far too focused on preserving Indian culture and neglected providing assistance in adjusting to the "mainstream of American life." Others charged that tribal rivalry thwarted the center's potential. Such social fissures and commitments to tribal identity persisted twenty years later when numerous Native people interviewed for a news story insisted that they had not retribalized as "Indian" people. A Choctaw woman mentioned that she felt alienated from Navajo friends because they so often spoke Navajo and generally did not do things the way Choctaw women did. One Cherokee community leader in Dallas claimed that other Native people from Arizona and New Mexico looked down on Indians from Oklahoma and called them "Okies."[37]

In 1971, disgruntled defectors founded the Dallas Intertribal Christian Center (DICC), a free health clinic on West Jefferson in the Bishop Arts District. Only six months after the DICC opened, roughly 10 percent of the DFW Indian

Site of the First Dallas American Indian Center at 722 N. Beacon Street, 2015.
Photograph by Douglas K. Miller.

population had visited for immunization, physical exams, nutrition classes, dental work, gynecology, eye treatment, and other medical needs. Some members of the community complained that they were still sick after clinic treatment, and sought a different form of healing. Navajo people, in particular, regularly raised money to send sick people back to Diné Country to visit medicine men. This worked, according to a non-Indian BIA counselor, who claimed that the people who adopted this approach almost always returned in an improved condition. Likewise, some Native women experienced great frustration with urgent needs for prenatal care. One Native woman appreciated the support of neighbors who pooled their money to help her get home to Phoenix, where she had her baby, after twice waiting all day long and still not seeing a doctor in Dallas. A second woman, while in labor, rode a bus home to Lawton, Oklahoma, to have her baby.[38]

A pillar of numerous Indigenous communities throughout Oklahoma, Indian churches also provided institutional and social support in DFW as people relocated with their faith, and sometimes their clergy, in tow. DFW congregations first met in rented houses or apartments. Then standalone chapels flourished, often beyond their identity as Indian churches. The popular Singleton Indian Baptist Church featured Muscogee Pastor Willis Knight, who preached from his pulpit to more than one hundred followers. A World War II Purple Heart recipient, Knight had studied at theological seminary in Fort Worth before leading the Singleton Church. He later returned home to Creek Country in Oklahoma.[39]

Indian churches functioned as more than just houses of worship. In addition to Sunday sermons and tribal hymns, the Dallas Indian Methodist Church offered powwows, potlucks, and basketball games. Core members could also frequently be found at the county courthouse attending hearings in support of fellow DFW Indian people. "The church may be a family substitute in the city," a member of the Fort Worth Baptist Mission suggested. About the Church, one non-Indian member from Fort Worth said, "This is where their friends are. Our people may know many other Indian people but it is to church members they will tell their desires, share their burdens, and really act close."[40]

Some Indigenous peoples in DFW formed community institutions not only to stay connected to each other, but also, and sometimes more importantly, to stay connected with people back home. Pursuant to repeal deadlines embedded in the 1959 Choctaw Termination Act, the Oklahoma Choctaw Nation faced the termination of their sovereign federal recognition on August 25,

1970. Choctaw people quickly formed the Dallas Choctaw Council to help fight against this catastrophic policy. To promote the group and recruit support the burgeoning council bought a full-page ad in the *Dallas Morning News* in hopes of reaching the paper's roughly one million readers. The ad included a form letter that readers could cut out and send off to their preferred U.S. senator or representative. This worked. With one day to spare, Congress repealed the act. From there the Choctaw Council continued its activism by directing attention to tribal elections back in Oklahoma as well as police brutality and discrimination in Dallas.[41]

Indians in Dallas also paid close attention to Indian Country writ large. At the invitation of Joan Ablon, a non-Indian Dallasite who studied with anthropologist Sol Tax at the University of Chicago and wrote about Indigenous peoples in San Francisco, a contingent of Indians from Dallas participated in the 1961 American Indian Chicago Conference, where tribal leaders from throughout Indian Country met to share survival strategies and craft a policy recommendation for President Kennedy. In Chicago, Dallas delegates informed attendees about their struggles with unemployment. They recommended greater care in screening program applicants, expanded orientation programs and health care, and Indian hiring at local offices.[42] Likewise, in 1973 the Native American League of Dallas (NALD) wrote the U.S. attorney general to protest any government plan to use force in eradicating Indian protestors from the Wounded Knee occupation in South Dakota. "Although we do not always condone the methods used by the American Indian Movement," Seminole chairman Matthew Taylor explained, "we, as American Indians, are all too familiar with the prejudice, injustice, frustrations and continued maltreatment of our people that led to this occupation." For the members of the NALD, urban and rural Indian people could not be divided and conquered.[43]

Some Indigenous peoples in Dallas–Fort Worth either felt uncomfortable with or did not know about the various Indian centers, clubs, and churches. Some among them instead found and supported each other in popular Indian bars, such as The Rainbow and Tom & Jerry's. These served as meeting spaces for breaks from the pressures of city living and the pains of missing home— places where people could talk about the "good times and the bad times," as a Lakota person in Dallas put it. Bars also functioned as social centers where one could get a job tip, cash a check, and pick up messages. As spaces of mutual aid, bars provided a sense of camaraderie and belonging. As Kent Blansett suggests about Indigenous peoples in San Francisco, Indian bars were the "first stop on the road to urban survival for many Native peoples." At Tom & Jerry's, situated at the infamous Peak and Bryan "Corner," relocated Indians could "find other Indians, brothers and sisters who have learned to survive in the strange, cold city," a Dallas reporter dramatized. "The Corner becomes his starting point, and the Indians who congregate there become his guides, as he begins his foray into the heart of the white man's world."[44]

At the same time, these establishments could be dangerous. So notorious was "the Corner" in 1975, one Northern Cheyenne man claimed that "Indians all over the country" knew about it. Indeed, the Dallas Police Department christened Bryan Street the "meanest street" in the Metroplex. During an interview in 1972, Dallas Indian Center Director Mary Williams mentioned that, over a recent period, police had arrested 357 people at the Corner, and 111 of them were Native American. According to police reports, during the first eight months of 1977 alone the Corner witnessed 42 assaults, 15 robberies, two murders, and one rape. The city's "most dangerous intersection" at Peak and Bryan also featured black, Chicano, and Nazi white supremacist bars, where some patrons competed in an extensive illicit drug trade that encouraged gangs and violence. On any given night, people who braved the Corner could score drugs, hire a sex worker, hear a gunshot, and see a bottle broken over someone's head. Occasionally, violence broke out between Indian and Latino groups, such as when six Indian men were shot—three critically wounded—during a fight with rival Latino men at Tom & Jerry's.[45]

According to Dallas relocation program director Robert Beams (Choctaw), three relocation program participants were killed at the Corner in a span of only three years between 1969 and 1971. "In one case in particular, the guy was just walking down the street and someone shot him," Beams mentioned. "[We] see evidence that some of our Indian young people may be rounded up and hauled in with the group because they were in a facility in the community where some sort of ruckus took place and they may get rounded up and sent in to jail with the group because they had been drinking but were not necessarily intoxicated," he explained. According to Beams, Indian people did not need to venture to the Corner bars for a violent encounter with the police. He recalled contacting the FBI to intervene in an incident of police brutality that started when they were called to an apartment complex to confront a Native family who had their stereo up too loud. The details surrounding the case are murky, but Beams said the Native residents "were roughed up quite a bit."[46]

In another example of Indian people being roughed up quite a bit by police, Choctaw Council leader David Harkens relayed a story about a fight that broke out in the local jail, during which a Latino man assaulted a white man. The police officers rushed in to break up the violence but committed their own when they inexplicably grabbed an incarcerated Indian bystander. "[T]hey had taken the Indian boy and taken him out of the cell. And when they brought him back, he was unconscious. . . . Well now this is nothing; I mean this is nothing new," Harkens explained. This was nothing new in many major cities where Native Americans were quite visible in arrest rates, while otherwise relatively invisible in the wider community.[47]

These incidents reflect racialized violence in the context of the United States' growing mass incarceration crisis. As with other minority groups, unequal treatment before the law was fundamentally about racialized attitudes toward Native Americans.[48] "Look at these whites, what they're doing, running to and fro with their automobiles, drunker than any Indian you've ever seen," one Native woman protested during public hearing. "You never saw an Indian as drunk as some of these whites." She continued:

> Monday morning you can't [find room to] walk [because of so many] Indians in the jailhouse. I went down the other day. What did they bring in with chains on them? Indians . . . I sat there and cried. Look, this is not a good picture, you might as well face it. Why didn't they put some chains on the white ones? They had fifteen white ones and seven Indians. Why didn't they chain up the whites?[49]

One of the worst potential outcomes of urban relocation, and one that Indigenous peoples living in urban areas still confront today, is that citizens of sovereign tribal nations, in their effort to increase their visibility, audibility, and rights as the original occupants of this land and improve their standard of living, became, in the minds of city, state, and federal officials and the general American public, another racial minority entitlement group who could not overcome poverty and achieve racial uplift, despite the non-Indian public's confidence that they had been given every chance to do so. The fact that some Indigenous peoples got caught in a web of homelessness and recidivism encouraged a confirmation bias among non-Indian observers and policymakers who failed to acknowledge structural oppression and the continuation of colonial violence. Indeed, potential violence at the hands of police officers notwithstanding, getting arrested could itself be a form of resistance, as for some it could be a safer alternative to the realities of street life.

"Hi. This is Cindy. And Dennis Wahkinney is here running the controls." So began each episode of the first incarnation of the radio program *Beyond Bows and Arrows*, which provides a rich example of how Indigenous peoples in and around DFW communicated with both non-Indians and each other in rapidly changing contexts. The show went on the air in 1983, and soon became a critical outlet for community news, job tips, Native music (White Fish Bay Singers, Haystack, Bad Medicine, Southern Thunder), and readings of speeches by famous Indian chiefs. Dennis and Cindy conceived the show as "an entertainment and educational program." The latter is reflected in the show's crossover appeal with non-Indian audiences who became interested in American Indians after seeing popular films such as *Dances with Wolves*. "Don't get me wrong—many myths remain," Dennis cautioned. "Some people still think we can make it rain, that we live in tepees, that we all speak the same language. When I go and speak to schools, they expect me to come in waving a tomahawk . . . I shock them when I walk in with a suit. But there seems to be more of a yearning to know, an appreciation and respect for our culture now."[50]

For Dennis, joining the show motivated him to learn about not only other Indigenous peoples' cultures but also his own. In 1984, he transferred from Oklahoma to Dallas with his IRS job. With no experience in radio and little fluency in Indian culture, he gave himself a crash course in both. The great-great-grandson of Comanche chief Quanah Parker, Dennis read books on Native American history, attended every powwow he could fit into his schedule, and taped powwow music to play live on the air. Growing up in Elgin, Oklahoma, he experienced racism and physical beatings by white schoolmates. He also struggled with the negative historical images of Indian people: "I grew up with an inferiority complex because of it, and for a while, when I was a young adult, I didn't really identify much with the Indian culture, because to me it was just problems. It lessened my image of myself, my self-esteem." He soon found his voice and carried the show for years. "Rise and be recognized," he used to sign off the air, "and let us grow stronger and stronger together."[51]

A stalwart pillar of the DFW Indian community, *Beyond Bows and Arrows* continues to broadcast Indigenous voices. One can still dial their FM radio to

KNON 89.3 and hear Indian music and Indian people talking about what is happening in the Indian community. Among its most loyal listeners are prisoners incarcerated in numerous institutions surrounding the metro area. They tune in every Sunday night at 6 P.M., current show host Albert Old Crow (Cheyenne) told me during a conversation live on the air. "This is their weekly escape," he explained.[52]

Other Native people turned to print and politics as a means toward achieving greater attention in DFW. In *The Raven Speaks,* a monthly community newsletter Raven Hail wrote and distributed for a yearly three-dollar subscription rate, she discussed major events in Native American history, told popular Indigenous stories such as "The Terrapin and the Fox," shared Bible verses, provided detailed background on Texas's Alabama-Coushatta people and reservation, and covered national contemporary Indian news, including the Alcatraz Occupation and the founding of D-Q University. She was so devoted to reaching and representing Indian people in Dallas that in 1972, while hundreds of Indigenous activists caravanned to Washington, D.C., on the "Trail of Broken Treaties" to demand treaty rights and protest conditions in Indian Country, she ran (unsuccessfully) for the Texas State House of Representatives from Dallas's district 33-B. "It is time for the Indians to have proper representation in the political structure of our country," she insisted. Her campaign adopted a relatively libertarian platform. "We cannot legislate against marijuana if everyone is smoking it. We cannot ban dirty movies if everyone is rushing to see them," she reasoned. She also advocated lower taxes and reduced government spending, and spoke against school integration busing programs.[53]

Coinciding with Hail's campaign, some Indian people put a premium on organizing an Indian voting bloc to function as a swing vote. In 1972, the Dallas Choctaw Council met with State Senator Mike McKool to discuss state politics. "We don't represent the voting power that the blacks do," meeting organizer Richard Lester suggested, fifteen years after he arrived as the first relocation program migrant to Dallas, "but that's the direction we'd like to go. If the Indian wants to get anything out of America, he has to put something into it, we figure."[54]

"God, no," Juanita Ahtone replied to a journalist's question about whether she planned to "die in Dallas." After her children finished school, she was "going home. We go home every chance we get." "I know whenever a tree falls on the old place," her husband Vernon added. Juanita spoke at length about "home" and its regenerative effect: "Well, for one thing, I'm going to go back to a brand new four-bedroom house out in the country. . . . I've lived in Dallas for many years and I've worked for twenty years and I think I'm going to retire where I can enjoy it. I don't want to go back home in a wheelchair. . . . When I go back home I see so many things in the Indian community that I feel like I can learn" When her interviewer asked if she initially imagined life in Dallas would be temporary, Ahtone did not hesitate, "I always knew I was going home."[55]

The Ahtones were not unique in their desire to one day leave Dallas and return to their real home. Many Native Americans not only maintained cultural connections to Indigenous homes but also planned to return from the city with new skills and experiences, and eventually retire among their people in tribal communities. Charlene Dodson (Navajo), for example, got along fine in Dallas, but she and her Navajo husband Kayo visited their reservation in Arizona as frequently as time and money allowed. "There we speak our native language," she said. "We load up on the food we miss, mutton stew and fry bread. Then we head back to Dallas."[56]

After attending Arizona State University in Tempe, and serving an administrative position at the Dallas Inter-Tribal Center, Rose Marie Rope still thought of herself as a San Carlos Apache person first. She dreamed of the day when she would return to San Carlos. "It's not safe here [in Dallas]," she explained. "At home, we leave the doors open." Vernon Tehauno (Comanche) shared a similar sentiment. "When I say let's go home, I mean Lawton," he said, despite having lived and worked in Dallas for thirty years. "They may come here and eke out a living," Dallas Inter-tribal Center Director Richard Lucero suggested in 1983, "but their heart is really back on the reservation."[57] "The more education you get, the more Indian you want to become," Nadine Valdez, a Sioux person from South Dakota living in Dallas, suggested. The city provided her the necessary skills and experiences to help her Indigenous people compete in 1970s America: "I would like to get my education, a knowledge of the laws, and go back and help my own people."[58]

Throughout its relocation program, the BIA gathered detailed statistical data, conducted random unannounced home visits with newly arrived families, followed up with reservation agency personnel, sent a steady stream of telegrams to

Washington, and commissioned private studies to evaluate its pet program. This was all done in an effort to measure its success at remaking Indigenous peoples as urban Americans. By "success" the BIA meant any individual or family who stayed in their new urban residence for at least one year. Meanwhile, the BIA missed the qualitative and holistic dimensions of Indian urban relocation. It missed how the eventual success of the relocation program, from Indigenous people's perspective, manifested in the continuation of Indigenous cultures in new social settings, the maintenance of community ties and obligations both to people locally and people back "home," and the new platform for encouraging acknowledgement of Indigenous peoples as capable of maneuvering within modernity, and deserving of self-determination and sovereignty recognition. In spite of the relocation program, these have been the wages of Indigenous survivance in the city.[59]

Success for relocated Native peoples meant so much more than program statistics, a terminal migration, or a postwar mainstream melting pot. For American Indians in Dallas–Fort Worth, success meant something more fundamentally human. At the Dallas Inter-Tribal Center, Choctaw behavioral health counselor Mike Frazier typically begins sessions with a question: "When's the last time you had some success?" "Wait," I stopped him during an interview. "How do you define 'success'?" "Well," he did not hesitate, "I like to use the dictionary definition: 'favorable outcome.' So I might ask our people: 'When's the last time you had a favorable outcome'? And that's what I mean by 'success.'"[60]

The approximately forty-five thousand Indigenous people who currently call Dallas–Fort Worth home have made lives marked by social and spatial mobility, cultural dynamism and resiliency, a relatively remarkable degree of visibility and audibility, and the occasional favorable outcome. But this was not guaranteed. Some Indigenous people made it with relative ease. Some missed their people, land, and homes too much. Some returned home for funerals and stayed there. Some disappeared. One person left Dallas to go work for the relocation program office back at the starting point in Oklahoma. The stories are highly subjective, but they overlap in their potential for razing stereotypes and partitions.[61] Since the 1950s, Indigenous peoples living in Dallas–Fort Worth gradually but actively transformed the Metroplex into a place of acceptance and reinvention, anonymity and rejection, and a space where generations of Indians living in a city coordinated new futures both across and beyond meanest streets that could always lead home. "At home, we leave the doors open," said one San Carlos Apache person living in Dallas.[62]

NOTES

1. "To Them Dallas Is an Interlude," *Dallas Morning News*, April 17, 1971.

2. Angela Young and Mike Frazier interview with author, Dallas Inter-Tribal Center, March 2018.

3. Young and Frazier interview.

4. See, for example, Renya K. Ramirez, *Native Hubs: Culture, Community, and Belonging in Silicon Valley and Beyond* (Durham, N.C.: Duke University Press, 2007); Coll Thrush, *Native Seattle: Histories from the Crossing-Over Place* (Seattle: University of Washington Press, 2007) and *Indigenous London: Native Travelers at the Heart of Empire* (New Haven, Conn.: Yale University Press, 2016); Nicholas G. Rosenthal, *Reimagining Indian Country: Native American Migration and Identity in Twentieth-Century Los Angeles* (Chapel Hill: University of North Carolina Press, 2012); Douglas K. Miller, *Indians on the Move: Native American Urbanization and Mobility in the Twentieth Century* (Chapel Hill: University of North Carolina Press, 2019); James LaGrand, *Indian Metropolis: Native Americans in Chicago, 1945–75* (Urbana: University of Illinois Press, 2002); Rosalyn R. LaPier and David R. M. Beck, *City Indian: Native American Activism in Chicago, 1893–1934* (Lincoln: University of Nebraska Press, 2015); and Ned Blackhawk, "I Can Carry on from Here: The Relocation of American Indians to Los Angeles," *Wicazo Sa Review* 11 (1995): 16–30.

5. Ramirez describes a Native hub as a place that supports "Native notions of culture, community, identity, and belonging away from tribal land bases"; see Ramirez, *Native Hubs*, 1. On the concept of Native nationalism, see Kent Blansett, *A Journey to Freedom: Richard Oakes, Alcatraz, and the Red Power Movement* (New Haven, Conn.: Yale University Press, 2018), 3. On third-space sovereignty, see Kevin Bruyneel, *The Third Space of Sovereignty: The Postcolonial Politics of U.S.-Indigenous Relations* (Minneapolis: University of Minnesota Press, 2007).

6. Other works that write against the pathological urban Indian trope include Blackhawk, "I Can Carry on From Here"; Thrush, *Native Seattle*; Rosenthal, *Reimagining Indian Country*; and Miller, *Indians on the Move*.

7. Official program destinations at various times included San Francisco, Oakland, San Jose, Los Angeles, Cleveland, Cincinnati, St. Louis, Salt Lake City, Chicago, Waukegan, Joliet, and Denver.

8. Ola Beckett to Sam Blythe (area relocation officer for Pawnee), June 25, 1962, Record Group (RG) 75, Records of Pawnee Area Field Representative, Records of Employment Assistance Officer, Studies and Telegrams, 1957–63, box 1, folder: Telegrams, National Archives and Records Administration at Fort Worth (NARA Fort Worth).

9. For essays that unsettle the "two-worlds" cultural binary, see C. Joseph Genetin-Pilawa and Jim J. Buss, eds., *Beyond Two Worlds: Critical Conversations on Language and Power in Native North America* (Ithaca, N.Y.: SUNY Press, 2014).

10. *Rosebud to Dallas*, directed by N. Jed Riffe (Jed Riffe Films, 2007 [filmed in 1977]). On fraught and violent relations between bordertown non-Indigenous and Indigenous people, see Thomas Biolsi, *Deadliest Enemies: Law and the Making of Race Relations on and off the Rosebud Reservation* (Berkeley: University of California Press, 2001).

11. "Dallas Bears Indian Sign of Hospitality," *Dallas Morning News*, March 19, 1958. In a larger sense, as Mark Rifkin notes, settler concepts of time have either "consigned Indigenous peoples to the past, or . . . inserted [them] into a present defined on non-native terms"; see Mark Rifkin, *Beyond Settler Time: Temporal Sovereignty and Indigenous Self-Determination* (Durham, N.C.: Duke University Press, 2017), vii. On military veterans forming a majority of the first wave of relocation participants, see Miller, *Indians on the Move*.

12. *Rosebud to Dallas*.

13. On the Collier administration's plan for an Indian urban relocation program, see Miller, *Indians on the Move*.

14. People who relocated to Dallas with BIA support prior to 1957 received a one-way bus ticket and a letter introducing them to the Texas Employment Commission. Jacob Ahtone, Anadarko Area Placement Officer, Monthly Employment Summary February–May, 1952, RG 75, Anadarko Area Office, Records of the Relocation Specialist, 1952–1957, box 1, folder FY 1957, NARA FW.

15. Other area offices were located in Alaska, South Dakota, Montana, New Mexico, Minnesota, Arizona, and Oregon. Relocatees Who Have Returned to Reservation, November 1957 Summary, RG 75, Records of Pawnee Area Field Representative, Records of Employment Assistance Officer, Studies and Telegrams, 1957–63, box 1, folder: 1957 Returnee Survey, NARA FW; Survey of December 1958, RG 75, Records of Pawnee Area Field Representative, Records of Employment Assistance Officer, Studies and Telegrams, 1957–63, box 1, folder: Special Studies on Returnees, FY 1958, NARA FW; Survey of December 1959, RG 75, Records of Pawnee Area Field Representative, Records of Employment Assistance Officer, Studies and Telegrams, 1957–63, box 1, folder: Special Studies on Returnees, FY 1959, NARA FW; Survey of December 1960, RG 75, Records of Pawnee Area Field Representative, Records of Employment Assistance Officer, Studies and Telegrams, 1957–63, box 1, folder: Special Report on Relocatees & RTs FY 1960, NARA FW; Billye Y. Sherman Fogleman, "Adaptive Mechanisms of the North American Indian to an Urban Setting" (PhD diss., Southern Methodist University, 1972), 2; Mary Williams interview on *TV Forum* with host Gene McIntire, February 12, 1972, Dallas, Texas, Dallas Indian Urbanization Oral History Project, Baylor University Program for Oral History (BUPOH), http://digitalcollections.baylor.edu/cdm/compoundobject/collection/buioh/id/3490/rec/1, accessed March 21, 2019.

16. Mary Louise Patrick, "The Bureau of Indian Affairs Relocation Program in Dallas: A Comparative Study, 1969–1971" (MA thesis, Baylor University, 1972), 45–48. This important study derives from interviews with Natives in DFW in the 1970s.

17. Patrick, "The Bureau of Indian Affairs Relocation Program in Dallas," 30–31.

18. Data and Stats on the Experience of the Muskogee Area Office with Respect to the Indian Relocation Program, 1959, RG 75, BIA Five Civilized Tribes Agency Office of Tribal Operations, Records of the Area Relocation Specialist, box 1, folder: Public Relations Relocation, NARA FW.

19. Richard G. Woods and Arthur M. Harkins, *An Examination of the 1968–1969 Urban Indian Hearings Held by the National Council on Indian Opportunity: Part III: Indian Self-Definitions* (Minneapolis: University of Minnesota, 1971), 4; Patrick, "Relocation in Dallas," 48–51, 67.

20. *The Raven Speaks* 1, no. 1 (April 7, 1968), Dallas Public Library Special Collections; Patrick, "Relocation in Dallas," 34–38.

21. "The American Indian in an Urban Community" (League of Women Voters of Dallas, March 1974), 12–13, in Dallas Public Library Special Collections.

22. I do not know the specific tribe of Pueblo people. Fogleman, "Adaptive Mechanisms," 67–69.

23. Oklahoma City's population eclipsed three hundred thousand by the late 1950s. "Dallasites Greet Indian 'Settlers,'" *Dallas Times Herald,* September 17, 1957.

24. Edmund Beartrack to Mr. Blythe and Staff, November 19, 1957, and Edmond (*sic*) Beartrack Home Counselor's Report, May 26, 1958, Anadarko Area Office, Records of the Relocation Specialist, 1952–1957, RG 75, box 3, folder: Correspondence FY 1958, NARA FW; Native American Obituary Index, Lawton Public Library, https://www .lawtonok.gov/sites/default/files/fileswidget/2018–02/Native%20American%20obit%20 Index.pdf, accessed July 15, 2018.

25. "White World Doesn't Fade Indian Spirit," *Dallas Morning News,* March 25, 1979.

26. On the history of anti-urbanism in the United States, see Steven Conn, *Americans Against the City: Anti-Urbanism in the Twentieth Century* (New York: Oxford University Press, 2014).

27. "Complex Housing Problems," *Dallas Morning News,* August 12, 1979.

28. "The American Indian in an Urban Community," 13.

29. Patrick, "Relocation in Dallas," 24–26.

30. "Dallas Soil Tainting: Relocation Urged," *New York Times,* April 25, 1983.

31. *Rosebud to Dallas.*

32. Between September 17, 1957, when the Lester family moved into Elmer Scott, through April 1961, 540 Indian families lived in the project. By April 1961, only 125 remained. Among those 540 total families, 331 left the project before the end of their first year there. As of 1972, only two Indian families remained at Elmer Scott. See Fogleman, "Adaptive Mechanisms," 56; James Goodner, *Indian Americans in Dallas: Migrations, Missions, and Styles of Adaptation*, sponsored by the Training Center for Community Programs in Coordination with the Office of Community Programs Center for Urban and Regional Affairs (Minneapolis: University of Minnesota, 1969), 11–12; "A Survey of the Occupational and Educational Needs of the American Indian in Dallas County" (Texas Education Agency and Dallas County Community College District, 1974), 12–17.

33. Woods and Harkins, *An Examination of the 1968–1969 Urban Indian Hearings*, 11.

34. I toured the area by automobile in spring 2015.

35. Kiowa Chief Lone Wolf led his people in defense of their homelands against settler invaders and the U.S. military during the 1860s–70s in present-day Oklahoma, before being incarcerated in Florida for over four years as punishment for protecting his people. Founded in 1944, the National Congress of American Indians became an important intertribal lobbying group in Washington and a vanguard for the defense of Indian sovereignty. Juanita Ahtone interview with Mary L. Patrick in Dallas, Texas, January 6, 1972, BUPOH; Fogleman, "Adaptive Mechanisms," 43; "Indians Organize their Own Club," *Dallas Morning News*, November 30, 1956; "NCAI Kicks Off Anniversary with Family Memories," *Indian Country Today,* October 22, 2018, https://newsmaven.io/indiancountrytoday/news/ncai-kicks-off-anniversary-with-family-memories-EdmnnLOPuoWlQDplWZVWqA/.

36. Ahtone interview, BUPOH.

37. Fogleman, "Adaptive Mechanisms," 116; Ahtone interview, BUPOH; Patrick, "Relocation in Dallas," 95–116; "Indians in Dallas Area Neither Cohesive nor Highly Visible," *Dallas Morning News*, November 19, 1989.

38. Fogleman, "Adaptive Mechanisms," 10; "The American Indian in an Urban Community," 10.

39. Goodner, *Indian Americans in Dallas*, 24–25; Willis Knight obituary, Hart Funeral Homes, http://www.hartfuneralhome.net/memorialpage.asp?id=69212&locid=94, accessed July 12, 2018.

40. Goodner, *Indian Americans in Dallas*, 29–34.

41. Patrick, "Relocation in Dallas," 136–38; Robert Beams (Choctaw) interview with Mary L. Patrick, January 11, 1972, Dallas, Texas, BUPOH; David Harkens (Choctaw) interview with Mary L. Patrick, January 22, 1972, Dallas, Texas, BUPOH.

42. Fogleman, "Adaptive Mechanisms," 46.

43. "Indians of Dallas Inactive but in Trouble," *Dallas Morning News,* March 11, 1973.

44. *Rosebud to Dallas;* Blansett, *A Journey to Freedom,* 89; "The Cement Prairie," *D Magazine* (November 1975).

45. Mary Williams interview on *TV Forum* with host Gene McIntire, February 12, 1972, Dallas, Texas, BUPOH, http://digitalcollections.baylor.edu/cdm/compoundobject /collection/buioh/id/3490/rec/1; "The Cement Prairie"; "The Meanest Street in Dallas," *D Magazine* (November 1977), https://www.dmagazine.com/publications/d-magazine /1975/november/the-cement-prairie/; "Six Persons Reported Shot," *Dallas Morning News,* May 4, 1977.

46. Beams interview, BUPOH.

47. Harkens interview, BUPOH. On disproportionate Indigenous incarceration, see Douglas K. Miller, "The Spider's Web: Mass Incarceration and Settler Custodialism in Indian Country," in *Caging Borders and Carceral States: Incarcerations, Immigration Detentions, and Resistance,* ed. Robert T. Chase (Chapel Hill: University of North Carolina Press, 2019), 385–407.

48. Kent Blansett notes that police in 1960s San Francisco's Mission District practiced racial profiling of Indian bars and arrested Native peoples at a higher rate than any other group; see Blansett, *A Journey to Freedom*, 89.

49. Woods and Harkins, *An Examination of the 1968–1969 Urban Indian Hearings*, 34.

50. "Native American Radio 'Beyond Bows and Arrows' Wins Listeners with Its Relaxed Approach," *Dallas Morning News*, June 10, 1991. In an excellent recent article on Indigenous radio, Josh Garrett-Davis discusses the *Indians for Indians Hour* radio program, which first hit the AM airwaves from Norman, Oklahoma, in 1941, and, after eventually moving to the FM dial and Anadarko, Oklahoma, still broadcasts today. The show aired in Indian stores, schools, gas stations, and hospitals. In the context of Indigenous peoples' dispersal to cities such as Dallas, the show helped build intertribal communities while functioning as an "audio message board" for news from Oklahoma Indian Country and beyond; see Garrett-Davis, "The Intertribal Drum of Radio: The *Indians for Indians Hour* and Native American Media, 1941–1951," *Western Historical Quarterly* 49, no. 3 (Autumn 2018): 249–73.

51. "Radio Host Speaks up for Indian Community," *Dallas Morning News*, July 11, 2000; "Urban Indians—They're Banding Together to Fight Big-City Problems and Maintain Cultural Traditions," *Dallas Morning News*, September 26, 1993; "Shattering Stereotypes—American Indian to Share Racism Experiences," *Dallas Morning News*, March 18, 1993.

52. Author interview with Albert Old Crow, KNON 89.3 Radio Studio, March 18, 2018.

53. *The Raven Speaks* 1, no. 1 (April 1968) through *The Raven Speaks* 4, no. 12 (March 1972); "Ms. Hail's Goal Is Rule of Majority," *Dallas Morning News*, March 5, 1972.

54. "Indian Vote Rally Schedule," *Dallas Times Herald*, January 14, 1972.

55. Ahtone interview, BUPOH; "To Them Dallas Is an Interlude."

56. "Dallas Indians Hold Wide Variety of Jobs," *Dallas Times Herald*, March 13, 1974.

57. "Indians Struggle to Conquer Urban Life," *Dallas Morning News*, November 14, 1983.

58. "Indians Solving Problems," *Dallas Time Herald*, March 10, 1974.

59. Gerald Vizenor tells stories of "survivance over dominance," in which *survivance*, unlike survival, is a continuing phenomenon, and not merely an historical one; see Vizenor, *Manifest Manners: Narratives of Postindian Survivance* (Lincoln: University of Nebraska Press, 1999), vii, 4.

60. Young and Frazier interview.

61. Individual Studies on Returnees, December 1959, RG 75, Records of Pawnee Area Field Representative, Records of Employment Assistance Officer, Studies and Telegrams, 1957–63, box 1, folder: Telegrams, NARA FW; Special Study of Returnees, RG 75, Records of Pawnee Area Field Representative, Records of Employment Assistance Officer, Studies and Telegrams, 1957–63, box 1, folder: Special Studies on Returnees, FY 1959, NARA FW.

62. "Indians Struggle to Conquer Urban Life."

10

NEEGINAN

The Struggle to Build an Indigenous "Enclave"
in Postwar Winnipeg

Slightly more than half a decade ago, a front-page headline in a widely circulated Canadian news magazine described the city of Winnipeg as the place
where "Canada's racism problem is at its worst."[1] In the accompanying article,
reporter Nancy MacDonald marshaled a broad range of anecdotal and statistical evidence to build a portrait of a city "deeply divided along ethnic lines,"
in which Indigenous people—who numbered roughly one hundred thousand
people, or about 12 percent of the urban region's total population—were "mani-
festly" denied equal opportunity, with many suffering "daily indignities and
appalling violence."[2] Her assessment of life in contemporary Winnipeg was
a bleak one.

While MacDonald's reporting accurately represented Winnipeg as a city
menaced by a stark racialized divide, her piece is riddled with analytic shortcomings, as a range of commentators have pointed out.[3] The most striking of
these is its failure to consider the robust and long-standing efforts of Indigenous

community organizers to contest the very sort of group-differentiated insecurities that her reporting describes. MacDonald's analysis is silent about the city's well-established status as one of North America's most important hubs of urban Indigenous political organizing and institutional development. It pays little attention to the complex web of Indigenous-led organizations that operated in the city and provided a range of social, linguistic, political, educational, religious, and residential services to its constituents. Ultimately, it leaves uninitiated readers with no sense of how Winnipeg is a place in which Indigenous people have thrived, often in the face of extraordinary adversity.

MacDonald's lapse is symptomatic of an enduring tendency amongst mainstream commentators to cast urban Indigenous experience as one primarily of victimization.[4] Like so many before her, she seems to have been unwilling or unable to see Indigenous people as active agents of the city's production.

By contrast, this chapter stresses how Indigenous people are integrally involved in the contemporary making of cities like Winnipeg by focusing on one particularly illuminating historical example. In keeping with the broad aims of this volume, and its commitment to challenging the narrative exclusion of Indigenous peoples from the development and social experience of North American urban life, the analysis that follows chronicles a multidecade effort by community organizers to establish an explicitly Indigenous quarter called Neeginan ("our place," in Cree) at the intersection of Higgins Avenue and Main Street, in the heart of Winnipeg's inner city.

As early as 1966, Indigenous organizers worked to establish an urban zone dedicated to providing social, cultural, economic, and residential opportunities to the Winnipeg's rapidly growing Indigenous community. Initially, the prospects for realizing this project looked very promising and, by the start of the 1970s, organizers had successfully persuaded public officials to invest in a series of planning exercises for the proposed zone. Setbacks emerged in the years that followed and by 1975 government support for the Neeginan concept had all but vanished (the history of state participation in the project is one of waxing and waning enthusiasm, as I demonstrate). Critically, though, Neeginan's backers were undeterred by these setbacks, and they continued to pursue support for the basic components of the original vision. By the 1990s, they had managed to resecure funding for a range of projects within the originally planned site. Their work facilitated the emergence of what is today one of the largest urban networks of Indigenous institutions in North America. In spite of these achievements, however, the sustainability of the de facto Indigenous community that now exists at the intersection of Higgins and Main (insofar as it has been realized) is menaced by a range of difficulties.

The research presented in this chapter offers a broad view of how Indigenous activists managed to shape an urban district in the face of considerable racialized adversity. As I argue, their work is significant not only because it challenges interpretive frames that imagine "urban" and "Indigenous" as radically incompatible categories but also because it disrupts the framing of the city as a settler space. By recasting the production of North American cities as a dynamic and contested process that has always included Indigenous actors, it becomes possible to disrupt what Penelope Edmonds calls "triumphal accounts" of urban history that stress "infrastructural progress" and the heroic deeds of visionary white men as the definitive ingredients of urban development.[5] This chapter, like the volume of which it is a part, attempts to tell a different kind of urban story by highlighting some of the ways that Indigenous organizers in Winnipeg sought to construct a different kind of urbanity in the heart of an inner-city neighborhood.

My discussion is organized into three parts. I begin with a brief contextualization of the geographical and historical setting, before turning to discussions of the history of the Neeginan project and, finally, to reflections on its broader political significance.

GEOGRAPHICAL AND HISTORICAL CONTEXT

Most North American cities are located on geographies that were well-established sites of Indigenous life well before settler-colonists began to transform them in accordance with their own objectives. Winnipeg is located at the fork of the Red and Assiniboine Rivers in a place that has been part of an Indigenous human geography for at least six thousand years. It is built on territories that are significant to both the history and contemporary lives of the Cree, Anishinaabeg, and Métis peoples.[6]

The first encounters between Indigenous and European peoples in the region occurred in the 1700s, as fur traders traveled through the vast northwestern region that Europeans called Rupert's Land, placed under the nominal control of the Hudson's Bay Company in 1670. From the late eighteenth century to the early 1870s, the area was home to the Red River Settlement, a largely Métis community grounded in a dynamic integration of Indigenous and European cultures and practices. For much of the nineteenth century, Red River functioned both as an urban Indigenous community in its own right and as an integral part of a broader Indigenous regional geography that included the life-worlds of Anishinaabeg, Cree, Oji-Cree, Dakota, and Dene communities.[7]

The relative peace and intercultural dynamism enjoyed by the Red River Settlement was not destined to last, however. By the late 1860s, the community's trajectory was radically altered as the British Crown offloaded Rupert's Land to the recently confederated Canadian state. In this context, the northern stretches of the Great Plains began to be reshaped by an ambitious project of predatory territorialization. Indeed, the period between 1870 and 1900 was an era of dramatic settler-colonial transformation.[8] By the late nineteenth century, ever larger waves of Euro-American settlers arrived in the western interior of North America and the syncretic arrangements that had existed between Indigenous and European peoples during the fur trade–era began to be radically undermined.[9] Places like the future province of Manitoba began to be rapidly, and violently, reconstructed as settler domains. Geographer Owen Toews distills the meaning of these changes to their elemental core: "Canada stole virtually all of the lands of the Indigenous peoples of the North-West and gave them to white men."[10]

These tectonic sociopolitical shifts were resisted by the residents of Red River. Under the leadership of Louis Riel, the settlement opposed incorporation into Canada and launched an independent Métis government. Of course, such an explicit challenge to settler authority proved intolerable to the fledgling Canadian state and that opposition was crushed with brutal force. The violence of Canada's suppression effort drove as many as ten thousand Métis people into exile, as the state took control of the region through the Manitoba Act of 1870. One year later, Canada signed the first of the numbered treaties (Treaty 1) and achieved formal agreement with the Anishinaabeg and Cree peoples.

The city of Winnipeg was incorporated two years later. As it began to grow, public policies were crafted to explicitly purge Indigenous people from cities. By the early twentieth century, First Nations populations across Western Canada had been largely removed to reserve territories that were intentionally sited at a distance from burgeoning cities and towns.[11] In this context, "reserves were viewed as temporary enclaves," writes geographer Evelyn Peters, "places where First Nations people would either be civilized through agriculture, Christianity, or education to take their place in emerging Canadian society, or where First Nations people could live in peace while their 'races' died out."[12] While cities like

Winnipeg boomed and emerged as key arrival cities for migrants, settlers often celebrated the removal of Indigenous peoples from urban life.[13] Historian Adele Perry demonstrates that in the late nineteenth and early twentieth centuries, the apparent absence of Indigenous people in Winnipeg was sometimes noted as a point of civic pride amongst settler constituencies.[14]

Consistent with these trends, census data suggests that a comparatively small number of Indigenous people called Winnipeg home between 1900 and the midcentury mark. While the city was being transformed by volatile moments of boom and bust (and shaken by labor unrest that culminated one of the fiercest general strikes in continental history in 1919), the urban region's population was the least Indigenous that it had ever been. Settler efforts to exile Indigenous people from the burgeoning prairie city appear to have been so comprehensive that only twelve First Nations people and roughly seven hundred Métis turned up in official counts of Winnipeg's population at the dawn of the twentieth century.[15] In the early 1920s, the recorded number of First Nations residents was only sixty-nine and it would take another thirty years for that figure to breach the two hundred mark (though issues with census information collection demand that these figures be treated with profound suspicion).[16] Determining the number of Métis people that were resident in Winnipeg during the first half of the twentieth century is complicated.[17] Recent research on an informal urban community called Rooster Town, however, confirms that Métis life persisted in Winnipeg in ways that aren't necessarily legible through state population statistics.[18]

Like other North American cities, Winnipeg was radically decentralized in the decades that followed the Second World War. Suburban development and the exodus of inner-city residents to the urban fringe resulted in a dramatic expansion of the city's boundaries. Winnipeg's geographical expanse nearly doubled in the period between 1960 and 1990, while its population grew only at a modest pace.[19] These transformations prompted inner-city districts to enter a period of protracted decline and disinvestment. Core area residential neighborhoods, particularly those north and west of the central business district, came to be associated with dilapidation, "slum" housing, and economic insecurity.

Postwar suburbanization coincided with a considerable uptick in Indigenous relocation to the city. Between 1958 and 1979, the number of Indigenous people living in Winnipeg grew dramatically, expanding at a pace of roughly 7 percent per year and breaching the twenty thousand mark by 1980.[20] This demographic growth continued in the years that followed, and today Winnipeg is home to the largest urban Indigenous community in the country, with about one hundred thousand residents identifying as Indigenous. Importantly, the language of "relocation" and "migration" is sometimes problematic in this context. As Evelyn Peters and others have pointed out, Indigenous people that moved to cities in the postwar decades did not "arrive" like migrants from other places. It is often more accurate to note that they were moving within their traditional territories.[21]

The reasons motivating individual moves to the city were as diverse as the movers themselves, but they certainly included the effects of chronic underinvestment in Indigenous communities and the discriminatory de-statusing of Indigenous women through midcentury reforms to the Indian Act of 1876, among other things.[22] Nevertheless, research conducted in the postwar decades suggests that the prospect of securing good employment seems to have been front of mind for many that left Indigenous communities for the city during this period.[23] In many cases, however, such ambitions remained unrealized as good jobs proved elusive. Deindustrialization had sapped Winnipeg of opportunities for unskilled workers, and Indigenous people arriving in the city often encountered a "wall of racism" when they applied for other work.[24] With limited economic prospects, most ended up in the low-rent housing of the core area neighborhoods mentioned above. An urban housing survey conducted by the Manitoba Indian Brotherhood in 1971 demonstrated that nearly 65 percent of Indigenous respondents were living in the inner-city.[25] For the Brotherhood, like other critical analysts, Indigenous concentration in "the lowest level of housing in the city" was so apparent that it was as if inner-city districts had become the "private preserve of the native populace."[26]

At the center of this emergent inner-city geography was an eight to ten block stretch of Main Street, one of the city's central thoroughfares, which extends north from the city center. From the 1960s on, this strip became home to a dense concentration of single-room occupancy hotels, beer halls, pawn shops, payday loan operations, and casual labor centers.[27] In spite of its mainstream reputation for insalubrity, however, the Main Street strip also emerged as an important cultural, social, and political hub for the city's growing Indigenous community. Through the 1970s, the strip was a key site for a robust Indigenous music scene and one of the main meeting spaces for Red Power organizing and other forms of anticolonial political work. By the 1980s, as key institutions were razed and replaced by a "sterile, authoritarian infrastructure," it was a critical part of the geography of Indigenous Winnipeg.[28]

Of course, the emergence of an inner-city district with a distinctly Indigenous character was not exclusively a reflection of the desire of Indigenous people to live in close proximity to one another. In their 1971 survey of housing conditions, Manitoba Indian Brotherhood researchers found that relegation to "slum" housing was part of a "chain of circumstance" by which the "newly-arrived Indian" was "shackled to an existence of hopelessness and degradation." And they argued that "the first link in this blighted chain of events is forged by the type of accommodation into which he is thrust."[29] In a contemporaneous report, the Manitoba Métis Federation concluded that much of the housing available to Indigenous renters had a "ghetto quality" that was every bit as "confining as the walls of any prison."[30] The language of "confinement" is significant here. Against those that would understand Indigenous concentration in the inner-city as the *cause* of core area decline, urban activists made it clear that Indigenous renters had merely inherited the low-quality housing abandoned by the participants in the exodus to the suburbs. "Members of the white community point their fingers at Indian-occupied slums and trot out the age-old stereotype of the Indian as one who feels at home in filth and disrepair," the Manitoba Indian Brotherhood observed. But if "such individuals could remove the blindfold which prejudice and ignorance have placed over their perceptual faculties, they would realize that these residences were in a decayed state prior to any Indian family assuming tenancy and that Indian people are occupying them through necessity rather than choice."[31] Most Indigenous analysts, including researchers with the Manitoba Indian Brotherhood, were keen to point out the spatial concentration of urban Indigenous residential life in the inner-city could not be explained without acknowledging the "ubiquitous and largely unchecked" racism that was shaping urban outcomes.[32]

Observations like these ones offer evidence of the long-standing significance of what researchers now describe as a form of "spatially concentrated, racialized poverty" that remains a key feature of Winnipeg's inner-city.[33] What is specific to this urban context and a handful of others, particularly in the Western reaches of the North American continent, is that this particular expression of concentrated insecurity cannot be understood without an explicit interrogation of its roots in enduring forms of settler-colonial violence. As researchers such as Elizabeth Comack, Lawrence Deane, Larry Morrissette and Jim Silver have argued, Winnipeg's crisis of "entrenched racialized poverty" can only be understood by interrogating the persistence of colonial inequity.[34]

THE NEEGINAN PROJECT

Indigenous organizers began the political work of building essential institutions in these contexts of demographic change and racialized adversity. As early as the mid-1960s, activists began floating the idea that Winnipeg's diverse Indigenous community would be better served by the establishment of a formally designated zone *within* the existing city. The "enclave" plan was motivated by the desire to establish a spatially concentrated hub that could meet the residential, recreational, cultural, commercial, and spiritual needs of the Indigenous community as a whole. At points, it was even suggested that the project might function with a degree of autonomy comparable to the Vatican City (vis-à-vis Rome) or District of Columbia (vis-à-vis the United States).[35]

The idea of constructing an urban Indigenous "village" was first publicly considered in 1966 at a meeting organized by the Winnipeg Indian and Métis Friendship Centre (IMFC), according to organization's executive director George Munroe.[36] On the heels of these preliminary discussions, the concept gained significant momentum and enthusiasts "consistently prevailed" on the IMFC leadership to begin moving it forward.[37]

Building on the first wave of community enthusiasm, Munroe and others embarked on the task of developing early plans and presented them to attendees of the 1970 edition of the annual Urban Native Conference, held at the St. Charles Hotel in Winnipeg's Exchange District. Conference participants were clearly impressed and gave the proposers the green light to move ahead with what would come to be known as the Neeginan project.[38] From there, Munroe and his fellow IMFC board member Tom Eagle enlisted the help of a University of Manitoba engineering student and began crafting sketches and a model for a development centered around inner-city land that had been initially developed (and since abandoned) by the Midland Railway company, a regional subsidiary of the Great Northern Pacific Corporation. To generate community excitement, Munroe and the other planners, including Bill Nanowin, held a number of meetings at the IMFC and dispatched Eagle to show off the display at other community meetings.[39]

But enthusiasm alone was not enough to bring the proposed development to fruition and supporters would need considerable financial support from at least one—and possibly all three—levels of government. Contemporary analysts doubted whether such funds would be forthcoming because state support for the urban Indigenous community had so far been decidedly minimal. The federal government, one observer predicted, would likely continue to "hide behind the Indian Act," which allowed it to "slough off" any responsibility for the welfare of Indigenous people not living in First Nations communities. Meanwhile, the provincial government could hardly be relied upon, since it had consistently abandoned the city in favor of rural investment. The comparatively low-revenue municipal government, he concluded, had little interest in social development programs, since it saw them as the responsibility of "senior" levels of government.[40]

Yet the 1960s and early 1970s were also a period of ambitious state action. In Canada, this is particularly true of the federal government, which attempted bold new forms of "engagement" in both its relationship to Indigenous peoples and, separately, its commitment to urban development.[41] While the former culminated in an (unsuccessful) proposal to terminate the distinct status of Aboriginal peoples with the notorious White Paper of 1969, the latter was expressed through the establishment of the Ministry of State for Urban Affairs (operational from 1971 to 1979) and new commitments to work with lower levels of government to address vexing urban questions. In both cases, bold plans were driven by a climate of federal "fiscal buoyancy" and a prevailing "readiness" to take executive action.[42] In short, this was a comparatively rare instance in which federal authorities were willing to take on new responsibilities.[43]

At the same time, a new municipal activism was beginning to take root, which, in turn, influenced federal initiatives.[44] Increasingly, urban policymakers were on the leading edge of efforts to address new social demands, albeit with minimal resources. In 1972, the Winnipeg urban region amalgamated as a single municipal entity, and some felt that this new initiative would give the city an unprecedented capacity to take social development seriously.[45] It was in this context that proponents of the Neeginan initiative turned to a municipal official to push the project forward. In the early 1970s, Bill Nanowin met with Earl Levin, Director of Planning at the City of Winnipeg, and invited him to convert the existing Neeginan vision into a formal proposal for the three levels of government.

Levin's report, finalized in June 1972, pulls no punches. It describes the exclusion and insecurity of Winnipeg's growing Indigenous population as the "single most urgent and difficult social problem that exists in the city."[46] In Levin's terms, Indigenous marginality was a multidimensional crisis in need of comprehensive remediation. He argued, in the first place, that the situation was urgent for Indigenous people themselves: "It is not merely that most of the Indians and Métis are poor," he wrote, but also that "the Indians suffer an additional tragedy of cultural disorientation. . . . They can find in the city . . . no basis of for self-identity and no basis for social or economic motivation."[47] But he also argued that the situation was equally urgent for the broader population: "If the migration of the Indians from the reservation into the city is continued at its current rate, and no adequate arrangements are made for receiving them . . . then the destruction of the city by men whose only outlet from the despair of their daily lives is violence, may well be the prospect for Winnipeg as it has already become the prevailing condition in many American cities."[48] Levin's appeal for state support has an ambivalent character, to put it mildly. It mixes genuine solidarity with patronizing caricature and alarmist hyperbole.

In spite of its significant shortcomings, however, Levin's report did attempt to persuasively pitch the "enclave" idea that Neeginan organizers had brought to him. Noting the widespread need among recent arrivals to be "with their own kind" in a "strange and hostile environment," the report argued that the enclave could function as an established site of community connection, analogous to a "Little Italy" or a "Chinatown."[49] While reserves had long functioned as sources of strength for Indigenous communities, he observed, the advent of accelerated urbanization demanded that a similar source of strength be constructed in the place where more and more Indigenous people were now living. The new "enclave," in other words, should be built *within* the city and, more specifically, "near the place where Indians are now concentrated."[50]

Building on the near unanimous desire of Neeginan activists to locate the project in the city center, Levin drew on his urban expertise to propose that the development could be situated on an inner-city "triangle of land" bordered by the Main Street strip to the west, the Canadian Pacific Railway (CPR) site to the north, and the Disraeli Freeway to the south. "It should be an ethnic quarter not unlike the other ethnic quarters in this and other cities," Levin wrote. "It should have its own schools and its own stores, and its own clinics. And it should be designed and built with the advice and participation of the Indians themselves."[51] Shrewdly, Levin's proposal offered a blueprint of how each level of government could contribute to achieving this vision. The municipal government should take care of planning and permissions, the provincial should build residential spaces through its already existing public housing schemes, and the federal should fund the construction of the cultural infrastructure, through a Secretary of State program designed to provide precisely such assistance.

Parenthetically, it is worth observing that by enlisting Levin's help and making direct appeals for the resources of the state, those behind the Neeginan project were taking a relatively moderate approach to the question of Indigenous exclusion from the prosperity of urban life. Their contemporaries in the Manitoba Indian Brotherhood, for example, were much more willing to publicly describe Indigenous exclusion as a direct outgrowth of white supremacy and settler colonial violence, even if that is not precisely the language that they used. Notably, Levin himself was dismissive of some of the apparently "naïve and hopelessly impractical" ideas that he heard emanating from more radical elements of the Indigenous community, including the notions that "the lands of their ancestors be returned to them, or that they be paid for those lands at current market values, or that they return to live in the bush, or that the white man has broken his treaty promises and has deprived the Indian of his aboriginal rights and these should be reestablished."[52] In a passage that drips with condescension, Levin notes that at a recent event hosted by the Indian Brotherhood, one speaker had the temerity to advocate "for a new Indian reservation ten miles outside of the city, where the white man would be forbidden and would enter at his peril."[53] While the "hatred seething in this idea is understandable," Levin conceded, how such a "scheme" would help to "solve the urban Indian's problem" was less clear.[54] Thus, while Levin is an important figure in this story, it is worth remembering that both his politics and his imagination were shaped by a narrow sense of what was possible.

Levin's report was, however, a significant interim step and the activists behind the project used it as a catalyst to continue pushing forward. In September 1972, the Neeginan concept was endorsed by a coalition of more than twenty Indigenous organizations.[55] IMFC organizers then submitted a formal request to the Ministry of Urban Affairs for funds to conduct a feasibility study. In his letter to Minister Ron Basford, the IMFC's George Munroe included a copy of Levin's report and noted that the proposal for a "native people's 'village' in Winnipeg" was the product of "many years" of preparatory labor. "The native people of Winnipeg are very enthusiastic and anxious to carry this project forward into its next stage," he added.[56]

In the months that followed, however, bureaucratic hurdles stood in the way of that progress. Officials determined that it was inappropriate for IMFC to be the coordinating force behind the project, compelling the project's proponents to regroup as an independent entity called Neeginan Inc. The significance of this development is largely legalistic, however, as the newly independent organization was governed by a board of activists with close links to the IMFC, including Bill Nanowin, Fern Courchene, and Stan McKay. And while these and other board members enlisted as "private citizens," they remained "extremely sensitive to the need for a continuing broad support in the community."[57]

In November 1973, the federal government agreed to fund the study and Damas & Smith Ltd. were contracted to conduct it. The study's terms of reference instructed the consultants to consider the development of a "community with a focus."[58] They suggested that the researchers should provide a comprehensive accounting of the "present patterns of living of native people in the City" and the "manner in which the migrant is accommodated and becomes familiar with his new environment." Most critically, however, the consultants were enlisted to test the feasibility of "creating a 'village' with linkages to native people throughout the City, where they now live or are likely to live in the future" and set to work on actually designing what that "village" could look like.

From the beginning, consultants Nick Damas and Bob Smith were made to understand that every level of their study needed to involve community feedback. To begin achieving their goals, they convened a task force that met every second Monday at the Winnipeg Native Club. It included members of Neeginan Inc. and other Indigenous community organizations, representatives from the city planning department, and occasional representation from the federal government, the broader Indigenous community, and legal advisors. At an early stage, Damas & Smith conducted a series of comprehensive community meetings, including one that was open to the city-wide Indigenous community. Participation was significant, and through this process the broad contours of the project proposal began to take shape. For example, the consultants quickly learned that Indigenous Winnipeggers—both as individuals and through their community organizations—were almost unanimously committed to two principles that should guide the project proposal. First, the development should be located in the inner-city. Site designs for suburban variations on the plan were met with far less enthusiasm than those that proposed to claim land in core areas.[59] Community members also stressed that the site should be accessible from the Main Street strip.[60] Second, the participants in the consultation process were far more excited about the proposed cultural and community service components of the project than they were about its proposed residential components. The consultants surmised that this was a reflection of a prevailing cynicism about the kind of investments that the various levels of the state were willing to make. With the exception of public investment in the Indigenous-led

Kinew Housing Corporation, there remained "a widespread feeling that the many bright promises of better housing made over the years have all come to naught," they wrote.[61]

In their final report, Damas & Smith concluded that the project should be pursued in two phases, beginning with the construction of an inner-city "Community Services Centre." This installation, they argued, would bring together a diverse range of Indigenous-serving organizations in ways that would promote unity and undermine the siloed nature of current activities. The new building would facilitate "closer and more frequent contacts" between groups and "contribute to a stronger sense of community."[62] It would also serve as a kind of focal point for Indigenous Winnipeg, providing a designated site where the urban community could "meet and mingle." Most critically, however, it would function as a kind of beachhead. If successful, it could inaugurate a broad transformative process that would ultimately yield an Indigenous "enclave" in the inner-city. Importantly, the consultants cautioned that the Community Services Centre should be more than another office building. Rather, it was "intended to have a deeper spiritual significance, and act as a symbol with which the native community can identify, linking them with the spiritual strength of their past, and pointing to a future where they can find anew their ancient qualities of pride and nobility."[63] Accordingly, designs for the complex incorporated a range of Indigenous motifs, including a "great central circle" intended to represent the "never ending continuity of the life of source of Indian and Métis in Manitoba" and splayed east and west courtyards intended to "recall the form of the Thunderbird."[64]

In spite of these promising beginnings, however, the proposal ultimately failed to win critical governmental support. Officials at various levels of government were unconvinced that the Neeginan scheme would do much to address the problems that they felt required remediation, and they criticized Damas & Smith for being short on practical information about what would be required to achieve the proposed vision. In one representatively disparaging report, an official concluded that the proposal would do little more than "reorganize present services under one roof with a few added facilities" and complained that the housing component contained in the original plan "was dropped to a later phase without too much study."[65] That official seems to have been unmoved by the community decision making process behind the decision to prioritize the proposed Community Services Centre first. In the end, a federal official informed Munroe that support was being "postponed indefinitely" and that it would be "unwise" for him to commit any more energy to the project.[66] By the summer of 1975, it seemed that the Neeginan plan was destined to go no further.

In the wake of this setback, progress on the Neeginan vision slowed. The initiative remained mostly dormant through the 1980s, though the implementation of the Winnipeg Core Area agreements (a partnership between the city and other levels of government) did set the groundwork for future development. In 1995, however, some of the central planks of the Neeginan vision began to be put in place, especially as the Winnipeg Development Agreement (WDA) was adopted as official city policy. The latter established a consultative body called the North Main Task Force, which sought new ideas about how to transform the Main street strip, including one of the target areas for the Neeginan site. Through this process, Indigenous community organizers, including some of those that had been behind the original project, managed to leverage enough funding to realize a portion of the original plan.

By the late 1990s, a number of the key components of the Neeginan vision had been realized, albeit in modified forms. Most significantly, the long-standing idea of building a cluster of Indigenous institutions at one inner-city location with easy proximity to the Main Street strip came to fruition on a parcel of land near the intersection of Main Street and Higgins Avenue.[67] The planned community services hub—which was so central to the 1975 plan sketched by consultants at Damas & Smith—came to life, in a sense, through the conversion of the former CPR station on Higgins Avenue into the Aboriginal Centre of Winnipeg. By 1999, the building was fully occupied by a range of Indigenous organizations and businesses, though the center's focus tended more toward the incubation of small businesses than on linking community service organizations. Meanwhile, the housing component of the original vision was partly achieved through the construction of Neeginan Village, a residential complex for students at the nearby Centre for Aboriginal Human Resource Development. Just as importantly, Circle of Life Thunderbird House, an architecturally significant spiritual center incorporating some early design elements, opened its doors in the lot across from the Aboriginal Centre building, just a few steps away from the headquarters of the Manitoba Métis Federation. These institutions are significant components of what has become a de facto Indigenous "village" in Winnipeg's inner-city, albeit one that differs significantly from the ambitious vision of Neeginan articulated in the 1970s. These and other Indigenous-led inner-city institutions are key bulwarks against the violence of "spatially concentrated, racialized poverty" that continues to menace the area.[68]

Despite these achievements, the vitality of the cluster of Indigenous activities located at Higgins and Main (and nearby districts) is routinely menaced by fiscal austerity. Both the Aboriginal Centre of Winnipeg and Thunderbird House are hard-won political achievements that rely on continuous public funding to be kept afloat. In recent months, the leadership of Thunderbird House went public about the dire state of their finances, noting that there has been no governmental help to maintain their rapidly deteriorating building.[69]

Just as distressingly, Indigenous achievements that have created a palpable sense of place in Winnipeg's inner-city are increasingly threatened by a policy climate of urban neoliberalism grounded in a commitment to "supply-side innovation, the undermining of social security infrastructure, and the privatization of land and public services."[70] In recent years, this toxic alchemy of commitments has had deleterious effects on the area around Main Street and Higgins Avenue, as Toews and I argue elsewhere.[71]

THE POLITICAL SIGNIFICANCE OF NEEGINAN

While the multidecade effort to realize the Neeginan vision has had important effects on Winnipeg's urban landscape, it is also significant in at least two ways that make it important for a broader consideration of the history North American Indigenous urbanization.

First, the Neeginan project offers robust empirical evidence for how Indigenous peoples have been (and continue to be) key participants in the contested production of urban space in settler-colonial societies like Canada and the United States. While this point may seem self-evident, it is worth repeating if only to counteract the widespread and enduring practice of imagining Indigenous life to have its proper place *outside* of the city.[72] By recounting historical narratives in which Indigenous urbanites are dynamic political contributors to urban production, we add to a body of evidence that stands against the problematic notion that Indigenous people are "out of place" in urban landscapes. Doing so not only complicates a tired set of stereotypes; it also chips away at the colonial conceit that cities are settler creations. It demonstrates that Indigenous people have long lived in and transformed urban spaces, often since the very beginning of city life.[73]

Second, the Neeginan project reminds us that cities themselves are part of the contested territorial arrangements that define contemporary North America. In so doing, it challenges the perniciously persistent idea of urban landscapes as either products of settler innovation or as multicultural melting pots where

Indigenous people are merely one "ethnic" group like any other. The latter contention operates to undermine the specific claims that Indigenous peoples have to North American urban space, naturalizing the settler colonial order of things and neutralizing the key questions of legitimacy that menace settler societies like Canada and the United States. The Neeginan project does precisely the opposite: it expresses the failure of settler colonial elimination by claiming Indigenous space in the city.

NOTES

1. Nancy MacDonald, "Welcome to Winnipeg: Where Canada's Racism Problem Is at Its Worst," *Maclean's*, January 22, 2015.

2. Community estimates suggest that there are about one hundred thousand Indigenous people living in Winnipeg. Statistics Canada figures suggest there were 92,810 people in Winnipeg Census Metropolitan Area (CMA) that identified as Indigenous (First Nations, Metis and/or Inuit) in 2016.

3. See Max Fineday, "What's Missing in the Maclean's Article on Racism?" *Briarpatch*, January 29, 2015; Jim Silver, "Winnipeg's Racism Challenge," *Winnipeg Free Press*, February 8, 2015; Heather Dorries, "'Welcome to Winnipeg': Making Settler-Colonial Urban Space in 'Canada's Most Racist City,'" in *Settler City Limits: Indigenous Resurgence and Colonial Violence in the Urban Prairie West*, ed. Heather Dorries, Robert Henry, David Hugill, Tyler McCreary, and Julie Tomiak (Winnipeg: University of Manitoba Press and Lansing: Michigan State University Press, 2019).

4. For a brilliant assessment of how MacDonald's piece reproduces what Eve Tuck calls "damage-centered" narratives, see Dorries, "'Welcome to Winnipeg.'"

5. Penelope Edmonds, "Unpacking Settler Colonialism's Urban Strategies: Indigenous Peoples in Victoria, British Columbia, and the Transition to a Settler-Colonial City," *Urban History Review* 38, no. 2 (2010): 4–20.

6. Adele Perry, *Aqueduct: Colonialism, Resources, and the Histories We Remember* (Winnipeg: ARP Books, 2016), 21–22.

7. Owen Toews, *Stolen City: Racial Capitalism and the Making of Winnipeg* (Winnipeg: ARP Books, 2018), 32.

8. Toews, *Stolen City*, 31.

9. For a broad perspective on these transformations, see Jeremy Adelman and Stephen Aron, "From Borderlands to Borders: Empires, Nation-States, and the Peoples in between in North American History," *American Historical Review* 104, no. 3 (1999): 814–41.

10. Toews, *Stolen City*, 31.

11. Evelyn Peters, "'Our City Indians': Negotiating the Meaning of First Nations Urbanization in Canada, 1945–1975," *Historical Geography* 30 (2002): 75–92, 75; Patricia Wood, "The 'Sarcee War': Fragmented Citizenship and the City," *Space and Polity* 10 (2007): 229–42.

12. Peters, "Our City Indians," 75.

13. There was, of course, an enormous amount of diversity amongst settler constitu-encies. For a consideration of some of the core class and ethnic fault lines of the city's non-Indigenous constituencies, see Jim Silver, "Winnipeg's North End: Yesterday and Today," *Canadian Dimension*, January 7, 2010; and Toews, *Stolen City*.

14. Jean H. Lagassé, *The People of Indian Ancestry Living in Manitoba: A Social and Economic Study* (Winnipeg: Department of Agriculture and Immigration, 1959), 47; John Loxley, *Aboriginal People in the Winnipeg Economy*, assisted by Bernie Wood, Louise Champagne, E. J. Fontaine, and Charles Scribe, prepared as part of the research program of the Royal Commission on Aboriginal Peoples ([Ottawa]: Royal Commission on Aboriginal Peoples, 1994, slightly modified 1996), 6, http://data2.archives.ca/rcap /pdf/rcap-105.pdf; Perry, *Aqueduct*, 24.

15. Loxley, *Aboriginal People in the Winnipeg Economy*, 7.

16. Loxley, *Aboriginal People in the Winnipeg Economy*, 7.

17. Loxley, *Aboriginal People in the Winnipeg Economy*, 7.

18. See David G. Burley, "Rooster Town: Winnipeg's Lost Métis Suburb, 1900–1960," *Urban History Review* 42 (2012): 3–25; Evelyn Peters, Matthew Stock, and Adrian Wer-ner, *Rooster Town: The History of an Urban Métis Community, 1901–1961* (Winnipeg: University of Manitoba Pres, 2018).

19. Richard Milgrom, "Slow Growth versus the Sprawl Machine," in *In-Between Infrastructure: Urban Connectivity in an Age of Vulnerability*, eds. Douglas Young, Patricia Burke Wood, and Roger Kiel (Kelowna, B.C.: Praxis Press, 2011); Chris Leo and Kathryn Anderson, "Being Realistic about Urban Growth," *Journal of Urban Affairs* 28 (2006): 169–89.

20. Loxley, *Aboriginal People in the Winnipeg Economy*, 7. These numbers are based on problematic census practices that were vulnerable to considerable undercounting. Loxley suggests they should be taken only as "rough orders of magnitude."

21. See Evelyn Peters, "Three Myths About Aboriginals in Cities" (paper presented as part of the Breakfast on the Hill Seminar Series, Canadian Federation for the Humani-ties and Social Sciences, March 25, 2004), 2–3.

22. On the latter, see Bonita Lawrence, *'Real' Indians and Others: Mixed-Blood Urban Native People and Indigenous Nationhood* (Vancouver: UBC Press, 2004), Evelyn Peters, "Subversive Spaces: First Nations Women and the City," *Environment and Planning D* 16, no. 5 (1998): 665–85.

23. Loxley, *Aboriginal People in the Winnipeg Economy*, 85.

24. Jim Silver, "Building Resistance: Aboriginal Organizations in Winnipeg's Inner-City," *Canadian Dimension*, January 7, 2009.

25. Manitoba Indian Brotherhood, *Urban Housing Survey* (Winnipeg: MIB, 1971), 2. The MIB was founded in the late 1960s as part of an effort to build a regional represen-tative body and is described by its successor organization, the Assembly of Manitoba Chiefs, as the "first common voice for First Nations in the province"; see Assembly of Manitoba Chiefs, "Assembly of Manitoba Chiefs and the MIB Early Beginnings," https://manitobachiefs.com/about/history/, accessed on April 1, 2019.

26. Manitoba Indian Brotherhood, *Urban Housing Survey*, 7.

27. Christopher Hauch, *Coping Strategies and Street Life: The Ethnography of Winnipeg's Skid Row* (Winnipeg: Institute of Urban Studies, 1985), 23–24.

28. Toews, *Stolen City*, 212–16. For many Winnipeggers, the Main Street strip remains stigmatized as a site of danger and illicit activity; see David Hugill and Owen Toews, "Born Again Urbanism: New Missionary Incursions, Aboriginal Resistance and Barriers to Rebuilding Relationships in Winnipeg's North End," *Human Geography* 7 (2014): 74.

29. Toews, *Stolen City*, 7.

30. Manitoba Métis Federation, *In Search of a Future* (Winnipeg: Manitoba Métis Federation, 1972), 41. The Manitoba Métis Federation was incorporated in 1967.

31. Manitoba Indian Brotherhood, *Urban Housing Survey*, 8.

32. Manitoba Indian Brotherhood, *Urban Housing Survey*, 22.

33. Elizabeth Comack, Lawrence Deane, Larry Morrissette, and Jim Silver, *Indians Wear Red: Colonialism, Resistance, and Aboriginal Street Gangs* (Halifax and Winnipeg: Fernwood Press, 2013), 7.

34. Comack et al., *Indians Wear Red*, 11.

35. Kurt Sargent, "Interview with Mary Richard, Chair, Thunderbird House" (transcribed), History of Urban Aboriginal Organizations Project, July 31, 2002, p. 12.

36. George Munroe, *Executive Director's Annual Report, 1974* (Winnipeg: Indian and Metis Friendship Centre, 1974).

37. Munroe, *Executive Director's Annual Report*.

38. Munroe, *Executive Director's Annual Report*.

39. Munroe, *Executive Director's Annual Report*.

40. Earl Levin, *Neeginan: A Proposal for the Urban Indians and Metis* (Winnipeg: City of Winnipeg, 1972), 4.

41. Frances Abele and Katherine Graham, "Federal Urban Aboriginal Policy: The Challenge of Viewing the Stars in the Urban Night Sky," in *Urban Aboriginal Policy Making in Canadian Municipalities*, ed. Evelyn J. Peters (Montreal: McGill-Queens University Press, 2011), 35. It is well beyond the scope of this paper to account for complexity of the intrajurisdictional struggles between the various levels of government. For a thorough review, see Evelyn J. Peters, "Developing Federal Policy for First Nations People in Urban Areas: 1945–1975," *Canadian Journal of Native Studies* 21 (2001): 58; and Abele and Graham, "Federal Urban Aboriginal Policy."

42. Abele and Graham, "Federal Urban Aboriginal Policy," 35.

43. Federal policymakers responded to the acceleration of Indigenous urbanization in the postwar period by creating some modest new programming. In doing so, however, they largely (and problematically) approached the phenomena as a kind of crisis of disorientation. Because Indigenous life was seen as radically at odds with urban modernity, federal efforts were primarily aimed at addressing issues of "adjustment" and encouraging Indigenous integration. For a thorough consideration of these questions, see Peters, "Developing Federal Policy for First Nations People in Urban Areas."

44. Abele and Graham, "Federal Urban Aboriginal Policy," 36.

45. Levin, *Neeginan*, 4.

46. Levin, *Neeginan*, 1.

47. Levin, *Neeginan*, 1.

48. Levin, *Neeginan*, 2.

49. Levin, *Neeginan*, 5.

50. Levin, *Neeginan*, 4–5.

51. Levin, *Neeginan*, 4–5.

52. Levin, *Neeginan*, 2.

53. For an analysis of the enduring challenges of building urban reserves in Winnipeg, see Julie Tomiak, "Contested Entitlement: Kapyong Barracks, Treaty Rights, and Settler Colonialism in Winnipeg," in Dorries et al., *Settler City Limits*.

54. Levin, *Neeginan*, 2.

55. By 1974, more than fifty such organizations would be involved in the planning process; see discussion in Toews, *Stolen City*, 217.

56. George Munroe, "Letter to Ron Basford, Minister of State for Urban Affairs," December 12, 1972.

57. Damas & Smith Ltd., *Neeginan: A Feasibility Report Prepared for Neeginan (Manitoba) Incorporated*, April 1975, 12.

58. Damas & Smith, *Neeginan*, 12–15.

59. Damas & Smith, *Neeginan*, 15–17.

60. Damas & Smith, *Neeginan*, 20.

61. Damas & Smith, *Neeginan*, 17.

62. Damas & Smith, *Neeginan*, 16.

63. Damas & Smith, *Neeginan*, 24.

64. Damas & Smith, *Neeginan*, 25.

65. Paul Scott, "Letter to Michel Barelo," June 17, 1975.

66. Barney Danson, "Letter to George Munroe, President, Board of Directors," July 9, 1975.

67. See Ryan Hildebrand, "Our Place, Our Home: Indigenous Planning, Urban Space, and Decolonization in Winnipeg" (MA thesis, University of Manitoba, 2012).

68. Comack et al., *Indians Wear Red*, 7.

69. Ryan Thorpe, "Thunderbird House Pleas for Help Ignored, Board Co-Chair Says," *Winnipeg Free Press*, July 10, 2018.

70. Hugill and Toews, "Born Again Urbanism," 72. For a thorough consideration of the intersection of racialized inequity and urban neoliberalism, see Toews, *Stolen City*.

71. Hugill and Toews, "Born Again Urbanism."

72. See Evelyn Peters, "'Urban' and 'Aboriginal': An Impossible Contradiction," in *City Lives and City Forms: Critical Research and Canadian Urbanism*, ed. Jon Caulfield and Linda Peake (Toronto: University of Toronto Press, 1996); David Hugill, "Settler Colonial Urbanism: Notes from Minneapolis and the Life of Thomas Barlow Walker," *Settler Colonial Studies* 6 (2016): 265–78.

73. Julie Tomiak, Tyler McCreary, David Hugill, Robert Henry, and Heather Dorries, "Introduction: Settler City Limits," in Dorries et al., *Settler City Limits*; and Hugill, "Settler Colonial Urbanism."

PART IV

INDIGENOUS URBAN FUTURES
IN THE TWENTY-FIRST CENTURY

DANA E. POWELL

NoDAPL ENCAMPMENTS

Twenty-First-Century Indian City

A CITY EMERGES

Situated on the south side of the Oceti Sakowin camp on the Standing Rock
Sioux Reservation, activists erected a directional pole symbolically orienting
a social movement aimed at stopping the Dakota Access Pipeline (DAPL). The
pole showed spatial alignments with villages and cities across the world as it
stood above the Cannonball River, a free-flowing tributary of the Missouri River
(Mni Sose)—the second longest river in North America—threatened by the
encroaching pipeline. Distance mattered: many water protectors, as they called
themselves, had traveled far to arrive here, while others had homes just down the
road. From nearby Fort Buffalo, distant Six Nations, Denver, and Flagstaff, or
transoceanic cities like Paris, Tokyo, and Edinburgh, people converged in rural
North Dakota to ally with citizens of the Standing Rock Sioux Tribe, who in
2014 had officially objected to the 1,200-mile crude oil pipeline cutting through

Directional pole at Oceti Sakowin. Photograph by Dana E. Powell.

their homeland. The pipeline, being built by Texas-based Energy Transfer Partners with a right-of-way from the U.S. Army Corps of Engineers, not only posed an environmental risk to the river but also a political threat to Lakota/ Dakota/Nakota sovereignty as its route breached legal treaties predating the state of North Dakota. In April 2016, under the leadership of Lakota historian

LaDonna Brave Bull Allard, members of the Standing Rock Sioux Tribe established a camp in the disputed territory.[1] They called it Sacred Stone Camp, and it became a site of watchful vigil, prayer, and direct action. Over the next ten months, with the support of the tribal government, two more camps—Rosebud and Oceti Sakowin—were established in the vicinity. The camps were a fluid social field, with people and objects increasingly flowing in and out, such that by November 2016 its inhabitants numbered nearly ten thousand, making the NoDAPL gathering the tenth largest population hub in South Dakota.

There are deep histories of Lakota camps assembling together for various reasons—ceremonial, political, economic—and this one captured some of that tradition of resistance and collaboration.[2] It became an international settlement, with more than one hundred Native nations and thousands of allies to put DAPL owners on notice that energy infrastructure would not pass through Lakota lands without resistance. They were focused on countering the global economy of intensive energy extraction and exposing what such threats meant for water and Indigenous sovereignty. In her assessment of NoDAPL epistemology, Joanne Barker suggests "water is an analytic" for historical violence.[3] The knowledge infrastructure of the camp, including internal oral communications, global social media missives, and prayer, worked to expose the layers of violence shaping Indigenous life in North America. I argue that through a standoff of infrastructures—the encroaching pipeline versus the encampment and its related knowledges—the camp transformed into a formidable urban hub.

In this essay, I argue that the NoDAPL camps—I'll focus on Oceti Sakowin camp—became an urban hub as a mode of political mobilization. Through everyday actions people built up the infrastructure of the camp, created relationships within it, and took the associated ideas with them when they left. In so doing they participated in a powerful critique of coloniality. To explore this, I pay close attention to the camp's infrastructure, artwork, lands, and public services as I encountered them. This ethnographic approach draws on primary source material I collected through collaborative research with Diné colleagues and participant observation during two separate trips to the encampment in October and November 2016, as well as more than forty on-site and follow-up ethnographic interviews from 2016 through 2017.[4]

This hub was both a physical place and idea. Take the directional pole. Materially, it is a work of art in its own right, handcrafted in the self-organizing DIY mode that defined the NoDAPL aesthetic. (And months later, just before the camp was forcibly evacuated by the U.S. Army Corps of Engineers under an executive order issued by President Trump, water protectors secured the pole's safe passage to Washington, D.C., where it remains an artifact of twenty-first-century Indigenous reorientation and resistance in the Smithsonian's National Museum of the American Indian). Symbolically, it connected the camp to other cities throughout the world, just as activists made the pole's colorful image go viral as they used Facebook and other social media platforms to promulgate the ideas of the NoDAPL movement around the globe. The pole disrupts persistent colonial tropes of Lakota/Dakota/Nakota peoples as somehow outside of modernity.[5]

The camp disrupted U.S. claims to territory. It was established to thwart a pipeline, witness and resist the expansion of capital, and assert a moral force against the settler state as a manifestation of Indigenous space. The pipeline carrying Bakken Shale crude oil had been rerouted through Standing Rock territory by the former governor of North Dakota, to avoid possible risks to the inhabitants of the capital city of Bismarck, should a rupture occur. The new route led right through unceded Lakota territory and under Lake Oahe, a sacred body of water for Standing Rock and other Sioux Nations, in addition to many other underwater crossings on its way to existing oil facilities in Illinois and then eventually to the Gulf Coast for export. This rerouting was a clear case of environmental racism.

It was also an issue of sovereignty, as the state of North Dakota refused to recognize the settlement as an assertion of unextinguished treaty rights. U.S. Department of Justice staff (under President Obama) visited and negotiated with water protectors within the camps, and in September 2016 they issued a statement arguing for improved government-to-government relations between Native nations and the federal government. The DOJ went further, even, to write that "this case has highlighted the need for a serious discussion on whether there should be nationwide reform with respect to considering tribes' views on these types of infrastructure projects."[6] Issued just a few days after activists suffered tear gas and dog bites from a private paramilitary security company, TigerSwan (employed by Energy Transfer Partners to protect the pipeline in the four states through which it was to pass), this press release offered a glimmer of hope not only for containing the immediate threat of one particular pipeline but also for advancing long-game, meaningful Indigenous consent (not simply "consultation") in large-scale development projects. Yet while federal primacy seemed, fleetingly, to uphold Native sovereignty, the state of North Dakota had a vested interest in seeing the pipeline built and deployed scores of county police in full riot gear to a bridge just north of the camps. One legal strategy of protection suggested in the camp would be to file with the state for incorporation as a town. The state's refusal to recognize the camps' claims for incorporation placed county-level law enforcement on the side of industrial extraction. Such state response is part of the ongoing threat of violence in the wider colonial landscape. As Melanie Yazzie argues, aggressive energy capitalism often gets recast as "development," in a way that dangerously obscures the structural violence of settler colonialism as well as the anticapitalist dimensions of Indigenous resistance. The pipeline was not just another artifact of "progress" but, rather, an extension of settler capitalism's means of production, for which Indigenous lands and waters constitute essential, yet expendable, resources. This crucial link between settler colonial injustice and environmental injustice became clear, as Kyle Whyte has shown, in the events of Standing Rock.[7]

Against these entangled threats, water protectors built a camp—board by board, and tarp by tarp—to enact a different mode of political life and to assert a moral argument and infrastructural force against the designs of the settler state. The settlement did not oppose itself to the countryside, try to become a self-contained system, or assert an ideal type—as the three central tropes of more orthodox notions of the "traditional city" would claim. Following David Wachsmuth, it was "a category of practice: a *representation* of urbanization processes that exceed it."[8] The empirical fact of the camp-as-city, as a "category of practice," challenged assumptions about the temporality of urban places as well as the fait accompli of capitalist dispossession. Likewise, in its transnational *hyper*visibility, Oceti Sakowin inverted the expected ontology of a city as a place of anonymity. It was constituted through the everyday practices of decolonial critique, a critical perspective that materialized through the building, crafting, organizing, procuring, and repurposing of the materials and the creative skills of the thousands that came and went over ten months, transforming a prairie watershed into a teeming, fluid center of global operations. The camp's "vibrant materiality" of visible and invisible actors (including rivers, tributaries, deities, port-o-johns, firewood, kitchens, internet boosters, solar panels, and water tanks) was central to the force that formed the NoDAPL movement, as was its experimental mode of craftmanship, highly self-conscious of constructing a kind of "design, that designs."[9]

In this essay, I show some of the ways in which Oceti Sakowin emerged as an urban embodiment of political and spiritual claims and was experienced as such by its inhabitants. I show how a certain mode of social practice anchored in relations, mobility, and infrastructure marks Oceti Sakowin as a historically significant, if fleeting, Indigenous *city*. As such, Oceti Sakowin exerted a geopolitical, infrastructural, and moral claim against the settler state. The infrastructure of the camps was established to *resist* the infrastructure of the interconnected settler infrastructures of dispossession: treaty violations, law enforcement that protects capital, territorial encroachment, and, of course, the pipeline itself, built to extract, transport, and export energy minerals that, to some Native nations, are the lifeblood of economic sovereignty.[10] This standoff of infrastructures is an ontological relation: it is a type of "colonial entanglement," following Jean Dennison, where certain "moments of complexity" are shaped by power dynamics that alternately advance, and impede, Indigenous nation building.[11] People within the camps established a set of relations from 2016 to 2017, which continues "to travel with the people through whom they are constituted."[12] Indeed, places become mobile attributes of identity and community even after they cease to exist.

THE POLITICS OF PLACEMAKING: RECLAIMING THE "CAMP"

"This is totally unprecedented," claimed National Public Radio commentators in interviews with water protectors: "the largest gathering of Native Nations in more than a century."[13] But despite these claims to novelty, I was tripped up again and again, on the ground, by the affective power of return, memory, intimate encounters, layered histories of resistance, and other points of reference that entangled in nonlinear ways, generating a sensorial field within the microworlds of the encampment, in which people tried—often through the errors inherent to experimentation—to embody and construct the kind of society they hoped to create. As Nick Estes details, there is a deep and complex history to violent removals and dispossessions (e.g., the Pick-Sloan or Flood Control Act of 1944) as well as to strategic resistances to settler colonial power. In Sioux territory and Standing Rock, events must be understood less as "unprecedented" as, rather, informed by that deeper historical context. In his history of Indigenous resistance, Estes writes "the past" to understand not only the present of the NoDAPL movement but also the possibilities for decolonial futures.[14]

Places reclaim histories and generate identities; they are sites of the working out of possible futures. Residents of Oceti Sakowin spoke of a sense of place and protection as the defining features of their newly formed urban space: people repeatedly shared analyses like, "the camp goes with me," or, "I carry Standing Rock camp wherever I go." Oceti Sakowin constituted itself—as a set of relations—by emerging as a distinctive place in a part of Indian Country that has seen its share of settler incursions and dispossessions, as well as long traditions of resistance.[15] Place came together, as well, through the embodied, intimate interactions among people who traveled in and out of the village across the four seasons of the encampments, and those who moved there and called it home. As with the world's earliest cities, the camp's core attribute, or identity, was protection: this was a city in defense of land and water, a city of strategy, security measures, and decolonization trainings. As Oceti Sakowin grew, becoming more intricately infrastructural, practices of bringing it into being further constituted it as a city.

Such practices included comparative reflections, reaching across space and time. Actions at Alcatraz in 1969 and Wounded Knee in 1973 were particularly salient points of remembrance for many people within the camps. Alcatraz was present in Oceti Sakowin through the explicit retention of specific tribal affiliations and identities, unsettling journalists' glossing of the action as "unprecedented" pan-Indianism. Differences mattered in the camp, and the microworlds of these sociopolitical differentiations manifested in the various enclaves of affiliated groups and allies. Native activists' reclamation of Alcatraz Island in the San Francisco Bay captured national attention through high-risk actions, high-profile leaders, and the sudden media attention brought about by negotiations with the Nixon administration. As Kent Blansett shows, the island itself became a camp of sorts, where activists explored the relevance of their significant differences as an intertribal coalition; and yet this intertribalism had to be worked out in practice: people wrestled with whether it helped or hindered the cause, and it was widely misread as a kind of "pan-Indianism" that homogenized significant differences.[16]

The 1973 standoff in the hamlet of Wounded Knee, South Dakota, on the Pine Ridge Sioux Reservation, was recalled as well by organizers and cooks, and water protectors and truck drivers, with whom I spoke. In one of Oceti Sakowin's several outdoor kitchens, the lead cook shared stories of riding bareback as a child in the American Indian Movement occupation at Wounded Knee, to bring supplies to activists: "I'd lay down flat on my horse's back, under a blanket, so no one could see me, and my horse just followed the wash, so it was out of sight."[17] The NoDAPL moment brought back such vivid childhood memories. For another veteran activist, part of the national strategizing network for NoDAPL, Wounded Knee's lessons were being rethought at Standing Rock: "And what we learned there, at Wounded Knee," she explained to me in a phone interview, "was that

Standing Rock had to be different. So you take this ancient concept of different bands coming together into Council, into camp, and of course the word 'camp' has such a charged meaning for so many Nations. So the idea this time was of experiencing something that was severed and lost and reclaiming it, through the camp."[18] Deeper histories of Indigenous camps across the West predate the settler "fort" and offer a temporal corrective to contemporary imaginings of what constitutes an urban center. As this activist's words indicate, there are important overtones to the word "camp" that are distinctly political, evidence of ongoing Indigenous presence and self-governance in the face of encroaching settler infrastructures of dispossession. The camp-as-city that Oceti Sakowin became conjured these and other historical antecedents.

The camp was infrastructure, and it emerged over ten months in tense relation with other kinds of infrastructure. The physicality of the camp was an experiment in designing another kind of world: the infrastructure of the camp was cobbled together month after month, with supplies arriving in Cherokee Nation semis and in Honda Fits with New Jersey tags—hammers, firewood, corrugated tin, military canvas, wood, clothing, art supplies, food, kerosene, and medicine, to become a residential, governmental, and strategic hub of operations. As the emerging field of critical design studies argues, the places we design, design us back. Such is the ontological politics of the built environment that challenges the very "structures of unsustainability" built into the modern city.[19] Against this, Oceti Sakowin labored to redesign ways of living, interacting, relating, and managing the resources of everyday life, from water to sewer, from food to shelter. It was not an undertaking made from asphalt and steel, guided by planners and politicians, but, rather, a vigorous experiment in what Arturo Escobar terms new forms of "habitability": efforts to "re-earth the city" through certain "spatio-territorial praxis."[20] A corral of pigs in Sacred Stone, the solar-powered portable audio system in Oceti Sakowin, and the open-sided kitchen in Rosebud that fed anyone who arrived at mealtime were projects to keep the world of militarized energy capitalism at bay; they also cultivated a different mode of living and relating within the settlement.

THE EVERYDAY LIFE OF DECOLONIAL ACTION

Camp Southwest was one of many hubs within Oceti Sakowin, like kitchens, art studios, medics' tents, clothing centers, and construction sites, offering spaces where conviviality, strategy, nourishment, wellness, and everyday life played out. Native hubs constitute nodes for resilient action, linking up across space and time to constitute senses of belonging and community.[21] Following the many hubs within the camp, as a methodology, makes visible the way that decolonial politics and action infiltrated the micropractices of daily life, from feeding to sheltering. Within Oceti Sakowin, each hub assumed a distinctive character, with various languages, styles, rhythms, dwellings, and inhabitants who moved in and out. The variability of life within the camp was vast. The residential hubs, much like neighborhoods, were DIY assemblages navigated by landmarks: a line of port-o-johns (the sanitation system provided to water protectors by Standing Rock tribal government), the looming white geodesic dome (site of Lakota-led decolonization trainings for newcomers), several horse corrals, a trailer of solar panels, and three or four medical and healing tents (offering biomedical and integrative techniques).

The central artery of Oceti Sakowin was a dirt road flanked by the flags of several hundred Native nations. Leading from the main highway down into Oceti Sakowin, the road was the only way for vehicles to enter camp. With single-entry/single-exit openings, flanked by volunteer security guards, the camp's blueprint invoked a walled medieval village more than a porous modern city. Colorful flags along either side of the road gave the entry a feel of grandeur; this was heightened when tribal leaders would arrive, entourage in tow, for photo ops next to their nation's flag. On the day of Navajo Nation President Russell Begaye's visit, he gathered with other Diné people—youth who had run to Oceti Sakowin from Flagstaff, and elders busy building sleeping quarters and meeting structures—for photos that would make headlines in the *Navajo Times* newspaper.

The flag-festooned road also offered a point of orientation and meeting, as cell phone signals were largely nonexistent within the camp, except for one sloping incline above the Veterans for Peace enclave that offered just enough internet connectivity to be known as "Facebook Hill." I taught one of my classes from this Hill, disorienting as it was to try to bring students in remote Appalachia into windy, vibrant camp life through a brief digital connection. This lack of web and cellular infrastructure did not stop enterprising creatives: someone hitched a stationary exercise bicycle to a small human-powered generator system, such that anyone could freely and vigorously ride the bike to charge their cell phones and laptops. Infrastructures like the device-charging bicycle became the site for other kinds of relations: friendships and alliances happened there, to advance the mission of the city.

Deep within Oceti Sakowin, everyday life was both mundane and urgent, the pace organized around getting things done, the procurement and distribution of food, fuel, and water, and various forms of care in off-grid conditions. Oceti Sakowin supported at least three large kitchens, each feeding hundreds of people three meals a day. Everyday life often was the front line of a political movement: nourishment, fire-tending, sorting donations of clothing and food, reinforcing canvas tents to withstand the high winds, making supplies lists on paper cups to send with volunteers driving up to Bismarck, goggles, a chainsaw, Velcro, rubber mats, rivets, batteries, and a reminder to take a shower (the Standing Rock Sioux Tribe opened its district building to water protectors for public showers). The other front line—at the base of a hill called Turtle Hill, flanking the Cannonball River, and on the highway bridge, a liminal space between the activists' camps and the riot-clad police—was far away for folks like this cook, who managed the life within, the feeding, clothing, warming, refueling of bodies who flowed in an out of her kitchen. Other chefs were hard at work inside the colorful tipi of the Shining Light Kitchen, a collective of New Orleans disaster-relief cooks who knew how to play music late into the night and how to prepare delicious meals in massive kettles atop propane burners to feed hundreds. Inside, I discovered an old friend—one of the founders of the Indigenous Women's Network—making gallons of herbal cough syrup to distribute through the camps and its medical clinics.

In yet another kitchen, a cook made guacamole for one hundred people in between forays to carry sandwiches to protectors maintaining a road blockade. At one point, the cook chained herself to a Nissan Pathfinder on the construction site in a coordinated action that yielded twenty individual arrests.[22] This clandestine movement of bodies and gear from the kitchens to the front lines was not spoken of publicly: while some knowledge was freely shared in the camp—like how to build, chop wood, walk around a sacred fire, repair a tent, cram foot warmers into your boots, connect a smart phone to a local signal booster, or understand treaty history—knowledge of high-risk actions was not. It would seem that the majority of the camp's residents, and the majority of people that I got to know, were largely unaware of and uninvolved with the "front line" toward which the camp's internal operations were all, ultimately, oriented. That front line served as a crevasse dividing civilian life from military force; it was the boundary marking inside and outside, and the line of tension which, as the camp's emcee reminded us, "the world is watching."

Indeed, we might speak of the interiority of Oceti Sakowin as an infrastructural world, an ambient environment of everyday life. People variously referred to it as a "city," "village," or "town" while living in it and reflecting upon it much later. It teemed with people busying themselves with warehouses of supplies, kitchens/outdoor dining rooms, free markets for clothing, medical clinics, roads, toilets, neighborhoods (like the International Lightworkers Union, the Two Spirits Camp, and Red Warrior Camp), forms of road signage, small-scale livestock (Diné people brought sheep to butcher and share), and even elementary education. Both Sacred Stone and Oceti Sakowin offered schools, with volunteer teachers and donated supplies. One of the schools' founders, Alayna Eagle Shield, recalled seeing the need and organizing to meet it: "I went around, with an Excel sheet and said to people, 'If you are willing to be a resource, can you write your name down?' One of the things that was evident was that our children needed somewhere to go."[23] She laughed as she recalled dashing between her professional role as bilingual educator on the Standing Rock Sioux Reservation and her activist-volunteer labor in the camps, all to extend the homeschool model she had found so useful for her own children's learning. Set apart from other housing, on the western side of Oceti Sakowin, the colorful yurt structure opened up to a grassy field for playing games and outdoor teaching.

PECULIAR ONTOLOGIES: INFRASTRUCTURAL POLITICS AND ENVIRONMENTAL JUSTICE

A peculiar ontological relation existed among the pipeline, the river, and the built world of the camp.[24] People built this relationship as they constructed a counterworld to the pipeline, making buildings and art, invoking prophetic teachings, and engaging in nonviolent direct action. The black snake in Lakota oral history linked the pipeline with other prophetic movements, like the Ghost Dances of the late nineteenth century.[25] As one Sicangu-Lakota citizen said, "Our elders have told us that if the black snake comes across our land, our world will end."[26] When I saw the line being laid, topsoil and surface peeled away to carve out its subterranean path, I recognized the snake: Its sleek build and thirty-inch "girth" seemed more svelte, however, than the monster that had loomed in my imagination. But its internal capacity to transport up to five hundred thousand barrels of crude oil per day connected it with the violence of "man camps" in the Bakken Shale oilfields. The source of this crude is largely the territory of the Mandan, Hidatsa, and Arikara (MHA) Nation, or Three Affiliated Tribes in northern North Dakota, whose former tribal leader, Tex Hall, led the way for this mode of nation building to create "sovereignty by the barrel."[27] Having worked closely with Diné colleagues for twenty years, I am familiar with the perils and potentialities of tribal economies committed to fossil fuels.[28]

The black snake worked its way every day toward its underground crossing at Lake Oahe. Its very pathway was an intrusion into unceded lands and waters. The 1908 *Winters* Doctrine affirmed Sioux possession of water rights to the river, as laid out in the Fort Laramie Treaties of 1851 and 1868 between the Sioux and the United States—and those water rights have never been legally diminished.[29] Images of the snake's fragmented body depicted in artwork around the camp echoed the actual legal dismemberment of the Missouri River, carried out by the U.S. Army Corps of Engineers and, ultimately, the "Finding of No Significant Impact" (FONSI) ruling. This legal feat was achieved by treating every one of DAPL's waterway crossings as a separate "impact," disaggregated from the entirety of the multistate transmission line.[30] This federal agency had thus strategically, and discursively, dissected the mighty Missouri River. Activists' attempts at dismembering the black snake occurred in Iowa and South Dakota, with evidence of blowtorches used on sections of pipeline before it came online.[31] Oil contamination of the Missouri River from the pipeline's possible—and quite eventual—rupture was not the only threat posed by DAPL.[32] Litigation by Standing Rock and Cheyenne River Sioux Tribes charged DAPL with the infrastructure's spiritual contamination, arguing that the very existence of the snake beneath Lake Oahe is a violation of the 1993 Religious Freedom Restoration Act, as its presence under the water will render the water impure and, thus, sacred rites impotent. Practitioners rely upon a certain spiritual integrity of the water for ceremonial efficacy.[33]

In all of this infrastructure, there was art, which became another kind of infrastructure. As cities depend upon infrastructures to come into being, so did the camp need to assemble around the built environment and its expressive dimensions. Vintage school buses repurposed as mobile homes and offices, and expertly painted with murals, became landmarks within the village of Oceti Sakowin. The *Dakota Skipper* mural became a landmark for me. On one side, a painting of a figure, eyes closed, long hair flowing and swirling like water; on the other, a painting of an insect against a bold sun, captioned, "The Dakota Skipper is a rare, beautiful, and endangered butterfly, whose habitat is being destroyed by the DAPL." Signed by R. Peet, #endangeredspeciesmurals. The Dakota Skipper, *Hesperia dacotae*—technically a butterfly, despite its mothy antennae—has a critical habitat that reaches across Standing Rock territory as far as Minnesota and into southern Canada. Since 2014, the Skipper has been listed as "threatened" under the Endangered Species Act. Peet's mural—at once

Dakota Skipper, mural by R. Peet. Photograph by Dana E. Powell.

an edifice, artwork, call to action, and unsettling question about multispecies environmental risk—was an image of life that the city sought to protect.

The Indigenous Peoples' Power Project (or IP3) Art Tent, at the far north corner of Oceti Sakowin, just below the highway bridge that led to the most acute point of confrontation with law enforcement, was the staging ground and workshop for artists. Collectively staffed by Native and non-Native silk screeners, puppeteers, painters, sculptors, and others, it oversaw the production of what became the NoDAPL aesthetic. Spray adhesive, masking tape, rotary cutters, silk screen ink, immersion remover, fabric, protractor, velum paper, and more were the raw materials—indeed, the infrastructure—of direct action, to accompany bodies to the front lines. But the IP3 artists workshop teemed with volunteers stretching cloth, screening, drying freshly painted banners, sketching out new designs on butcher paper, and downloading images from artists around the world that were being sent in electronically. I talked to a man from L.A. who, like me, had wandered to the tent to take a peek at the hub of artistic production. The person who appeared to be the day's team leader wrote up a shopping list for more supplies and handed it to us—she needed one of us to get to Bismarck and return soon with the materials. The resultant artworks were highly valued, but, like all other objects and services in the camp, nothing was for sale. The most coveted were the silk-screened patches, which had to be "earned," as many water protectors told me, by making a venture as part of an action to the front line. Artist workshops proliferated outside of the IP3 Tent, spreading into self-organized events where students from Standing Rock and other tribal high schools were bused in with their teachers for workshops on sculpture and watercolor; and the Pine Ridge Reservation's "Rolling Rez Arts" bus offered a space for arts workshops and a pull-down screen, and generator, for outdoor films.

There were periodic building workshops in camp, for example, how to turn old oil drums into woodstoves for the tipis, "tarpees," and wooden structures like our Diné hogan (the traditional east-facing, circular, log dwelling of Diné people). And no one missed the irony of the oil-drum-turned-heater smack dab in the middle of a camp resisting the expansion of oil infrastructure. One particular structure, the tarpee, received praise from a builder in the camp as an "extraordinary construction" and a "symbol of a new kind of activism."[34] Imported by an Indigenous designer from the Pacific Northwest, the tarpee was a ready-to-build tipi-like structure made from tarps assembled to a circular pinnacle for smoke release. Unlike the tipis in camp, most of which were made of canvas and therefore less suitable for the North Dakota winter (and several had leaked badly and caught on fire), the tarpee used more robust materials and was made for a central woodstove rather than an open fire. Nor did it require hand-hewn poles. It could be assembled with lumber components and inexpensive hardware. Proponents of the tarpee embraced its low cost of approximately $350 (for all materials and final touches) and the fact that it could be assembled in a few hours, rather than days. Tarpees spread through camp as winterization ensued, expanding the encampment's ability to house the hundreds that continued to flow in, despite the oncoming winter.

Similarly iconic in the Oceti Sakowin landscape, the geodesic dome was the site of daily "decolonization meetings" and orientations for non-Natives and new arrivals to camp. The large, white dome, built of metal poles and stretched industrial canvas, led to mimetic designs at smaller scales: one was built with PVC pipe, bright blue tarp, and duct tape by Camp Southwest residents. Sam, a truck driver from Pine Ridge and Vietnam veteran, served on the security force for Oceti Sakowin and would periodically deliver reports from "the sacred fire"—the fire that burned and was tended all day and night at the main entry to the camp, the central node of trickle-down communiques. Communications within the city were spread sometimes by the camp's emcee as public announcements but, more often than not, traveled by word-of-mouth relay to key hubs within the camp. People would gather at these hubs, often around a fire, to hear the decisions of elders who served as the authoritative voice on whether or not direct action would proceed.

The camp also housed an "infrastructure" of readiness in the daily direct-action trainings and teach-ins on nonviolence theory. We learned chemical-weapons emergency first aid: Pour water sideways into the patient's eyes to flush thoroughly, and never wear goggles with foam seals—the foam absorbs tear gas and burns the skin. Keep a water-soaked bandanna on you at all times. Other preparatory infrastructures included artistic mural and banner making, or the making of colorful wind socks on long sticks, lifting the message "Mni Wiconi" high above the heads of hundreds of vigilant bodies walking to stand face to face with police officers in silence. Artists made the protection camp a space for performance, turning art into infrastructure in the protection of nature and bodies in ways that activated the camp's sense of transformative potential. Artist Cannupa Hanska Luger (MHA Nation/Lakota) grafted an idea he found in 2014 women-led resistance movements in the Ukraine into the NoDAPL actions: he created mirror shields for water protectors to defend themselves against rubber bullets, water cannons, tear gas, and other munitions of law enforcement that would also, ingeniously, reflect the faces of individual officers back on themselves.[35] The mirror shields created a living work of performance art that went viral through social media, along with a how-to video, so these reflective shields could be built by anyone.[36]

THE BUILDER'S NOTEBOOK

On the last Sunday in November, a blizzard hit and Camp Southwest lost two hundred pounds of potatoes to the freeze. Upon waking to a foot of snow, we quickly moved plastic bins of canned food, rice, kerosene, and other supplies from the outdoor makeshift kitchen into a large, enclosed plywood hogan, repurposing it as a storage and cooking shelter. The previous week, I'd watched as eight men built the spacious building in less than two days. It dwarfed a smaller hogan nearby, in which my Diné friends had offered me a prime sleeping spot, between the woodstove and the power strip for charging cell phones and tablets (supported by a generator and an internet booster). Hunkered down in our sleeping bags, we could read digital media for breaking news on the encroaching pipeline and confrontations with police, trying to make sense of the burgeoning megalopolis in which we were embedded. Outside, snowplows cleared the main road and firewood deliveries continued to roll in.

The encampment had not only surged in numbers since my first visit in October; it had been transformed from a haphazard gathering of three-season camping tents, military-issue canvas huts, and several aging school buses and Plains-style tipis to a formidable village of insulated housing, RVs, and small wooden bunkers. Volunteers from the camp's "construction staging area," a hangar-like arrangement of shelving, lumber, and tools, strategically erected structures legally classified as "semi-permanent" to avoid state building codes. Jerome Begay led much of this labor. A self-described "Navajo Cowboy," Jerome was a rodeo rider who had followed the NoDAPL movement on Facebook from his mother's home in Sheep Springs, New Mexico, on the Navajo Reservation. After seeing images of Energy Transfer Partners' armed mercenaries setting dogs and pepper spray on activists, which went viral in the first weekend of September 2016, he made the twenty-hour drive to Standing Rock to join the occupation. He recalled:

> I came for a weekend of selfies, but I wound up staying and building the camp, becoming director of construction for Oceti Sakowin. I knew how to use wire, duct tape, two-by-fours—how to haul water and chop wood— all that stuff you learn growing up on the Rez. People needed housing and they needed stoves, so I said 'okay,' and I led others and we got them built. And I wanted to build a camp for my people—for Navajos—so that's how we made Camp Southwest, with the hogans, deep in the center of Oceti Sakowin.[37]

Qualitatively different than the hundreds of photographs, videos, and textual accounts of the camp—made famous by the *Guardian, New York Times, National Geographic, Vice News*, and social media—Jerome's notebook may be the only detailed material record of this particular infrastructural world. It is a ledger of the temporary Indigenous city that gripped global attention for ten tense months. One month later, Jerome showed me his notebook. In his handwriting were lists of essential building supplies, alongside the carefully printed names and phone numbers of individuals and families who were requesting shelter to enable them to remain in the camp through the North Dakota winter. It struck me as the field notebook of an ethnographer or, as Michael Taussig says,

Jerome's notebook. Photograph by Dana E. Powell.

a mimetic sketch, or list, that is part-diary and part-description but is "always written for the spirits."[38] I take such lists and list-making seriously, as Jerome himself records and attends to the seemingly mundane details of everyday life, the records of designing a sustainable city and microeconomy, one shelter at a time. These are the details that elicit power: as the city grew, so did the federal threat of removal.

The notebook was a catalog of stories: how person or family so-and-so came to Oceti Sakowin, seeking shelter (often an improvement on where they'd come from), provisions, and the relational possibilities that the camp offered. The notebook detailed an infrastructural world as it emerged, a material record of two-by-fours, oil drums, cell phone numbers, and penciled designs for a place whose presence grew in the notebook, then grew on the ground. Jerome's notebook offers a material portal into the infrastructural world of the pipeline that gave rise to the city at Standing Rock. The notebook, however, and its many shopping lists, sketches, names, and reminders, seemed to haunt Jerome: in one public retelling after the physical occupation and after the camp was broken up, he expressed the affective force of this artifact, of a once very material world, as "heartbreak." Its worn yellow pages offer a record of occupation and absence; it is a ledger of desire, disappointment, and design as resistance. But it is also a ledger of locality, in Hugh Raffles's sense: of the "ongoing politics" and "density" of Standing Rock, which has traveled with Jerome (and thousands of others) in the dispersion of water protectors that some described as a "diaspora." Clearly, the dwellings of Oceti Sakowin were not simply utilitarian shelters. Many provided dignified, warm housing and free and culturally appropriate health care for people who did not have that where they came from. Some structures were themselves works of art or canvases for art, always "made in prayer," as builders and water protectors would say. Like Jerome's notebook that now serves as their mimetic connection to the present, they indeed were made "for the spirits." Other things were small-scale materializations of the kind of politics many in the camp wanted to see: supporting solar photovoltaics powering small generators, as well as the main portable audio system for Oceti Sakowin, which sent out the camp emcee's daily wake-up call, traveling through the earliest minutes of dawn across the city, followed by the shrill, ceremonial songs of Lakota singers.

Readying for the certain onset of winter as well as the increasingly palpable threat of state violence, Jerome made an uncanny presentation to those of us in Camp Southwest one morning: piles of brightly colored, foam squares (children's flooring tiles?) bought at Wal-Mart in Bismarck, with instructions on how we might repurpose them into rubber bulletproof vests. In other techniques of self-protection, we participated in nonviolent direct-action trainings, emergency medical trainings, decolonization meetings with often hundreds of participants, and many of the nearly daily organized "prayer actions," which might send hundreds of vehicles, or thousands of bodies, to create a roadblock or bear silent, nonviolent witness at one of the front lines facing the pipeline's serpentine progress. In more mundane moments, we washed dishes and chopped wood, hauled water and sorted clothing donations, supporting the everyday survival of thousands in this temporary autonomous zone.

REASSEMBLING THE CITY: RELATIONS, MOBILITY, INFRASTRUCTURES

President Trump's executive order in January 2017 overturned a ruling and impact statement process put in place by President Obama in December 2016, enabling the U.S. Army Corps of Engineers to grant the final easement required by Energy Transfer Partners to complete the North Dakota portion of the pipeline. Facing forced eviction a few weeks later, water protectors held prayer ceremonies before setting fire to the camp, rather than have their buildings, ceremonial structures, and artwork confiscated or destroyed by federal agents. *How to end a city?* People on the ground saw Trump's election as a failure, and Obama's previous concessions as a failure, but regarded the encampment as a success—even as its remaining infrastructures went up in flames. The eviction on February 23, 2017, witnessed 33 arrests of water protectors, like Jerome, who held ground in the camp until the very end.

The camp-as-city, in its ten-month existence and through its extended life that carries on through those it touched and transformed, challenged the logics of broader colonial landscapes and settler infrastructures of dispossession. This was an urban world of social and political life, where lived risks and embodied realities of long-term, large-scale mineral extraction (from cancers to asthma, from employment in the mines to resistance at the mines) inflect the common understanding of what remains at stake in the complexities of settler-Indigenous relations in North America: the ability to control the built environment—and its infrastructures of energy—as one crucial enactment of state power.[39]

Seeing Indigenous-designed dwellings and the notebook that survives them as central crafts of a movement, and remains of an Indigenous city, this chapter is part of a wider conversation among scholars and activists regarding how global capitalism (powered, in large part, by fossil fuels) materializes and is experienced in internal spaces of dispossession within the settler state. Championed by the NoDAPL movement of 2016–17 and the long-standing anti-extractivism movements in the Great Plains, Southwest, and beyond, "Water is Life" emerges as an affective refrain and an existential claim provoked by and also resisted through infrastructure. And though Oceti Sakowin no longer breathes in that *particular* politico-ecological place (of unceded Sioux territory, along the Missouri River), it indeed still occupies a significant affective space that persists: a *locality*. It was not only an institution but an idea, as well as a place that was made through skilled practice, design, and a critical stance against the dispossession of Indigenous lands and waters.

On the ground, within the camp, a city emerged: but not the city of the nation-state. Rather, a city designed to *challenge* claims to land, life, and water made by the settler state. Standing Rock was powerful because the stakes of sovereignty, treaty rights, and decolonial action were understood; when it ended, none of that ceased to be. Networked and mobile, these commitments traveled and continued on, with water protectors and through social media, and in other sites of resistance to energy infrastructure (the Enbridge/Line 3 in Minnesota, the Atlantic Coast Pipeline in Virginia and North Carolina, and the Bayou Bridge

Pipeline in Louisiana, to name only a few). The city that was Oceti Sakowin is not remembered as a failure by people on the ground or by scholars.[40] Rather, it was part of a longer, and still ongoing process of decolonial analysis and lived experience—in a word, decolonial praxis. In everyday practices like trainings, free food and medicine, building Indigenous-designed structures, and teach-ins on treaty history, decolonial praxis was embedded into the making of the city. And decolonial praxis was also at the front line, where unarmed protectors faced police who deployed rubber bullets and water cannons in subzero temperatures. All the while, the NoDAPL movement narrated itself, told its own story and self-archived images and text that exposed capitalist dispossession and treaty violations. The archive persists online (https://www.nodaplarchive.com) even as the protectors have dispersed elsewhere, applying their experience in new locales. A young protector that I knew in Camp Southwest, citizen of the Eastern Band of Cherokee, near my home in North Carolina, described NoDAPL as, "something that lives on, isn't over, and is inside of us wherever we go."[41]

ACKNOWLEDGMENTS

I would like to thank editors Kent Blansett, Cathleen Cahill, and Andrew Needham for their careful comments on earlier drafts of this essay. Insights from Maurice Crandall, Mishuana Goeman, Sasha Suarez, Jennifer Nez Denetdale, and David Hugill were also particularly helpful for my revisions. Thanks goes as well to my 2016–17 research assistant on this project, Ricki Draper. Funding for this research was provided by a University Research Council grant and a Claassen Research Award from Appalachian State University.

NOTES

1. I only identify individuals by their actual names when, as in the case with Allard, they have been highly visible and on public record for their positions and statements. More than forty one-on-one, private ethnographic interviews inform this chapter, and all of those names are replaced with aliases both in the text and footnotes unless the person has expressly requested their real name be used.

2. Nick Estes, *Our History Is the Future: Standing Rock versus the Dakota Access Pipeline, and the Long Tradition of Indigenous Resistance* (London: Verso, 2019).

3. Joanne Barker, paper delivered at Indigenous Feminisms panel, Department of Gender, Women, and Sexuality Studies, University of North Carolina at Greensboro, 2018.

4. I am deeply informed by the work by Nick Estes, Kyle Powys Whyte, and Temryss MacLean Lane. Their projects underscore the politics of Indigenous sovereignty, justice, gender, and political difference at stake at Standing Rock.

5. Philip J. Deloria, *Indians in Unexpected Places* (Lawrence: University Press of Kansas, 2004).

6. "Joint Statement from the Department of Justice, the Department of the Army, and the Department of the Interior Regarding Standing Rock Sioux Tribe v. U.S. Army Corps of Engineers," U.S. Department of Justice, September 9, 2016, https://www.justice .gov/opa/pr/joint-statement-department-justice-department-army-and-department -interior-regarding-standing.

7. Melanie K. Yazzie, "Decolonizing Development in Diné Bikeyah: Resource Extraction, Anti-capitalism, and Relational Futures," *Environment and Society: Advances in Research* 9, no. 1 (2018): 25–39; and Kyle Powys Whyte, "The Dakota Access Pipeline, Environmental Injustice, and U.S. Colonialism," *RedInk* 19, no.1 (2017): 154–69, 168. See also Teresa Montoya, "Violence on the Ground, Violence Below the Ground," *Fieldsights*, Hot Spots, Society for Cultural Anthropology, December 22, 2016, https://culanth.org /fieldsights/violence-on-the-ground-violence-below-the-ground.

8. Wachsmuth poses a question for which Standing Rock/NoDAPL offers a compelling empirical example: "how to reconcile the explosion of the city form with the tenacity of the city concept?" The "explosion of form" that I witnessed on the ground, within the camps, stretches the imagination for what a transnational and diverse, yet Indigenous-led, urbanism might yet be; see David Wachsmuth, "City as Ideology: Reconciling the Explosion of the City Form with the Tenacity of the City Concept," *Environment and Planning D: Society and Space* 31, no. 1 (2014): 75–90, 75 and 76.

9. Jane Bennett, *Vibrant Matter: A Political Ecology of Things* (Durham, N.C.: Duke University Press, 2009); and Arturo Escobar, *Designs for the Pluriverse* (Durham, N.C.: Duke University Press, 2018).

10. Andrew Curley, "*T'áá hwó ají t'éego* and the Moral Economy of Navajo Coal Workers," *Annals of the American Association of Geographers* 109, no.1 (2019): 71–86. See also Dana E. Powell and Dailan Jake Long, "Landscapes of Power: Renewable Energy Activism in Diné Bikéyah," in *Indians and Energy: Exploitation and Opportunity in the American Southwest*, ed. Sherry L. Smith and Brian Frehner (Santa Fe: School of Advanced Research Press, 2010), 231–62.

11. Jean Dennison, *Colonial Entanglement: Constituting a Twenty-First-Century Osage Nation* (Chapel Hill: University of North Carolina Press, 2012), 7.

12. Hugh Raffles, "'Local Theory': Nature and the Making of an Amazonian Place," *Cultural Anthropology* 14, no.3 (1999): 323–60.

13. National Public Radio, October 2016.

14. Estes's book offers a detailed history of the Pick-Sloan Act and a firsthand account and critical analysis of the Indigenous-led movement at Standing Rock. It is essential reading for this specific topic and any project related to contemporary Indigenous treaty and territorial rights; Estes, *Our History is the Future*.

15. Estes, *Our History is the Future*; and Dina Gilio-Whitaker, *As Long as Grass Grows: The Indigenous Fight for Environmental Justice, from Colonization to Standing Rock* (Boston: Beacon Press, 2019).

16. Kent Blansett, *A Journey to Freedom: Richard Oakes, Alcatraz, and the Red Power Movement* (New Haven, Conn.: Yale University Press, 2018); Paul Chaat Smith and Robert Allen Warrior, *Like a Hurricane: The Indian Movement from Alcatraz to Wounded Knee* (New York: New Press, 1996); and Paul Chaat Smith, *Everything You Know About Indians Is Wrong* (Minneapolis: University of Minnesota Press, 2009).

17. Tweetie, interview with the author, Oceti Sakowin, October 13, 2016.

18. A national NoDAPL organizer, telephone interview with the author, Minneapolis, Minn., February 20, 2017.

19. Escobar, *Designs for the Pluriverse*.

20. Arturo Escobar, "Habitability and Design: Radical Interdependence and the Re-Earthing of Cities," *Geoforum* 101 (May 2019): 132.

21. Kent Blansett, "How Alcatraz Became a Powerful Monument for Indigenous Peoples," *Washington Post*, November 20, 2019; and Renya K. Ramirez, *Native Hubs: Culture, Community, and Belonging in Silicon Valley and Beyond* (Durham, N.C.: Duke University Press, 2007).

22. Anonymous water protector, phone interview with Ricki Draper (research assistant to the author), May 7, 2017.

23. Interview with Alayna Eagle Shield, Oceti Sakowin, October 18, 2016.

24. Infrastructures have what anthropologist Brian Larkin calls a "peculiar ontology: they are material things, but they are also the relation between things," a duality that renders them "conceptually unruly"; see Brian Larkin, "The Politics and Poetics of Infrastructure," *Annual Review of Anthropology*, no. 42 (2013): 327–43, 329.

25. Mark Rifkin, "Among Ghost Dances: Sarah Winnemucca and the Production of Tribal Identity," *Studies in American Indian Literatures* 31, nos. 1–2 (2019): 170–207.

26. Thom Hartmann, "Will the Lakota Tribe's Black Snake Prophecy Come True?" Thom Hartmann Program, August 19, 2016, https://trofire.com/2016/08/19/will-lakota-tribes-black-snake-prophecy-come-true-thom-hartmann-program.

27. Angela Parker, "Sovereignty by the Barrel" (paper delivered at the Native American Indigenous Studies Association [NAISA] Annual Meeting, Austin, Tex., May 30, 2014).

28. See Dana E. Powell, "'The Rainbow Is Our Sovereignty:' Rethinking the Politics of Energy on the Navajo Nation," *Journal of Political Ecology*, no. 22 (2015): 53–78; Dana E. Powell, "Toward Transition? Challenging Extractivism and the Politics of the Inevitable in the Navajo Nation," in *ExtrACTION: Impacts, Responses, and Alternative Futures*, ed. K. Jalbert, A. Willow, D. Casagrande, S. Paladino, and J. Simonelli (Walnut Creek, Calif.: Left Coast Press/Routledge, 2017); and Dana E. Powell, *Landscapes of Power: Politics of Energy in the Navajo Nation* (Durham, N.C.: Duke University Press, 2018).

29. Nick Estes, "Fighting for Our Lives: #NoDAPL in Historical Context," *The Red Nation*, September 18, 2016. https://therednation.org/2016/09/18/fighting-for-our-lives-nodapl-in-context/; and Estes, *Our History Is the Future*.

30. The U.S. Army Corps of Engineers assumed jurisdiction over dams and waterways in the United States as part of the Pick-Sloan or Flood Control Act of 1944. This Act made the U.S. Army Corps of Engineers the federal agency with oversight of development

projects impacting rivers and waterways such as DAPL; see "Dakota Access Pipeline Final EA and FONSI Released for ND Section 408 Crossings," U.S. Army Corps of Engineers (news release no. 20160728–001), July 28, 2016, http://www.nwo.usace.army .mil/Media/News-Releases/Article/878649/dakota-access-pipeline-final-ea-and-fonsi -released-for-nd-section-408-crossings/.

31. Steve Almasy, "Dakota Access Pipeline Vandalized Before It Comes Online." *CNN* March 21, 2017, https://www.cnn.com/2017/03/21/us/dakota-access-pipeline -vandalism/.

32. Since 1995, more than two thousand significant accidents have occurred involving oil and petroleum pipelines, and since 2009, accidents have increased by 60 percent according to data from the U.S. Pipeline and Hazardous Materials Safety Administration; Associated Press, "Federal Data: As Oil Production Soars, So Do Pipeline Leaks," *Chicago Tribune,* May 22, 2015, http://www.chicagotribune.com/news/nationworld/ct -oil-pipeline-leaks-20150522-story.html.

33. The Cheyenne River Sioux Tribe's legal briefing emphasized that perhaps DAPL could exist elsewhere but that the currently located pipeline threatens a body of water (Lake Oahe) held in trust for the tribe by the federal government; see Robinson Meyer, "The Standing Rock Sioux Claim 'Victory and Vindication' in Court," *The Atlantic,* June 14, 2017, https://www.theatlantic.com/science/archive/2017/06/dakota-access -standing-rock-sioux-victory-court/530427/.

34. Phone interview with Ben MacFayden, Poland, February 20, 2017.

35. For details on the Mirror Shield Project, see Cannupahanska at www .cannupahanska.com/mniwiconi.

36. Thank you to my colleague Marc Kissel for helping me find my way back to the Mirror Shields' creator.

37. Jerome Begay, interview with the author, Santa Fe, N.Mex., March 28, 2017.

38. Michael Taussig, *I Swear I Saw This: Drawings in Fieldwork Notebooks, Namely My Own* (Chicago: University of Chicago Press, 2011). See also Brian Massumi, "The Autonomy of Affect," *Cultural Critique* 31 (Fall 1995): 83–109.

39. For more on this idea, see Dominic Boyer, *Energopolitics: wind and Power in the Anthropocene* (Durham, N.C.: Duke University Press, 2019); Cymene Howe, *Ecologics: Wind and Power in the Anthropocene* (Durham, N.C.: Duke University Press, 2019); Timothy Mitchell, *Carbon Democracy* (London: Verso, 2011); and Sherry L. Smith and Brian Frehner, eds., *Indians and Energy: Exploitation and Opportunity in the American Southwest* (Santa Fe: SAR Press, 2013).

40. Estes, "Habitability and Design"; Temryss MacLean Lane, "The Frontline of Refusal: Indigenous Women Warriors of Standing Rock," *International Journal of Qualitative Studies in Education* 31, no.3 (2018): 197–214; and Whyte, "The Dakota Access Pipeline, Environmental Injustice, and U.S. Colonialism."

41. Elvia Walkingstick, public comments at panel "Water Is Life/Mni Wiconi: Indigenous Responses to Standing Rock," Appalachian State University, Boone, N.C., 2017.

12

"BUILDING THE PERFECT HUMAN TO INVADE"

Dikos Ntsaaígíí-19 (COVID-19) from Border Towns
to the Navajo Nation

On March 17, 2020, international attention turned to the Navajo Nation in the American Southwest as Navajo reporter Arlyssa Becenti relayed that a forty-six-year-old Navajo man had tested positive for COVID-19.[1] The Diné had a travel history and the man was from Chilchinbeto, Arizona, a community that would be spotlighted in national and international news as a virus hot spot when it was revealed that Navajos had attended a Nazarene Zone Rally at the Chilchinbeto Church and then returned to their own nearby communities of Cameron, Coppermine, Kaibeto, LeChee, Tonalea–Red Lake, and Navajo Mountain. Two Diné died, one confirmed to have attended the rally, and both had respiratory symptoms associated with the novel coronavirus.[2]

The novel coronavirus disease (or COVID-19), caused by severe acute respiratory syndrome coronavirus 2 (SARS-CoV-2), was first identified in December 2019 in Wuhan, China. By January 12, 2020, the World Health Organization declared the virus a pandemic.[3] On July 20, 2020, the Centers for Disease Control and Prevention (CDC) reported 3,106,932 cases of COVID worldwide, with 59,260 new cases for that day, 132,855 total deaths, and 799 deaths for that day. On April 10, 2020, COVID-19 cases on tribal lands were more than four times the rate than that in the rest of the United States. By May 18, 2020, the Navajo Nation's rates surpassed those of all states, including New York's, which had been the pandemic's U.S. epicenter. By June 1, 2020, the Navajo Nation reported 5,250 positive cases, 1,745 recoveries, and 241 deaths. On February 12, 2021, the Navajo Department of Health reported that 29,098 Navajos had been tested and 1,097 had died from COVID.[4] It is difficult to determine how many Navajos in border towns and urban cities have died from COVID, so the numbers of infections and deaths are likely much higher. After six months, with a lull in infection and death rates, we experienced another bout of the virus's spread. Navajo Nation president Jonathan Nez repeatedly ordered weekend lockdowns and weekday curfews while the border town of Gallup, New Mexico, set up roadblocks to deter traffic from the Navajo Nation because visiting Navajos increased the town's population of 22,000 by tens of thousands every weekend. As expressed by Navajos like Johnnie Henry, the roadblocks meant to keep them out are part of Gallup's long history of racism: "They targeted people around here. They're going to be coming to Gallup to shop, so they put a stop to that." Henry revealed that two of his relatives were infected at their place of employment in a hospital. Being shut out of Gallup carried stigma for Navajos who claimed that they were being targeted as virus carriers.[5]

For June 26, 2020, in Rapid City, South Dakota, health data revealed that 53 percent of people with confirmed COVID cases in Pennington County were tribal members, and that statewide Native Americans accounted for 14 percent of all cases though they constituted only 9 percent of the population.[6] Native peoples in South Dakota established roadblocks to regulate travel through their territory while Governor Kristi Noem threatened them even as she refused to address the growing numbers of infections in her state.[7]

By July 2020, the fifth month since the coronavirus's onset in Navajo communities, a second wave of the disease surged as the Trump administration absolved itself of any responsibility for rising infection and death rates. The virus, without a cure (though, as of this writing, there are vaccines), has ultimately become a source of profound political division that re-entrenches economic disparities across racial divides, especially manifest in communities of color subject to the highest infection and death rates. Across the United States, tribal nations followed the CDC's guidelines and enacted some of the strictest safety measures and protocols even as they battled with the federal government for funding to address the virus's spread. In New Mexico and Arizona, counties with significant Native and specifically Navajo populations, leaders closed roads to their communities and enacted weekday curfews and weekend lockdowns in efforts to slow the virus's spread.[8] The public offered money, food, water, and personal protective equipment supplies as part of the relief effort. Significantly, Native nations' public health efforts, based upon sovereignty and science, were stymied by a host of uneven measures by towns, cities, and state governments, especially in Republican-dominated areas. There, conservative Christian whites called for a faith-based approach and protective measures, especially the wearing of masks in public, were met with physical and verbal assault.[9]

The U.S. pandemic was cause, ironically enough, for much of the rest of the world to ban Americans from their borders. By August 14, 2020, the United States had the highest confirmed number of COVID-19 cases in the world, according to Johns Hopkins University's COVID-19 dashboard.[10]

On January 8, 2021, Navajo Nation health officials reported 237 new coronavirus cases and 22 deaths for the day. Health officials said more than 213,000 people had been tested for COVID-19 on the reservation and more than 12,600 had recovered. The latest figures increased the Nation's totals since the pandemic began to 24,776 cases and 866 fatalities. Reports of some of the new deaths were delayed. Deaths not related to COVID, long-term illnesses, or old age exacerbate our sorrow.

The virus has left very few of my relatives untouched by the scourge. One of my uncles did not survive and his children reported that his last words to them were that he didn't have the strength to fight it. Their father was buried in the veteran's cemetery with only pallbearers on hand. In the Shiprock area, three siblings buried their mother, father, and brother, and watched the burial service remotely because they also had contracted the disease. I answered a call from a relative in tears because several members of her family had contracted the disease and I listened quietly as she sobbed. I cried along with the Navajo Nation as we learned of the death of a popular local band's lead singer. In my extended kin relations, over the span of five months, three siblings have died, one from COVID, one soon after recovery from COVID, and one from other illness. We wonder, who will be left to care for home places established by parents who came of age during the livestock reduction of the late 1930s and 40s?

COVID-19 FROM BORDER TOWNS TO THE NAVAJO NATION   293

This essay offers an analysis and personal account of the still-unfolding effects of the pandemic on the Navajo Nation, the second largest Indigenous nation in the United States. It places the virus' spread within the contexts of settler violence to demonstrate that the failure of federal Indian policies and laws sustains continual American colonial violence against the Diné. The United States remains a settler society whose ostensibly multicultural and liberal- democratic forms of governance reinscribe Indigenous elimination again and again. This settler "project" is always cloaked in the state-sanctioned rhetoric and practice of the so-called gifting of sovereignty and democracy to Indigenous peoples; this "gift," however, always manifests itself in settler terms and requires Indigenous peoples to bend to settler sovereignty, its laws and unitary authority. In turn, it renders Indigenous life invisible and therefore expendable.[11] Yet such treatment spells not the end for Indigenous peoples, including the Diné, for we have mapped our way out of multiple life-threatening crises—and I invoke the generative scholarship and community organizing practices of Lakota scholar Nick Estes and Diné scholar Melanie K. Yazzie, who, collectively, declare that struggles over life and death shape the Indigenous refusal of liberal "developmental" violence. Estes calls out "terminal narratives," which amount to a settler "obsession with [the] death, disappearance, and absence of Indigenous people rather than their continued, visible presence and challenge to colonialism," while Yazzie celebrates Diné refusal to die in a tradition of refusal and resistance and that values Iiná or life.[12]

Hit hard by COVID, Navajo country caught the interest of national and international media. Journalists and photographers rushed to document and memorialize the pandemic's onset. What quickly became clear was that the lack of infrastructure on the Navajo nation is deadly. Sunny Dooley, storyteller and keeper of traditions, relates living conditions on the southern side of the homeland: "My hogan [home] has electricity but no running water. My brothers bring me water and they put it in a 75-gallon barrel. I drink that water, and I wash with it, but I also buy five gallons of water for $5, in case I need extra. I typically use a gallon a day, for everything—cooking, drinking, and washing up." Dooley also relates local health conditions or, better, local conditions of death:

We have a lot of cancers in our community, perhaps because of the uranium. And we have may other health issues . . . that make the virus so viable among us. We have a lot of diabetes, because we do not eat well, and a lot of heart disease. We have alcoholism. We have high rates of suicide.

We have every social ill you can think of, and COVID has made these vulnerabilities more apparent. I look at it as a monster that is feasting on us—because we have built the perfect human for it to invade."[13]

Dooley's stories indicate that the colonial conditions that made possible the monsters feasting on us—social, health, and economic disparities—also opened a space for the novel coronavirus to spread rapidly through Navajo communities.

Diné journalist Sunnie Clahchischiligi makes similar observations in her travels across the homeland, interviewing our relatives experiencing the traumas of the disease. As she notes, "There is no safe haven today on the Navajo Nation, where generations of families have lacked running water, food, electricity, indoor plumbing, safe housing, and access to health care—the basic necessities for fighting disease." Her interview with elder Chili Yazzie of Shiprock, New Mexico, known for his advocacy for Navajo civil and human rights, reveals how people are coping: Everyone knows someone who has struggled with COVID-19 or died from it. Each day brings a new round of worry, grief, and fear. Yazzie says, for him, it's been a time of reflection, of trying to understand what is happening. As he says, "The world is in great disorder; the equilibrium of the Earth is greatly upset. . . . Perhaps the pandemic is the great discipline whip of the Earth, from having irretrievably damaged the Earth. . . . This virus is a force to be reckoned with. . . . It is alive with death."[14]

Dooley's and Yazzie's narratives become the occasion to reflect on U.S. treatment of Indigenous peoples, namely, the systematic theft of Indigenous lands and natural resources, and the genocidal policies intended to destroy us as Indigenous peoples. It is this tortured history that created the "conditions of death" for the monster to feast upon us. A theorizing of settler colonialism and its twin monster, racial capitalism, spotlights the devastation of communities of color and Indigenous communities.

Diné health officials and leaders named COVID-19 Dikos Ntsaaígíí-19 (the Big Cough) after consultation with those who hold knowledge of the old stories and who connect the virus to our creation stories of monsters who wrought havoc and killed our people.[15] For the Navajo people, COVID-19 is one of the many monsters of the old stories who plagued the People until Changing Woman birthed her sons, the Hero Twins, who brought a new era in Navajo history of harmony and balance. It is these old stories that the Diné look to for answers. The stories tell us that there have always been monsters among us, but we also have a web of kinship networks of care, compassion, and generosity that refuse conditions of death.

Dikos Ntsaaígíí-19 raises the specter of Navajo experience with epidemics and pandemics such as influenza and tuberculosis, inviting a historical view on Indigenous peoples' experiences with calamitous diseases. Upon arrival to the "New World," European carriers of smallpox brought death to about 90 percent of the Indigenous population. Indigenous peoples have never recovered from early "contact." According to Nick Estes, Indigenous deaths from Old World diseases wiped out anywhere from ten to one hundred million Indigenous people in the Americas. He notes, "There is a common myth in U.S. history that most Indigenous people did not die because of active killing, warfare, and genocide, but rather as a result of outbreaks: smallpox, measles, and cholera. However, these epidemics occurred and intensified in times of war, which means mass starvation, depravation of resources, such as access to sanitary conditions— water, food, shelter—or the dependence on rations as the means of survival."[16] As is apparent, Indigenous peoples are familiar with bioterrorism. As so many of our people relate, the conditions that make the virus "alive with death" are the structures of settler colonial practice, what Achille Mbembe terms, a sovereign's right to dictate who may live and who may die—in a word, to eliminate Indigenous peoples.[17] As Patrick Wolfe argues, the logic of elimination not only refers to the summary liquidation of Indigenous peoples but also practices that "remove Indigenous people from their lands through miscegenation, the breaking-down of Native title into alienable individual freeholds, native citizenship child abduction, religious conversion, [and] resocialization." Elimination also includes the failure to provide the means necessary to prosper, including access to decent living conditions like health care.[18]

Navajo Studies scholars note the federal government's public health efforts served as convenient excuse to simultaneously introduce Western medicine and health practices and eradicate Navajo medicine and health practices. Historically, the Diné were decimated by foreign diseases at the Bosque Redondo concentration camp from 1863 to 1868. Then from the 1880s to the early twentieth century, Navajo children died from the diseases that ran rampant at boarding schools.[19] At the turn of the twentieth century, the Navajo battled the influenza pandemic of 1918, which decimated 2,000 Diné—literally, one-tenth of the Diné population. The influenza pandemic killed 50 million people worldwide, with Indigenous peoples suffering mortality rates four times that of others. Smallpox spread among schoolchildren, and trachoma infections among adults and children raged for at least two decades, patently revealing the inadequacies of federally run health care systems.[20] The government's response to the epidemics and pandemics that afflicted Navajos did not improve health care and, as Robert Trennert notes, the "devastation of the flu epidemic failed to produce any significant improvement in government health care for the Navajo."[21] The Diné suffered disproportionately because of federal neglect. In 1993, the hantavirus infected two dozen Navajos, with half of them dying. Navajos reported racism directed at them in border towns where non-Indians claimed that they were carriers of the disease.[22] In 2009, during the swine flu epidemic, Navajos died at a rate of four to five times higher than other Americans.[23] The history of U.S. health care, then, reveals the long roots of failed federal government response to the COVID pandemic among Navajo communities. This failure is but one aspect of a larger legacy of Indigenous peoples in the Americas as the survivors of a 500-year-old war that has not ended. Now, war is waged through the subtler means of laws, policies, and governance.

Indigenous leaders, community organizers, and scholars were quick to recognize that the virus's rapid spread to communities with marked socioeconomic disparities spelled disaster. Against those who naively asserted that the virus was indiscriminate in its victims, they argued for the virus as no equal-opportunity killer: We have been exposed to "deceptive and deadly information. The perception that this is a jet-setters' disease, or a spring breakers' disease, or a 'Chinese virus,'" the last as President Trump has called it, must be refuted. "The idea that this virus is an equal-opportunity killer must itself be killed."[24] The national media's attention on the virus is tainted by elitism, and we participate in it by similarly rebuking of people of color who cannot seem to stay home, who must for survival go to their jobs, who live in crowded housing conditions, and who now expose their vulnerable bodies to even more scrutiny and control because of socioeconomic disparities. In the nation's cities, many predominantly Anglo white-collar professionals ensconced themselves in remote work and "pods." Within cities already deeply unequal, COVID-19 raged particularly among racialized service workers who did not have the luxury of space and who were frequently blamed for failing to protect themselves and public health more generally. Navajos were subjected to similar criticism, including observations that several generations live in one house or a one-room hogan. So-called commonsense notions that "tradition" has played a role in the spread of the virus in Navajo lands are confirmed by interviews with Navajos who allow images of their homes to accompany the stories written and circulated about them. Ironically, homes are often dilapidated and several generations live under one roof not because it is "traditional" but because it is almost impossible for Navajos to build homes on Navajo land—a proposition made difficult by myriad challenges, including antiquated Navajo Nation land use laws and policies, high unemployment, and poverty.

Exacerbating the coronavirus's spread through Navajo communities, the Navajo Nation's poor infrastructure is also to blame. Poor infrastructure is reflected in high unemployment, few businesses, and a mere thirteen full-service grocery stores across more than 27,000 square miles, a land base often compared to the state of West Virginia. Because of these conditions, the U.S. Department of Agriculture calls the Navajo Nation a "food desert."[25] A poor infrastructure makes it necessary for constant travel to border towns and cities for even the most basic of necessities. These round-trip drives take anywhere from an hour to four to six or eight hours. Because homes are so remote and often do not have electricity, fresh foods don't have longevity. A reliance on canned and processed foods contributes to health disparities. Even though the Navajo Nation holds robust water rights under the *Winters* doctrine, at least 40% of households do not have running water.[26] Rather, our natural resources of water, coal, gas, and oil, and the vast open expanses of unpolluted air, have been hijacked to feed the monster of capitalism.

Like elsewhere, in mid-March 2020, we began to hear about the virus and warnings to sanitize your surroundings and wash your hands. I took my last plane trip to Winnipeg, Manitoba, to visit with Indigenous faculty and students, a trip I considered a brief break from 24-hour care for my mom who was courageously battling cancer in my home. Upon my return, mom was sent to the hospital emergency room again. I could not be with her because I had been out of the country within the last fourteen days. In what would be the last days of her life, she listened to my sisters and I talk about the public health concerns, the hoarding of toilet paper, sanitizing groceries, and storing extra food. Mom suggested we buy canned goods and powdered milk, marking her familiarity with lean years during the Depression, when Navajos transitioned from self-subsistence to dependence on outside sources. That time is also known as the livestock reduction era when U.S. Indian Commissioner John Collier ordered the removal of 50 percent of Navajo-owned horses, sheep, and goats as a response to decades of federal concern over overgrazing on Navajo land.[27] The post–livestock reduction era led to massive social engineering of the Navajo people across all aspects of Navajo life.

My parents were the last generation of Diné integrated into a livestock economy where sheep, goats, and horses were life—Iiná. To the Diné, "Sheep is Life" is a phrase that invokes a value of life based upon a land tenure system where k'é, "a complex and sophisticated code of ethics," stipulates how one cares for one's relatives, one's livestock, the land, and how to relate to the universe. This land ethic predates American colonization when Navajos had expanded their territories and owned hundreds of thousands of sheep, goats, and horses.[28] Life based upon the movement of sheep and goats meant seasonal movement to grazing lands and watering places, what Nick Estes and Melanie K. Yazzie expansively term a "relationality (with other humans, with sheep, and with the land itself) that dictates how different family and political units are meant to share space and approach mutual land use practices."[29]

This history of U.S. federal Indian policies and laws sets the stage for the pandemic's effects on Native peoples, including the Diné, so that they would be as Sunny Dooley terms it, "the perfect human(s) to invade." The livestock reduction stands out in Navajo collective memory because it attacked the measure of self-sufficiency that many of our people had regained after returning to their homeland in 1868. Like other Indigenous peoples, the Diné experienced the American invasion of their homeland. They were defeated and forcibly relocated to a concentration camp (Fort Sumner, New Mexico) hundreds of miles from their homeland. In 1868, a treaty signed with the United States allowed their return to a portion of their traditional territories, a land base that would always be too small for the ever-increasing population. From the end of the nineteenth and to the early twentieth centuries, traders established posts on and around the reservation while Hispanic and white settlers seized the best lands for cattle and farmland near waterways. Spaces beyond the boundaries of designated Navajo reservation lands became border towns, where settlers enriched themselves through the Indian trade.[30] In the 1970s, as part of the politics of self-determination, Navajo leaders responded to the exploitative practices of traders who opened posts on Navajo land by passing laws and policies that forced traders into bordertowns where they continued to traffic in predatory businesses with Navajos as their major consumers. At present, border towns remain violent spaces for Indigenous people and, regrettably, facilitators for the spread of COVID-19 to the Navajo Nation.

John Collier was Commissioner of Indian Affairs from 1933 to 1945. His determination to "rehabilitate" Navajo land was spurred by decades of federal reports warning that drought conditions and Navajo livestock had denuded the land. Federal concern was also driven by fear that silt from Navajo land might clog the reservoir near Hoover Dam. Diné Studies scholars note, "Many non-Navajos pictured Navajos as a people unable to conserve land, and who would thus allow both their own and their livestock population to increase to such a point that they would have to encroach on their neighbors' land. Navajos were blamed, similarly, for mismanaging their land to such an extent that it was washing away into the Colorado River and silting up the newly dammed lakes."[31]

The devastation of a subsistence system led to the grotesque social engineering of Navajo life, from so-called land reforms to a transformation of governance, health, education, and domestic/intimate spaces, with the intentions of recreating Navajos as ideal citizens of not only their own nation but also of the United States. As Melanie K. Yazzie points out, such federal policies intended to remake Diné into nuclear family units, the building block of individualist capitalism. Development, then, meant an integration into the material and psychic structures of American life as the natural progress of social development. Yet, as Yazzie notes, "development is not a natural process, but rather a form of politics that stakes a claim within a field of power conditioned by the inequalities and violence of prevailing structures of global capitalism, U.S. imperialism, and colonialism."[32] As the same time that federal officials and white reformers sought to remake Navajos in their image, Navajo resources were targeted for extraction to create the urban Southwest of today.[33] Diné scholars John Redhouse, Andrew Curley, and Melanie K. Yazzie each offer incisive analyses of how and why the Navajo Nation is rendered a "third world" country where Diné Bikéyah is mined for natural resources to benefit settler towns and cities, in fact, creating settler towns and cities.[34] Yazzie draws upon the work of Redhouse to present a vast network of connections between multinational corporations (with their relentless pursuit of natural resources), tribal governments, U.S. politicians, and other vested interests that systematically robs the Navajo and Hopi people of their natural resources—what Redhouse calls the "grand plan" for the colonization of the Navajos. It is this network of relationships to settler colonial institutions that leads to the conditions of life or, rather, conditions of death, for the Diné in the present day.[35] The cities of Los Angeles, Albuquerque, Phoenix, Las Vegas, and Tucson exist because of the theft of Navajo and Hopi land and resources, including coal, uranium, and water.[36] The devastation of

Navajo subsistence economies was engineered by federal officials in collusion with corporations that collectively raped the land for its resources, created the urban Southwest we see today, and paved the way, years later, for COVID's feeding insidiously on our bodies.

It is this death plan, to systematically rob Navajos and Hopis of their coal and pristine waters, that led to the second largest relocation of Navajos when Congress passed the Navajo-Hopi Land Settlement Act in 1974 and those who found themselves on lands awarded to the Hopi Tribe were forced to leave their residences in Big Mountain, in northern Arizona. Over 12,000 Navajos relocated with many moving to sundry border towns and cities.[37] John Collier's post–livestock program to transform Navajo life is his bitter legacy to the Navajo people and it includes a forced (yet decried) dependency on the U.S. government, integration into the wage economy, the migration of our people across imaginary boundaries (thought to separate the Navajo Nation from U.S. border towns and cities) in search of waged employment, and the constant search for basic supplies such as food, clothing, gasoline, shelter materials, and grain for livestock.[38] Collier's legacy, ethnic cleansing in all but name, also includes the appalling number of our people living on the streets of these towns and cities as well.

Border town histories, whether they involve the boundaries of the Navajo Nation or other Indigenous nations in other states, have commonalities in terms of how they grant non-Indigenous peoples predatory access to Indigenous peoples and their resources, including their commodified labor. In turn, our people have become dependent on these towns and cities for basic necessities.

The seemingly recent phenomenon of border towns has roots in the federal government's policy to settle the West and to develop the land according to settler notions of land use and its development. As Nancy J. Owens maintains, "Whites benefited from many federal programs, including federal troops to wrest land from Indians, homestead laws, allotment of Indian lands which reduced the Indian land base and made more land available to whites, federal subsidy of the railroads encouraging settlement."[39]

One example of how a border town feeds on Diné (and thus constitutes part of the multiple structures, from the economic to the everyday experiences of racism and discrimination, that define Diné life in these spaces) is the history of Page, Arizona, on the northwestern boundary of the Navajo Nation. As Owens argues, urban development on the fringes of these reservations did not result in a significant improvement in the Indians' standard of living. Rather, the Navajo

Tribe possessed four resources: land; water rights to the Colorado River; coal, jointly owned by with the Hopi Tribe; and clean air, stolen through legal means to create the urban Southwest. Page began in 1957 as a boomtown to accommodate construction workers brought in to man the coal mines on Navajo land at Black Mesa and Kayenta. Planners refused to consider establishing work sites and living spaces for the non-Indigenous workers in the closest Navajo community of Kayenta, because it was inconceivable for whites to live on Indian land. By 1958, wage labor provided 68 percent of all income for Navajos, with income from employment in nearby towns and from various federal programs. By 1960, Page boasted a population of 6,000. Navajos entered the work force in the lower echelons of the wage economy, even though it was Navajo resources that fueled the border town economy in the first place. Owens's study is but one of how Indians lost control of their resources and shifted from reliance on their own resources for livelihoods to reliance on low wage labor, marginalizing Navajos within their very homelands.[40] In border towns, the pandemic became an occasion—and excuse—to reinforce Indian marginalization and whip up anti-Indian sentiment, as vividly demonstrated by Page's mayor delivering a slur against Navajo Nation President Jonathan Nez.[41]

These historical conditions shaped Diné life and facilitated the appearance of the monster Dikos Ntsaaígíí-19. COVID-19's rapid spread to Navajo communities is directly connected to migration from places on the Navajo Nation to border towns and more distant cities. These migrations become the norm for Navajos because of the need to survive. The virus migrates across imaginary boundaries, carrying infected bodies back and forth in much the same way that other diseases like alcoholism work. Refusing imaginary boundaries that separates the "rez" from the "urban," the virus's spread between Navajo land and border towns and cities raises the specter of settler colonial violence and how it continually recreates itself to eliminate Indigenous peoples. Border-towns demonstrate how we as Diné become not only lawless but also rendered invisible and, in the present day, not worthy of the care needed to survive.[42] It is necessary for scholars to move past dated paradigms that impose imaginary binaries such as rez/urban; studies of border towns and urban spaces reaffirm, rather, that Indigenous peoples, and Diné in particular, are always in the spaces of their homelands, regardless of settler efforts to eliminate them and erase their presence. This is reinforced by the fact that approximately 70 percent of Native people live off designated Native nations and so the pandemic is not confined to proscribed geographical areas.[43]

Meanwhile, the *Gallup Independent,* a border town newspaper that offers some Navajo and Native news, reported possible exposures to the virus at the "drunk tank" (a.k.a. the Na'nizhozhi Center, or "the Detox"), where its occupants were admitted to local hospitals.[44] By mid-April, eighty-nine "clients" of the detox center had come into contact with a person who tested positive. Health care officials expressed concern that this person may have infected eighty-nine other people whose locations were then unknown. Just as that person traveled to the Navajo Nation from an urban place and infected others who would then take the virus home to their families and relatives, these exposures facilitated the spread to communities within the Navajo Nation. The migratory movement back and forth across imaginary boundaries marking off Navajo land and border towns and other urban spaces enabled the virus spread. On social media and through stories, the Diné felt as beleaguered as their kin newly returned from the city and sometimes carrying contagion.

Border town leadership and residents were unwilling to humanely deal with the very conditions they created—including unsheltered Indigenous people on the streets and rampant alcoholism—and are directly responsible for the invasion of the monster. The Gallup Indian Medical Center (GIMC) is one of several Indian Health hospitals providing limited medical treatment because they are always understaffed and underresourced. In Gallup, GIMC and Rehoboth McKinley Christian Hospital provided care for coronavirus patients. But they became so strained that medical staff at Rehoboth protested working conditions.[45] According to Diné, the hospital and the Detox personnel were unprepared and allowed infected patients to leave their premises where they then moved through the town's business district and impoverished areas and then communities on the Navajo Nation. The Rehoboth hospital accepted 22 patients infected with the virus from the Detox Center in May 2020.[46] For decades, Diné community organizers like Larry Casuse, John Redhouse, and Earl Tulley have challenged the chronic anti-Indianism that characterizes border towns like Gallup. These towns depend on Navajo resources to enrich themselves—Gallup has a number of millionaires whose wealth was made off of Navajo consumers, including pawn and payday loan businesses, while the townspeople do their best to erase Diné out of spaces made from our original homelands.

Almost a year later, we see the devastation COVID has caused. As Navajo Nation council delegate Amber Crotty relates, "Everyone has been impacted. Some families have been decimated. How can we go back to normal when we've lost so many after so many layers of trauma? It's unbearable." Former Navajo Nation president and Arizona state representative Albert Hale died from the virus on February 2, 2021, bringing the Navajo Nation's death toll to 1,038, the equivalent of losing one in every 160 people in our nation.[47]

At this moment, with an already failing economy on the brink of collapse and a health care system strained to the limit, Black Lives Matter confronts racialized police violence. The demands of young black people to end racism, police violence, and poverty and to address other inequalities and injustices resonate with Indigenous communities who stand with their black brothers and sisters in solidarity while calling for Indigenous liberation. Ironically, the federal government and state leaders rushed to confront protests and call up state and city law enforcement and the National Guard (spending millions in the process), while neglecting the coronavirus. As Keeanga-Yamahtta Taylor observes:

> State leaders have been much more adept in calling up the National Guard and coordinating police actions to confront marchers than they were in any efforts to curtail the virus. . . . We have to make space for new politics, new ideas, new formations, and new people. . . . If we are serious about ending racism and fundamentally changing the United States, we must begin with a real and serious assessment of the problems. We diminish the task by continuing to call upon the agents and actors who fueled the crisis when they had opportunities to help solve it. . . . We have the resources to remake the United States, but it will have to come at the expense of the plutocrats and plunderers, and therein lies the three-hundred-year-old conundrum: America's professed values of life, liberty, and the pursuit of happiness, continually undone by the realty of debt, despair and the human degradation of racism and inequality.[48]

As the pandemic rips through our communities, Diné poet Jake Skeets asks, about the nostalgia some express about life before the pandemic, "what we are grieving for?" More to the point, why do we long for a time before COVID-19, when, in truth, our people were already suffering greatly. He further asks, "Every month, there are numerous headlines announcing the deaths that occur in border towns around the reservation. So if we yearn for the time before this virus, are we also yearning for those ills as well? Or do we yearn for the post-pandemic, which will include either further disaster capitalism or the so-called end times, both of which would be catastrophic for families in the United States?"[49] Skeets goes on to affirm the integrity of our stories to address our grief, to mend ourselves, and in that process, revitalize our spirits. Our stories reflect our relationships to the land, which tell us how we are related to all living beings through k'é (kinship).

Yet Indigenous people's dreams of freedom do not lie in the possibilities that the settler state will ever transform itself; rather, its colonial-capitalist structures will always be violent and anti-Indigenous because that is what is required for its survival. Rather than accommodating the settler state, oppressed communities build relationships to extend kinship beyond the human to include all living things.[50] The Diné who have shared their stories with media express this very idea. We have always turned to the strength of our ancestors, and we do so now.

Recently I spent the better part of a week filling out an application for funding on behalf of a distinguished elder who holds traditional knowledge about the cycles of life and death. We plan to facilitate our people's return to traditional forms of knowledge, to help our people remember that we have our own concepts of life, death, and the afterlife, as well as the proper preparation for burials. It is a turn away from capitalism and the carnivorous reach of border town predatory businesses. After studying this issue and doing the research, I realize that this topic is sensitive, but I must support a person who is a holder of our knowledge. After working with this traditional practitioner for nine years, having him offer prayers for my family's well-being, I affirm the wisdom of our ancestors, my parents, and my father. Our ancestors' words also resonate in those of our thinkers like Leanne B. Simpson and Melanie K. Yazzie. Here I quote Simpson: "We cannot carry out the kind of decolonization our ancestors set in motion if we don't create a generation of land-based, community-based intellectuals and cultural producers who are accountable to our nations and whose life work is concerned with the regeneration of these systems"[51] Their voices carry the wisdom of my ancestors. We come from a long tradition of resistance. It is not new knowledge to me, for my late father was a healer who prayed for our relatives every day.

The stories that my relatives share on social media, in interviews with journalists, with me and with each other reveal that the Diné rely upon networks of kinship that have deep roots in our traditional narratives. For example, consider what a single Navajo mom posts on her Facebook page:

> Women are holding space. Our Navajo, Indigenous women, doing the work and holding lifelines. Yes, this pandemic hit us hard. Small business

owners on the reservation, such as our food sales were literally our bread and butter. We are navigating our way through. And yes, we need to improve our infrastructure. We have children with lack of internet service. We live in a food desert. And it is going to take us, as a community to hold space, speak up, advocate, lend a hand and throw a lifeline. We are all in this, wear your mask, stay 6 ft or more apart and wash your hands.[52]

Sunnie R. Clahchischiligi shares Diné elder Chili Yazzie's thoughts on revitalizing ourselves: "While the staggering numbers have left many feeling hopeless, some in Shiprock have found solace by looking to history, traditions, and family stories to push back against the pandemic. They are returning to a way of life depicted in tales passed down by elders, generation after generation." Yazzie continues, "For the first time in a long time I'm a farmer again. It's always been my therapy. . . . As a community leader it's overwhelming to know that there's very little that you can do proactively to prevent or mitigate the impact of the virus. We've just been scrambling around doing what we can, trying to keep people from not going hungry and making sure they're OK." Another Diné, Zefren Anderson, who has survived COVID and begun thinking about returning to former self-sustaining practices such as farming and weaving, has also shared his story.[53] So many of my relatives around me show me again and again the power and strength of our people, of our determination to live in freedom.

The counter to devastation and death is Iiná (life) and its cultivation through relationships that extend to the natural world and all beings. Through such relationships, we will revitalize our communities.

ACKNOWLEDGMENT

As I revise a final draft of this essay, I note the shifts in how Diné are responding to the pandemic and new hopes that perhaps the worst is behind us. Like so many of our people, I received the Pfizer vaccine at the Gallup Indian Medical Center after growing weary of waiting for the New Mexico Department of Health to schedule me for the vaccine. I drove one hundred and forty miles one-way to receive the vaccine. As a Diné who lives in Albuquerque but often visits home in Tohatchi, I am used to driving long distances for necessary services. As I take stock of where we are in the spring of 2021, almost a year to the day when we first learned of the virus, we hear of the COVID-related death of Albert Hale, a former president of the Navajo Nation, and note the number of obituaries still appearing in local newspapers. Even as we mourn our losses, which are immense, we greet the sunlight of each dawn with prayer and thankfulness.

NOTES

1. Arlyssa Becenti, "First Diné Tests Positive for Coronavirus," *Navajo Times*, March 17, 2020, https://navajotimes.com/reznews/first-dine-tests-positive-for-coronavirus/.

2. Krista Allen, "Virus Strikes at Rally: Chilchinbeto Church Gathering May Be the Source of Outbreak," *Navajo Times*, March 25, 2020, https://navajotimes.com/coronavirus-updates/two-deaths-in-western-may-have-been-covid-virus-spread-at-church-rally/.

3. "Novel Coronavirus—China," World Health Organization, January 12, 2020, www.who.int/csr/don/12-january-2020-novel-coronavirus-china/en/.

4. The Navajo Department of Health updates its data daily on COVID infections, the number of tests, number of deaths, and Navajo Nation public health orders. Data dashboard available at https://www.ndoh.navajo-nsn.gov/COVID-19/Data.

5. Morgan Lee, "Gallup, New Mexico, under Extreme Lockdown Due to Massive COVID-19 Outbreak," *HuffPost*, May 8, 2020, www.huffpost.com/entry/gallup-new-mexico-covid-19-shutdown_n_5eb5d44dc5b6dea39d55ace6.

6. Associated Press, "Tribal Health Board: Native Americans Hit Hard by COVID," *U.S. News & World Report*, June 26, 2020, www.usnews.com/news/best-states/south-dakota/articles/2020–06–26/tribal-health-board-native-americans-hit-hard-by-covid-19.

7. Morgan Matzen, "Data: Native People Disproportionately Affected by COVID-19 in County, State," *Rapid City Journal*, July 18, 2020, https://rapidcityjournal.com/news/local/state-and-regional/data-native-people-disproportionately-affected-by-covid-19-in-county-state/article_7c08443f-bc34–5b9e-a93c-ed57de4529a9.html.

8. James Bikales, "Native American Tribal Nations Take Tougher Line on COVID-19 as States Reopen," *The Hill,* June 21, 2020, https://thehill.com/homenews/state-watch/503770-native-american-tribal-nations-take-tougher-line-on-covid-19-as-states.

9. James Joyner, "Republicans Refuse to Wear Masks," *Outside the Beltway*, July 13, 2020, www.outsidethebeltway.com/republicans-refuse-to-wear-masks/.

10. Michelle Baran, "Europe Extends Its Travel Ban—and Americans Are Still Not Allowed In," *Afar*, August 14, 2020, www.afar.com/magazine/europe-finally-set-to-reopen-but-not-to-us-travelers.

11. Audra Simpson, *Mohawk Interruptus: Political Life across the Borders of Settler States* (Durham, N.C.: Duke University Press, 2014), 12.

12. Nick Estes, "The Empire of All Maladies: Colonial Contagion and Indigenous Resistance," *The Baffler*, 52 (July 2020), https://thebaffler.com/salvos/the-empire-of-all-maladies-estes; and Melanie K. Yazzie, "Decolonizing Development in Diné Bikéyah: Resource Extraction, Anti-capitalism, and Relational Futures," *Environment and Society: Advances in Research* 9, no. 1 (2018): 25–39.

13. Sunny Dooley, "Coronavirus Is Attacking the Navajo 'Because We Have Built the Perfect Human for It to Invade," *Scientific American,* July 8, 2020, www .scientificamerican.com/article/coronavirus-is-attacking-the-navajo-because-we-have -built-the-perfect-human-for-it-to-invade/.

14. Sunnie R. Clahchischiligi, "Planting Hope amid a Plague," *Searchlight New Mexico,* June 3, 2020, https://searchlightnm.org/hitting-home/shiprock/.

15. Arlyssa Becenti, "Dikos Ntsaaígíí dóóda! Nation Musters Defense against COVID-19," *Navajo Times,* March 12, 2020, https://navajotimes.com/reznews/dikos -ntsaaigii-doodaa-nation-musters-defense-against-covid-19/.

16. Yoav Litvin, "Indigenous Leadership Points the Way Out of the COVID Crisis [An Interview with Nick Estes and Justine Teba]," *Truthout,* May 5, 2020, https://truthout .org/articles/indigenous-leadership-points-the-way-out-of-the-covid-crisis/.

17. Achille Mbembe, "Necropolitics," *Public Culture* 15, no. 1 (2003): 11–40.

18. Patrick Wolfe, "Settler Colonialism and the Elimination of the Native," *Journal of Genocide Research* 8, no. 4 (2006): 387–409.

19. Gerald Thompson, *The Army and the Navajo* (Tucson: University of Arizona Press, 1976); and Jennifer Nez Denetdale, *Reclaiming Diné History: The Legacies of Navajo Chief Manuelito and Juanita* (Tucson: University of Arizona Press, 2007).

20. Wade Davies, *Healing Ways: Navajo Health Care in the Twentieth Century* (Albuquerque: University of New Mexico Press, 2001); Robert Trennert, *White Man's Medicine: Government Doctors and the Navajo, 1863–1955* (Albuquerque: University of New Mexico Press, 1998); and Brianna Johns, Michael Caslin, Michael Lewis, Karletta Chief, and Madhusudan Katti, "Settler Colonialism and Pandemics: Native Americans Misrepresented in Health Data Pay a Heavy COVID-19 Price," *Science for the People* 23, no. 3 (Winter 2020), https://magazine.scienceforthepeople.org/vo123-3-bio-politics /native-americans-health-data-covid-19/.

21. Trennert, *White Man's Medicine,* 127.

22. Sue Anne Pressley, "Navajos Protest Response to Mystery Flu Outbreak," *Washington Post,* June 19, 1993.

23. Jeva Lange, "The Navajo Nation Outbreak Reveals an Ugly Truth behind America's Coronavirus Experience," *The Week,* April 2, 2020, https://theweek.com/articles /909787/navajo-nation-outbreak-reveals-ugly-truth-behind-americas-coronavirus -experience; and Andrew Siddons, "The Never-Ending Crisis at the Indian Health Service," *Roll Call,* March 5, 2018, www.rollcall.com/2018/03/05/the-never-ending-crisis -at-the-indian-health-service.

24. Charles M. Blow, "Social Distancing Is a Privilege," *New York Times,* April 5, 2020, www.nytimes.com/2020/04/05/opinion/coronavirus-social-distancing.html.

25. Alan Mozes, "COVID-19 Ravages the Navajo Nation, but Its People Fight Back," *U.S. News & World Report,* June 9, 2020, www.usnews.com/news/health-news/articles /2020-06-09/covid-19-ravages-the-navajo-nation-but-its-people-fight-back.

26. Melanie K. Yazzie, "Unlimited Limitations: The Navajos' *Winters* Rights Deemed Worthless in the 2012 Navajo–Hopi Little Colorado River Settlement," *Wicazo Sa Review* 28, no. 1 (Spring 2013): 26–37.

27. Richard White, *The Roots of Dependency: Subsistence, Environment, and Social Change among the Choctaws, Pawnees, and Navajos* (Lincoln: University of Nebraska Press, 1983).

28. Brodrick Johnson, ed., *Stories of Traditional Life and Culture, Ałk'idáá Yéek'ehgo Diné Kéédahat'inée Baa Hahane'* (Tsaile, Ariz.: Navajo Community College Press, 1977).

29. Nick Estes and Melanie K. Yazzie, "Introduction: Settler Colonialism in Turtle Island," *The Funambulist* 20 (November–December 2018): 14.

30. Jennifer Nez Denetdale, "'No Explanation, No Resolution, and No Answers': Border Town Violence and Navajo Resistance to Settler Colonialism," *Wicazo Sa Review* 31, no. 1 (Spring 2016): 111–31; and William Y. Adams, "The Agent, the Trader, the Missionary, and the Anthropologist: Rival 'Godfathers' of the Colonial Era," *Diné Be'iina': A Journal of Navajo Life* 2, no. 1 (Fall 1990): 67–79.

31. G. Mark Schoepfle, Kenneth Nabahe, Angela Johnson, and Lucie Upshaw, "The Effects of the Great Stock Reduction on the Navajo," *Diné Be'iina': A Journal of Navajo Life* 1, no. 2 (Winter 1988): 62.

32. Melanie K. Yazzie, "U.S. Imperialism and the Problem of 'Culture' in Indigenous Politics: Towards Indigenous Internationalist Feminism," *American Indian Culture and Research Journal* 43, no. 3 (2019): 101.

33. Charles F. Wilkinson, *Fire on the Plateau: Conflict and Endurance in the American Southwest* (Washington, D.C.: Island Press/Shearwater Books, 2004); Andrew Needham, *Power Lines: Phoenix and the Making of the Modern Southwest* (Princeton, N.J.: Princeton University Press, 2014)

34. John Redhouse, *Geopolitics of the Navajo Hopi 'Land Dispute'* (Albuquerque: Redhouse/Wright Publications, 1985); Andrew Curley, "Unsettling Indian Water Settlements: The Little Colorado River, the San Juan River, and Colonial Enclosures," *Antipode: A Radical Journal of Geography* 53, no. 3 (April 2019): 705–23; and Yazzie, "Decolonizing Development."

35. For a theoretical take on settler colonial dispossession and elimination that structure U.S.-Indigenous and U.S.-Diné relations, see Yazzie's "Decolonizing Development." Yazzie builds upon the brilliance of John Redhouse, who simultaneously mapped the geopolitical structure of Diné dispossession and proposed a model for Indigenous and, specifically, Diné liberation; see Redhouse, *Geopolitics of the Navajo Hopi*; and Redhouse, "Getting It Out of My System" (self-published, 2014). Redhouse's papers at the Southwest Research Center in the Zimmerman Library at the University of New Mexico contain a copy of this self-published memoir.

36. Wilkinson, *Fire on the Plateau*; and Needham, *Power Lines*.

37. Jerry Kammer, *The Second Long Walk: The Navajo-Hopi Land Dispute* (Albuquerque: University of New Mexico Press, 1980); and David M. Brugge, *The Navajo-Hopi Land Dispute: An American Tragedy* (Albuquerque: University of New Mexico Press, 1994).

38. For histories of Navajos during the livestock reduction era, see Donald L. Parman, *Navajos and the New Deal* (New Haven, Conn.: Yale University Press, 1976); Colleen O'Neill, *Working the Navajo Way: Labor and Culture in the Twentieth Century*

(Lawrence: University Press of Kansas, 2005); and Marsha Weisiger, *Dreaming of Sheep in Navajo Country* (Seattle: University of Washington Press, 2011).

39. Nancy Owens, "The Effects of Reservation Border Towns and Energy Exploitation on American Indian Development," in *Research in Economic Anthropology*, vol. 2 (Greenwich, Conn.: JAI Press, 1979): 303–37, 305.

40. Owens, "The Effects of Reservation Border Towns."

41. Associated Press, "Navajo Nation Leader Urges Unity after Page Mayor's Alcoholism Comment," *Fox 10 News,* May 3, 2020, www.fox10phoenix.com/news/navajo -nation-leader-urges-unity-after-page-mayors-alcoholism-comment.

42. Nick Estes, Melanie K. Yazzie, Jennifer Nez Denetdale, and David Correia, "I Can't Fucking Breathe," in *Red Nation Rising: From Border Town to Native Liberation* (Oakland, Calif.: PM Press, 2021).

43. Litvin, "Indigenous Leadership."

44. Richard Reyes, "Possible Exposure at NCI Detox," *Gallup Independent,* April 8–9, 2020.

45. Morgan Lee, "Outbreak on Edge of Navajo Nation Overwhelms Rural Hospital," *Las Cruces Sun News,* May 20, 2020, www.lcsun-news.com/story/news/2020/05/20 /navajo-nation-outbreak-overwhelms-rural-hospital-edge-gallup/5226002002/.

46. Lee, "Outbreak on Edge of Navajo Nation."

47. Nina Lakhani, "Exclusive: Indigenous Americans Dying from Covid at Twice the Rate of White Americans," *Guardian,* February 4, 2021, www.theguardian.com/us -news/2021/feb/04/native-americans-coronavirus-covid-death-rate.

48. Keeanga-Yamahtta Taylor, "How Do We Change America? The Quest to Transform This Country Cannot Be Limited to Challenging Its Brutal Police," *New Yorker,* June 8, 2020, www.newyorker.com/news/our-columnists/how-do-we-change-america.

49. Jake Skeets, "The Other House: Musings on the Diné Perspective of Time," *Emergence Magazine*, April 29, 2020, https://emergencemagazine.org/story/the-other-house/.

50. Nick Estes, "The Empire of All Maladies."

51. Leanne Betasamosake Simpson, "Land as Pedagogy: Nishnaabeg Intelligence and Rebellious Transformation," *Decolonization: Indigeneity, Education & Society* 3, no. 3 (2014): 13.

52. Anerie Tachiinii, Facebook, October 18, 2020, https://www.facebook.com/eiren .begay.

53. Clahchischiligi, "Planting Hope."

CONTRIBUTORS

KENT BLANSETT is a Cherokee, Creek, Choctaw, Shawnee, and Potawatomi descendant from the Blanket, Panther, and Smith family lines. He is Langston Hughes Associate Professor of Indigenous Studies and History at the University of Kansas and author of *A Journey to Freedom: Richard Oakes, Alcatraz, and the Red Power Movement* (2018). The first biography of Akwesasne Mohawk leader Richard Oakes, his book weaves together the methodologies of Indigenous biography and urban history to explore the rich histories of three modern Indian cities: Brooklyn, San Francisco, and Seattle. Beyond Indian cities, his scholarship explores the histories of Native nationalism, intertribalism, Red Power, and global Indigenous experience. Blansett serves as the founder and executive director for the American Indian Digital History Project (www.aidhp .com)—a digital history cooperative that strives to expand both free and open access to critical Indigenous research and archival materials.

CATHLEEN D. CAHILL received her PhD at the University of Chicago. She taught at the University of New Mexico for thirteen years before moving to Pennsylvania State University, where she is now Associate Professor of History. She is the author of *Recasting the Vote: How Women of Color Transformed the Suffrage Movement* (2020). Her first book, *Federal Fathers and Mothers: A Social History of the United States Indian Service, 1869–1933* (2011), won the Labriola Center for American Indian National Book Award and was finalist for the David J. Weber and Bill Clements Book Prize. Her work has also appeared in *American Indian*

Quarterly, American Indian Culture and Research Journal, Frontiers: A Journal of Women's Studies, Journal of Women's History, and the *Journal of the Gilded Age and Progressive Era.*

MAURICE CRANDALL is a citizen of the Yavapai-Apache Nation of Camp Verde, Arizona. He is Assistant Professor of Native American Studies at Dartmouth College, and from 2016 to 2017 he was the Clements Fellow for the Study of Southwestern America at the Clements Center for Southwest Studies at Southern Methodist University. He is a historian of the Indigenous peoples of the U.S.-Mexico Borderlands. Crandall's first book, *These People Have Always Been a Republic: Indigenous Electorates in the U.S.-Mexico Borderlands, 1598–1912,* was published in 2019.

JENNIFER DENETDALE (Diné) is Professor of American Studies at the University of New Mexico. She received her PhD in History from Northern Arizona University and is the author of three Navajo histories and numerous articles and essays. She is the first Diné to receive a PhD in History. She has been recognized for her scholarship and community advocacy with several awards, including the Rainbow Naatsiilid True Colors for her support and advocacy on behalf of Navajo LGBTQI persons and the UNM faculty of color award for her teaching, research, and service to the academy.

C. JOSEPH GENETIN-PILAWA received his PhD at Michigan State University and is currently Associate Professor of History at George Mason University. He is the author of *Crooked Paths to Allotment: The Fight over Federal Indian Policy after the Civil War* (2012) and the co-editor of *Beyond Two Worlds: Critical Conversations on Language and Power in Native North America* (2014). His articles have appeared in the *Journal of Women's History, Western Historical Quarterly,* and *The Capitol Dome,* as well as several edited collections. Genetin-Pilawa's current research examines the visual, symbolic, and lived Indigenous landscapes of Washington, D.C., especially the ways that Native visitors and residents claimed and reclaimed spaces in the city.

MISHUANA GOEMAN, Tonawanda Band of Seneca, is Professor of Gender Studies and American Indian Studies, and an affiliated faculty member of Critical Race Studies in the Law School, UCLA, and Community Engagements Program. She is also the author of *Mark My Words: Native Women Mapping Our Nations*

(2013) and a Co-Principal Investigator on two community-based digital projects, Mapping Indigenous L.A. (2015) and Carrying Our Ancestors Home (2019).

NATHANIEL F. HOLLY is an independent scholar and Acquisitions Editor at the University of Georgia Press. He has published articles on Indigenous urbanism, the eighteenth-century Southeast, transatlantic Indians, and the preservation of Cherokee places in *History Compass, North Carolina Historical Review*, and *Early Modern Women*. His research for this essay was supported by the North Caroliniana Society, Georgian Papers Programme, National Society of the Sons and Daughters of the Pilgrims, American Philosophical Society, American Historical Association, William L. Clements Library, and Huntington Library. He holds a PhD in Early American History from the College of William & Mary.

DAVID HUGILL is Assistant Professor of Geography and Environmental Studies at Carleton University in Ottawa. He is author of *Settler Colonial City: Racism and Inequity in Postwar Minneapolis* (2021) and coeditor of *Settler City Limits: Indigenous Resurgence and Colonial Violence in the Urban Prairie West* (2019).

ARI KELMAN is Chancellor's Leadership Professor of History at the University of California, Davis. He is the author of *Battle Lines: A Graphic History of the Civil War* (2015), *A Misplaced Massacre: Struggling Over the Memory of Sand Creek* (2013), and *A River and Its City: The Nature of Landscape in New Orleans* (2003). Kelman's essays have appeared in the *Journal of American History, Journal of Urban History, Nation, Slate, Times Literary Supplement*, and many other venues. He is now working on a book titled, "For Liberty and Empire: How the Civil War Bled into the Indian Wars," and editing the journal *Reviews in American History.*

DOUGLAS K. MILLER is Associate Professor of Native American and United States History at Oklahoma State University and a former Clements Center research fellow. His first book, *Indians on the Move: Native American Mobility and Urbanization in the Twentieth Century* (2019), discusses the dynamic and consequential motives and outcomes for generations of Native American peoples who moved to cities, both through and around the federal urban relocation program, while preserving important ties to home, and often returning there. He is currently developing a book about legendary Kiowa musician from Oklahoma City Jesse Ed Davis, who played his way to the top of the rock world.

ANDREW NEEDHAM is Associate Professor of History at New York University, where he is the director of the Minor in Native American and Indigenous Studies. He is the author of *Power Lines: Phoenix and the Modern Southwest* (2014), which explores how resources from the Navajo and Hopi Nations underlay the development of Phoenix and other cities in the U.S. Southwest. *Power Lines* won awards from the Western History Association, American Society for Environmental History, and Border Regional Library Association. He is currently working on a book about Indigenous dispossession and the U.S. petroleum industry in the early twentieth century.

ELAINE MARIE NELSON (PhD, University of New Mexico) is Assistant Professor of History at the University of Kansas, where she teaches courses on the American West, Women and Gender, and the Great Plains. Her published work appears in the *Great Plains Quarterly* and *South Dakota History*, and she is completing her first book manuscript on tourism, performance, and memory in the Black Hills. Nelson has presented her work at several professional conferences and received fellowships and grants for her work from the Andrew Mellon Foundation, Newberry Library, Huntington Library, Buffalo Bill Historical Center, American Heritage Center, Charles Redd Center, and American Philosophical Society. She is also the Executive Director of the Western History Association, since 2017.

DANA E. POWELL is a cultural anthropologist working on issues of environmental justice, "extractivism," energy development, and coloniality in Native North America and the Navajo Nation, in particular. Her first book, *Landscapes of Power: Politics of Energy in the Navajo Nation* (2018), tracks the rise and fall of a controversial coal project and the everyday entanglements of sovereignty, environmentalism, and natural resource development. Powell is Associate Professor of Anthropology at Appalachian State University, where she directs the undergraduate program in Social Practice and Sustainability. Her current collaborative projects focus on using water as an analytic to understand toxicity and transition in the Navajo Nation, and on social movements addressing biogas and biomass proposals in rural communities in eastern North Carolina.

SASHA MARIA SUAREZ (White Earth Ojibwe descent) is Assistant Professor of History and American Indian Studies at the University of Wisconsin–Madison. She received her PhD in American Studies from the University of Minnesota in

2020. Her work examines White Earth Ojibwe women's community organizing and placemaking in twentieth-century Minneapolis.

DANIEL H. USNER is Holland N. McTyeire Professor of History at Vanderbilt University. His books include *Indians, Settlers, and Slaves in a Frontier Exchange Economy: The Lower Mississippi Valley before 1783, Indian Work: Language and Livelihood in Native American History,* and *American Indians in Early New Orleans: From Calumet to Raquette.* He is currently completing work that centers on the Chitimacha Tribe of Louisiana, tentatively titled "The Arts of Survival: How Basket Diplomacy Saved a Louisiana Indian Nation."

INDEX

References to illustrations appear in italic type.

Red Lake Nation, 216n13
Red Middle Voice, 79
Red Power Movement, 13, 169, 212, 251
Red River, 59, 248–49
Red Rock Country, 140, 150, 156, 158n9
Red Warrior Camp, 277
Rehoboth, N.Mex., 302
Rehoboth McKinley Christian Hospital, 302
Reid, John Phillip, 26
Religious Freedom Restoration Act, 278
Relocation Authority (Bureau of Indian Affairs), 10
relocation programs, 10–13, 16–17, 144, 212, 219–30, 235–36, 238–40, 250–51, 300
Remembering the Children, 195n32
Republican Party, 77, 81, 85–86, 129, 292
Rhodes, Dennis Sun, 214
Rice Creek, 79
Rickard, Jolene, 104
Riel, Louis, 249
Rifkin, Mark, 103
Rimrock, Ariz., 139, 150, 155
Rio Verde Reserve, 142–44, 146, 160n32, 160n40
Rock Creek, 130
Rodning, Christopher B., 27
Roosevelt, Theodore, 128, 164n106, 176
Roosevelt Dam, 139, 163n106
Rooster Town (in Winnipeg), 250
Rope, Rose Marie, 239
Rosaldo, Renato, 98–99
Rosebud Bill, 176, 193n23
Rosebud Lakota, 224
Rosebud Reservation, 173, 176, 178, 181, 223, 229, 269, 274
Rosebud Sioux, 223
Rosenthal, Nicholas G., 11, 13
Rouquette, Adrien, 62
Rouquette, François Dominique, 62
RSR Corporation, 229
Rupert's Land, 248–49

Russell, Daisy Quesada, 162n72
Russell, Henry, 164n106
Russell, Ned, 158n10

Sacred Stone Camp, 269, 274, 277
Sah-Kah-Tay (Sunshine) Club, 204–7
Saint Aulaire, Félix Achille Beaupoil de, 61
Saint-Domingue, 54
Saint Paul, Minn., 78–82, 84–88, 199, 202
Salt River Canyon, 142
Salt River Materials Group, 164n109
Salt River Pima Maricopa Indian Community, 164n109
San Carlos Reservation, 16, 144–51, 162n75, 239, 241
Sand Creek, 2, 88
Sanderson, Frances, 13
San Francisco, Calif., 234–35, 245n48
Santa Fe, N.Mex., 1
Santa Fe Railway, 222
Santee, 87, 170
Satala, Lucy, 144, 160n34
Sauk, 6, 115–16
Seattle, Wash., 10, 13–14
Second Bull Run, 85–86
Sedona, Ariz., 146, 150, 156
Sellers, James D., 152
Seminole, 7, 234
Seneca, 16, 96–97, 101, 110–12, 121
Seven Days' Battles, 85
Seventh Street (Rapid City), 179
Seven Years' War, 56
Shawnee, 59
Sheep Springs, N.Mex., 282
Shenandoah Campaign, 85
Sheridan, Thomas E., 160n35
Sherman, Mark, 192n18
Shining Light Kitchen, 276
Shiprock, N.Mex., 292, 294, 305
Shoshone, 121, 127, 169
Sibley, Henry Hastings, 84–85

Printed in the USA
CPSIA information can be obtained
at www.ICGtesting.com
CBHW031822210324
5657CB00002B/91